Financial Pathways for Ministry Leaders and Christians

PROVISIONS FOR THE VISION

Dr. Festus K. Akinnifesi

PROVISIONS FOR THE VISION
Copyright © 2021 by Dr. Festus K. Akinnifesi
ISBN 978-1-8382191-9-2

All rights reserved.
No part of this publication may be reproduced, stored in a retrieval system, or transmitted in any form or by any means, electronic, mechanical, photocopying, or otherwise, without prior written consent of the publisher except as provided by under United Kingdom copyright law. Short extracts may be used for review purposes with credits given.

Main translation in use: NKJV
Scripture quotations marked NKJV are taken from the New King James Version®. Copyright © 1982 by Thomas Nelson. Used by permission. All rights reserved. Scripture quotations taken from The Holy Bible, New International Version® NIV® Copyright © 1973 1978 1984 2011 by Biblica, Inc. ™ Used by permission. All rights reserved worldwide.

Scripture quotations from The Authorized (King James) Version. Rights in the Authorized Version in the United Kingdom are vested in the Crown. Reproduced by permission of the Crown's patentee, Cambridge University Press.

"Scripture quotations taken from the (NASB®) New American Standard Bible®, Copyright © 1960, 1971, 1977, 1995, 2020 by The Lockman Foundation. Used by permission. All rights reserved. www.lockman.org"

Published by
Maurice Wylie Media
Your Inspirational Christian Publisher

Publishers' statement: Throughout this book, the love for our God is such that whenever we refer to Him, we honor with capital letters. On the other hand, when referring to the devil, we refuse to acknowledge him with any honor to the point of violating grammatical rule and withholding capitalization.

For more information visit
www.MauriceWylieMedia.com

Contents

Acknowledgment	09
Preface	11
1. Knowledge, Provision, and Vision	15
2. Financing Your Vision	26
3. Jesus Taught Money	43
4. The Kingdom Investors Mindset	61
5. Take Your Wallet With You	79
6. Taking Your Provisions	97
7. Faith for Finances	110
8. Financial Miracles	132
9. Fundraising for Ministry	149
10. Developing a Fundraising Campaign	161
11. Earning to Finance Your Ministry	177
12. Making a Difference	201
13. Marketing Your Talents and Skills	225
14. Repositioning Yourself to Earn More	242
15. Blooming in a Financial Wilderness	263
16. Developing Your Financial Plan	278
17. Building Your Financial Networth	293
18 Pathways to Financial Freedom	305
19. Financial Decision Guide	320
20. The Grace of Giving	335
21. Tithing in the Modern Church	349
22. Financial Reforms for 21st Century Church	372

Bonus Section

1. Financial Growth and Opportunities   388
2. Receiving Your Start-up Investment Capital   401
3. Auto-piloting Your Investment   428

Contact   447

Endnotes   448

Disclaimer

The author's role is to support and assist you in reaching your own goals, but your success depends primarily on your effort, motivation, commitment, and follow-through. The author cannot predict and does not guarantee that you will attain a particular result, and you accept and understand that results differ for each individual. Each individual's results depend on his or her unique background, dedication, desire, knowledge, motivation, actions, timing, opportunity, and numerous other factors. You fully agree that there are no guarantees as to the specific outcome or results you can expect from using the information you receive through this book.

The information contained in this book is not intended to be a substitute for legal or financial advice that can be provided by your own attorney, accountant, and/or financial advisor. Although care has been taken in preparing the information provided to you, the author cannot be held responsible for any errors or omissions and accepts no liability whatsoever for any loss or damage you may incur, as the book is not an investment or financial advice. Author encourage the reader to do its own due diligence and seek financial and/or legal counsel relating to your specific circumstances as needed. In reading this book, you agree that the information is not providing legal or financial advice.

Dedication

This book is dedicated to Dr. Uzodinma Adeogo Obed, truly a general of God for this generation, who has left an indelible footprint in the sands of time. More importantly, Heaven rejoiced on the day in 2019 when he finished his race with joy and went to be with the Master. As a true shepherd, he has held me by the hand as I walk the trail of bi-vocational ministry over the years. With unreserved gratitude, I say, Thank you.

Acknowledgements

Within this book, hundreds of great minds converge on the pages. Many of these authors are credited directly, but some insights of the others have been blended, adapted, modified, and integrated into the text in such a way that specific acknowledgment would be difficult. However, to all of these individuals, I would like to say thank you.

I am greatly indebted to Pastor Uzo Adeogo Obed and Pastor (Mrs) Chy Obed. They have not only taught me the heart of Jesus on financial stewardship, but have also demonstrated it in their lives and ministries.

Many thanks to late Dr. Jack Hatcher, Former Vice President and Provost, Christ for the Nations Institute (CFNI), his wife Professor Alta Hatcher, and his son, Pastor John Hatcher, former Director of Advanced School of Leadership and Pastoral Ministry at CFNI and was also my professor, for their encouragements in ministry. Thanks to Pastor Robert Summers, Sr. Pastor Mount Greek Family Church, Dallas, for his shepherding heart and encouragement.

I also want to thank all the pastors, elders and leaders, and brethren of all churches and ministries where I have had the privilege to teach on this subject worldwide. In particular, His Excellency, Dr. Lazarus Chakwera, President of the Republic of Malawi (former President of the Assemblies of God in Malawi.) I am grateful to Pastor Charles Makata, Sr. Pastors of Area 18 Assemblies of God, Lilongwe, Malawi;

and Pastor Chiudza Banda, former Vice President, and Sr. Pastor Assemblies of God Zomba, Malawi—both of whom I served under as a Bi-vocational Minister. Ambassador (Dr) & Mrs. Olaniran, Sr. Pastors, New Covenant Church, Rome, Italy; Pastor Michael and Mrs. Ellen Mwale, Assemblies of God, Lilongwe, Malawi—my co-laborer in the vineyard, and anointed interpreter of Chichewa, in Malawi; Pastor Sunday Awe, Christ Proclaimer's Global Ministry, Ibadan, Nigeria, for his encouragements; Beloved Pastor Benson and Mrs. Felicia Ekakitie, Frosinone, Italy—bi-vocational ministers; Bishop Solomon and Rev. Comfort Adebayo, Life Changers International Church, Lilongwe, Malawi; Pastor Jacob Adekunle Aderibigbe, Redeemed Christian Church of God, Lilongwe, Malawi; Pastors James and Mrs. Yellena Onibonoje, International Christian Fellowship, Dallas, United States.

I would also like to appreciate the editorial support by Rev. Polly Harder of CFNI, Dallas, and her prayerful encouragements.

Special thanks to my age-long and bosom friend, bi-vocational minister, Dr. Oluyede, and Mrs. Deola Ajayi, Pastors, Redeemed Christian Church of God, Arnhem, Netherlands.

Special thanks go to my beloved wife, Adetutu, and our children for their encouragement and support over the years so I could have the mental and physical space to see this work through.

Keeping the best to the last, I want to thank the Lord Jesus, my Chief Shepherd, and the Holy Spirit, my Teacher, for the inspiration in writing this book over the past number of years. Without His help, it would have been a mere mirage.

Preface

What would it be like if Christians, missionaries, and ministers were able to walk in their calling without financial constraints or for them to have sufficient finances to meet their family needs while supporting God's work financially?

Provisions for the Vision is not another book on prosperity or wealth creation but is targeted to those whose passion is to achieve financial freedom through biblical understanding of 'How would God do it.' After all, Jesus died for us to be free from the entanglements of this world. Yet church members are suffering financial drainage, as their money leaks out of their lives and binds them to debt.

My journey with finances began with a burden for world evangelization, realizing that many who have been called, trained, and ordained have been financially ill-equipped to have a major breakthrough in their calling. It challenged me to ask a trillion-dollar question, **"Is it possible that Jesus could have left the Church with such a huge task of evangelizing the world without providing a financial clue as to how to finance this great task?"**

It was such a question that drove me into prayer while earnestly seeking the Word of God for answers.

I had read hundreds of books on spiritual and secular investment, but without doubt, the Bible remains the most remarkable book on financial directives, and therefore, the source and underpinning to what you are reading.

What I discovered in studying God's Word on finances changed me forever and transformed many ministers within my circle of influence, especially those who sat under my teaching over the years as God graced me with insight from His Word.

There have been times when I wondered was Jesus disappointed when He said that the children of the world are wiser than the children of the Kingdom? He also said, *"Because it has been given to you to know the mysteries of the Kingdom of Heaven, but to them, it has not been given"*.[1] This clearly informs us that it is God's will for you and I to know the mysteries of the Kingdom.

With this in mind, we need a set of fresh new lenses to ask the question, "What is the Church missing on the subject of finances?" For example, how to cultivate, grow, and multiply money without making it our object of worship. Jacob never succeeded until he discovered the keys of success and applied them. Unlike some ministries who would crave money, Solomon was not given a blank checkbook or an anointed handkerchief from God to create wealth. Instead, they were given keys to financial wisdom by God.

The Church seems to be torn between two worlds: The conventional paradigm for making money demands that believers operate in either the secular world view of money-making, which considers money a measure of success. This has led to the current trend, which is infiltrating the Church—secularizing the spiritual and spiritualizing the secular on wealth-making approaches. This includes the extreme "prosperity gospel," which sees everything through a money lens. That leads to excess, greed, corruption, and exploitation of the flock of God.

The second is the religious worldview—which sees money as a hindrance or a snare to one's spiritual growth and sanctification. So it completely opposes and shuns any wealth-making interests. These two world views often clash in their values, principles, and methods, and none of them has sufficient backing in the Scriptures but are products of human invention that are motivated by hypocrisy, greed, and guilt, or even fanaticism.

Many have considered these two as separate routes: you either pursue secular ways of money-making and miss God, or you can be overly spiritual by neglecting God's wealth-creation principles and remain poor and miserable. Let me tell you that both standpoints are extreme! You cannot follow the selfish money-acquisition method and please God. You also do not displease God by having financial means for preaching or supporting the Gospel as a prudent financial steward. However, what is important is how you make money and how you spend it. How much do you value money, and where do you place money in your heart?

We can follow God's Words and achieve financial success while maintaining an unfailing loving relationship with Him. As ministers, we can accomplish great things for God, and yet, we can possess financial means by using the talents, wisdom, skills, time, and opportunity God has given each one of us. We can know how to abound in and how to lack finances, but all for His glory.

If you are looking for a 'get-rich-quick' or an *abracadabra* type of money-making in the ministry, this book does not provide such a recipe. Instead, it provides a Spirit-inspired, meaningful, practical way of getting you out of debt, meeting your expenses, and showing you how to invest and grow your income; not only for your future but for your children's future, and supporting God's work as well as remaining a committed Christian, or minister.

The chapters of this book are structured into three unmarked parts. The first part is on financial wisdom. It details many of the problems which have created negative mindsets that have prevented believers from attaining financial freedom. It defuses the misunderstanding on the subject of finance—prosperity, money, riches, and poverty. It recalls Jesus' commands on finances for the Gospel and draws from the practices of the Apostles and veteran Christian workers.

The second part opens with financial miracles and how to move from earning to significance in the Kingdom. It includes how to market your talents better in the workplace and offers financial models, as well as how to bloom in your financial wilderness.

The third part details the practical aspect of investment methods—how to grow and multiply money earned from regular income or savings for expanded ministry work. This includes helping the reader know how to estimate financial net worth, develop a financial plan, acquiring start-up capital for investment, financial pathways, and offering financial decision guides for Christians.

Throughout this book, I have highlighted details, strategies, and disciplines that will help you achieve your financial goals allowing a holistic approach, integrating the whole-counsel of God on finances.

Chapter 1 Overview
Knowledge, Provision and Vision

Ministry Issue

Receiving a call to preach is the easy one because it comes by grace and not by work. Fulfilling the vision is the work, but without financial resources, a vision becomes a mirage.

Ministry Lesson

To fulfill the vision requires knowledge and wisdom based on the Word of God and practical application of integrated knowledge to bring necessary provisions that make the vision blossom.

CHAPTER 1

KNOWLEDGE, PROVISION AND VISION

"Where there is no vision the people perish..."[2]

Getting It Right With Finances
"And where there are no financial resources, the vision perishes." John Maxwell[3]

In 1998, as a visiting professor teaching Students of Masters Programme in Agroecology at the State University of Maranhao, Brazil (Universidade Estadual do Maranhao), and bi-vocational minister in the beautiful Island of São Luis, Maranhão, Brazil, I went to the "Centro"—city center.

The central market was a very busy place with rivers of people streaming in all directions on a shopping spree. As my wife went shopping in one direction, and I hurried to get what I wanted before rush hour traffic became more difficult to get through; a man intercepted me. He was beaming with enthusiasm and joy of the Lord as he started to converse with me in a fast-paced Portuguese language.

"Are you a born-again Christian?" he asked. "Yes, I am." I smiled with joy that someone cared for evangelism without being intimidated by the rowdiness of the area.

He asked, "What church do you go to?" probing further. Replying, I said, "Assemblies of God." He put a tract into my hand that was for growth and maturity, and bidding him farewell; I hurried away.

As I hurried off, I heard… "Brother!" I looked back as he called to me. As he got closer, he asked, "Can I have 'two *reais from you?*" (Two US dollars.)

I felt a bit upset inside. Several questions roamed through my mind. Could this man be selling tracts for profit? Concluding that he may be, I told him, "Another time, brother!" I left him and hurried away, rushing back to where my wife was waiting in the car.

As we drove away, I heard a voice of the Holy Spirit compelling me to go back and give him the money. To go back was difficult with the traffic now building, but I had no choice, so I obeyed and turned around. When I reached the man, I pulled out my wallet and gave him far more than he had asked for. Looking at the money, he jumped up, raise his hands up to Heaven, and started praising the Lord loudly. He then told me that he had not eaten all day! Do you ever feel shame? That day I felt a mixture of both shame and joy. I felt ashamed of myself for being selfish and judgmental the first time he had asked me for money, but I was glad that the Lord compelled me to do the needful.

Over the years I became more aware of many ministers, missionaries, Christian workers, and the average believer, who suffers and wallows in abject poverty and lack—the lack of money to put food on the table, pay the rent, pay the kid's school fees, transportation costs, and to keep their families together. Pastors who have sat with me and told their stories of how they have been kicked out of their houses for failing to pay rent. One of these pastors, his wife, was about 7-months pregnant. The landlord knocked on the door and commanded them to leave, then put a new lock on the door.

Having traveled to over 40 nations around the world and lived in six of them, including Nigeria, Brazil, Malawi, Belgium, and the United States, and Italy, I have also realized that poverty among Christians and Christian workers is not just limited to third-world countries. The only difference is the level of poverty. On the extreme side, there are affluent churches in both rich and poor nations, but these are just an oasis in the desert among the hundreds of thousands of poor churches that cannot pay their bills or support a pastor, not to mention missionaries.

In 2012, Tim Peters reported a survey where he listed ten reasons pastors quit the ministry too soon in the United States. According to him, "Every year 4,000 new churches are planted, and 7,000 churches close." According to the article, 1,700 pastors leave the ministry every month. One of the top five reasons is financial pressure—70% of the pastors feel grossly underpaid and cannot provide for their families."[4] Matthew Fretwell actually lists finances as the number one reason pastors quit ministry.[5] When they come to a crossroads, pastors get angry and complain, "Lord, I have fully obeyed you. I left my job, went to seminary, and planted a church. Why are things not working out for me? Have I missed something?" Can I ask, does this sound familiar?

The number one reason for arguments in a marriage is money. Sadly, many divorces are also caused by problems with cash flow.[6] The Christian family is not spared from this any more than a non-Christian.

On 26 August 2020, the Barna research reported that one in five churches in the United States could close in the following 18 months due to the impact of the COVID-19 pandemic on their finance. For instance, there are 300,000 evangelical churches in the United States, and tithing remains their main financial engine. While church attendance generally declined and online attendance increased, church giving was severely hit right from the beginning of the pandemic. The report indicates that with online churches, the way people look at the Church—their donation and relationship with local churches will change after the pandemic, and a fifth will close.[7]

Over the last 20 years, I have taught many church congregations and groups through Sunday school series, mid-week series, lunch hour meetings, seminars, conferences, and special events, on the subject of finances. At first, it was purely teaching on the subject of biblical finances for believers. During intensive studies, the Holy Spirit started to open my eyes to a more balanced understanding of the subject of money and finances. Because the Church has been mystified about it for so long, we've alienated unbelievers from coming to the Church in the way we conduct business when it comes to money. They are quick to spot our unbiblical approaches of overemphasizing money and pressurizing people to give at every opportunity. Worse still, the Church has alienated the majority of Christians from participating in the Great Commission for the same reason—we have demonized the subject of money and have over-structured our approach to giving, fundraising, and budgeting in churches and ministry.

About a decade ago, I was invited by the President of the Assemblies of God in Malawi to give a seminar to ministers and leaders at the National Annual Convention of the Assemblies of God in Malawi. The event took place at the Assemblies of God headquarters in Lilongwe. The two-hour session was titled "Mobilizing Finances for Ministry."[8] After the sessions, I returned home to rest. Then I heard the Holy Spirit drop the title of this book into my spirit, saying, *"Provisions for the Vision."* I jumped up, wrote it down, and meditated on what I knew would be a book to help Christians achieve financial freedom.

I realized the Lord wanted me to write a book about how Christian workers can fund their God-given vision and how Christians can position themselves to achieve financial surplus and to be able to finance God's work. That became my focus as the ideas on the content and structure of the book started to take shape in my heart. I became more burdened and started to pray and ponder more on how the book could benefit more Christian workers in ministry—full-time ministers, career missionaries, tentmaking (bi-vocational) ministers, marketplace ministers, and every Christian of any vocation around the world—with the chief goal of creating more money to finance the Great Commission.

It is vital for us as Christians, to understand that God doesn't send anyone to the battlefield without empowering them—spiritually or financially. After all, He is a good Father. If God has called you, every financial support you need has already been fully provided in the call—**there's provision in the vision.** You only need to discover how to access your provisions for the vision. He has called you to do!

You may, as a Christian find the following statement hard to take, but in truth - everything rises and falls on money. Ignore money or take money out of the Gospel, and you have an empty, beaten, confused, weak, and limited Church. God-fearing ministry leaders don't go into ministry to make or raise money, but they soon realize that money is essential if they are going to succeed. But how will God meet both our personal and ministry needs? Will He drop money down from Heaven, or send a fleet of ravens to our brook, or send an angel to us with bread and meat on hot coals, or take us on a gold-exploration tour to Heaven?

God has a way that we do not seem to fully embrace or know of in the modern-day Church. Yes, God can perform miracles, but most often, He simply gives you the *power* to make wealth by using the wisdom and abilities He has already given you. That was all He did for Solomon after promising that He would be the richest man on Earth.[9] Yet, this truth is an aspect that is still *veiled* to many ministers, and our actions affect the believers who follow us because we fail to teach the whole counsel of God on finances.

No matter how anointed you are, you won't go far without the financial resources needed to birth the vision and sustain it.

Provisions follow a Divine Vision
The word of the Lord came to me for the second time when He said, "Knowledge, Provisions, and Vision" Again, I prayed and meditated on it. People perish for lack of knowledge (Hosea 4:6). Also, *"Where there is no vision, the people perish"* (Proverbs 29:18). John C. Maxwell adds, "And where there are no financial resources, the vision perishes."[10]

Vision dies in the hands of half-hearted trustees—those who have no knowledge of how to protect and actualize the vision, thus sending it to the grave prematurely.

We need to acquire knowledge about the provisions God has given for the vision He gave us. Joseph received God's vision, but his knowledge, wisdom, and skills carried him through. He was responsible for key decisions each time he got to a crossroad. Many Christian folks think the knowledge they need is only spiritual knowledge, but man is a total man, not a half or a quarter of a man. How many truly called ministers have put down their battle-ax and drowned in the mud of financial poverty? Their understanding or mistaken belief that Jesus wants just to minister to the poor has limited their vision.

Did you ever consider how Jesus paid for His ministry? He first acquired knowledge until age 30, including working as a carpenter and studying theology at the same time. Both were done before He launched out into a full-time, earth-shaking ministry for a little over three years. His vast knowledge on agriculture and food systems is evident in His parables. He learned how to have enough provisions and pursued the vision His Father had given Him. He did not go out with an empty stomach, bare-footed, homeless, or naked. He actually relocated to Galilee at some point—a bigger city and resided in Capernaum in a home with a team.

As the Lord stepped out, more provisions followed Him. He knew when to multiply cooked fish and bread, when to send His disciples out to the field to pick grains, when to ask them to cast their nets for a catch, when to get money from the mouth of a fish, when to receive into His ministry from voluntary givers, when to send them out to request a furnished banquet hall, or to untie a donkey. He sent them on short evangelism missions at some point, and each mission had important lessons to teach them. All these fit into the short-term mission He was assigned to by His Father. Yet, none of these methods was to be repeated by the disciples as their only means of getting provisions for their calling. They needed creative financial wisdom on provisions.

Get Knowledge, Get Understanding
We need knowledge of the Word of God to understand how to get provision to achieve the vision; as Proverbs tells us, *"The discerning heart seeks knowledge"* (Proverbs 15:14). Have you been called into ministry? Do you want to do something tangible for the Lord? Do you want to be a Christian who participates in sending out missionaries or supports churches and ministries for the world harvest? If that is the vision you have, then you need knowledge to accomplish it. Get knowledge, get wisdom, and get understanding. Why do Christian workers fail? Because they stop at prayers.

Remember that God told Moses that He specially filled Bezalel and Aholiab with "the Spirit of wisdom, knowledge, and understanding"— the specialized skills and workmanship needed for the building of the most magnificent Temple that has ever been built on earth. There is a place for prayer and anointing, but there is also a place for knowledge, understanding, and wisdom to produce quality products and services. It is often said that the best way to control your destiny is to confront it with action. Do not just see an opportunity; you must seize it. Do not wait for an opportunity to come: you are the opportunity. Jesus said to His disciples, *"The knowledge of the secrets of the Kingdom of Heaven has been given to you, but not to them. Whoever has, will be given more, and he will have abundance"* (Matthew 13:11-12). But why is it that many do not know the secrets of the Kingdom in the area of finances? Why is our knowledge so warped in this area, and why do we continue to pursue practices that further alienate the very ones we are supposed to be bringing into the Kingdom?

Perry Noble said, "Many leaders who are facing an under-funded vision do teach about money, but only from the perspective of giving. While it is extremely important to put God first, simply teaching people how to give more in order to increase churches income is not the biblical basis to winning with money God's way."[11] Please read this statement carefully, and let it soak in. We can do more than just ask people to give. We can teach people how to make money and be a cheerful giver afterward, which means you can teach them how to do both—if you are a Christian, you should be able to give and know how to make money.

One of the common reasons that unbelievers cite for not coming to church is how we handle finances—they were able to spot what is unethical about our attitude toward money. They feel uncomfortable and could not trust us with their finances. When they sit in the assembly of believers, we make them feel uncomfortable with our invisible hands that forcefully search their pockets through the way we frequently plead for money until they become embarrassed. Sometimes ministers use even subtle threats for those who had nothing to give or need to give everything in their pockets. They see their purses and not their souls as Jesus sees them. That's why we count numbers and appoint leaders or give people attention based on their tithe cards. Just sit in front of a Christian television program for only thirty minutes, and you can hardly escape without desperate requests for donations. Nearly every church or ministry website has a donation call attached to it. It is all about *donate, give,* and *sow,* regardless of how rich that church or ministry might be. Seminars and conferences require registration at a cost. Why should people have to pay just to hear the Word of God, be healed and delivered from satan? At what point did Jesus charge?

We say that Jesus is our example, but if so, then something is fatally wrong with our methods and financial practice. When Jesus met a rich young man, instead of exploiting him, He actually told him to give away what he had to the poor (not to Jesus' ministry!). Based on much of the prosperity teaching content today, Jesus should have manipulated the man to give directly to Him while slapping them with "Malachi 3:8-9." Yet, Jesus warned us not to commercialize the gospel: *"Freely you received, freely give"* (Matthew 10:9). Do we still hold that value in churches and fundraising today? Can we say, like Paul, that we have preached the Gospel free of charge?[12]

Whether secular or spiritual, money plays a vital role in any human endeavor. In today's civilization, the Great Commission depends on money, and that there can be no revival without plenty of financial costs to implement it. Gone are the days when a preacher could just walk into the street, pull large crowds, and then look for one of them to take him home with them for a couple of days or weeks, gladly feeding him and paying for his return boat ticket. Trekking, riding donkeys, or jumping on a boat for long-distance travel cannot deliver the goods anymore. A deliberate, structured financial action plan is required.

The open space for the preaching like the *Hall of Tyrannus* [13] that Paul used in Ephesus probably was free. Then there may not be too many Peters who would gladly allow us the free use of his boat as a platform to preach from at the lake. The Ethiopian Eunuch of our day will not stop his limousine car for a poor pedestrian preacher who is running after him. He will probably suspect that someone was attempting to rob or assault him and tell the driver, "Go faster Jack!" or "Faster, Addisu! I suspect that fellow wants to catch up with us to steal from the car." The million-dollar cathedrals of today are no longer without constraints and rules that alienate '*freelance*' preachers of the Gospel even if you are an ordained *rabbi* like Jesus or Paul with freshly minted, distinguished certificates from Gamaliel's Seminary, and possess faith that moves mountains.

The preaching of the Gospel has become more sophisticated, just like any other field of human endeavors over the last 2,000 years. The audience wants some gospel music, comfortable seats, and an air-conditioned hall or church, too. The villagers want you to bring free food and distributions in crusades that take them away from work, to show films, and to give away free books. The 'minstrels' will no longer do it for free. The crowd will no longer stay under the sun, rain, and snow for three days; or crowd into the lounge of a three-story building to hear the Gospel being taught throughout the night, as in Troas. There is a constant cry for more comfort, more entertainment, compensated services, quick fixes, and advanced technologies everywhere. The preachers can no longer pull the crowd or go to the mission field without extra sandals, extra tunics, and bags.

It takes two years to prepare an average missionary for the field. It is almost easier for a terrorist to get a job at the White House than to be accepted as a missionary with some agencies, even when you may have to raise your own money and meet 100% of your budget.

Ministry today requires money. Money is needed. Yet, Jesus said, "Go, I have sent you?" If you are still waiting for someone to foot the bill, it may take a pretty long time for an angel to show up. Even after sending out thousands of mass mailers and making financial appeals, many have not been able to raise the money needed and are sometimes frustrated. Doesn't God have a better way?

Today, many leaders spend hours on fundraising activities or filling out funding applications. Our prayers do not need to be dominated by crying out for finances every day and focusing and coveting partners or members who are capable of giving large checks.

No matter how many excuses we have on finances, the truth is that the Gospel must be preached on all the Earth until the end comes.[14]

Chapter 2 Overview

Financing Your Vision

Ministry Issue
How can a Christian worker finance their God-given dream of making Kingdom exploits?

Ministry Lesson
The starting point is to have the right mindset about finances.

CHAPTER 2

FINANCING YOUR VISION

Fine-tune Your Financial Mindset
"Every man ought to have money on his mind. No man ought to have money on his heart." Larry Burkert and Ron Blue[15]

The great evangelist, teacher, and writer, Gordon Lindsay, who pioneered the Voice of Healing Ministry, which later became Christ For The Nations Institute (CFNI), said in his book:

> "The main hindrance to the world's evangelization has not been for the want of devoted missionaries, nor is it for the lack of trained nationals, which was a serious problem for many years. The hour has come when we have an eager army of Gospel-ready individuals to launch out in faith and to preach the apostolic Gospel, and they are doing it! Nor is there a lack of people responding to the message…Where then is the lack? It is in the lack of necessary financial assistance that often is not available at the moment the Spirit of God moves in a community."[16]

This statement is still valid today. Supposing the church's income, the ministers' income and an average believer's income increased two-fold, five times or ten times above what we currently have, what impact would that have made on the Great Commission?

Brother Kenneth Hagin asked the question, "How many projects have remained in the dreaming or planning stage because the money to turn them into a reality was never available?"[17] Is this not still true?

As far back as 1888, T.S. Linscott wrote in his book, "We find the Church of God descending to using business methods in order to raise enough money to pay its expenses; hence, we have tea-meetings, bazaars, concerts...and all sorts of schemes to raise money—while the vast majority rob God of His tithes...If Christian people would live up to the Bible, there would be no need for such methods of raising money—there would be enough and some to spare.... We have men and women whose hearts God has touched and whose souls are aflame with missionary zeal. We also have a Gospel that meets all sorts of requirements of all kinds and conditions of men...but how can they be sent without money? And how can they get the money unless it is given to them in God's appointed way..."[18] He decried the commercializing of the Gospel in the name of fundraising. These practices are not really the 'business method,' but a coward's choice.

If these statements were valid in the days of Linscott, when he wrote them in 1888, of Gordon Lindsay in 1961, and Kenneth Hagin in 2000, then they are even more pertinent today and beyond. The problem with world evangelization, church planting, and global revival is not the lack of preachers or a lack of missionaries and Christian workers at home or overseas; it is the lack of financial resources—a truth we must all admit and address.

This is a perennial problem with the Church, and it must be faced with boldness, honesty, and determination. The Church can no longer wave aside the challenge of finances for world evangelization with excuses of the current and past abuses of finances by some corrupt elements of the Church or by a lack of funds. Every generation has its problems, and each must find creative ways of accomplishing the Great Commission and generating enough money to carry out what Christ has commissioned. That is the bottom line. How can they go unless they are sent? How can they be sent without money? How will dreams not perish unless there is money?

How Can I Finance My Vision Or Calling?
A ministerial vision is a picture of what God wants us to achieve while we are here on Earth. It is the unique thing that counts in a person's

life, and it makes him or her distinguishable. James, in his Epistle, says it is a sin if we know how to do good and we fail to do it. What is needed in this generation is a man with a vision from God, passion to fulfill it, and the finances to birth it. But finance can challenge your faith when it comes to obeying the calling.

When someone has been called by God, trained or is zealous to preach the Gospel and do God's work, the first major question the enemy raises in his mind is: "How will you fund that vision and your plans? Don't you think you are being overly ambitious and have too high expectations?" This is the billion-dollar question on why the Great Commission is lagging behind. There is no doubt money is the biggest obstacle to global evangelism. The more we try to ignore that question, the more it haunts and troubles us, regardless of how much we try to suppress it. When you leave that question unanswered, you will live to face it again sooner or later.

Today, there exists a huge 'poverty monster' that plagues the mind of the Church, and it prevents the believer from attaining financial freedom. This limits the effectiveness of preaching the Gospel and achieving the Great Commission in general. Without resources, the Church will continue to make little impact; the lost will continue to be unreached; the ripe harvests will continue to rot and be unharvested, and the harvester will continue to be unmotivated because of the lack of provisions. Much of the advice that ministers, as well as the Body of Christ, receive from Christian authors on "prosperity" is somewhat faulty, manipulative, and misleading. They have no clear solution to obtaining provisions for the vision without becoming an impostor. They further dash people's hopes of accomplishing God's purpose for their lives.

Christians are simply told to bring more money in order to get more money—the 100-fold formula—but many Christians wonder how that works for them. The same believers who have been instructed to shun money-making methods are expected to bring their checks and do endless "sowing." The reason is that believers are not taught how to draw their wisdom from God's Word to generate finances and to manage their money.

Turning to secular authors doesn't help, either. In fact, it can cause more harm because they tend to hype up the process of money-making in order to hook the reader. Now their 'captive audience' can pay even more to buy their continuously rebranded products, attend their ongoing, expensive seminars, and pursue money-making schemes in unrighteous ways. Many are led astray in the process, trying to become millionaires in a nanosecond! That there's always a secret to money-making. The truth is, there is no new secret of money-making that has never been known before. Every wealth book is a product of what has already been said or done in the past.

People are easily drawn to bad advice as long as it is presented as a *new secret*. It is not that we cannot learn from the corporate or business world, but we need to know how to separate the wheat from the chaff and eat fish without the bones. This is the greatest challenge to Christians who want to use worldly wisdom as their guide. Much of the literature on money is lopsided—largely written by atheists and those who do not hold true Christian values or believe in God.

How the Church has Embraced Lady Poverty
There is a new rise of a movement in the Church that advocates a "Poverty Gospel." It may sound fashionable to denounce money and adopt the so-called "Adversity Gospel," also known as "apostolic poverty." At least on the surface, that is what it looks like. In reality, most of those who condemn the "Prosperity Gospel" actually promote and practice it in a different but smarter way. They are the same folks who commercialize the Gospel and ask Christians to pay for registration to attend their meetings. They will have a long list of partners they raise money from, ask for donations, or get the government to fund their

para-church projects. Yet, they are not Prosperity-Gospel inclined. I am not supporting an extreme "Prosperity Gospel" that exploits people and corrupts leaders, but there is a point I want to make here.

Now we need to understand that it is guilt that has motivated the overly hypocritical embrace of the "Adversity Gospel" in this generation of waste and surplus driven by consumerism. The concept of self-imposed poverty or "Adversity Gospel" is like an act of 'penance'—trying to punish oneself in order to earn God's approval and to appear holy to others. Salvation is by grace and not by works![19]

A zealous leader of a mega-church in the United States once said he had led his church to remove their cushioned benches and replaced them with hard benches. This was a way of proving that he is not a prosperity preacher. That is either fanatism, hypocrisy, or both, and the motive can be questioned unless there is proof the proceeds from the sale of those cushioned benches were sent to a poorer church.

Sitting on cushion benches is not a sin in any way. In some cases, a church would announce the celebration of an ultra-modern cathedral costing $40 million dollars, and five satellite campuses at $25 million dollars each, and then turn around and trumpet that they have sent $1,200 to a church in Honduras, South Sudan, or Ethiopia, or $500 to a native missionary in India for their annual support or to build a church. They proudly announce this in the same way a villager, who has just killed a lion or an elephant, would boast. They expect to be praised for doing good.

Now, how can you preach the "Adversity gospel" to people who are already poor? We can harm the Gospel when we teach people too much about poverty, especially where people look to God on a daily basis for all their meager needs—health, jobs, food, and shelter. The Gospel is not supposed to be a life sentence, but the good news!

On the other hand, the Church in the southern hemisphere is struggling even to financially support their workers. Many meet in borrowed or rented buildings, sheds, shade trees, whether it's rain or shine—without shelter, in villages. Others meet in homes and underground churches to learn God's Word, to worship, and to fellowship. Under such situations, teaching the "poverty gospel" is sheer insensitivity. Believers want to know God's Word and trust Him for all their needs. We must even go past teaching to show that our teaching worked for us. That is where "Faith living" makes real sense, and we must not despise the poor.

That was why Paul had to teach people that God can supply all their needs beyond their expectation and imagination and is able to make all grace abound so people can have enough and plenty to share with others.[20] He was not just talking about them giving but also receiving. It is in agreement with Scriptures, too—God can give us more than we give to Him—He can open the windows of Heaven and pour out such blessing that there will not be room enough to receive it.[21] That will happen if we acquire knowledge on His financial wisdom.

The truth is that God doesn't fail to do financial miracles any more than He fails to do healing miracles. He can heal poverty, just like He can heal sicknesses or heal the land. This book is not about either Prosperity or Adversity teaching. I am just trying to strike a balance with the perspectives here and challenge what we have come to accept as the *status quo,* and present a refreshing paradigm on financing the ministry.

The Church has gone through historical cycles of lopsided 'adversity-prosperity,' starting from the 'communal wealth distribution,' which temporarily met everyone's needs, and then was followed by an extreme 'austere' in the Jerusalem church. This moved on to a balanced teaching and practice on finances in the Pauline-led churches. However, following the Constantine Edict of A.D. 313, the medieval church became overly materialistic, and Christianity became a money-making machine. The priesthood became not just an alternative job but the most lucrative one, compared to medicine, law, or any other professions of that day. Those were the days when relics that were claimed to have been recovered from the apostles were sold in the Church to raise huge wealth, and Certificates of Indulgence were sold for the forgiveness of sins for specified monetary amounts. That situation continued for nearly a thousand years until the time of reformation. It was a major financial scandal.

A Long Journey of Poor Scriptural Application
A flashback to the apostolic handling of finances in the Early Church in Jerusalem leaves a model that cannot be adopted today. Out of their zeal to experience the Sermon on the Mount, the believers, in self-denying joy of fellowship, had voluntarily sold off what they had and brought the proceeds to the apostles' feet. These blessings were shared, and everyone's needs were met in the short term.[22]

Jesse L. Hurlburt puts it like this:
"We read a surrender of property on the part of the richer disciples so general as to suggest the extreme of socialism in a community of goods. But concerning this aspect of the Pentecostal Church, it should be noted that it was entirely voluntary, not under the compulsion of law, not the poor demanding the property of the rich, but the rich of their own accord giving to the poor. It was tested in a small community, all dwelling within one city…to reproduce the principles of the Sermon on the Mount. It arose in the expectation of a speedy return of Christ, at whose coming, earthly possessions might be no longer needed.

As a financial experiment, it was a failure and was soon abandoned. It left the church in Jerusalem so poor that, for a generation, collections were taken abroad for its relief. Also, the system developed its own moral evils, as in the selfishness of Ananias and Sapphira. We are still on the Earth and need the spur of self-interest and of necessity. This spirit of liberal giving is to be commended, but its plan may have been unwise."[23]

That was a summary of the financial practice in the Jerusalem church. Nonetheless, the generosity of the brethren was to be commended. Those who teach against tithing and advocate a return to early church practice on finances should read that again. It is simply not a model that can be used in the modern church.

Dr. Bruce Shelley, in his book, *Church History in Plain Language*, provides a beautiful insight on how the Church arrived at the 'Prosperity-Poverty' schism today, in a chapter entitled, *A Song to Lady Poverty*.[24] The biography of St. Francis of Assisi indicates how devotedly and ardently he gave himself to poverty. According to the story, Francis was told by two old men that Lady Poverty lived in the mountains. So he went with his companions in search of her until he found her "on the throne of her neediness." She convinced Francis that she was with Adam in Eden and that she had become a homeless wanderer until Jesus came to make her His "elect one." That through her, believers multiplied, including monks, until her enemy's avarice made them rich and worldly. So she withdrew from monasticism. Enchanted by her story, Francis vowed to be faithful to her and made her his bride.

Many other admirers joined in the 12th and 13th centuries. In those days, their mandate was clear-cut: "Sell all you have, give it to the poor, and come follow me." This medieval "Poverty Movement" broke into two camps—heresy or orthodoxy, sometimes with little difference, but at the heart of it was spiritual hunger. Is Lady Poverty truly the Bride of Jesus—the Church? That's what the advocates of voluntary poverty believed. To them, a life of penance and poverty was an indication of purity. There are Pentecostal and evangelical Christians who still pitch their tent here today.

Under the leadership of an abbot, Arnold of Brescia, the gospel of voluntary poverty drew its strength and sympathy from the corruption of the Church of that day. This movement actually seized power for about ten years, but the Abbott was executed by burning in A.D. 1155.

Soon after this, a rich merchant, Peter Waldo, another advocate of "apostolic poverty" from Lyons in eastern France, arose with a strong "voice of poverty." In search of how to live like Christ, a priest pointed him to Matthew 19:21, "If you want to be perfect, go sell your possessions and give to the poor, and you will have treasure in Heaven.

Then come, follow Me." Peter Waldo, enchanted by the poverty spirit, left his new bride on the night of his wedding and went to the Holy Land. After Waldo gained some followers, he sent them out to preach, and they practiced voluntary poverty, calling themselves "Poor in Spirit." This movement is known as Waldenses.[25]

Years later, Waldo was so emaciated due to a life of denial that no one could recognize him. He lived on scraps from the family table and only revealed his identity as he lay dying—too late to be restored by the grieving family.[26] The movement of "apostolic poverty" had aimed to bring the Church back to the Bible, but it didn't apply the whole counsel of God. Jesus is looking for a Christian who is truly *"poor in the spirit,"* not a bunch of beggars or some radical poverty movement.

The Two Hair-Splitting Camps
Because of this supposedly weird, financial apostasy, among other factors, the reformation leaders of the Church saw money as an enemy to be avoided; of course, it was justified by unbalanced and out-of-context Scriptural supports. The result was the division of a naturally invincible and indivisible Body of Christ on concepts, principles, doctrines, and authority. One of the areas of such great contention is finance.

Out of this rubble came two camps. The first is the advocate of the so-called "Prosperity Gospel."—This is generally perceived as having an emphasis on wealth, healing, and deliverance from demonic forces. It is based on the premise that God has provided for all needs of humankind through the atonement of the Cross—through the suffering and death of Jesus Christ. However, there is a wrong impression that the prosperity gospel ignores the cross and does not teach salvation. This is an understanding that is questionable. Prosperity Gospel has put God back in the center of Christian experience by teaching that God is more than able to meet all needs. It offers a holistic view of salvation rather than the dualistic view of salvation that is devoid of power and provision. The challenge, however, is that the prosperity gospel has tended to swing to the extreme of the pendulum by promoting faulty and unscriptural practices and doctrines. In some quarters, prosperity is synonymous with greed and materialism, and consumerism.

The second camp embraced with a new resurgence the unsung but implied, "Adversity Gospel." In an attempt to separate themselves from the prosperity gospel, the adversity gospel movement has tried to throw the baby out with the bathwater, with the danger of veering away from biblical and theological facts on God's provision. Provision, healing, and expectation that God can meet the needs of believers beyond their ability are part of the Gospel of Jesus. Neither of these two camps is the true Gospel, and we need the whole counsel of God to stay on middle ground. The Bible is the middle ground—far from both extremes. It calls for reflection. It calls for balance. It calls for a return to the true teaching on the subject of money from the whole counsel of God.

Never, in the history of the Church, has there been such confusion, heresies, misunderstanding, and conflicts, regarding the application of biblical concepts on finances as there is today. The word "prosperity" has now been increasingly abused and bastardized by the "Prosperity camps" to raise more money from unsuspecting crowds. On the other hand, the word "prosperity" is being shunned and demonized by the "Adversity camps," which are fed up with the former. These result in gross misunderstandings and counterproductive ways of viewing and handling money by the Church, even among the Charismatic, Evangelical, and Pentecostal believers of the 21st Century.

The Scriptures are often twisted, mutilated, misquoted, and misapplied by both camps in order to either promote or denounce financial prosperity—as evil or as good. All these further result in distrust, dishonesty, chaos, abuses, and heresies. Consequently, there are many who want to have nothing to do with teaching on finances for fear of being called a prosperity preacher. I am sure no one wants to be called an "Adversity Preacher," either. If you find one in your city, just go ask for the keys to his car and home before he goes too far with that claim. So I want to be called the "Whole-Counsel" teacher or preacher or a "Whole-Counsel Christian." How about you?

The advocates of 'Adversity Gospel' promote avoiding anything to do with finances as if it is a sin or leprosy or plague. They teach believers to cherish poverty and always to remind themselves that wealth is sinful. Why? Their easy answer is to quote James, *"woe unto you that are rich"* (James 5:1-6). A bible teacher interpreted that to mean that Jesus had cursed the rich when He said, "But woe to you who are rich, for you have received your consolation." But that is half-truth unless you read the whole text. So were Nicodemus, Joseph, and Zacchaeus cursed as they were rich? Context matters in every biblical interpretation. You will realize the type of rich people James was addressing here: those who made their money through fraud, corruption, cheating, oppression, and even murdering the innocent for money. The camp advocating the "Prosperity Gospel" emphasizes and presents money as an object of worship and as a measure of success and spirituality. They measure God's blessing and achievement by dollars and success in terms of the crowds. The result is consumerism—spending church money for self and members' enjoyment, entertainment, and luxury, and not for the Great Commission. It results in leaders staying in $6,000 hotel rooms per night and flying private jets to preach. That is also an undesired extreme that must be avoided. All they need to do is to put God's stamp on the excesses. Although both camps still extract money from the pockets of believers, the only difference is their approach to it. How long must people continue to dishonor God, thinking they are honoring him with ignorance, poverty, and wrong attitudes?

The backlash of these half-truths is that missionaries are caught between the two camps and are left confused. The result is that either there are insufficient funds to do God's work or there is a surplus or abundance of money that is hoarded by a few rich mega-churches and their ministers for internal consumption—in multimillion-dollar cathedrals and monumental structures, Hollywood state-of-the-art musical equipment, and artificial Heaven-like stages.

Many Christians in the Pentecostal churches in most third-world countries are poor. One reason is that Christianity appeals more to the poor than it does to the rich, and that is why Jesus had placed the poor in very high esteem in His ministry and teachings.

On the other hand, many believers who are wealthy are often ill-informed and misguided in the way they must acquire and spend their money. Many clergymen spend more time managing the wealth of their members than they do in equipping and releasing them for the service of the Kingdom. They create the impression that once you are financially prosperous, you are doing well in the Lord—He is shining His face upon you. This concept is very dangerous.

The sound biblical teachings, principles, practical models, and paradigms on financial wealth creation, wise investments, and financial stewardship have been deliberately avoided in the Church to avoid reducing the church's income. If we must restore the Church to the position of Christ's vision, we must retrace our steps back to the Bible—that is where we can encounter solutions for a financial breakthrough.

When God calls a believer to the ministry, whether it is as a missionary, a pastor, an evangelist, or any of the five-fold ministries, they are preoccupied with the thought, "How will my needs be met?" This single question has split families as spouses disagree with the calling because of the financial responsibilities and possible unmet needs. Some ministers truly called and trained have remained in their shells, withdrawn in their comfort zones because of unmet needs.

Many Christians who sense God's calling are afraid to say, "Yes Lord, here am I, send me." Some in the full-time ministry, who have been struggling, even question whether or not they should go back to doing secular jobs again. Those who felt called often feel trapped, and the fact that they cannot leave their job for one simple reason: "What will happen to my family if I leave this job? How will my needs be met?" Yet, the Word of God and His wisdom provide answers to every situation. What we need is the right balance and the knowledge of how to apply God's Words. If we must have doctrines, we must base them on sound biblical counsel—the whole counsel of God.

Christians need to be enlightened about how to acquire and manage finances and then how to spend it to the glory of God and the expansion of the Kingdom. Therefore, *Provisions for the Vision* is not a book on traditional prosperity myths or just another book on wealth creation magic bullets. It's a heuristic treasure that allows Christians and leaders to discover self-learned, practical ways of applying God's Word to create, multiply, retain wealth, and apply financial stewardship. It aims at unlocking the secret of financial freedom without compromising biblical standards or one's Christian integrity.

Improve Your Financial Mindset
In 2004, as I was about to conclude my teaching at the Assemblies of God Church, Lilongwe, Malawi, a young man who was sitting on the back row raised his hand and blurted out his frustration. "These are conflicting messages of 'prosperity' preachers, and I am confused. You are saying that it is not a sin for Christians to have money. Did the Bible not teach us that Jesus Himself was poor? He was born in a manger, He did not own a house, He rode on a borrowed donkey, had a banquet in a borrowed hall, and He died and was buried in a borrowed tomb? Is Jesus a good model to follow?" The classroom was stunned. There was dead silence.

This young man had a wrong mindset about why Jesus was poor.

Then I began to show him how everything that was predicted about Jesus had been fulfilled in each of his statements. That Jesus, who was rich, chose to become poor—so we could be rich, not that we should be poor!

King Solomon said, "As a man thinks, so he is." You cannot be greater than your mindset when it comes to finances. If you are wealthy, a wrong mindset can set your finances into a reverse motion; this is why people with poor mindsets that win the lottery lose the lottery money. Wrong thinking causes wrong management.

Many Christians are overly spiritual, and they generally view money as the 'root of all kinds of evil.' They may not say so directly and even understand what Paul said, but their actions imply exactly otherwise. But is money the root of evil or the love of it?[27] Many Christians omit the word "*the love of* money..."; instead, they say money is the root of all evil. Also, James said in his biblical epistle, "Now listen you rich people, weep and wail because of the misery that is coming upon you. Your wealth is rotted, and moths have eaten your clothes. Your silver and gold are corroded...."[28] Read the rest!

Who was James talking about, believers or the worldly rich? If we choose to label anyone who teaches on money as a "prosperity preacher" and despise money altogether, we are not faithful to God's Word, and the Gospel will suffer. Kenneth Hagin put this in context, "It has been my experience that with every biblical subject, there is a main road of truth with a ditch of error on either side of the road. The Church has not always been a very good driver, often having difficulty in staying in the middle of the road. Just about anywhere you go on the Bible pathway you'll find people off in the ditch—on one side or the other. There are those in one ditch who teach that Jesus lives in abject poverty, that money is evil, and that biblical prosperity has nothing at all to do with material things. And in the other ditch, there are people who are preaching that biblical prosperity is the main focus of our faith, that God's main concern is your material well-being, and that money is the true measure of spirituality. Where is the truth? It is found far away from both extremes, on much higher ground." The difference between the rich and the poor is simply in their financial mindset.

Money is Needed for the Gospel

One of the stumbling blocks to missions is, "We don't have enough money to fulfill the vision."[29] Comes with this realization is then the Church will have to raise its own finances, as the world or satan will not do it for her. No government, not even in Israel or America, will even set funds apart for evangelism and teaching the Word of God. And if that were to happen, you can expect that the Church would be secularized in no time. How many believers have ever asked God to make us a part of the financial investors in the Kingdom; not just 'donors,' but those who will deliberately invest their money, their heart, and their lives into the expansion of Christ's Kingdom on Earth, with the aim of getting eternal returns? As we should expect, to increase the realization of the work of the Holy Spirit in evangelizing the world, we must not forget the importance of money.

Let's come to face the fact that the word "prosperity" is not a worldly term but a scriptural term. The word prosperity actually litters the entire Bible, and God's own Words pronounce or promise prosperity hundreds of times. There is no other book I know of that you can find the word 'prosperity" being used and promised more than in the Bible. And prosperity is beyond finances—it includes our physical, material, and spiritual wellbeing, *"Beloved, I pray that you may prosper in all things and be in health, just as your soul prospers"* (3 John 2). Why do we then want to shun the word and blessing for believers and demonize it just because some preachers have gone overboard? Do we shun the calling of pastors just because some shepherds are actually wolves? Or do we shun visiting the hospitals and doctors because there are some bad ones out there? In all things, there are counterfeits and the same within the church. But we must not despise God's Word because of counterfeits as God's Word cannot be broken.

Prosperity is the sum of material and spiritual well-being for the believer that brings joy, peace, and thanksgiving to God.[30] On the other hand, poverty is the reverse. It is a situation of want, insufficiency, austerity, and hardship. Have you ever met anyone who truly wishes to be poor? No, I have not. I am yet to see anyone who truly loves to be very poor.

The evil one satan has led the Church to believe that money is dirty. In turn, he can hold the Church hostage as believers they are bound and unable to run the race that is set before them.

Chapter 3 Overview
Jesus Taught Money

Ministry Issue
What did Jesus actually teach on money and investment?

Ministry Lesson
Removing the negative stereotype from what Jesus taught on money, with regards to preaching the Gospel. Uncovering the fundamentals of financial stewardship and investment wisdom contained in the teaching of Jesus.

CHAPTER 3

JESUS TAUGHT MONEY

Financial Wisdom in The Gospel

"Again, it will be like a man going on a journey, who called his servants and entrusted his property to them…each according to his ability… The man who had received the five talents went at once and put his money to work and gained five more" Matthew 25:14-16.

"To see a man humble under prosperity is one of the greatest rarities in the world."[31] John Flavel

One of the most amazing metaphors describing the Gospel of Christ in this century was appropriately coined by Brian Zahnd in his book, *"Beauty Will Save the World."* In the book, Pastor Zahnd powerfully argues for a rediscovery of the allure of Christianity—how the Gospel of Christ could enchant those it captivates to the Kingdom of saving grace, even where truth and goodness fail to win the heart of the people. Unless Christians learn to discover the breath-taking story of Jesus and let their lives truly be the mirrors of Him as His ambassadors, that enchanting beauty of the cross will remain obscured. We must see the Gospel preached from the total counsel of God. We must tell His story and tell it well.

We cannot tell it well when thousands of churches permanently close their doors every year due to financial challenges. Or when many churches meet under trees, open spaces, uncompleted buildings, and leaking roofs, and falling walls, and when many Christians cannot afford personal bibles in their hands. Or when missionaries are abandoned in the mission field, or when pastors and leaders must spend most of their private time meditating, praying and fasting, and worrying about how to make ends meet, than use the time to preach or teach, intercede for souls and minister to the needy. That is one of the chief strategies of the enemy: he simply empties the Church of financial resources.

Message on Money Confuses Christians

Jude was a 37-year-old millionaire that I met some years ago during an advanced leadership and evangelism training at The Haggai Institute, Hawaii. He is an amiable personality, an excellent Christian, and is zealous for God.[33] We spent a lot of our free time talking about ministry, vision, and entrepreneurship. One evening, Jude humbly explained how his financial worth was worth tens of millions of dollars at the time. He had started very well in both corporate achievement and investment. With a solid background as a computer analyst and an MBA, he rose very quickly to become the CEO of a rapidly expanding company in his country when he was only 28 years old. Early in his career, he started to invest in real estate and had bought dozens of houses and paid them off while streams of income flowed to him, especially from large amounts of rent each month. He also bought businesses.

The worth of these properties had increased astronomically. Within fifteen years, his real-estate investments had multiplied more than ten times in the market. His stock had soared, also. Money continued to flow to him from sales, rent, and equity, also from the stock market and businesses.

He said to me, "Festus, to confess to you; I have too much money. I can even buy an airplane. I am afraid that I have too much money. I also spend too much. You can't imagine how I spend. I am convicted that I have been sinning by having too much money! When I return to my country, I want to sell all my real estate properties. I will invest in only one company to reduce my wealth." Jude said, with much confusion, soberness, and 'charismatic guilt' in his voice.

"Jude, what made you think you have sinned by having a lot of money?" I probed.

"Well, because I have too much money, I have so many real estate properties that I have paid off, owing nothing. Rent flows to me from many of them, and I am still working and earning. I have many properties, and some of them have increased 1000%! The values of the properties have multiplied more than ten times since I bought them."

"But, I can't really see where the problem is," I said, trying to calm him down.

He responded, "The Bible says it is a sin to have too much money. I am sinning. I have read through the New Testament that it is a sin to be rich. I am convicted and do not know what to do."

Now he really felt it was a turning point in his life, and he must do something about it. How he was going to do it was the real challenge to him. I realized that we both had just read some materials, and one of them was a fundraising book. The author had interpreted the Bible in the "Poverty-is-good" and "Give-all-you-have" mentality. I tried to explain why he shouldn't reason that way, but he wouldn't be convinced otherwise. He was only one step away from embracing Lady Poverty as his new bride.

Then I said, "Alright, Jude! What are you planning to do, now that you seem to be convinced that you are sinning because you have too much money? I am forced to agree with you that you are a sinner because you have too much money, but don't quote me. I am driving at something here. Now, tell me more. What are you planning to do now?" Before this, I had tried to convince him, abortively, for over 30 minutes; but he was adamant about his perception.

"Yeah…When I return to my country, I want to sell some of my real-estate properties and give the money to charity to help the poor. I want to buy a small company. I need to reduce my wealth. I feel really convicted. I know you are a wise man and a mature believer; I need your advice." He nearly sounded a bit confused. I could see that his struggle has not shifted to deciding between selling all his assets and reducing the assets to enable him to do some charity. He did not even talk of supporting the Kingdom.

Smiling at my friend, I said sarcastically, "Well said; I have a better idea. If you really want to be perfect, I recommend that you go and sell everything you possess, leave nothing out—your properties, your businesses, your shares, and close your accounts and all your savings and give the money to the poor. Give all to charity or the Church, then keep serving Jesus, and you will live." Note that I deliberately included, "If you want to be perfect, and you will live" so he can be sure there was scripture to back it up. Then I watched his reaction.

"No! I can't do that! My family will suffer." He was blunt about this. I realized that his countenance immediately looked pale.

"Then you are not ready to obey what Jesus said to the young rich man. You are a young man and zealous about following Jesus, and you also want to be perfect. Why wouldn't you sell all your properties and give to the poor?"[34] He was quiet. So I laughed to break the silence that followed. Jude was now calm and sober. He was ready to listen to me.

I now started to help Jude see the Scriptures and the subject of finances in a more constructive, biblical, and holistic way. I asked him the following questions, and I also want to ask you…

(You may want to write your answers down.)

- How many pastors, missionaries, or Christian workers have you supported, and how much per month?
- How many bibles or scriptural materials have you bought and give to others in need or new believers?
- How many churches have you supported or even built?

- How many Christians have you housed, paid their rents or offer hospitality?
- How many orphans or poor people had you helped?
- Have you ever helped believers in difficulties in your own church or elsewhere?
- What are your ministry goals, plans, and giftings?
- What is your vision for ministry—what is God calling you to do for the Kingdom?
- Do you know about the *supply-line* and *front-line* concept of the Kingdom troops?
- What are your retirement plans and goals in life? Will you continue to give after your retirement?

I realized that although Jude really loved to serve God, he had not yet identified any clear calling in the ministry, but he had a zeal for God and some interests. He was also an elder in his church, but his Christian leadership experience and depth of the Word needed some time to reach maturity, according to his own confession. I helped Jude tease out some ideas on how he could still be an entrepreneur and contribute more effectively to the Kingdom. Like Lydia from the church of Philippi, entrepreneurs have an important role to play in the Kingdom. She was a dealer in purple cloth for the wealthy. She became an instrument of God for promoting the Kingdom.

I also advised him to start changing his prayers henceforth and to start asking the Lord Who had endowed him with the power to make wealth and use it for His glory, what He really wanted him to do with this wealth to direct him to where he could partner with God in the work of the Kingdom—either in the frontline or supply line or both, rather than taking a panic measure and unguarded emotionally-driven steps.

"Are you now on board?" I asked. "Yes. Thank you for the wisdom and your time. I really appreciate it." His mindset had changed as he realized God will not give us anything without a purpose for it.

The Mindset Trap

Newton Richardson had received a newly-minted MBA degree from Harvard University, and he had great potential in the business world.[35] Within five years, he had become a mini-CEO of a growing toy-making company. Then he sensed a calling into the ministry and went to Bible college where he obtained a Master's degree in Evangelism and Leadership; he was ordained as a minister. He was a visionary, Spirit-filled, and an evangelistic firebrand who wanted to preach the Gospel and win his generation.

While in College he sat under a visiting teacher and was 'baptized' into the adversity, anti-money gospel. He argued that Jesus was not interested in crowds or playing gimmicks when He boldly declared that anyone who would follow Him should first abandon everything—his finances, his needs, ambition, his family, and even his own life, and then carry his cross and follow Jesus.[36] Yes, in Luke 9 and 10, He had also told His disciples not to take anything with them.

Having read about the story of the man Jesus told to go and sell all he had and give them to the poor and then follow Him, he concluded that Jesus hates any form of wealth connected to those who choose to follow Him. He also read in James' epistle, a rebuke to the rich who hoarded wealth, lived in luxury, indulged themselves and defrauded their workers of their pay, and who even murdered the innocent.[37] So he concluded that James and the apostles hated money and the rich, as well.

Newton's desire was to please God and be pure, so he believed if he hated money, that was the answer. He sold his car, his house and other possessions and distributed all the money to a charity organization catering to the poor. His wife could not cope with the hardship she experienced and quit the marriage. He went to the mission field in India with only his transport money and refused to ask for help from any man. Nevertheless, he did not completely starve because of God's grace. Two years later, Newton was back in town, vowing to never return to ministry again, never to be called a pastor, and became a manager in Walmart. How many visions have died in the hands of bad trustees in this way? Half-gospel is sometimes worse than no-gospel.

On the other hand, Robert Kaiser[38] was a medical doctor who had been practicing for eight years. He had a clinic of his own and made a very good income. He took off two years to study at a Spirit-filled bible college that taught balanced words of God. He was taught financial principles and ethics and bi-vocational ministry. He launched a church plant at weekends with some of his own resources. He engaged two of his co-ministers and even supported them financially at the beginning. They trained new leaders in gifts identification, development and deployment, and missional church planting. Each year they conducted evangelistic meetings and planted at least one new church. Within ten years, a dozen vibrant churches had been planted with membership ranging from fifty to over a thousand, and most were pastored by home-grown leaders.

After twelve years, Dr. Kaiser was led to serve God in a full-time position. He sold off his clinic and invested the proceeds in diversified investment options that generated passive income for him. His church plant also supported most of his other major ministry expenses. Today, Pastor Kaiser leads a church with well over 500 branches, with balanced teaching on the Great Commission. This would have been impossible without knowledge and money to implement the vision.

Here two people went to Bible college and were zealous for God, but their motivations, and understanding of God's Word on money, were somewhat different. One killed his own vision out of ignorance, and the other had nurtured and grown his vision into fruition. We are responsible for understanding the teachings of the Scriptures and applying them correctly to our lives and ministry.

Nearly half of all the parables of Jesus touched on finances—giving, investment, entrepreneurship, stewardship, and sacrifice. Therefore, it is an injustice to the teachings of Jesus if we just use them to disenfranchise believers from participating in the world harvest because of our veiled and skewed interpretations.

What Does Jesus Really Say About Money?
We need to discover the secret of God's wealth on earth and how to finance the Great Commission. Jesus was rich, but He became poor that we might be rich.[39] Paul said this in reference to money, not just about spiritual richness. Jesus didn't become poor so the Church could be poor. But that is what the "Adversity Gospel" promotes. On the contrary, He became poor that we may be rich. We need to change our mindset on what we wrongly thought Jesus expects and focus on what He actually said. Rather than surveying literature on what Jesus taught on money, investing, and finances, I want to package these into timeless investment principles that will help us develop and enlighten our financial view.

For instance, Jesus had taught on various subjects that related to finances in, but not limited to, the following:

- He taught against financial greed and the love of worldly wealth. (Luke 12:13-21)
- He advocated for financial sacrifice—selling everything was to test the heart. It tests how you value or prioritize the Heavenly and earthly wealth; (Luke 12:33; 18:22)
- He commended and encouraged financial sacrifice, giving, and stewardship; (Luke 12: 42-45; Luke 6:38)
- In understanding the cravings of the hearts of men for material wealth, He contrasted between Heavenly and earthly wealth—your heart is where your money is; (Luke 12:33-34)
- With the Samaritan man's example, He showcased the need for doing good with money and having compassion for the needy:

the man paid the inn with two silver coins. (Luke 10:35) If the man was poor, he would not have been able to pay.
- Jesus asserted that ministers of the Gospel deserve their pay. (Luke 10:7; 2 Cor. 9:13-14) Paul agreed with this as well. (1 Cor. 9:13-14) It is not wrong for ministers to receive financial gifts or income from the local church or from those they minister to.
- Mustard seed is a form of investment that grows. The Church is a living organism that can grow. The word of God is the seed.
- The parable of the sower and parable of the talent or minas are classical investment models. (Luke 8:8; Matthew 25:14-30) Jesus used these to teach on the Kingdom of Heaven and what we must do until His return.
- A woman who lost her coin and rejoiced when she found it. (Luke 15:8-10). This has important investment and kingdom implications.
- The two parables of the treasure and the pearl are investment wisdom. (Matthew 13:44-46)
- The story of Lazarus and the rich man was a teaching on the attitude to wealth, humility, and kindness, and doing good with money. Jesus did not condemn the rich man for being rich, but because of his unkind behavior. He never condemned his friends who had means: Lazarus welcomed Him in his house with food for Him and His disciples; the wealthy Nicodemus who buried Him, and Joseph whose tomb was used; the rich Pharisees who entertained Him; Zacchaeus was wealthy.

Let us try to expound on these and distill key investment lessons and principles from some of the teachings of Jesus, including some of the ones listed above.[40]

Lesson 1. *Honor God with your money and goods*
Jesus taught that believers should invest in a Heavenly bank where moths cannot destroy, *"But store up for yourselves treasures in Heaven, where moths and vermin do not destroy, and where thieves do not break in and steal"* (Matthew 6:19-21). In other words, we must honor God

with our money by giving to God's work. Paul supported this statement by saying that God loves a cheerful giver. No matter what you believe, if you do not give to God's work in your church and support the Great Commission, you are disobedient to the Gospel.

Jesus expects us to give. Paul recalled the Word of the Lord, *"...It is more blessed to give than to receive"* (Acts 20:35). More than that, we are to give and to also expect to receive back from God in good measure.[41] If Jesus expects every Christian to be poor, why would He expect us to give and to expect to receive back from God? Without giving, there is nothing to receive back. Without sowing, you cannot reap. Solomon said, *"Honor the Lord with your wealth, with the first-fruits of your crops; then your barn will be filled to overflowing and your vats will brim over with new wine"* (Proverbs 3:9-10). Jesus expects us to have money and in turn, be able to give.

One day as Jesus saw the rich putting their gifts into the temple treasury he also saw a poor widow put in two very small copper coins. *"Truly I tell you,"* He said, *"this poor widow has put in more than all the others"* (Luke 21:1-3). According to Jesus, giving is about sacrifice, not the actual amount that is given. The formula of asking people to give a flat rate negates Jesus' principle of sacrifice. Paul said to give according to what you have, not what you do not have.[42] Giving should be in proportion to your wealth or income and not your credit card or loan required to be taken out.

Lesson 2. *Pay your tax*
The Pharisees wanted to test Jesus on issues of taxation, so they asked whether it was right or not to pay tax to the Emperor Caesar. Jesus asked them to show Him whose image was on the silver coin. They agreed it was Caesar's; then He said to them, *"Give back to Caesar what is Caesar's and to God what is God's"* (Mark 12:17). The fact that we pay tax on our income is not a good excuse not to give also to God. In the United States and probably some other nations, the money

given to the Church or a charity is tax-deductible—meaning part of it could be reclaimed and deducted from the tax. It is considered a charitable donation, and as long as you have a receipt or a written acknowledgment, it is tax-deductible.

For countries where that is applicable, the tax-deductible policy should make Christians much more generous than we currently experience in the Kingdom because it means you can actually give to the Church and deduct it from what you ought to have paid Caesar (the Government). Here Caesar is generous and allows you to take that out. I also wish other Christian nations could emulate that tax-deductible giving orientation that can be channeled to the cause of the Gospel and for doing good. Nevertheless, only a quarter of Christians give at least ten percent of their income, and on average 2-3%, as has been reviewed earlier.

A second time came about when the Pharisees cornered Peter and asked if his Master paid the temple tax. He told Peter, *"But so that we may not cause offense, go to the lake and throw out your line. Take the first fish you catch; open its mouth and you will find a four-drachma coin. Take it and give it to them for my tax and yours"* (Matthew 17:27). So if our Lord, Himself, paid the 'temple tax'[43] and instructed that people pay the 'government tax,' it is a blessing to obey those commands.

Lesson 3. Pay your debts and be willing to forgive debts

Jesus told a parable of a king and a debtor who owed him 10,000 talents (equivalent of 600,000 denarii)—it is conservatively put at more than US $15-billion today.[44] The story is recorded in Matthew 8:23-35. The king wanted to sell the man, his wife, and children to get back his money. He decided to have pity on the man because he was unable to pay, so the king forgave the debtor. But this same man saw someone who likewise owed him a hundred denarii[45] (one talent of gold was worth 6,000 denarii), but was unable to pay him back. He appealed, but the man immediately ordered that he, his wife, and his children should all be sold to repay the debt.[46] When the king heard of this wicked man's behavior, whose debt had been canceled but who in turn did not have mercy on his own debtor, he turned him over to the jailers. That is why forgiveness is very important to God because Jesus has paid the price that we cannot buy with money.

The picture of someone begging the lender, or being sold to pay a debt, was pitiable and was surely not God's will for His people. Believers are not supposed to live in debt, whether it's from credit cards or loans. These must be paid promptly. King Solomon said, *"The rich rule over the poor, and the borrower is slave to the lender"* (Proverbs 22:7). Nonetheless, believers are expected to be lenient to borrowers, and to be willing to help other believers, and, when it is in our power, to cancel debts for those who owe us and are unable to pay. *"And forgive us our debts, as we also have forgiven our debtors"* (Matthew 6:12). Believers are encouraged to write off debts from believers if we can, especially when we are convinced that our brother or sister is having difficulty and may not be in a position to repay, yet have the desire to do so. Jesus said, *"There was a certain creditor who had two debtors. One owed five hundred denarii, and the other fifty. And when they had nothing with which to repay, he freely forgave them both. Tell Me, therefore, which of them will love him more?" Simon answered and said, "I suppose the one whom he forgave more." And He said to him, "You have rightly judged"* (Luke 7:41-43).

When you cancel someone's debt, it will bring joy and rejoicing in the Lord.

Lesson 4. *Spend your money wisely and avoid losses*
Let us examine related parables of Jesus for the concept of avoiding financial losses. A woman had ten silver coins and lost one of them. She spent a lot of effort looking for the lost coin until she found it—lit a lamp, swept the house, and searched for it carefully.[47] When she eventually found it, she rejoiced and celebrated with her friends, saying,

"Rejoice with me; I have found my lost coin" (Luke 15:9). A coin sounds like small money today, but we must realize that the temple tax was just half of a shekel coin—a coin of two shekels and was the wages of a person for one week! (a man would earn 30 shekels in four months in Jesus' time.)[48] Jesus used this parable to teach how Heaven rejoices when a soul is saved. The investment lesson is how to value what we have and to avoid careless financial losses.

The parable of the prodigal son was also about recovering losses. The most financially relevant parable on recovering what was lost was that of a shepherd who lost one of the sheep and decided to go and look for it. Also, there was a dishonest manager who was accused of wasting his master's possessions and was faced with being fired from his job. Although paradoxically, this rogue was commended for his shrewdness; it is a profile that believers should avoid when God has entrusted any job into our hands. A day of reckoning will surely come. The prodigal son squandered his wealth—a good investment capital that he ought to have multiplied, and as a result, to have become wealthy. Instead, he became a pauper and paid dearly for his foolishness.[49] Imagine if he had asked his father for an investment seed money and diligently grown it and brought his returns to his father. We must be wise with our money and not squander it.

Lesson 5. *Invest your money wisely and expect returns*
The parable of the sower is one of the best examples of a farmer's investment and return of investment. A farmer went out and sowed his seeds in different growth environments: the wayside, rocky surfaces, thorny and fertile soils.[50] The Lord interpreted this in Matthew 13 verses 18-23. The seed is the message or Gospel of the Kingdom (the Word of God), which is preached to everyone. Those seeds that fell by the wayside and were eaten up by birds of the air—are those who have the Word of God snatched away from their hearts by the devil; those that fell on the rocky surfaces had no root and easily withered. These people accepted Christ but soon fell away (backslid) due to trouble or

persecution. Those seeds that fell on thorny places represent believers who allow worries of life and deceitfulness of wealth to choke the word of God in their hearts and made them unfruitful.[51] The seed that fell on the good soil and yielded 30, 60, and 100-fold, are believers who hear the Word and obey! The good soil is a Christian who understands the message and nurtures it and becomes fruitful in the Kingdom. How we value and nurture the Word of God in our hearts will affect the extent of spiritual fruits we bear. This is exactly how an investment works.

So let us now apply this parable to investment.[52] Farmers are investors who want to make a profit from their farming enterprise. But the soil and growth environment of the seed (investment)—where it is sown and what it experiences will determine the financial outcome. Returns on the investment require adequate financial security (protection from birds), a good investment instrument (good soils), good investment space (no rocky depth), and less competition (no thorns). The key investment return depends a lot on the type of investment instrument and the environment that allows profit-making or otherwise. There are vanity investment grounds—where an investor cannot expect profits; there are also thorny, rocky, and fertile investment grounds.

The investor needs to make careful decisions. There are unavoidable losses due to poor performance and even bankruptcy of companies, and obvious gains with good stocks. Note that the farmer's focus was to produce crops, hence the sowing on different qualities of soil. He is happy to find fertile land that can produce bountiful crops. In investment terms, the lesson here is that an investor should invest wisely, be prepared for losses, but minimize them, and identify the fertile soil—a suitable investment environment for making more profits.

Second, Jesus spoke of how a treasure investor found one pearl at a great price; he secured it, sold all that he had, and bought the field.[53] This man was adjudged to have made a wise investment decision by liquidating all his possessions and converting them to cash in order to make a higher value investment. The parable teaches that the Kingdom of Heaven is a priceless treasure that believers must be prepared to give everything in their hearts for in order to acquire it.

Third, Jesus said to His listeners, *"Hear another parable: There was a certain householder, which planted a vineyard, and hedged it round about, and dug a winepress in it, and built a tower, and let it out to husbandmen, and went into a far country"* (Matthew 21:33). This man made an investment into his property, he converted it by planting a vineyard in it, and he further added value by constructing a winepress, digging a tower, and a hedge around it. The building of a hedge and tower is for security reasons. Financial protection is important today (insurance against loss). He rented it out for a return on his money equals profits.

Fourth, in a similar parable, Jesus said, *"Then he said to the keeper of his vineyard, 'Look, for three years I have come seeking fruit on this fig tree and find none. Cut it down; why does it use up the ground?"* (Luke 13:6-9).

God wants fruits from His people—we must be profitable. Likewise, every investor is interested in returns from every investment they made. If you keep investing in one investment and there is no profit, sometimes there is a need to move your money to a more profitable enterprise or stop putting in more money.

This is a no-brainer in knowing that what Jesus said more than 2,000 years ago is still a valid investment decision today. In this, we learn that God is the Owner of money, and all possessions, the Earth, and its fullness belong to Him.[54] He gives us the power to make wealth.[55] We are the managers of God-given resources, including money, and we have the responsibility to manage it well.

Lesson 6. Plan for your investment
There is a saying that failing to plan is planning to fail. Every investor knows that it is imperative to plan before embarking on a project. Plan

your financial life. Jesus gave an excellent example, *"Suppose one of you wants to build a tower, won't you first sit down and estimate the cost to see if you have enough money to complete it?"* (Luke 14:28). Kingdom investors need financial goals, and financial plans are developed based on that vision God has given us. You cannot be a good steward if you do not know how to invest. Joseph was a good steward, and he had success because he had an investment mindset. The investment principles of Joseph began from planning ahead. Believers, ministers, and the Church need to have a diligent plan for the money we receive, and we must use it wisely and grow it. We must also teach and empower believers to manage their money wisely. Churches hold marriage courses, but when was the last time your church held a financial management course?

Lesson 7: Money is important for the Gospel
Let's be straight here … Jesus did not hate money; He used money in His ministry. Judas was His treasurer, and he often stole the money—which meant the Lord's ministry treasurer was a thief.[56] Jesus also gave to the poor; otherwise, the disciples would not have thought Jesus was telling Judas to give to the poor.[57] When financial lack was expressed by Philip in feeding the multitudes, Jesus performed miracles to show He is the Lord of provision. Jesus taught that money is important in the ministry, but the anointing is vitally important.[58] Jesus taught that He could sustain a minister who wholly lives by faith and also by empowering him or her through financial investments and their jobs. That was the reason the Lord asked the disciples whether they lacked anything when He sent them out without money, and they answered, "Nothing." We will discuss this in detail in the next chapters.

Oswald J. Smith was once driving along the highway when he pulled his car to the roadside to hear the broadcast of Sir Winston Churchill to the American people as he spoke on the BBC radio station. The British Prime Minister spoke for only about three minutes and said:

"We shall not fail or falter; we shall not weaken or tire. Neither the sudden shock of battle nor the long-drawn trials of vigilance and exertion will wear us down. Give us the tools, and we will finish the job."[59]

"Give us the tools, and we will finish the job." From that day, Oswald Smith got his own slogan for the resource mobilization campaign. He mobilized many congregations and denominations to financially support 44,000 Protestant missionaries, using those same words of Mr. Churchill. He would say, "That is what I say to you now. As fast as the money comes in, the message goes out. We have the workers. We have the organization. All we need are the funds with which to do the work ... may God help you to do what you can. Give us the tools, and we will finish the work."[60]

What the Church lacks today is not people to preach the Gospel, but the "tools" for impacting the missionary field and world evangelization—a financial lever for preaching the Spirit-empowered Word. You, too, can respond to that call of giving Christian workers the tools, so that we can finish the King of kings' work. When Presidents Barrack Obama, Donald Trump, and Joe Biden of the United States of America called for money respectively in 2012, 2016, and 2020, it flowed in by the millions. The Georgia State election in the USA raised about half a billion US dollars. The COVID-19 pandemic gulped several trillions of dollars around the world. All these are for temporary societal values. But when King Jesus calls—for what matters most, everyone puts "the widow's mite" in the offering basket.

Chapter 4 Overview

The Kingdom Investors Mindset

Ministry Issue
Why did Jesus think and communicate His teachings with an investor's mindset?

Ministry Lesson
Kingdom business is an investment, and Kingdom subjects should think as investors and be profitable.

CHAPTER 4

THE KINGDOM INVESTORS MINDSET

Investment Wisdom in Jesus' Parables
"The Kingdom of Heaven is like a treasure hidden in a field. When a man found it, he hid it again, then in his joy went and sold all he had and bought that field" Matthew 13:44.

Dr. Doug Carter affirmed a well-known truth when he said, "The Bible has more to say about money and possessions than any other subject—more than two thousand verses, compared to five hundred on prayer, and even fewer on faith. It is an established biblical fact that Jesus taught about money consistently—He actually taught more on the subject of money than most other topics in the gospels. Sixteen of His thirty-eight parables deal with it."[61] The most obvious fact about money is for spreading the Gospel and how to obtain it through investments seems to have strangely escaped the Church. I is surprising to realize how much the Church has continued to accept and affirm tradition, rather than applying the Words of Jesus on money for missions.

First, Jesus knew that money reveals the heart of a person. Second, He knew that without money, the Great Commission could not go far or be accomplished—the preacher, provisions, and the message go hand-in-hand in soul-winning. Third, He knew that the attitude of a Christian about money would either limit or open ways for Kingdom expansion. Money can both be a blessing or a curse to the cause of Christ. It can be a faithful servant, as well as a shrewd master.

Have you ever thought ... why did Jesus think and communicate His teachings with an investor's mind? He related faithfulness to financial investment, forgiveness to debt cancellation, salvation to discovering treasure, or recovery of lost money. God sending His Son to the Earth as an investment; God's view of Heavenly reward to hiring and paying laborers, etc. The lesson here is that the Kingdom of God is like an investment—there is the investment and the profit end of everything—no matter how spiritual. The Kingdom subjects will do well if they reason as their Master did and think as investors.

Paul asserted, "*...But we have the mind of Christ*" (1 Corinthians 2:16). Christians need to have the mind of Christ in all aspects of faith. In this chapter, we want to get the mind of Christ on money, finances, and investing—to think as He thought and act as He would have acted or had us act.

The parable of the talent is one of the best examples of sound investment decisions that are implied in Jesus' teachings.[62] The talent was literal money of that time. A rich man had entrusted his money to his servants to invest: To one, he gave one talent, to another two, and to another five talents. Then he went on a long journey. When he returned, each of them came to settle accounts with him. One talent in today's money is worth more than 500,000 U.S. dollars.[63] Often, when we think of this money today, we think it is a small amount of money. So to have given even one talent to someone was not a small investment capital.

The story goes like this:
> "*Again, it will be like a man going on a journey, who called his servants and entrusted his property to them. To one, he gave five talents of money, to another two talents, and to another, he gave one talent, each according to his ability. Then he went on his journey. The man who had received five talents went at once and put his money to work and gained five more. So also, the one with the two talents gained two more....*" But the man who had received

one talent went off, dug a hole in the ground, and hid his master's money" (Matthew 25:14-18).

The rich man gave appropriate investment capital to his servants to leverage their ability to make money. God is that rich man, and He has endowed every one of us with what to invest and profit—talents are our money, gifts, abilities, skills, and of course, time. What have you been doing with your talents and your time? Time scarcity is not the problem for people who complain of not having enough time or lacking enough money to live. Everyone has 24 hours of time as talents to invest; how is your time investment doing?

The master returned from his journey and settled his account with them. It means he had given them the investment talents for a ***purpose***—so they could invest and make ***profits***. The first servant with five talents invested his money and came out with ten talents; he said, *"Master, you entrusted me with five talents. See, I have gained five more"*(Matthew 25:20). He had doubled his investment capital—100% profit! The master said to him, *"Well, done, good and faithful servant. You have been faithful with a few things; I will put you in charge of many things. Come share your master's happiness"* (Matthew 25:21). The man with two talents likewise traded and came back with four talents—100% profit. The master said the same words of commendation to him as well.[64]

Then the man with one talent came and said, *"Master, I knew you are a hard man, harvesting where you have not sown and gathered where you had not scattered seed. So I was afraid and went out and hid your talent in the ground. See, here is what belongs to you." The master replied, "You wicked, lazy servant! Well then, you should have put my money on deposit with the bankers so that when I returned, I would have received it back with interest. Take the talent from him and give it to the one who has ten talents. For everyone who has will be given more, and he will have an abundance. Whoever does not have, even what he has will be taken from him"* (Matthew 25:24, 26-30).

If you have never invested what God has given you—financial, material, and spiritual, you must learn from this sobering judgment of this wicked, lazy, and unprofitable steward.

The investment principles shown in the parable are timeless and priceless. Jesus, obviously, had an investor's mind. Let us attempt to explore these fundamental truths.

Principle 1. God expects the investment of our talent

Although the parable is about the return of Jesus and the reward for faithfulness, it has taught us about great investment principles. In this parable, Jesus gave investment insight into what believers can do with what they have—their money, their time, their skills, their talents, and their spiritual gifts. He wanted us to know that God owns all the money and stewardship is needed. We will have to give account for them. There's an entrepreneurial expectation from the Master.

Financial investment is not worldly wisdom but biblical. It operates on the same principle as spiritual or Heavenly investment, and both intersect. Your financial turnaround can come by studying God's Word and applying it to investments.

In this story, Jesus did not blame the lazy man who refused to invest because he had not made as much profit as the others or because he had no skills to undertake the business. His error was he failed to do what he had the ability to do. In Luke's account, when the master gave them the money, He instructed them to *"Put this money to work"* (Luke 19:13). He expected them to put the money to work. Failing to invest the money was an act of disobedience. Jesus implied that money could work for you and generate some returns. It is possible to do God's work part-time or full-time in ministry and yet, put money to work as your slave instead of the opposite.

Richard H. Fessler said, "In my many years of helping people to achieve a better life, I have time and time again learned that failure is not caused by what a person does not have, but by failing to use what they do have. Failure is not caused by what a person cannot do, but by failing to do what they can do." What can you do with what you have?

The master expects everyone to make a profit with his talents, *"Then he sent for the servants to whom he had given money, in order to find out what they had gained with it"* (Luke 19:15). In this case, God gave talents to each one, and God expects us to make a profit by using the gift. The master in the parable gave capital assets for the purpose of trading and making profits. He commended those who traded and made a profit equally, regardless of the amount they made. He said, *"Well, done, good and faithful servant. You have been faithful with a few things; I will put you in charge of many things. Come share your master's happiness"* (Matthew 25:21,23). It is not how much profit you make that matters but how well you use your talents. In this case, both servants had invested and doubled their investment. You can also double or triple the gifts, talents, and money God has given to you. The master trusted these servants, and he promised to entrust many things into their hands. They were good stewards because they accounted for what he gave them. Do we give account to the Lord for what He has given us?

On the other hand, the master condemned the man who did not trade as an unprofitable servant, a lazy and wicked man. Why? The master asked why the man did not invest the money with the usury (bank) and gain some interest on his investment. He said, *"You should have put my money on deposit with the bankers so that when I returned, I would have received it back with interest"* (Matthew 25:26-27). We got an insight into the mind of God here concerning investment. Trading with what God has given you to make a profit is not a sin. It is actually expected, *"Do not forsake wisdom, and she will protect you: love her, and she will watch over you"* (Proverbs 4:6).

None of the disciples of Jesus was called when they were idle—they were all busy working and doing something. Jesus used the picture of a man who did not invest to teach to those who do not use their gifts. But why did He use money as the illustration in the parable? It is because this principle is timeless, and it applies to both spiritual and Heavenly investments, as well as financial investments.

Principle 2: *If you cannot engage in direct money-making, then invest to earn interest.*
The master said, "You should have put my money on deposit with the bankers so that when I returned, I would have received it back with interest" (Matthew 25:26-27). Jesus indicated that even though this man was not ready to invest the money directly, he ought to have invested it indirectly with bankers and at least be able to earn interest for the master. Obviously, the man was either ignorant of these opportunities, or he was too risk-averse to apply them. He remained lazy and poor because he was judgmental.

For many believers, we remain ignorant because we are judgmental of those who trade with their money and talents. We call them names and consider them worldly. Some wonder why God did not give them money like unbelievers or some other believers who have money. They will always have reasons why they cannot win souls or do anything else for God. They become critical instead of investing.

God wants us to be engaged. The Master said, *"Occupy till I come!"* or *"Do business till I come"* (Luke 19:13). Whatever your hands find, do it with all your heart. A believer ought to be entrepreneurial in his life and ministry. To be entrepreneurial is to be profitable. If God gives you any gift and it is not used, He will take it back.

When an opportunity is acted upon, it can be converted to wealth, *"The man who had received the five talents went at once and put his money to work; he gained five more"* (Matthew 25:16). The man with two talents gained two more. They both traded and sowed the investment seeds, and they yielded financial fruits from them. Why was the Lord unhappy with the man who went to hide his talent? Because he did not invest and multiply it as he ought. The poor, lazy man had sowed nothing, and he reaped nothing—nothing ventured, nothing gained.

We are responsible for investing the finances God has provided us, and I would be happy one day to see us telling God: "Lord, thank you for granting me the privilege and opportunity to have those resources. This is how I have spent and invested what you gave me. Ten percent of it I gave back for my tithing, an additional ten, twenty, or even thirty, I gave back to your work; Forty, I spent for my family and helping people. The remaining twenty percent or more I invested in diverse investment options to grow it, so I could continue to accomplish what you have called me to without bringing a reproach to Your Name. Lord, here is your money, your spiritual gifts, your unique talents, and the time you have given me. I have invested and have doubled, or tripled, and quadrupled them. Take them back, with thanks, O Lord." Then I would give my crown back to Jesus, as well, at His feet.

Principle 3: *Much is expected of those to whom much is given.*
The master will give more to those who have invested profitably. The most dramatic part of the story was what happened after the lazy servant went and dug out the talent. The Master was upset with the lazy and unprofitable servant; he commanded that they take away the one talent he had and give that to the one who had ten talents. Wait a minute. The master did not ask the man to give the extra talent to the one with the two talents who has made four so he can at least have half the resources of his friend. This is what democracy would argue as equality and justice, but God is a just God. The Kingdom of God is not about democracy. He is not a democratic God. He is Theocratic.

What is the financial wisdom the Lord was teaching us here? Listen to Jesus' response: *"For whoever has will be given more, and they will have an abundance. Whoever does not have, even what they have will be taken from them"* (Matthew 25:29). Luke even added that *"...what they think they have will be taken from them"* (Luke 8:18). The man who thought he had too little and did not want to invest, what he thought was too little was taken away from him; maybe he forgot about *"do not despise small beginnings"* (Zechariah 4:10). It was given to the one who had so much, so he could have even more abundance.

It is about receiving back what you have sowed with increase. Money flows to those who know how to put it to good use. Money flees from those who despise or misuse it.[65] It is the same for all the gifts of God—financial or spiritual. If you have a talent as an artist, sportsman, or musician and you do not use it, after some time you will realize you are not as good as you used to be.

In the first place, why did the master not share the talents with them equally before he traveled? It is because he knew each man's ability. God deals with us as individuals, not as part of a group. The Holy Spirit gives gifts according to our abilities. Investment is about risk-taking, and the man with ten talents has a bigger heart for taking risks and for harnessing every opportunity to make profits. He is able to trust God for bigger things. There are those God will give five souls to and those He will grant millions of souls to, *"...From everyone who has been given much, much will be demanded..."* (Luke 12:48). If God has given you many resources, money, talents, gifts, and abilities, don't squander them because He will demand and expect more from you. Much more investment is expected from you. Much more sowing and reaping in the Kingdom, much more giving is expected from you. There are those He will bless with just enough, and there those who will have more than enough. Everything depends on our relationship with the Master and our faith.

Regarding the untrustworthy manager, the Lord said,

"Whoever can be trusted with little can also be trusted with much, and whoever is dishonest with very little will also be dishonest with much. So if you have not been trustworthy in handling worldly wealth, who will trust you with true riches? And if you have not been trustworthy with someone else's property, who will give you property of your own? No servant can serve two masters. Either he hates one and loves the other, or he will devote to the one and despise the other. You cannot serve God and Money" (Luke 16:10-13).

What can God trust you with? Jesus wants us to 'handle' wealth or money faithfully and use it, not to be its slave. Don't serve mammon (money). Make it your servant and ride it as you would a horse!

Principle 4: The size of your talent or your profit is not important. One would have expected the master to have commended the man with five talents much more than the rest. When Jacob was praying for his children, he gave extra to Joseph because he loved him more.[66] He even adopted two of Joseph's children to have the same share as his own sons. So Joseph got a double portion of his father's inheritance—Manasseh and Ephraim were counted as part of Jacob's descendants.

God does not judge like humans. For example, God did not choose Joseph to be the tribe through which the Messiah would come; instead, He came through Judah. In Heaven, we will be surprised to see the man who had won millions of souls receiving a similar reward to the one who has won five souls. It is based on what God has called you to do. There are many who did signs and wonders that will not qualify to enter the Kingdom. Jesus will simply tell them, "I do not know you." What really matters in Heaven is not how many souls you won or how much profit you made. What really matters is what was in your heart when you carried out the will of God.

This is a powerful investment lesson from Jesus. The Rich Man gave investment capital to his servants. Remember, Master Jesus is that Rich Man—God is the richest Being on Earth and in Heaven. The master in this parable had traveled on a long journey, just as Jesus has traveled on a long journey to Heaven, and He has left us here on earth as stewards of the talents He gave us. One day, He will return and ask about what He had committed into our hands. He will come back in His glory and judge this world, according to what each one has done.[67]

The Master left us to manage the investment capital He gave us. How are you managing yours?

Let us reflect on the Lord's judgment of the unprofitable servant. He condemned the one who did not trade as an unprofitable servant, a lazy and wicked man. Why? Because the man did not invest. Therefore, God does not permit a believer to just receive Christ and be warming the benches and chairs in the church auditorium every Sunday without doing anything for the advancement of the Kingdom.

Let me paraphrase what the Master said to the man: "Regardless of what you think about Me, I consider it a terrible foolishness for you not to have invested the money I gave you because My money should have yielded interests over time if I had applied it to other investments, if I had given it to that other man who had five talents, or if I had just kept my money in a bank or the stock market. Therefore, because you are good for nothing, unprofitable and non-enterprising, you are, indeed, very lazy and useless. Now, you will have to pay for your sin of omission and commission for your foolishness and for your wrong and judgmental attitude. Now, give the talent to your neighbor, who is more profitable than you are. And get out of my sight."

Principle 5: *Each person receives from God according to our ability.*
Except for the amount of talents the three men in the story received the same amount of opportunity. Likewise, the Holy Spirit gives each of us

spiritual gifts, according to our ability—He is the one who determines who receives what. We are not supposed to be worried about what we do not have or what God has given to others. We will only account for what He has given to us, not what we do not have.

The amount of your investment capital is not as important as your motive, your investment effort, and your entrepreneurship. Surprisingly, the master commended the two men in the same way. To the one that had two and had multiplied his investment into four, the master said, *"Well done, good and faithful servant. You have been faithful with a few things; I will put you in charge of many things. Come and share your master's happiness"* (Matthew 25:21). Likewise to the one that had five talents and had multiplied it to ten, he also said, *"Well done, good and faithful servant! You have been faithful with a few things; I will put you in charge of many things. Come and share your master's happiness"* (Matthew 25:23). Exactly the same commendations. Be faithful to what God has called you to and to the resources He has endowed you with.

Principle 6: *Your attitude to financial opportunity determines your success or failure.*

The key to financial independence is not how much money you have for the investment but how well you have put it to use. Having a million dollars to invest doesn't guarantee that you will not be poor again. Roberts Kiyosaki and Sharon L. Lester told the story of three people who were supposed to have been millionaires based on the opportunities they suddenly had.

First, was William Post, who won $16.2 million from the Pennsylvania lottery in 1988. Within a year, he was $1 million dollars in debt, and as of 2005, he was said to be living quietly on $450.00 a month and food stamps.[68] Second, was the story of a lucky boy, Ken Proxmire, a machinist who won $1 million dollars in the Michigan lottery. Within five years, he had filed for bankruptcy.[69] Evelyn Adams also won the New Jersey Lottery—twice (1985, 1986) to the tune of $5.6 million; the money was all gone, and she was said to be living in a trailer.[70]

Money flows to those who know how to put it into good use. Money flees from those who despise or misuse it. As Scripture states, *"For everyone who has will be given more, and he will have an abundance. Whoever does not have, even what he has will be taken from him"* (Matthew 25:29). Isaiah said, *"If you are willing and obedient, you will eat the good things of the land"* (Isaiah 1:19). This man was not willing to invest and grow his income. He remained poor. Why? Because he hated to invest what was bestowed upon him. He had a wrong attitude about his Master. Many have wrong attitudes about God, about Jesus, and the Holy Spirit. Investing requires a change of mindset, hard work, and diligence. It is the same for all of God's gifts.

Principle 7. Financial wealth creation is about seizing an opportunity at the right time.

Dr. Howard Stevenson of the Harvard Business School defined entrepreneurship as "exploiting an opportunity, regardless of the resources currently available." This perspective, according to him, is to "focus on opportunity rather than resources."[71] I would like to also mention that the willingness to seize the opportunity is the primary issue and having the amount of resources is secondary. John E. Girouard said, "Risk is not about losing money, but losing the opportunity for profit."[72]

The lazy servant was not being rebuked for making investment blunders or for incurring losses, but because he had refused to take the risks and seize the opportunity to make profits for his master; as a result, he missed the opportunity of making a profit. These were the golden investment or entrepreneurial lessons implied in Jesus' teaching in the parable of the talents.

Why did the lazy man not invest?

The unprofitable servant had the talent, but he failed to use it because of three reasons:

1) The man was afraid of losing the principal capital.[73] Fear is a terminator gene, and there is little chance of achieving the right results through fear. Many Christians do not venture into what God is calling them to because of fear of the unknown. In turn, they buried their gifts and talents. In the same way, many people could not venture into entrepreneurial investments because of the fear of losing their money.

2) The servant did not trust his master. He had a wrong view of the master. He himself was not trustworthy. If you can't trust God, you do not deserve His trust, either. It means you are not trustworthy. Many have failed in the ministry because of wrong perceptions of the Word of God and of the Kingdom. The man had a wrong notion of his master. He had thought of him as a Scrooge who reaped where he did not sow and gathered where he did not scatter. What is your view of your parents, your mentors, your pastor, or God? Christians place constraints on themselves and misinterpret what God has said in His Word. They cannot trust anyone with their money, not even the bank. Do you trust God with your investments?

3) The man was wicked and lazy, according to the master. God hates laziness.[74] There are many who go to the ministry because they found other jobs and careers more demanding. Some actually think ministry is an easy job, but they are wrong. Any truly called leader, who is fully committed, knows that there is no more demanding job than being a minister—it is a 24-hour job. Sometimes I hear someone share his testimony that "I have tried everything I could, but nothing worked for me; so I knew God wanted me to serve Him fully." Another one will say, "I spent six years looking for a job until I became tired, so I decided to try ministry." There is no precedence for that in the Bible. Does God look for every unsuccessful person and call them into the ministry? How will they be productive in the ministry if they go with the same attitude of giving excuses for their failures? Jesus called His disciples from the workplace, not from lying about playing games all day.

No Investment, No Possession!

The greater revelation of the parable of the talents is recorded nicely in Luke 19. When the man with ten minas came to the master with ten more that he had gained as profits, the master replied, *"Well done, my good servant. Because you have been trustworthy in a very small matter, take charge of ten cities"* (Luke 19:17). He also told the one with five minas likewise, *"You take five cities"* (Luke 19:19). The two servants were said to be trustworthy by the master. Then he said they should take cities, according to their level of investment.

Did you notice the parable moved from talents to taking cities? This is very interesting. Preaching the Gospel is about taking cities by force from the kingdom of darkness and establishing the Kingdom of light. The Master will entrust more cities to those who invest their talents and make profits on their investment money given to them. What did the servants invest in the parable? Money! Money matters in the Kingdom. Kingdom workers and Kingdom takers ought to have an investor's mindset. Without investments, there will be no Kingdom possession. We must think and act as an investor; invest and make financial profits. Invest in the Kingdom. Preach the Gospel.

Parable of the Workers in the Vineyard

There are also some investment principles from the Parable of the Workers in the Vineyard.[75] Jesus described the Kingdom of Heaven as an estate farmer who hired laborers into his vineyard at various times of the day and at an agreed wage—first in the morning, then at the third, sixth, and eleventh hours. Those he hired later were standing in the marketplace doing nothing there, and no one had hired them, so the estate owner promised to pay whatever seemed right to him—not to them. They had no bargaining power because it was only a favor. In the evening, the owner of the vineyard said to his foreman, *"Call the workers and pay them their wages, beginning with the last ones hired and going on to the first"* (Matthew 20:8). He decided to pay everyone a flat rate—a denarius!

Those who were first hired were expecting to receive more pay but were surprised to realize that they had received equal pay with those who had come to join them later. They started to grumble against the landowner to protest an "injustice." They argued, "These men who were hired last worked only one hour, and you have made them equal to us who have borne the burden of the work and the heat of the day." The owner did not budge to their pressure; instead, he firmly said, *"Friend, I am not being unfair to you. Didn't you agree to work for a denarius? Take your pay and go. I want to give the man who was hired last the same as I gave you. Don't I have the right to do what I want with my own money? Or are you envious because I am generous?"* (Matthew 13-15).

What are the investment truths from this parable?

Truth 1. You must see your investment as a contract.
The early laborers wanted to change the contract. Those who deal with the financial market know that bargains are only possible at the initiation of a contract; you do not change the goalposts along the line, as fraudulent people like to do. If you are buying a bond, fixing money in a CD, buying shares, or investing in the money market, the terms will apply accordingly.

Truth 2. Financial freedom is not about how hard you have worked but His grace.
The race is not for the swift, and the battle is not for the strong.[76] The master did not consider how much someone sweats in the heat of the day, how long the period of waiting was, but rewarded each person equally. God is the rewarder, and He is generous. His reward is not based upon your sweat but on His nature. The master said to them, "Don't I have the right to do what I want with my own money?" Let me illustrate this with the stock market. If investor A had bought stock with Microsoft in January 2001 and had invested $10,000 at $10 per share, and the market increased to $15 a share in 2012, and Investor

B had bought $15,000 worth, by 2014, when the market declined to $5 per share, and that is when Investor C bought his $5,000 worth to enter the market. If by 2020 the market price of the stock increased to $30 per share, who will get the most money?

- Investor A bought $10,000 in stock at $10 per share, so she has bought 1000 shares.
- Investor B bought $15,000 in stock at $15 per share, so she has 1000 shares.
- Investor C bought $5000 in stock at $5 per share, so she has 1000 shares.

In 2020, all three investors will receive the same amount of increase on their stock. Each will sell and receive $30,000! (minus the dividends the company paid, if applicable.) Would you not have felt that was an injustice? How can investor C receive the same amount as investor B, who had paid $10,000 more, and Investor A, who had paid $5,000 more and had stayed for twenty years? That is how it works! You cannot sue Microsoft for being partial; it is a contract. That race is not for the swift; there is an element of risk and chance involved. It is the same principle that applies when a new believer comes to Christ in a church, and there are others who had come to Christ at different times—1, 3, 6, 15 years before this fellow. It is similar to the parable of the vineyard workers.[77] After five years, a newcomer can be so much more endowed with gifts and grace than those who had come to Christ earlier.

Paul was an excellent example. After his conversion, he became an apostle, and when he was invited to the church of Antioch, he became one of the teachers, along with those who had come to Christ long before him. Later, he became more gifted than even Barnabas and was able to confidently correct Peter of hypocrisy![78] He wrote a third of all the epistles. God doesn't look at the size or the year but the heart. That was the reason Jesus had commended the woman who gave a mite.[79]

Truth 3. Never invest your effort in an unknown investment.
In the parable, these men who came later didn't know what the owner was going to pay. They had no bargaining power and were at the mercy of the landowner. We are safe in the hands of God because He is a just God. Learn to trust and depend on Him. He will reward us accordingly, even when the landowner is not as good as the one in this parable. God can bring favors to you. To investors, reliable market information is crucial for wealth creation. You need to know your market well—no surprises.

In the next two chapters, I am going to show you what you have never really realized that Jesus taught about how to fund world evangelization. It will change your perspectives on the traditional way of doing ministry.

Chapter 5 Overview

Take Your Wallet With You

Ministry Issue
How does Jesus expect Christians to find the needed finances for the Great Commission?

Ministry Lesson
Trusting God for our finances in short-term or full-time ministry. Jesus' vision of Church finance revisited. How to apply creative financial wisdom of God and using our talents, abilities and skills.

CHAPTER 5

TAKE YOUR WALLET WITH YOU

Leveraging Ministry With Your Talents

"Then Jesus asked them, 'When I sent you without a purse, bag, or sandals, did you lack anything?' 'Nothing,' they answered. He said to them, 'But now if you have a purse, take it, and also a bag; and if you don't have a sword, sell your cloak and buy one" Luke 22:35-36.

In wartime scenarios, there are two main lines of offense—the frontlines and the supply lines, and both are crucial. In the battle for souls against the kingdom of darkness, the mission field is the frontline or frontiers where the battle is usually the fiercest. Many faithful believers throughout the centuries have recognized the wartime parallel of the great commission.[80] The general rule in the military is to 'obey the last order' you have received until you get new orders from your commander or superior. If you receive a contradictory order from your superior, the military rule requires you either to obey the orders in the order you receive them or obey the last order first. This is necessary because the superior may have new information about a changed situation.

So when Jesus our Commander gave the Church the last command on finances, what was it?

The *first order on financing the great commission—Luke 9 and 10*, Jesus had instructed the disciples not to take money or any extra provisions when He sent them out to preach the Gospel around Galilee, Judea, and Samaria, and He gave that same instruction twice![81]

In the *second order on financing the great commission—Luke 22:35-36*, however, He commanded them to take necessary money and provisions along with them, if they have any, as they take the Gospel to the nations. That was the last order on finances for global evangelization before He faced the cross. As we will see later, this last command didn't seem to stick—the disciples didn't really get it. Neither did the great troops that would mushroom out of their blood trails and continue their calling get it, either. The pre- and post-reformation church didn't get it either. The Church has never really gotten this last command right, and it is still a major limitation to the world's evangelization. The enemy has really blinded the eyes of the Church from seeing this truth in our finances.

The Forgotten Check Book

When Jesus was ascending to Heaven, He had finished all the work He needed to do. He had brought the secrets of the Kingdom of Heaven and the keys of the Kingdom to the disciples and the Church.[82] He had demonstrated the power of the Kingdom to preach the Gospel to the poor, heal the sick, cast out devils, and deliver the oppressed from captivity. He had given that same authority to the disciples to practice and use it and had gladly listened to their wonderful testimonies of how the devil had obeyed them.[83] He had demonstrated to them that He is indeed the Messiah—the Son of the Living God and that He has power over sin, the devil, hades, and death.[84] He was resurrected from the dead and spent forty days with them. He had commanded them to preach the Gospel, demonstrate it with signs and wonders, and make disciples of all nations.[85] He had promised them to expect the coming of the Holy Spirit in a few days' time. Then He led them out of Jerusalem and ascended up into Heaven in their sight, and they all had worshiped Him.[86]

Now, the fire burned in their hearts, and they couldn't wait to receive the power of the Holy Ghost and to preach the Gospel which would take place in the Upper Room. Five thousand men, or more than 15,000 people—including women and children, were now crowding into Solomon's Colonnade following Peter's preaching and signs and wonders by the apostles.[87] The first mega-church and mother of all churches to come had been born.

"Oops! Wait a minute! How will they finance the work? If Jesus expects us to reconcile the whole world to God through the power of the Gospel, how come He has forgotten something so crucial? He didn't give a clue as to how to get the money—tons of silver and gold, billions if not trillions are needed. If the world needs hundreds of billions to address climate change, fight terrorism, hunger, and poverty, and trillions of dollars to combat COVID-19 pandemic, and many times over to run the nations, how much does Jesus need to get people of the world in every generation saved? The Lord had said, *"And this Gospel of the Kingdom will be preached in the whole world as a testimony to all nations, and then the end will come"* (Matthew 24:14).

Yet He didn't leave the Church with a checkbook, a treasury bill, a bank, or even tell the church where to get the money to preach the Gospel." I am surprised that none of the disciples remembered to ask Him these questions. They had asked many questions, but none of them asked Him how to finance the Great Commission He had given them. How come they forgot to ask?

Assuming that Jesus suddenly shows up in your closet as you are praying, and you have a golden opportunity to ask Him about the forgotten money for the work He had commanded, wouldn't you be tempted to ask Him, "Lord, you have given all the blueprints to implement your Great Vision—the Great Commission on Earth. With your Divine power, we seem to have all the spiritual resources we need—to walk in godliness and to participate in your Divine nature.[88]

The Holy Spirit is present and powerfully moving in our midst. The Word of God is so rich that we have no lack in what to preach and teach, and the people are eager to believe You and be saved. We also have many ready workers. You have sent us as Your Father had sent you, and we are more than willing to go.

"Did you not instruct that we should sell all we have and not to go with money in our wallet or extra bags? But Lord, how can we go without money—without finances our family and us? Where do we get money for organizing crusades and evangelism events, for moving our teams, and starting our church plants, and to do good? How about the money to pay our staff's salaries, buy all the equipment, and support prospective leaders in Bible Schools or seminaries, and to send missionaries who are waiting to go to the field, to help the poor and needy in our midst, or even feed those who have come to hear Your words with empty stomachs?"

What do you think His response would likely be? Will He say, "No, you are completely wrong? I do not expect you to spend a dime. You will have voluntary givers all the time. Go to the nearest bank around you and ask the cashiers to unload the money into your pocket or bag as much as you need. Anyone you meet on your way, just tell them by faith, "Give me your money, your car, and food. The Lord has need of it." And they will give to you. Did I not command you? Don't you know that no one fights a war at his own expense? So, you will fight this war at My full expense. Be abundant, and be full. Go, gather them from the streets, and highways, so that My house may be filled. As My Father has sent me, I send you. Go now, in peace."

Is that like what Jesus would say? Your guess is as good as mine. However, the truth is that Jesus never left anything unaddressed. He could not have left such a crucial issue unaddressed. We are either veiled or ignorant. He will probably say, "Read My words in the book of Luke and understand it. Read My parables and understand them."

In this chapter, we want to find out how Jesus really expects us to finance the Great Commission. Like David, we ought not to give sleep to our eyes until we have found this hidden secret. Let us explore these truths.

Jesus' Specific Command on Finances

Early in my studies on the subject of money, I thought the New Testament tended to emphasize more on poverty and shunned prosperity, and that the Old Testament was the opposite. My worry was more on how to do the Great Commission without money. Was Jesus expecting a bunch of beggars to preach the Gospel? But as I prayerfully studied the New Testament, I discovered an all-important insight into Jesus' actual position and command on how to fund the Great Commission. This key is loaded into a single Scripture verse and may never be fully understood until now. I want the reader to try and look out for that verse by the time we get to the end of this chapter.

Jesus called his twelve apostles to Him and gave them power and authority to drive out all demons and cure diseases and to preach the Gospel. He then commanded them:

"Take nothing for the journey—no staff, no bag, no bread, no money, no extra tunic. Whatever house you enter, stay there until you leave that town" (Luke 9:3-4).

They went from village to village and preached the Gospel, cast out demons, and healed the sick everywhere. They then reported back to the Lord.

As the news was still going around among His larger group of disciples, they must have wondered if they also could heal the sick. Some must have said, "I think those apostles were specially anointed. No ordinary disciple could heal the sick like Jesus." Jesus knew their hearts, so again, He appointed and sent out 72 other disciples. He paired them two-by-two and sent them out to every town where He wanted to go, with the following commands:

"Do not take a purse or bag or sandals; and do not greet anyone on the road. When you enter a house ... Stay in that house, eating and drinking

whatever they give you, for the worker deserves his wages. Do not move around from house to house. When you enter a town and are welcomed, eat what is set before you..." (Luke 10:4-8).

They returned with the same results!
Let's first try to understand verse 4 from different Bible translations:

- The King James Version, *"Carry neither purse, nor scrip, nor shoes."*
- The New International Version, *"Do not take a purse or bag or sandals."*
- The Amplified Version says, *"Carry no purse, no provisions bag, no [change of] sandals..."*
- New Life Version says, *"Take no money. Do not take a bag or shoes."*
- American Standard Version, "Carry no purse, no wallet, no shoes; and salute no man on the way."

In all of these translations, we understand that Jesus clearly commanded them not to take any provisions—no money, no luggage, or any extra things for the journey—just go as you are, empty-handed. He said, don't even take your purse or *wallet*. And He repeated it twice.

Twice, the Lord forbids them from taking either money or extra provisions for their upkeep. Why? We do not know how long the journeys took in both cases, but we know these were short-term missions, probably same day, a few days or weeks, and within commuting distance. They probably didn't have to cross the ocean, board a ship, or travel overseas. This was a specific *instruction* to the disciples of Jesus for a purpose. It was clear that He wanted them to trust God for all their food, provisions, and their financial needs as they went out. They would be fully provided for wherever they went. His anointing would meet their needs, and angels would stand by them, open doors for provisions and financial favors. But remember: these were short-term missions.

As you would later see in a chapter on 'financial miracles,' Jesus can and still does meet the needs of Christian workers in miraculous ways today. Paul puts this clearly, *"And my God will meet all your needs according to His glorious riches in Christ Jesus"* (Philippians 4:19). Their testimonies proved that Jesus knew what He was doing. They had great exploits and were all well provided for by their hosts.[89] None of them had lacked anything.

What was Jesus teaching the disciples in these commands, not to take the money and provisions in these two short-term missions? We need to understand this as a principle for the Great Commission.

Principle 1: Ministry is not an alternative job; it is a calling.
On the first instructions, twice, the Lord had commanded them not to take a purse, bag, or any provisions. It was to give them a picture of what to expect in the mission: they may either be accepted or be rejected. They may have finances, and they may lack. In a calling, you can expect an abundance or lack, but you will still go ahead and do what God wants you to do. Paul said, *"I know what it is to be in need, and I know what it is to have plenty. I have learned the secret of being content in any and every situation, whether well fed or hungry, whether living in plenty or in want"* (Philippians 4:12). Nonetheless, the Lord was able to show them that He can meet the needs of those who obey His calling.

Take no money—This was the hardest part—to take no wallet. With money, you could buy whatever you needed or even a coffee in today's age, but what can you do without it? He had wanted them to depend fully on the providence of God. Without money, you are stripped of your self-sufficiency and have to depend fully on God.

Take no bag—They must not go with extra provisions, sandals, or even extra clothing. The bag, knapsack, or luggage is where we pack our extra provisions—clothes, books, money, shoes, confectioneries, etc. Depending on how long our journey is, we make provisions in the bag for the journey. But Jesus told them not to take anything, not even toothbrushes or sandals. Here they would have to depend completely on whatever was provided for them. Yet, Jesus ensured that their needs would all be met—72 people, in 36 groups! No one came back with complaints about how badly they were treated, how they had been hungry, or how they were stranded at the lakeshore because of a lack of money to pay their fares. Every need was fully met. Jesus asked them, "When I sent you without money, bag, knapsack, and sandals, did you lack anything?" So they said, "Nothing." They were to depend on the generosity and hospitality of their hosts. That really helped them to bond easily with the local people in those towns and villages they had evangelized. Bonding is an essential element of cross-cultural missional work.

Take no staff—The staff represents a support to lean on. They must not rely on any personal or external support they had. He even instructed them not to greet anyone on the way, probably to avoid asking people for help.

Wow! No money, no provision, and no self-sought human support? What was the Lord teaching the Church here? By sending out both the apostles and the seventy disciples, Jesus proved that 'faith-living' fully depends upon God's providence for missions, and it is not just for the twelve apostles, five-fold ministers or clergies, but for all Christian workers who have no alternative provisions. They all can depend on Him. The key message from Jesus in Luke 9 and 10 is that He is able to meet all the needs of Christian workers when we have no other source of support. It means you can preach the Gospel without money or provisions.

Principle 2: Without money and no provisions, you can still preach the Gospel (in the short-term.)
The Lord was actually training His disciples in the early part of His

ministry on how to preach the Gospel as a soldier going to battle. A soldier will not take his television, car, sofa, refrigerator, or certificates, along to the war front. Paul encourages Christian workers to endure hardships, *"Endure hardships as a good soldier of Christ. No one serving as a soldier gets involved in civilian affairs—he wants to please his commanding officer"* (2 Timothy 2:3-4). He cannot draw from his bank accounts, or go with many of his expensive suits.

That was why the Lord said, *"If anyone comes after Me, he must deny himself and take up his cross and follow Me"* (Luke 9:23). He taught them how to not look back.[90] When they encounter danger, they must be as wise as the serpent and gentle as the dove.[91] This principle of not taking your purse also exemplified the full-time ministry where the minister has no work or means, because God goes ahead to prepare the means they need. *"When you enter a house, first say, 'Peace to this house.' If a man of peace is there, your peace will rest on him; if not, it will return to you. Stay in that house, eating and drinking whatever they give you, for the worker deserves his wages. Do not move from house to house"* (Luke 10:5-7). This is powerful.

A worker in the Kingdom has a certain anointing power from God that brings peace to anyone she or he encounters. That peace is what heals the sick, casts out demons, calms storms, and brings God's blessings. How does anyone in the house receive the anointing of peace? When they respond favorably to the servant God has made to be a dispenser of His grace, power, and blessing, then peace will flow to them. You become a man of peace who has brought the Kingdom news to them, i.e., a blessed one. If you are a man or woman of peace, God wants to use you to meet people's needs.

God Can Pay the Bill.
The second part says we should eat and drink whatever is offered to us, and the Lord added a justification, *"The worker deserves his wages"* (Luke 10:7). Some believers are always fond of looking at whatever is offered to the minister/pastors as being undeserved. Some even don't think anyone

who is not an *ordained* pastor deserves anything—they think a lay pastor doesn't deserve his wages. But who really ordains a minister, man or God? Jesus was not even talking about pastors alone in this command. He was talking about all Christian workers—that is, everyone who does God's work, especially those who preach the Gospel, whether as a pastor, evangelist, missionary, or in any other way.

Peter, John, and James deserved their wages, just as Paul, Barnabas, Silas, and Timothy deserved theirs. Paul also said, 'The worker deserves his wages.' The preacher deserves his wages; the pastor deserves his wages, the evangelist, the missionary, the teacher, the worship leader, the trainer, the church, or ministry workers, etc.

If you preach the Gospel, then you deserve your wages, and God can pay you. He can meet your needs. This applies to all those who receive one form of remuneration or another in the ministry. Missionaries and Christian workers who have left their families, their homes, their land, or their jobs also deserve their wages. If they truly serve the Lord, they deserve their wages. They have neither purse and nor bag. They need someone who is the '*man of peace*' to provide for them. When you open your house, offer your food or water, or money to these Christian workers, you qualify as a man or woman of peace.

There was a good example of a woman of peace in Philippi. Her name was Lydia.[92] Such were many who supported the ministry of Paul. Such are all of you who pay your tithe, offering, and support the ministry of men and women of God in your church. Those who support missionaries and ministries to do the Great Commission, and those who open their house to Christian workers, be it missionary or evangelist, or pastor, will all receive your reward.

Principle 3. There is a need to outgrow your self-sufficiency.
One of the reasons Jesus had asked the disciples to go without provisions was to enable them to "experience the hospitality of the local people and to be dependent upon them."[93] It is cultural arrogance that makes

us think that occasional dependence on God and others or occasional vulnerability or stress is a bad thing. It is actually a good thing when it is not a regular pattern. It develops our spiritual stamina. When we make ourselves vulnerable to other people and put them in the position to help us, and we are willing to depend on their hospitality, generosity, or support, it creates trust and a two-way exchange of love in a new relationship. However, no one wants to be the only receiver. We should sometimes deliberately make room for other people to help or give to us, not because we do not have, but to raise their self-esteem.

When I ministered in Malawi to over 30 churches and more than 35-40 events a year, I always returned the money that was offered to me as a 'love offering' in an envelope. This was because I was a bi-vocational minister who was already earning enough income from my professional work. Sometimes, I would even give money to my hosts or their family, or the church. However, one thing I will not do is to refuse food when it is offered to me. We eat the food provided by our host, and we eat with them, not because we lack or are hungry, but to fellowship with them and make them enjoy the joy of being a host. In some cultures, such refusal can be considered as pride or rudeness, especially after or during ministration for several hours or even a few days. Jesus spent time with the Samaritans and enjoyed their hospitality when they begged Him to stay.

As ministers, we should receive our host's hospitality and appreciate it. It is a powerful missionary tool to not only minister to people but also to allow them to minister their generosity to us, as they desire. If we don't give that opportunity, we let them feel inferior or guilty that they have not properly taken care of God's servant. That was the grand missionary lesson Jesus wanted to teach the disciples in that short-term missionary assignment. However, long-term missionary work cannot be operated on dependency on other's generosity alone unless it is a church.

That flexibility was what Paul exemplified in his ministry. There were places he would let people take care of him and provide for his needs, such as in Philippi. The reason was that the brethren in Philippi were generous. Lydia had invited Paul to stay in her home, voluntarily.[94] The jailer also provided food for Paul and Silas at his house after their whole family was saved.[95] He also stayed in the house of Carpus in Troas.[96] Sometimes, however, Paul asked and trusted friends for support. In other places where dependency would have jeopardized his ministry, he decided to work as a bi-vocational missionary. Instead of receiving, he became the giver, such as in Corinth. The people didn't complain because their culture enjoyed receiving and not giving.

Whichever way, the important thing is for the Gospel to be advanced. The blanket application of dependency on others can cause more harm to the Gospel today, especially in some cultures. It is not that people do not like to give, but it is not considered ethically right to be without work unless you are clergy, where the majority of people can barely make ends meet. That was why Paul had to command the people in Thessalonica to work. A long-term missionary in that city may not find ready support.

Principle 4. *The Last Instruction on Money is to Take Your Finances Along!*
On the last night, Jesus had with the disciples—the very night He was being arrested, tried, and crucified—He had another discussion about finances and missions. The Lord had just finished the last supper with His disciples. He knew the Great Commission was to be financed. So He did not make the mistake of leaving this aspect unfinished as He said to them:

> *"When I sent you without purse, bag, or sandals, did you lack anything?" "Nothing," they answered. He said to them, "But now if you have a purse, take it, and also a bag; and if you don't have a sword, sell your cloak and buy one"* (Luke 22:35-36).

Plainly, Jesus told them that they could take all the money they wanted and any provisions they wanted to take. What a contradiction from Luke 9 and 10. It is safe to assume that the command from Luke 22:36 superseded the previous commands—which implies that to take your money is a superior command to not take money. The disciples in Jerusalem rarely understood this Last Instruction on Finances, yet soldiers are meant to *obey the last order.*

How About the Swords?
The disciples were caught in another divine equation they wouldn't be able to solve for a long time to come— *"But now if you have a purse, take it, and also a bag; and if you don't have a sword, sell your cloak and buy one"* (Luke 22:36). No one had dared to ask the Lord to clarify that command. It seemed so simple but most confusing and difficult, just as many of His teachings had caused some of the disciples to desert Him. Taking money and swords for preaching the Gospel?

Peter was an impulsive man. He acted on the last part. He thought he understood: he grabbed two swords he had kept and showed them to Jesus, saying, *"See, Lord, here are two swords." Jesus replied, "That's enough"* (Luke 22:38). I can picture Jesus smiling and shaking His head as if He were saying, "Oh, poor folks; they didn't get this important command at this time. Alright, I'll let it go. They will understand it later. Or at least someone will, some day." Well, Paul got it, at least that is one person. What about you, are you understanding it? Taking the Sword implies being equipped with the Sword of the Spirit, which is the Spirit-empowered Word of God! (Ephesians 6:18). Having a Word of God is the most important aspect in our preplanning of mission or preaching the Gospel.

The Day the Free Manna Stopped
The story of the Israelites illustrates a powerful lesson for today's Christians on financial provisions. If God could provide for the Israelites in the wilderness on their way to the Promised Land, and they didn't

lack food for 40 years, then He can provide for His children and servants when they are busy preaching the Gospel.

Nonetheless, the free manna was not to be a permanent source of food for God's people at any time; otherwise, the Jews would never have needed to work for food. As soon as the Jews crossed over into the Promised Land and harvested food in the land for the first time, the manna stopped falling from Heaven the very next day.[97]

Why did the manna stop? The manna stopped the day after they ate the produce of the land because the Lord expected them to work and cultivate the land for their daily livelihood. Was God tired of raining the manna and quails from Heaven forever? Not at all. They had reached the Promised Land, and the *'manna-treatment'* had to stop. Man was never expected to live on free food, free money, and free provisions. This is why God told Adam and Eve to tend the land, cultivate it, work it, and take care of it; then, they could eat the fruits of the land for their food.[98] The word "Eden" means royal garden (*pardes*). It was meant to be worked and cultivated.

Likewise, believers and Christian workers should not expect daily provision of manna as God's standard. He can provide the manna at any time, especially in our wilderness, but don't expect it as the norm. If God has been giving you manna in the ministry, it will last for a while, but eventually, that ministry must generate enough finances to support you and achieve God's purpose; otherwise, your dream cannot be fulfilled. Pro-vision follows a vision, and if it doesn't, we must check our method or the vision again.

We must listen to His Spirit to know His best will for us. It is possible to be instructed by the Holy Spirit not to work, or not to rely on your savings, or even to dispose of our assets and depend on God in the ministry. But this is a rarity and not the norm. This can also happen when God realizes we are putting too much of our attention and expectation on those financial means instead of focusing on Him.

Money for the Gospel?
In those two brief evangelistic missions, Jesus had taught them how to have "faith for finances."

- The Lord taught them not to expect help to come from their friends or acquaintances. That is why He said they should not even greet anyone on the way. When you don't greet anyone, how will you tell them about your financial problems?

- When we receive a call to mission or to preach today, the first thing people do is solicit financial help from everyone we have ever met. It simply requires boldness to send out emails, not a strong faith. The real faith is in asking God and depending on Him whom we cannot see, and without looking at men who we can see.

- The Christian worker (missionary or minister) deserves whatever he or she is given voluntarily, and God will bless whoever blesses them. When Jesus commanded the disciples not to take money, He did not say they should ask people. He said they should eat whatever gifts they were offered voluntarily and accept the hospitality of their hosts.

- We must note that that was also a brief mission. But many Christian workers stopped at Luke 9 and 10 and did not apply Luke 22—*take your purse!* That was Jesus' last instruction on finances. However, it is conditional, "If you have, take it." First, the Sword—Spirit empowered *Word of God*, is a compulsory weapon for the frontline soldiers! Second, is the *Provisions* (pulse, albeit it is conditional: "If you have." The Lord is saying that although finances can follow the vision, even if you do not have enough but have the Word. But a Christian worker will do better if there are provisions to achieve the vision.

A Jingling Purse for the Gospel

In ancient times, money was generally denominated in coins—copper, silver, and gold. These coins were loaded in a long hollow purse and tied around the waist under the robe. Remember, there were no trousers in those days, so men wore robes and had to girdle them with 'a belt'—usually a long strip of cloth. The banks of those days were the money-lenders, and they had to physically protect their money with weapons or guards.

To have an idea of the ancient language of a 'purse,' George S. Clason puts it in his Babylonian parable of wealth:
"I tell you my students, a man's wealth is not in the coins he carries in his purse. It is the income he buildeth, the golden stream that continually floweth into his purse and keepeth it always bulging. That is what every man desireth."[99]

The measure of wealth in those days was how fat or lean your purse was. A poor man had a lean purse, and a rich man a fat purse.

The jingling of the purse was an indication of wealth in ancient times.

Today, it means fat wallet or fat bank account. The command "take your purse," which is also interpreted as take your 'money bag,' is not to be interpreted as small amounts of spendable money. The purse was your wealth or income. In other words, Jesus was saying, "If you have a wealth or income source, take it with you, and if you have provisions, take it as you go to preach the Gospel." In plain language, it also means that if you are wealthy or have a profession to earn a steady income and you want to preach the Gospel, take the money, and use it.

But before we are able to take our purse and get a sword, we have resigned our jobs, closed our accounts, sold our estates, and distributed it—we have emptied ourselves of 'mammon' and run with the Gospel, but only too soon realize that we cannot go far. As much as we pray for the *power stream* of the Holy Spirit to go with us, we also need an *income stream* of money with us.

With the 'Sword of the Spirit,' Peter drew crowds into the temple and the streets of Jerusalem and raised Dorcas from the dead. This is what made a woman called Lydia offer her house to Paul in Philippi, persuading him and Silas, saying, *"If you consider me a believer in the Lord, come and stay at my house"* (Acts 16:15). She had perceived the anointing power of God in these men—they were the fragrance of the knowledge of Christ and the aroma of life to those who are saved.[100]

However, the requirement of a missionary today is more than where you stay and what you eat; there are other family and ministry needs that a generous host like Lydia would not be able to provide. Only a few people will be as generous as Lydia, especially if the guest is spending more than a few days.

Chapter 6 Overview
Taking Your Provisions

Ministry Issue
What are the ways Jesus expects Christians to finance ministry?

Ministry Lesson
The application of Jesus' command on finances is modeled by the ministry of Paul, characterized by a three-tiered but intertwined approach.

CHAPTER 6

TAKING YOUR PROVISIONS

Three-Pronged Financial Blueprint By Jesus

"But now if you have a purse, take it, and also a bag; and if you don't have a sword, sell your cloak and buy one" Luke 22:36.

"Nobody can do everything, but everybody can do something, and together, we can change the world."[101]

When it comes to getting finances for ministry, one size doesn't just fit all. Many wonder whether those who are called to the ministry should or shouldn't work to meet their livelihood needs. Can all Christian workers always expect their expenses to be met or their incomes to be paid out of a church's budget? Or should all Christian workers always depend on generous giving by other Christians, so that they can do ministry? My take on this is that every minister or Christian worker will have to depend on God's specific instruction for his calling and let the Holy Spirit guide each one of us in the financial route we should take. However, the Bible is clear about how to obtain finances for ministry, and we will constructively explore these possibilities.

Having read the amazing testimonies of how many have received finances by faith (financial miracles) and my knowledge of how others struggle to make ends meet in the name of 'living by faith' in the ministry, I have come to a conclusion that Jesus doesn't expect every Christian worker to operate in the same way.

Today, instead of prayerfully seeking a more robust way of doing God's work, many Christian workers take the easy path: let someone else pay the bill.

I am talking about Christians or Christian workers who simply do not want to work; they remain idle, and still expect others to meet all their needs. In some poor nations, there are Christians who move to what they consider "wealthy churches"—where they think there are wealthy believers who will take care of their expenses. Sadly, some Christians feel resentment when well-off believers do not shoulder all their bills. They consider them to be worldly and guilty of hoarding wealth, reminding them in a roundabout way of the Scriptures commanding the rich to give to the poor.[102]

This attitude can easily develop into covetousness—coveting the wealth of other believers because they are better off. Oftentimes, these individuals choose to do ministry, not because they are called, but because they see it as an easy way of paying their bills. Those were the ones Paul rebuked in 1 Thessalonians 3:12 when he commanded that they should earn their living. If this is your way of thinking, you will always be disappointed.

If you consider those who work in secular jobs while doing ministry, or those who are financially endowed, to be less spiritual, you do not understand Jesus' instruction on finances. That should be the starting point for young Christian workers—learning to earn so we can give generously. With that training, we will better appreciate generous givers in the Kingdom.

There are many Christ's ambassadors who labor in the ministry and therefore could get their living from the church or the ministry in which they work. This is purely biblical and does not qualify as living on a hand-out because they are being paid by God (as their direct employer) through the church, the same way a factory worker is paid by his employer. Those who do creative fundraising to support active ministry do not belong to that group because they too work for the Lord and deserve their wages. Although, in many cases, the effort put into doing fundraising is more than the actual effort spent on the ministry. The Bible supports strategic asking for finances or provisions for ministry. We will come back to this issue later in another chapter.

The *El Shaddai* As Provider

The story of the Israelites illustrates a powerful lesson for today's Christians on financial provisions. Have you ever thought of the huge resources the children of Israel had to use on their way to the Land of Canaan? *"The silver and the gold are Mine..."* (Haggai 2:8). God is known as El Shaddai, i.e., the God of providence—riches and honor belong to Him.[103] Let me quickly prove it to you below.

First, the New Jerusalem is an opulent place. Let us see how John described it.
"The construction of its wall was of jasper; and the city was pure gold, like clear glass. The foundations of the wall of the city were adorned with all kinds of precious stones: The twelve gates were twelve pearls: each individual gate was made of one pearl. And the street of the city was pure gold, like transparent glass" (Revelation 21:18-21). Just think of the beauty of these precious stones and rare gems!

Second, is the cost of "Operation Israeli Rescue" from Egypt that was championed by God through Moses. The Israelis came out with great possessions as God had earlier promised Abraham.[104] It was recorded that "They took a lot of flocks and herds for meat and for sacrifices, and all their livestock, and plundered the Egyptians of much good."[105] How much did that war and the plunder cost God? According to Elizabeth Bumiller of the New York Times, "The conflicts in Iraq and Afghanistan have cost the United States of America a staggering $1 trillion dollars to date, second only in inflation-adjusted dollars to the $4 trillion dollar price tag for World War II."[106]

Third, the Israelites ate for forty years on God's account—they ate manna and quails and drank water until they entered the border of the land of Canaan.[107] Can you imagine the enormous amount of food, meat, and water, and energy (wood) they must have consumed on their journey? Let us do some arithmetic here:

Jacob's family had increased from 15 people to 66 by the time he relocated to Egypt.[108] By the time they left Rameses in Egypt, "The Israelites had journeyed from Rameses to Succoth. There were about six hundred thousand men on foot, besides children. Many other people went up with them, as well as large droves of livestock, both flocks, and herds."[109] This account says at least 600,000 men, excluding wives, daughters, and male boys under the age of 20. Also, the foreigners were not counted. Let's put some value to the forty years of the Israelites' journey in the wilderness.

Population—Now, if we assume an average of 10 people per household (men, women, children, their non-Israeli slaves, and friends), it means at least 6,000,000 people had left Egypt.

Water—*They needed 880 billion gallons of water for 40 years!* [110] On their way, they even had to buy water.[111] That would cost $44 million U.S. dollars today.[112]

Food—*They needed 50 million metric tons of grain for 40 years!* [113] That would cost $17.7 billion U.S. dollars today.[114] Yet they did not grow one acre of wheat; God rained manna.

Wood—*They needed 43 million tons of fuel—wood to cook their meals.*[115] The energy supply would have cost $860 million to $3.4 billion U.S. dollars in modern-day.[116] That would require thousands of miles of well-stocked wooded savannah or forests. In a desert, that was not a simple provision, but God met all their needs.

Health—*How about their medical and insurance bills?* They were healthy for forty years. "He also brought them out with silver and gold, and there was none feeble among His tribes."[117]

Can you imagine that as the Jews were eating manna every day, the people on the other side of the border of the Jordan river (Canaanites) never even saw or knew what manna meant?

If God could provide for the Israelites in the wilderness on their way to the Promised Land and they didn't lack food for 40 years, then He can provide for His children and servants when they are busy preaching the Gospel.

We must take note that as soon as the Jews crossed over to the Promised Land and harvested food in the land for the first time, the manna stopped falling from Heaven, the very next day as Scripture states, *"… The manna stopped the day after they ate this food from the land; there was no longer any manna from the Israelites, but that year they ate of the produce of Canaan"* (Joshua 5:12).

Why did the manna stop? The manna stopped because the Lord expected them to produce food—work, and cultivate the land for their daily livelihoods. Was God tired of raining the manna and quails from Heaven forever? Not at all! But manna from Heaven was not God's original plan for the Jews' livelihood. Even Adam and Eve were not in vacation mode under God; they were to work—take care and cultivate the Garden.

Manna was God's 'emergency provision' for people transitioning from the wilderness to the Promised Land. He can provide the manna at any time, especially in our financial wilderness times, but don't expect it as just handouts. Each ministry must generate enough finances to support itself and achieve God's purpose; otherwise, visions cannot be fully fulfilled. Provisions follow a vision, and if it does not, we must check our method or the vision again. God wants us to step out.

Jesus never asked the disciples to live on the miracle 'bread-multiplication' for ministry, even though He had multiplied bread twice in His ministry. Some Christians think it makes them more spiritual if they can believe and receive financial miracles.

God will provide miracles when most needed because He is a good God. Yet Jesus didn't expect miracle fish and bread to be the regular source of food; otherwise, He would not have rebuked the Jews when they expected Him to multiply bread again to prove He was the Messiah.[118] Also, none of the disciples had attempted to repeat that miracle of provision. Why? They knew that miracle bread, miracle fish, miracle coin, a borrowed donkey, and a borrowed banquet hall were only emergency and temporary provisions. Living on daily manna is not for the mature Christian as those who ate the manna still didn't believe God, and many did not even make it to the Promised Land.[119] Let me be clear, daily-manna Christianity doesn't build up our faith; it makes us less willing to play our part.

Fat Wallet, Lean Wallet
Today a lean wallet will not take one far. If we have a fat wallet, then it has finance available to it, like a good credit/debit card backed by a good bank account. The command *"take your purse,"* which is also interpreted as taking your 'money bag,' is if you have money, take it, and if you have provisions, take it as you go to preach the Gospel." In plain language, it also implied that if you are wealthy or have means of income or financial provisions, and you are called to preach the Gospel, take the money and use it. Go with your fat wallet. Go with your provisions.

Putting Jesus's commands from Luke 9, 10, and 22 in perspective, we have the foundation for the three fundamental approaches:

1. Take No Provisions (Money). Here Jesus taught the Church how Christian workers could do the work of the ministry sometimes, without financial means and instead, relying on the power of the Gospel (the Spirit-wielded Word of God) to meet all the needed provisions. This can be accomplished in two ways. First, it can be through faith for finances and expecting God to meet the needs miraculously. We must note that this was for a short season, just as when the Lord sent out the 12 and 72 disciples on short mission trips. In the second approach, a Christian worker can take no provision when there is a body of believers who can supply the needed resources. I am not talking of fundraising, but where the Church can fully provide the needs of the minister or Christian worker. Unfortunately, many pastors do not believe the Church should provide for evangelists, missionaries, and other non-pastoral callings. In some countries, only full-time pastors deserve to be paid, not missionaries or evangelists, even if they do not have other work. This is an oversight.

2. Take Your Provisions (Money). In Luke 22:36, Jesus commanded that the Christian workers should deliberately plan for, create, and use their own money if they can. This is the most neglected aspect of this command and one that can make the most impact in the Kingdom. There are three known God-honoring ways of acquiring the money or provisions to take for the ministry:

First is deliberate "tentmaking" for funding ministry.[120] This includes working to earn money. This includes any type of work where a minister can earn decent money and still serve the Lord. This involves marketing personal services, ideas, abilities, or products. It doesn't mean that every Christian earning to make a living is a "tentmaker." Only those who work and do the Great Commission are qualified to be "tentmakers". We will discuss this in full in a later chapter. There are two types of "tentmakers." The first are those who work for a company or an employer to earn their income. This includes professionals of all types, skilled, artisans, and general workers. The second type are those who are self-employed by investing in businesses, real estate, or capital markets. This has been covered in more detail in other chapters of this book. The advantage is that at some point, it is possible to autopilot the investment and let the money work for us while we do the work of the ministry.

3. Fundraising—you can raise money by raising financial partners. The third way of getting money for the ministry is through fundraising. This is the art of inviting other Christians, Churches, or Kingdom investors to participate in the vision through their financial contribution. This is biblically valid also. However, most Christian workers tend to start off ministry with fundraising. It is encouraged that Christian workers should explore the first two approaches early in ministry. It is much easier for others to partner with us when there are already tangible and compelling results. To obtain such results, we can use our own funds, or voluntary individual or church support, or work as a "tentmaker." Fundraising is most God-honoring when it is short-term and targeted to important work in the ministry, such as mass crusades or evangelism events, or where there are no other means of support, and there is no opportunity to make money. Personally, it is my opinion that fundraising should be for expanded ministry when the work is beyond what your personal fund can support. God has not called us to only do what we can achieve on our own.

Three Ways of Raising Finances for Ministry:
To fully understand the Scriptures and carry out ministry according to the New Testament, we have to see our doctrines and practices through three lenses, an appropriate order of authority:

First is the command of Jesus. That is the highest level.

The second is the apostolic practices and teachings. Ideally, the apostles' teachings were what they heard directly from Jesus and their practices as

He commanded them.[121] However, we cannot place these at the same level as Jesus' direct commands, because like us, the apostles were not always perfect.[122] Only Jesus is perfect.

The third level is Church practices, customs, and traditions. Some of these are largely human traditions and customs that have no sound New Testament basis. They are not always bad, some are important, good, or at least they cause no harm. However, we need discernment to know which of these are God's will, and we can only know through His word and the His Spirit.

Table 6. The levels of authority on church practices and approaches to finances.

Authority	Workers' Wage	Wallet-Taking	Fundraising
Jesus' commands	Worker deserves his wages—Jesus has ordained that everyone who works for the Gospel will be provided for by God, if they do not have money. [123]	Take your money, and your provisions—Jesus desires that a Christian worker have or can earn their own income, and use the money for the Gospel.[124] The parable of the talent is about investment.[125]	You can expect God to provide finances by asking churches or individuals in the body. "Ask, and it shall be given to you."[126]
	Those who preach should be sustained by provisions from the Gospel.	Invest your talent—you can invest the money God has given you to earn a profit.	Jesus asking for a banquet hall and a donkey, suggests that workers can be led to ask.

Apostolic practices	Those who preach should be sustained by provisions from the Gospel.[127]	Tentmaking is the best-known model—the Apostle Paul, Barnabas, and many of the leaders of the Gentile churches worked for a living.[128]	The Apostle Paul did fundraising to support the Jerusalem church.[129]
	There was an indication that the Apostles in the Jerusalem church had depended on regular income from the Church.[130] The Scripture justified this that those who serve the temple get their food from the temple.[131]	Expanded tent-making work modeled by Paul, Luke, Aquila, and Priscilla, whereby they were able to do their ministry without being fully engaged in the work. This is where auto-piloting plays a role.	Occasional request to strategic partners by Paul supports fundraising for personal support, but it was limited.
Church traditions	Vowing not to receive money from anyone but God. There is no biblical precedent in the NT. Selling of properties to enter full-time ministry, and never to work.[132]	Church companies, investment, and commercial units. These are not bad as long as they do not compromise the integrity and effectiveness of the Gospel.	Many of the modern pressurized fundraising approaches that raise questions are auctions and the sale of items supposed to have spiritual powers. Others are frequent TV shows to raise money. This is not bad, but there is a thin line between legitimate fundraising and exploitation that can jeopardize the Gospel.

We want to describe the key approaches to funding ministry in terms of their levels of biblical authority.

i) *Workers' wage* approach (the worker deserves his wages.)[133]
- Salaried worker (church/ministry jobs.)
- Unsalaried worker (depending on faith for finances through generosity *ad hoc* gifts from other believers, church, or provision in miraculous ways.)

ii) *Wallet-taking* approach[134] (Bi-vocational ministry and financial investment,) and:
- Conventional bi-vocational tentmaking (working to earn and do mission.)
- Auto-pilot tent-making (putting investment instruments to work while doing ministry.)

iii) *Fundraising* approach (mobilizing financial partners—other believers.)
- Mobilizing funds for personal support.
- Mobilizing funds for expanding the ministry.

The Worker's Wage Approach
The "workers' wage" represents the income or source of finances received by all Christian workers who work in the ministry full-time. They base their motivation on Jesus' command, *"Do not take a purse...when you enter a house...stay in that house eating and drinking whatever they give you, for the worker deserves his wages"* (Luke 10:4-7; 9:7-9). This worker does not need to move from house to house but accepts whatever is offered to him or her.

In modern times this remuneration may be in terms of i) employment in the Church or a ministry that pays a salary to the worker, or ii) a non-salaried work where the worker has to raise his or her own income. This is *ad hoc* support that is not obligatory but based on God's daily providence. The difference between the first and second is that the remuneration is structured and is certain in the salaried job—usually with a letter of appointment and terms of references by the employer (church or ministry) stating a fixed amount of income to expect and what benefits are covered. It is not too different from the marketplace employment, except that the money comes from the Church or ministry budget, whereas the non-salaried worker has no fixed or structured remuneration. Income depends on voluntary gifts, love offerings, honorariums, and unusual financial miracles in times of need. Some people call it "living by faith," but I prefer to call it "faith for finances."

All finances by Christians are supposed to be by faith anyway, even for those secular professional jobs. These are doors opened by God, and He can determine our benefits and promotions. And here I speak from experience, and assert that there has been no job I worked in that was not already confirmed by the Holy Spirit, and in most cases, He would tell me about that job before I knew about it, confirming "That is your next place of assignment from here." This is because all the other workers using approaches such as tentmaking, investment, and fundraising described in this book, are also living by faith, in a sense. They all expect God to intervene, except that the level or kind of faith required differs.

Chapter 7 Overview
Faith For Finances

Ministry Issue
Can Ministers Fully Depend on Faith-for-Finances?
Do Supernatural Provisions Work?

Ministry Lesson
God will work supernatural miracles when we are in His will and are in critical times of need, especially when there are no other ways of meeting those needs. Learn more in this chapter.

CHAPTER 7

FAITH FOR FINANCES

Provisions Through Financial Miracles
"The ravens brought him bread and meat in the morning and bread and meat in the evening, and he drank from the brook"
1 Kings 17:6.

Divine provision is one of the ways God provides for His people throughout the Scriptures. It works when we know and follow His divine principles for provision. Many ministers who have committed their lives and ministry to faith living or exercising "faith-for-finances" have experienced incredible testimonies that cannot be pushed aside, except by a blind skeptic. However, many of these financial testimonies that God gave to His children from time to time have sometimes been misapplied, miss-presented, and abused by greedy ministers who manipulate God's word and promises to exploit believers or a captive audience in gatherings.

The way some Christian leaders have presented the faith-for-finances message has been inadequate. As a result, a large part of the Church has alienated itself from anything that is suspected to mean getting money from God in fear of it being associated with the "prosperity message." With good intention, there are those in the Christian faith who think that avoiding money and embracing self-inflicted adversity, sometimes called "apostolic poverty" or "adversity gospel," is a virtue. But this is nothing other than sheer legalism and fanaticism. It is similar to some religious adherents who hold the belief that the practice of 'penance' imputes holiness.

Out of sheer ignorance, a theologian, McConnell, once described "healing and prosperity" as "cultic" and a "different gospel."[135] The enemy has been using half-truth theologies to fight any move of God through division on important biblical issues like money and health. Its goal is to limit the flow of resources to the church and to stop the flow of the Spirit power. Let's face it; if we took away God's promises and the power to heal and meet needs, the Gospel would become nothing but traditions and an empty shell. We have to embrace the supernatural. The ministry of Jesus is the ministry of the supernatural, to heal and to cast out demons, and provisions must follow the ministry of Jesus. It appears naïve for the church to be ignorant of such important aspects of the Gospel, which can even determine the success or failure of the Great Commission. Denying the supernatural in provisions and bundling it as "prosperity gospel" is to hide away the fact that we no longer believe what God has provided freely and demonstrated as part of the Gospel.

Let's remember one of His last instructions on finances, *"If you have your money, take it, and your provisions too, take it. If you do not have the Sword, sell your cloak and buy one"* (Luke 22:36).[136]

You need money. You need provisions. You also need the Spirit-empowered Word of God (the anointing,) to preach the Gospel. You cannot do the ministry of Jesus successfully without money, provisions, and the anointing for healing and miracles. You cannot impact the Kingdom if you exclude supernatural provisions.

No matter how we view finances, they cannot be removed from the Gospel, just as the anointing for healing and miracles cannot be removed. Failing to believe God's provision itself can lead to financial failure because it is only those who are willing and obedient that will eat the good of the land.[137] We must be willing to be blessed and obedient to His words. The word of God cannot be broken.

As we have already reviewed in the previous chapters, we know that Jesus instructed us about money. In the parable of minas or talents, the Lord particularly taught about the need to trade your God-given talent and natural abilities in order to make a profit.[138] This applies both literally and spiritually. Just because someone hates the 'prosperity message' cannot stop God from performing financial miracles to those who believe in His divine providence to the church. Derek Prince wrote in his book, "Blessing or Curse: You can choose one!"[139] He expatiated the blessings and curses in Deuteronomy 28, revealing we have a choice; which one will you choose, Blessing or Curse? I choose blessing. This is why it is important for the church to be taught and why we need a well-balanced and rightly divided word of God on this subject.

Financial Miracles are the Sovereign work of God.
God can surprise us with financial miracles, and God can do things beyond our imagination. Paul knew this well when he said, *"And my God shall meet all your needs, according to His glorious riches in Christ Jesus"* (Philippians 4:19). Jesus demonstrated to us that He could provide finances supernaturally, just as He could multiply bread to feed the multitudes. When the Pharisees were pressuring Him through His disciples about the payment for the temple tax, Jesus asked Peter to go get the money from the mouth of a fish: *"... Take the first fish you catch; open its mouth, and you will find a four drachma coin. Take it and give it to them for My tax and yours"* (Matthew 17:27). However, this was never repeated in His ministry or those of His Apostles. So, we cannot take it as an everyday practice. The principle remains that nothing is too hard for God. Practice can change, but the principle doesn't.

Many people like to hear about God sending a tall, strange-looking fellow to them at the end of the street who would stuff some money into their hands or drop a bag of money at their doorstep and vanish. God rarely works that way—He never did that before; although, He can do it at His discretion. When believers pray for a financial miracle, they start to look around for the one God will likely use to answer that prayer, and many have waited forever. Some even go ahead and ask their target if God is telling them something about their needs. There's nothing more laughable.

As a matter of fact, if we go deeper, we will realize that each of the men and women of God who had experienced many financial miracles also had periods of financial lack or anxiety in the time of waiting. I don't believe God expects our prayer life to be dominated by financial intercessions when we should be interceding for souls, for health and healing, for love, and unity in the Church, for workers, and for God's glory on earth.

When you depend only on financial miracles for your survival, it is not good to look at mankind or who will do it. We know God has a way of blessing whoever will obey Him to achieve His purpose.

Story 1: Wider Is the Hand that Gives
Paul quoted Jesus, who said that *"It is more blessed to give than to receive"* (Acts 20:35). A renowned minister in the United States testified about how another pastor had come up to him one day and gave him $100 as an offering. As he was going away, he said, "Pastor so and so, I will still come back and give you $1,000." He had said it by faith. A few months later, he returned and stuffed $1,000 into his hand. As he was walking away, he said, "Pastor so and so, I will still come back and give you $10,000." He didn't know why he said it, but then he walked away. Months later, he came back with a check for $10,000. As he was walking away again, he said, "Pastor so and so, one day I will still come back and give you $100,000. What made him say that? A few months later, he came back with the check of $100,000. As he was going, he said, "Pastor so and so, I will still come back and give you $1 million dollars." When he left, he felt that he was now in deep trouble. How would that happen? Nonetheless, the $1 million dollar check came after some time. This was a real-life story, and I heard it first-hand from this recipient pastor.[140] I strongly believe this was God in action.

I must mention here that it is not about using the right words or about proclaiming any 'faith formula' that had worked for the man. What worked for him was faith in the God of Providence. When we are moved by the Holy Spirit, we can speak by faith, and God will honor it. This man had the testimony of what Jesus had done for him, and he went to acknowledge that by giving a tenth to the servant of God (it is also not about him giving the tithe,) but rather that he spoke by faith, and God honored his faith, *"For the testimony of Jesus is the spirit of prophecy"* (Revelation 19:10).

It is the underlying faith of the pastor above that had worked for him, because the Holy Spirit had moved that faith into action. It was what he believed in his heart that he had spoken out, by faith, even though the amount was unbelievable to his mind when he spoke it. It is the object of our faith that matters, not the size of our faith or the manner we use to articulate it.

Imagine how some other ministers could easily make it a doctrine. Many would try to share that testimony to spur people into making foolish promises of giving to them what they cannot afford: promises that are not backed by faith or the revelation of God. There are also believers who might easily be trapped in making unwise vows because they want to become millionaires overnight, without working. We did not hear the rest of the story, especially how exactly God had done it for this pastor. We do not know his level of intimacy and consecration to God. We do not know what business he was involved in; all we know is that God did not allow this pastor's words to fall on the ground. I am persuaded to believe that God must have known that this pastor was a faithful servant.

Since this specific case of an unusual financial miracle, along with many others in the Scriptures cannot be repeated, it cannot be made into a doctrine because it has no biblical support. We must shift emphasis away from the emotionally charged messages that focus on methods that worked for us or someone else, and speak about the unchangeable, Kingdom's principles on finances.

Another pastor shared a powerful testimony on a television program about how he had wanted to buy a property for his church. The property was selling for $25 million, but the Holy Spirit told him to offer $7.7 million. It was first rejected outright, with some insults. Later, they called him back and offered it to him at the same price he offered. Now, at the time he was making the offer, he did not even have the money. Just after they had called him, someone walked up to him and said, "Pastor, God woke me up this morning and told me to give you $7.7 million dollars!"

Again, we are dealing with the operation of a gift of faith-for-finances when our spirit is moved by the Holy Spirit to believe for divine provision, which usually comes at a critical time of need. That is how God can partner with us to get His purpose accomplished. Many times, we are preoccupied with the how and where to get the money, but instead, if we learn how to know God's mind, we will have solutions to our finances. Miracles are simply miracles—that is, the act of God through the Holy Spirit to do the unusual thing that our human reasoning cannot comprehend, and we cannot remove miracles from the Gospel. God can do exceedingly more than what we can think or imagine, according to His Spirit that works in us.[141] A true miracle must surprise us and build our faith in God. When God has called you, He has provided the provisions for the calling somewhere, and somehow—there are also Provisions for the Vision. Believe it!

The most confusing part of the subject of financial freedom that has led many to reject or scoff at divine provisions is the delivery—the way it is communicated, taught, and handled in the Church. In general, Christian leaders have not been faithful in teaching the whole counsel of God based on money; rather, we have made it appear as if financial provision is a type of magic to the simple Christian. We expect them to take everything by faith, but there is very little logic in the way we have presented the facts. We leave people with the guilt that it is because they lacked faith that they have not received financial miracles. Miracles are God's sovereignty.

Financial provision can come to us by faith. I have experienced divine provision several times in the marketplace in times and ways one can only attribute to the provision of God, and God only. Over the years, I was favored in mobilizing a large amount of funds for my employers in my research and development career by faith and prayers, several times and at critical times. I can actually write a whole book on financial and other miracles in the marketplace. It is the same God who works within the Body of Christ that works at the marketplace. As a matter of fact, whether we received finances by faith, by investments, or by working for money through God's wisdom, it doesn't matter because it is still God who gives us the *"power to make wealth"* (Deuteronomy 8:18). It is only the way He has achieved it that may be different, so we must not limit Him. We must never attribute any of them to our own efforts.

God's word works better when we understand the principles and not the methods. Those who follow methods easily become dogmatic and frustrated, and those who teach it are prone to leading others into errors.

Jesus gave several parables to teach on the principles He used, not the methods. We can benefit more from the Bible when we develop the skills and wisdom to understand the principles. Let us look at some biblical methods and local examples of divine provisions that could be packaged into global principles. These key principles reflect the way God deals with His people during both Bible times and in our day.

Principle 1: You can wholly depend on God in times of desperate lack

In the days of Elijah, he had challenged King Ahab by declaring that there would be neither rain nor dew in the land for the next few years until he would reverse the statement.[142] Immediately afterward, the Lord instructed him to escape to the Brook Cherith (also called Kerith Ravine), in the east of Jordan. God told him, *"You will drink from the brook, and I have ordered the ravens to feed you there"* (1 Kings 17:2-4).

The ravens faithfully brought food: bread and meat to him in the morning and in the evening, and he also drank from the brook.[143] Can God still do this in our day? Yes, but He will not necessarily send a raven. If you are waiting to see literal ravens bring your meat and bread, you may wait forever. Yet, God can send a figurative raven to bring our provisions, whether as a job, as a business, direct supply, or other financial sources, in time of need.

What are the lessons here?
First, Elijah was completely in the will of God and on a divine assignment. God must absolutely provide for him. Elijah could not have been farming, trading, or going around asking people for food. To make things worse, he himself had prophetically shut the window of Heaven from raining or giving dew, so that no crops could be grown. It means there would be a great famine in the land, and Elijah himself might have starved. He will have to face the music of his own prophecy unless God acts and supplies his needs.

Staying in the land means he would either be killed by the angry king or by the mob who knew that he was the cause of their calamity, or he would have been ravaged by famine in his hiding place. God alone can deliver the goods here. It means when you have no option left, you can depend on God. If you are in His will and you have a personal relationship with Him, He will provide for you in any way. When the brook Elijah had depended on for water dried up, God relocated him to where he could eat and drink and have a suitable shelter for as long as he needed to stay.

Again God said, *"Go at once to Zarephath of Sidon and stay there. I have commanded a widow in that place to supply you with food"* (1 Kings 17:9). He was again being provided for by a new host, a widow, in Zarephath. There was no one around in the wilderness because Elijah had walked a day's journey away from the city into the desert where no one lived. Only God could feed him there, and it was not going to be ordinary food. God sent an angel who fed him twice a day with food and water, and he traveled for forty days on the strength of that food![144]

When your brook dries up, God is able to supply your needs, or He could relocate you to a new realm of provisions. When Jesus multiplied the bread and fish, it was because there was a desperate lack, and He had compassion on the people. If He fed the crowd who just came to hear Him, some of whom didn't fully believe, why would He not take care of their needs?[145] This is why He said we shouldn't worry because God knows all of our needs.[146] Later, when some Jews expected the Lord to multiply bread and fish again and demanded that the He bring manna from Heaven as proof of His messiahship, Jesus sharply rebuked them.[147] Manna from Heaven is an exception rather than a norm. So also, relying on financial miracles for all our needs is an exception in the Scriptures. Nevertheless, God will always answer the prayers of the faithful in times of real need.

Story 2: The Woman at Counter Number Eight
One of the most amazing testimonies I have ever heard on financial miracles was the story of an old woman in Brazil, a pensioner, and how her 'brook' suddenly dried up. The story was told by a visiting pastor at the Assemblies of God church in Joao de Deus, Sao Luis-MA, Brazil. The guest pastor knew this woman personally. She was a faithful giver and a retiree. Suddenly, there was a prolonged delay in the payment of her retirement benefits for a few months. She had nothing and no one to help. She was on the brink of starvation.

One day, after she had been praying and crying out to the Lord, the Holy Spirit spoke to her, "Go to such and such shopping mall and do your shopping there. I will pay your bill." It was one of the largest shopping malls in the city. She thought God was probably going to have someone or an angel give her money. Off she went.

As she entered the shopping mall and waited, the Lord told her to go in, take a big shopping cart, and make it a full shopping trip. She knew she heard Him. When she picked up one loaf of bread, the Lord would tell her to 'pick up four.' When she picked up one tablet of her favorite soap, He said, 'take a whole pack.' When she picked up oil, He said, 'pick up two gallons.' When she picked up one kilo of chicken, He told her to pick up another one and some beef also. When she picked a few oranges, He pointed out the bananas to her. She was just obeying and loading the trolley until it was over-flowing. She had everything she needed in the trolley. Then she looked at what she had picked up and laughed at herself. She thought she was going crazy![148]

She comforted herself that she really had heard God. She pulled the heavy shopping cart aside, waiting there in case the Lord was going to send someone to give her the money. I can imagine her smiling at every person that was coming in her direction and looking expectantly, but nothing happened. At one point, the Lord urged her to step into the queue and said (in Portuguese,) "*Go to counter number 8.*" She obeyed, but as the queue reduced, she started to panic—her legs were shaking. The last person at the counter paid and left, and she was the next in line. She looked back; nobody was coming.

"Next!" The attendant called to her.

She hesitated and wanted to turn back, but the Lord told her to move in and pass every item through the machine and that He would pay for her.

As she was obeying, she wondered if she was being deceived by satan. Although the voice spoke clearly to her that she should not fear, she was trembling. She was looking around in case someone was coming to make the payment, but she saw nobody. Then as the clerk took the last item in her shopping cart, the electric power went off, and an alarm rang loudly.

At the end of the alarm, a voice spoke in Portuguese, "We have just completed a secret lottery. The woman in Counter Number 8 has just won the jackpot. She will not have to pay anything! Congratulations, Madam!" Everyone was saying, "Parabens, Senhora!"

She was perplexed and felt as if she were dreaming. Everyone came to embrace her and helped her move the shopping cart. Someone volunteered his car to drive her to her house. She fed on that provision for at least two months, and before that food was finished, all her retirement income and the past arrears were fully paid by her employer. God is faithful!

Can anyone just go to the shopping mall and have the same faith for God to repeat this woman's testimony in the same way? If you believe you can repeat it, you go try it at Walmart and come back to tell your testimony. God will do that once in a while, but you cannot depend on it as your permanent means of survival or financial strategy. That also applies to all forms of financial miracles—they are for critical times of need. In sum, we must always trust God.

Lessons learned:
- God deals with individuals on financial miracles in unique ways.
- There is no silver bullet for miracles; it depends on your situation and faith.
- No situation is beyond God.
- You must be sure you heard God! Stand on God's word.

- Act on what God says, even if it makes little sense; be wise and discerning.
- Avoid emotional drive and baseless fanaticism.

Let us draw a few more principles on financial miracles.

Principle 2: There is sacrifice in trusting God for finances

The first question that comes to mind when entering a full-time ministry is how do I meet my needs? Can a believer or minister completely depend on God? Yes, but there are specific situations where this may be warranted. Depending on God for finances does not come on a platter of gold, as many think. Many of those whom God has been faithful with in finances have been men and women of God who had been very faithful to God, obeying His voice in little and great things. It comes with sacrifice, anxiety, and uncertainties, also.

For instance, Dr. John G. Lake, as I have shared with you, was formerly a millionaire in terms of his financial net-worth. He resigned from his professional job and donated his savings and investments to charity. He paid the price by jumping into the dark and went into a full-time ministry, trusting God only. He did not even receive offerings or fundraise in his ministry as most missionaries and evangelists do today. He solely depended on voluntary giving. John G. Lake received some of the greatest financial miracles in the revival era. It is not that he never experienced lack. He did, and his wife and family actually suffered a great deal from it. His house was often lacking enough for the large family—he had seven children and many visitors they had to receive, but it was the price for the great work God did through him. Pastor E.A. Adeboye, General Overseer of the Redeemed Christian Church of God (RCCG), felt led to divide his pension into three parts and give it to three different recipients. God told him he should depend solely on Him. He obeyed. He already had paid the price by relinquishing his career as an Associate Professor of Mathematics when he went into full-time pastoring. Did an angel bring money to him the following week? Not at all. He actually suffered for some time initially, but the Lord took care of him, supplied all his needs, and gave him a great ministry. God blessed the ministry, and it prospered greatly. Paul said, *"And my God shall supply all your needs according to His riches in glory by Christ Jesus"* (Philippians 4:19). Before then, Pastor Adeboye had times he could not find money to fuel his car or take a taxi after he resigned from his job and distributed and gave away his pension. Nonetheless, God met all his needs in His own way.

One day this great servant of God was praying to God to give him a house of his own. God replied that He would not give him a house but a city. Anyone who knows the Redeem Camp or Redemption City, in Ogun State, near Lagos, Nigeria, will know that God has fulfilled that promise. It is a City within a City.

The Apostle Paul paid the price of following Jesus. He considered all his achievements as a loss in order to gain Christ.[149] He knew how to abound in provision and how to be in lack.[150]

What price have you paid that justifies wholly depending on God? What relationship do you have with the Lord? While you were earning, did you spend or use your money to please God? We must also remember that the Lord can actually tell us to give away our income if He realizes that we are focusing too much on it as our source in the ministry. If you value money so much, the Lord will ensure He shifts your eyes from it until you have no options left, except Him. We must simply obey. He will demand that you do away with what is between you and Him. That was what He did to Abraham when He told him to offer Isaac, his only son, to Him.

This was the reason Jesus told that young man to go and sell all he had and follow Him. The man had asked the Lord how to be perfect. Jesus looked at him and loved him, and said, *"One thing you lack,"* He further said, *"Go, sell everything you have and give to the poor, and you will have treasure in Heaven. Then come, follow me"* (Mark 10:21). The specific instruction of Jesus to this man was not a general command to every Christian. Otherwise, the Lord would have asked Nicodemus, Lazarus, or Joseph Arimathea to sell their possessions, too. Throughout church history, people have misunderstood and misapplied this story.

The man was sad because his wealth was more important to him than the privilege of following Jesus. How about you? If God asks for your Isaac, what would you do? Some people naturally purge or strip themselves of financial security as a way of sanctifying themselves to avoid the trap of mammon. That was what John G. Lake did. It is not a requirement by God for His ministers, but if anyone feels led, I believe it is pleasing to the Lord.

The wisdom here is that it is better not to do anything rash unless the Lord leads us to do so. This is because the money you have can be put to use in God's work to advance the Kingdom. The energy we spend being anxious and praying in faith for the needed finances can be channeled to other important Kingdom priorities. But if the Lord leads us to dispose of our income or wealth, for His sake, and we are sure it is God Who is speaking to us, woe to anyone who refuses to obey that command.

It is very easy when we share the testimonies of how the Lord has done things in the past. But what we quickly forget is that when you are re-watching a football game, after it is over, the anxiety is not the same as when you are watching it live for the first time. There is a price of anxiety in most faith-for-finances situations, especially when the days are approaching, and the hours and minutes are ticking by ... before God shows up. That was why King Saul missed what God was doing; he gave up because he thought Samuel had delayed and he took a wrong decision.[151] If faith-for-finances is your route for ministry, don't give up and learn to depend wholly on God. When we depend on God this way, it truly builds our faith in Him. Weeping may endure for the night, but joy comes in the morning.

Lessons learned:
- There is a price to pay. It is not just anyone who can expect God to meet their needs—to expect God to meet 100% of their finances all the time. Your relationship with God and whether you truly know the Lord counts.
- You must be sure you heard God lead you to operate this way. If you do, that will keep you going, even in times of difficulty.
- God may require that we shift our focus from money and focus on Him. In that case, He may ask us to dispose of our wealth like the young, rich man. However, this is an exception rather than a rule. Instead, God can actually use that income to achieve His purpose. That rich young man was not even a minister or follower of Jesus.
- God honors those who honor Him. When we have a good relationship with God, have been called to His work, and depend on Him, He never fails. He provided for Peter and the rest of the apostles in Jerusalem through generous giving by the church.
- Faith is not completely without anxiety or pressure, and the final test comes from the waiting time. Those who depend on God for finances must be prepared to pay the price of waiting anxiously by holding on to Him in faith and seeking. God does not fail.

Principle 3: Faith-for-finances grows.
God doesn't start a believer with millions overnight or in one day. He moves His people step by step in what He has called them to in faith. Abraham had stepped out in faith, trusted Him for his promises, and faced troops, believing God for his safety, victory, and prosperity. Many believers want to do what others have done without really knowing where they are coming from in their relationship with God, and faith, and a life of consecration.

One day, a young man who later became the great evangelist Reinhard Bonnke started believing God for his needs as a student at college.[152] He felt led to give all the pocket money he got from home to a missionary who would come. He obeyed and then prayed to the Lord that he wanted to be a man of faith. He started to practice faith living. His faith had to grow from little things—getting the needed postage stamp, later, a bus transport fee, and then, a traveling ticket.

For the bus fees, he and his friend had just traveled to a place to preach, but they had no money to return back to the campus. They met a minister who invited them for lunch, but they thought God was going to use him to give them the money. Unknowingly, the minister paid the bills and shook their hands, and they parted. At the last hour, a woman ran after them. She said that she had enjoyed the preaching of the two young men. She stuffed two coins into their hands. It was the exact amount of money they needed for transport back to the campus. His faith for finances started to grow from here. Faith grows. If you can believe God for 100 dollars, you should be able to believe Him for 1,000 dollars. To God, the amount does not matter.

Today, most of those who claim to practice faith living do not keep it between themselves and God when or what they need. They actually solicit until their hearers become embarrassed and start to do something about it in the flesh. If you have faith, God will meet your needs; you don't have to go and ask people for it or tell them you believe God will meet your needs through them. That is helping God. That was what Sarah and Abraham connived together to do, and Ishmael was the product. That was only God's permissive will, even though God had promised them a son of their own. Much of what people call "faith-for-finance" is nothing but an Ishmael alternative to the true faith because they had sought help from people. The credit goes to God—to God wholly. But God does not want His glory to be shared with another.

When I hear exhortations for finances before an offering is received, I recognize an Ishmael method in our fundraising. When I hear,

"God told me there is someone here who God is speaking to right now to give for this project. Don't resist; just obey." I see another Ishmael on the way. Can we seek more of 'Isaac' in the church? Abraham didn't need help for Sarah to bring forth Isaac, but their anxiety in trying to help God gave them Ishmael. Although God wasn't worried about it, it was not His best for him. Yet, He still blessed Ishmael, anyway.

To depend on God, we must not expect it like magic all the time. There are times God will treat us as the eagles treat their young before getting us to the level of faith-for-finances. It doesn't come overnight. We can learn from this Scripture: *"As the eagle stirs up its nest, hovers over its young, spreading out its wings, taking them up, carrying them on its wings, so the Lord alone led him, and there was no foreign god with him"* (Deuteronomy 32:11-12 NKJV)

The eagle trains its young ones by first pushing them out, with their wings, one after the other. As the eaglet rolls down, she flies over it. Imagine how they must cry from the fear of striking the ground. Just as the baby bird is about to crash, she swoops down and picks it up, putting it on her wings and taking it back to the nest. At a point, the eaglet begins to wiggle its wings until it starts to fly. But instead of flying upward, it goes downward; then the eagle hovers over it and grabs it. She does this repeatedly until the eaglet is able to fly.

This is a wonderful illustration of how God trains our faith for anything, including finances. You will not wake up and believe God for one million dollars if you cannot believe Him for $100. You can't believe Him for a house if you can't trust Him for your rent. Faith must grow, but God will not forsake the righteous. Faith-for-finances does not mean there will be no time of need. The Christian worker must know that our faith will always be tested.

Lessons learned:
1. Faith living can grow, as we know God, just as our faith-for-finances can grow.
2. Faith-for-finances does not mean a lack of anxiety, but we must hold on to God.
3. God has pleasure in how we trust Him.

Principle 4: God can meet our needs through both faith and blessing our work.
Paul had great faith in God, and he heard from Jesus directly; yet, he had to plan and work for his living. There were moments he lacked and moments when he had surplus. Think about that for a moment. According to him, *"I know what it is to be in need, and I know what it is to have plenty. I have learned the secret of being content in any and every situation, whether fed or hungry, whether living in plenty or in want. I can do all things through Him who gives me strength"* (Philippians 4:12-13).

Apart from Jesus, no one else in the New Testament had taught on faith and on the subject of money more than Paul. But the Apostle said here that he was acquainted with lack and plenty, yet he was content in every situation he found himself in. Instead of doing a *'name it and claim it,"* he depended on the grace of Jesus. We must reflect and think about that statement each time we want to go overboard to *abracadabra* Pentecostalism.

In your ministry, whether you have a source of income or not, it is important to trust God. He can meet your needs, and His plan for you is to have enough and plenty more to share.[153] As a matter of fact, most of those who have their needs met probably started in other ways until they were able to gradually depend on God. If your church is regularly paying your income as a salary in sufficient amount, there is not much of a faith walk in that. You simply need to deliver on what your church board wants and the income is guaranteed. Today, many pastors and church workers apply for jobs and conduct interviews with specified benefits, just as those in secular, professional careers do. Some senior pastors or 'presidents' also fire and hire other ministers like CEOs. That is the extent to which we have secularized Gospel work. So, where is faith-for-finances in that? Faith comes even when that income is not enough, and we believe God to supplement our specific needs.

God can meet all our needs because all the gold and silver, the earth, and its fullness belong to Him. God doesn't encourage laziness and foolishness, and there are times He wants to shift our focus from money to Himself. Paul was the best New Testament teacher on *divine finances*—sowing and reaping,[154] but he himself had to work for a living, along with Barnabas, and Aquila, and Priscilla, when the situation permitted him.[155] It is not unbelief to work for your living and do God's work as a minister. There is no pride in claiming to work full-time but ending up harassing or embarrassing church members or those we minister to with a prolonged plea for money or apply unacceptable gimmicks to extract money from people when we are under pressure. We cannot meet our needs at the expense of causing hardships to others without reproaching God's Name.

For the vast majority of ministers, they will have to be supported by the church, or they will have to work. This also is not a sin or greed. The Bible is very clear on the need to support ministers—pastors and those who minister to us.[156] Some churches like Corinth were not generous givers to Paul, and others were. He wrote to them and said, *"Don't you know that those who work in the temple get their food from the temple and those who serve at the altar share in what is offered in the altar? In the same way, the Lord has commanded that those who preach the gospel should receive their living from the gospel"* (1 Corinthians 9:13-14).

Paul himself wrote this, despite his being a bi-vocational minister, earning a living from tentmaking wherever opportunity permitted.

The situation in Corinth might have made it difficult to receive offerings. He said the above to the Corinthians in order to not abuse his privileges, and he believed it was more honorable when he did not ask them for money.[157]

Paul's situation in Corinth is where the teaching on tent-making and how to grow our income becomes very relevant to workers in the Kingdom. With investment, it is possible to receive passive income that can support personal ministry. We will discuss this at length in another chapter. This is possible if we have or are willing to learn and apply the necessary skills in investing.

Usually, at the beginning of a ministry or church, when the income is not forthcoming, it makes sense to do some income-generating work. Many ministers can also obtain extra income from writing books, CDs, and other materials, but these should not be our main focus. The Gospel must be preached.

Let me say this: whether we do the ministry full-time or part-time, the most important thing is that the Gospel message must be preached. If Paul preached part-time as a 'bi-vocational evangelist' and reached the whole world with the Gospel, we have no excuse. Jesus advised those who think they cannot preach the Gospel until they have all their needs met and have finances guaranteed for the next five years not to focus on those things as unbelievers do.[158] We must not crave wealth the way pagans crave it because, *"For where your treasure is, there your heart will be also"* (Luke 12:34). We must guard our hearts against loving money and serving the god of mammon.[159]

The purpose of generating financial wealth should be to enable us to preach the Gospel; anything else will be a distraction. When you do not have to run around for money or spend the early hours wondering how to make ends meet, or shed secret tears because you are unable to feed or pay your children's fees, you will have more quality time studying the Word of God, interceding for the afflicted and doing evangelism. But when we overly focus our heart on accumulating money, we must not be shocked if Jesus tells us to rid ourselves of it and focus on Heavenly things.

Lessons learned:
- There is no contradiction in God's Word, with regards to depending on God wholly as a minister or planning for your finances with God's wisdom and power to make wealth.
- The great commission needs the money, whether it is earned directly by you or not. You can use your God-given skills and talents to make wealth for His glory.

Often, money will follow the power of the Gospel. However, ministers must avoid self-aggrandizement and exploitation of the power of God. The Gospel money must be spent on the Gospel, and self must be last, instead of first.

In the next chapter, I want to present some of the most amazing financial miracles of our times in the last century. They will build your faith and challenge you. God is still the God of miracles.

Chapter 8 Overview
Financial Miracles

Ministry Issue
Does God still perform financial miracles today?

Ministry Lesson
God is faithful in healing, just as He is faithful in provisions.

CHAPTER 8

FINANCIAL MIRACLES

Amazing Financial Miracles Of All Time

"Elisha said, "Go around and ask all your neighbors for empty jars. Don't ask for just a few. Then go inside and shut the door behind you... Pour oil into all the jars..." 2 Kings 4:3-4.

"Have you got any water?" Wigglesworth asked Harrison calmly. "Yes, I keep a can for topping off the radiator." "Put it in the petrol tank," he ordered." [160]

Financial miracles are a sovereign act of God, which He does when He pleases. We cannot arm-twist Him with our emotions when our human nature wants free money. It doesn't work that way. God will not magically produce money for us as if He were a mystic or a magician. He will only act when He needs to, and His methods are usually not the same, nor are they always predictable, but His principles are the same. The problem is that we want God to repeat practices but change His principles; this He will not do. The Jews asked Jesus to bring manna from Heaven so they can believe him.[161] Even as nothing is impossible to Him, He did not do it. He is a sovereign God.

Therefore, we need to ask, "Is it possible to depend on God without having to work or do any other investing?" Not every minister must operate by tentmaking or by the investment route, just as it is not every minister who can work full-time without any financial source and succeed. Some people will have to work full-time, while others will have to work as bi-vocational ministers, but both can also be investors. We will focus on the investment part in another chapter, but here I want us to further look at some amazing financial miracles when ministers trust God.

A lot will depend on your calling, your faith, and your circumstances. God's Word supports both full-time ministries and wholly depending upon God when we do not have other sources. His Word also supports and actually prefers that we raise or generate our own funding for ministry. This is done through investing the talents, money, resources, time, and opportunities He has given us, and also by partnering with Him. Some people have no money, but they have people who are willing to support their ministry with little effort. That is good news. Take it!

However, the truth is that the money may not always flow into the ministry. No matter where you live, people are becoming stingier when it comes to supporting the work of God. There are times when the Christian worker will just have to trust God alone for his next meal.

Yet, the Christian Church is generally skeptical about fully trusting God for finances. The reason is that we have taken the supernatural out of the Church, and we now preach and teach the Gospel without the supernatural—substituting the supernatural with human methods, political and theological correctness, or well-figured out methods, all of which require little faith, but reliance on people and on brainpower.

There is danger in moving from Kingdom ways to mental persuasion.

The following stories will help to reinforce the assertion that God is still the same and He can provide for anyone who trusts in Him. They are amazing and will build your faith as you read them.

Story 1: How God Provided for Dr. John G. Lake
I am always amazed at the great healing ministry of John G. Lake and how God backed him up supernaturally. I mentioned him briefly in the previous chapter. Most of the time, when people talk about his ministry, it is about healing miracles, and we rarely talk about financial miracles. He was doing well financially as an insurance executive, a successful

businessman—one that you could even describe as a millionaire in his day. He had substantial assets in real estate properties and stocks. His income, savings, and pension were enough to support him indefinitely in the ministry if he had chosen to depend on that money. However, with the Christian belief of that day about the calling of God,[162] he decided to sell all his estates and distributed the money to charity. Then, he went into full-time ministry in the Lord's timing.

It must be noted that Dr. John G. Lake actually started out his ministry as a tentmaker. In 1891, he was admitted to the Baptist School of Ministry in Chicago and was appointed to pastor a church in Peshtigo, Wisconsin by October of that year, but he declined the offer. Instead, he moved to Illinois and founded a local newspaper business, "The Harvey Citizen." In 1901, he moved to Zion City to study divine healing under Apostle John Alexander Dowie. John Lake was preaching at night and studying during the day, and also working for Dowie as his building manager. Following Dowie's financial crisis and a huge loss from Lake's investment there, he relocated to Chicago and bought a seat with the Chicago Board of Trade. It is remarkable that Lake never criticized Apostle Dowie in any of his many writings nor regretted the time he served under him. On the contrary, he revered the great anointing of God on the man. Over the next year, he had accumulated $130,000 in the bank and $90,000 in stocks. He also formed a trust with one of the three largest insurance companies in the United States and was making $50,000 per year as a top executive business consultant. Without doubt, he was a millionaire by today's standards.[163]

At the same time, he was able to combine his secular work with ministry. He did not go to full-time ministry immediately, as Roberts Liardon would comment:

> "By the turn of the century standards, John G. Lake was now making a fortune…for a while, he was able to juggle his great success and grow in God. Some people think that if you are called

to the ministry, you must leave your secular job *immediately*. But as was true with Lake, this is not the case. By learning to commune with God from within his spirit, Lake continued to progress toward the perfect timing for his ministry. He didn't venture out ahead of God or cause his family to suffer. Then when the timing was right, he was able to sell everything because he had learned great faith from his years of walking with God as a businessman. In 1907, John and Jennie disposed of their estate, their wealth, and their possessions. In a great move of faith, they determined to be entirely dependent upon God. Now it was time to preach."[164]

As we can see, for about 16 years (1891 to 1907,) John G. Lake was operating as a bi-vocational Evangelist or tentmaker. He also developed and trained himself in ministry while still working as a businessman. He did not go into full-time ministry, believing God for the finances, until he had learned to walk with God in faith. This is the reason I recommend early starters in ministry to first work before going into full-time ministry unless God says otherwise. During that period, we will be able to learn how to depend on God and also know how to undertake ministry and fund it.

After he had emptied himself of his resources, he was immediately being led to conduct evangelistic campaigns in Indianapolis and to also prepare for missionary work in Africa.[165] The time had come for a vision he had received much earlier to be fulfilled.

With seven children and a wife, Dr. Lake was led to South Africa as a missionary, and he had less than $2. After prayers with his partner, an unknown person sent in the needed $2,000 for the tickets for the two families' bill for the one-way journey to Johannesburg.

On their arrival, they needed to pay $200 as a requirement before they would be allowed to disembark the ship. By faith, he joined the queue, not knowing where to get the money, but he trusted God would not fail him.

Just before it got to his turn, another person, whom he did not know, called him aside on the queue and told him God had instructed him to give Dr. Lake $200 to support his ministry.

Just before they could clear at the port, the Lord sent an elderly American woman with specific instructions to look for a missionary couple with seven children who would be arriving at the port that day and to provide a home for them.

Mrs. Goodenough had a large, well-furnished cottage, and she was living alone. The Lakes became her guests at the Lord's provision, and they lived in that house for some years; they had great memories of the love of God through this woman during their ministry in South Africa.[166] Now, that is what I call true "faith-for-finances!" It is different from sending out emails to thousands of people to solicit personal financial support and displaying photographs of starving children in war-torn Africa or in some poor Asian nations, as our strategy for raising a meal ticket—to garner emotion for steady, financial support from partners.

Those who claim to depend on God should truly depend on God. Some claim to 'live by faith' and wholly depend on God, but in reality, they're looking up to people. Imagine how Dr. Lake lived this way, by absolute faith for years without directly asking anyone for money, and he was successful in his ministry. Faith for financial miracles cannot be different from faith for healing. If anyone can believe God for healing, they should also be able to believe Him to provide miraculously. That was the secret Dr. Lake probably knew better than most of us.

Story 2: Provisions through a Financial Covenant with God
Smith Wigglesworth, the great healing evangelist from the 1880s,

gave the last payment he received from a plumbing fee back to the old woman he had worked for as an offering to the Lord. He closed his business and entered into full-time ministry with a conviction that God, as his partner, could not fail. He made the following covenant with the Lord: "Lord, my shoe heels must never be a disgrace, and I must never have to wear trousers with the knees out." I said to the Lord, "If any of these take place, I'll go back to plumbing."[167]

God never failed to do His part, and Smith never had to return to plumbing. He also did not have to ask for money or do fundraising of any form. There are those who don't believe this is possible, but I believe that with God, all things are possible—nothing is too hard for God![168] In those days, it was almost regarded as a sin to collect offerings in Pentecostal circles, but God provided for every one of the ministers.

Water Turn into Petrol
Colin Melbourne wrote an article on one of the most amazing miracles I have read about the great legendary evangelist, Smith Wigglesworth. It wasn't just about healing or the miracle of raising the dead that we all know about. This miracle was when he turned water into refined petrol.[169] What a mystic cannot do, God can do.

The story is paraphrased as follows: When Smith Wigglesworth was in his eighties, he was still preaching the Gospel wherever God led him. It was wartime in Britain, and traveling was dangerous and challenging. Petrol was strictly rationed by using allowance coupons. The black market ran mainly on military bases, and the servicemen required bribing and buying at inflated prices. The petrol and other liquid fuels were dyed by the authorities according to type, source, and location. The policemen monitored the use of petrol. If they stopped someone in a red zone and realized he was using the green petrol, he was arrested. Coupled with the fact that for ethical reasons, Christians would not bribe someone to buy on the black market, they had to make do with the legitimate quota they were allowed.

Pastor Harrison of Sutton, in Ashfield, Nottinghamshire, had saved his petrol ration for a special event. Smith Wigglesworth had committed to coming on the condition that the Pastor would come and pick him up from a neighboring town where he had a preaching engagement. As they reached the middle of Sherwood Forest, the Morris Eight car sighed as the engine juddered, sputtered, and brought itself to a halt—the car was out of fuel, and they were still 17 miles away from their destination. It was dark, at night, and dangerous in the middle of bomb-blasted England. Harrison was gravely embarrassed for having invited a world-renown evangelist to his church and yet, got him stranded in the middle of the forest at night.

As Pastor Harrison mulled over his options, which seemed futile, Smith Wigglesworth already received a solution from God about what to do.

"Have you got any water?" he asked Harrison calmly.
"Yes, I keep a can for topping off the radiator."
"Put it in the petrol tank," Wigglesworth ordered. Now that was God-sized faith!

Harrison did not argue; he just obeyed. He took the half-gallon can of water from behind the driver's seat and poured it into his car's gas tank while he whispered some prayers between his clenched teeth. When Harrison engaged the engine, it roared and burbled miraculously to life. Harrison sped off with amazement, reaching their destination without incident. Wigglesworth sat quietly until they arrived, and he preached his message as planned. What a wonderful God we have!

Later, Harrison took the can to a mechanic workshop to scoop and withdraw some of the liquid from the tank. They discovered it was pure petrol, with no trace of water. It also had the exact color that was allowed legally for Nottinghamshire. Jesus said it all, and Wigglesworth believed that *"Things which are impossible to man are possible with God"* (Luke 18:27). All things are possible to those who believe. This was a case of total consecration, faith, and dependence because we know the God we serve.

Story 3: The Testimony of How God Sustained Brother Kenneth Hagin

Similarly, many times the great teacher of the Gospel, Brother Kenneth Hagin (as he was fondly called,) also shared incredible testimonies of how God was sustaining him in ministry. Like thousands of other ministers around the world, I have traveled from Malawi to Tulsa, Oklahoma. In 2003, I went just to listen to his teaching and unsurpassed wisdom, just like Sheba went to hear Solomon. I also bought dozens of his books. His teaching on the subject of faith ministry was legendary, and his testimonies of faith for finances were incredible.

He had developed such a relationship with God that he could even ask Him for a particular amount of money by faith. He often got the exact amount or more. God honored him throughout his ministry, which lasted for nearly half a century.

The ministry prospered, and Rhema Bible School, led by his son, Rev. Kenneth Hagin, is a monument to his great faith. He never had to work, and God met all his expenses week after week and gave him a great ministry. The Lord actually taught him how to fully trust Him for all his finances: to believe and be willing, in order to eat the good of the land. He depended fully on God and never lacked. If you truly know your God, and you have been truly called, God is able to provide all you need to accomplish the Vision He has given you. You only need to believe God and ask Him where to locate your own "acres of diamonds." There are many like Brother Kenneth Hagin. The Lord will honor their ministry with signs and wonders, and money will flow in naturally with less effort.

Story 4: How God taught Reinhard Bonnke about Faith for Finances

Reinhard Bonnke had learned about 'faith living' from his bible college. In that college, students had to believe and pray for everything they needed until they got an answer from God. They were not to ask anyone. This is the faith ethic that does not come with the 21st-century 'faith living'—people ask and use various ways to mount pressure on anyone who they suspect could give, yet claim to live by faith.

Reinhard started to believe God for all his needs. Later in life, he mentioned that he could believe God for one million dollars the same way he would believe Him for one hundred dollars back then. One day, after he had packed his bags, he waited on the Lord for the money to come, and the time was ticking away. Colin Whittaker puts it this way:

> "His friend Tunis found him on his knees. Reinhard invited his friend to pray with him. Reinhard bags were packed; everything was there except the money. If praying depended on the loudness of their cries, Heaven must have surely heard! But Heaven remained as brass. The situation was desperate. Then the words of the chorus came to mind, and he started to sing, 'There's nothing too hard for Thee…I'm trusting alone in Thee… It's never too late for Thee, dear Lord." As they were singing the last verse, something happened in his head. He suddenly knew that God had answered. He could not explain it, but there was an inner certainty, and he believed it. Tunis was startled when Reinhard stood up and shouted, 'The money is there!' Tunis asked, "Where?" he said, "I don't know, but I know it is there!"[170]

A friend came and asked, "How much money do you need?" He was sure God was about to meet his needs through this person. Reinhard believed it was inconsistent with faith to tell him the amount. He answered, "God knows the amount, I am not telling you."[171] Tim handed him some bills and left; when he counted it, it was the exact fare he needed! This happened as the relationship between Reinhard and God deepened.

Story 5: Doing God's business, God's Way

The great revivalist Katheryn Kuhlman preached as an evangelist without any financial support from any denomination. She believed in a big God whom she served. It was during the great depression. She told Hewitt, her campaign manager, to act as if they had one million dollars, to get everything ready in a big way.

When Hewitt hesitated because they only had $5, Katherine said, "God is not limited to what we have or who we are. He can use our $5 and multiply it as easily as He multiplied the loaves and fishes. Now, go to Denver. Find me the biggest building you can. Get the finest piano available for Helen. Fill the place up with chairs. Take out a big ad in the Denver Post, and get spot announcements on all the radio stations. This is God's business, and we're going to do it God's way—big!"[172] That's God-sized faith-for-finances! She trusted in God and let Him do it His way. God didn't fail her.

Story 6. Radical Faith By Evangelist R.W. Schambach

The great healing evangelist R.W. Schambach narrated a very radical testimony of how he was able to buy a church building by faith using the inspired Word of God.[173] He had just preached on Deuteronomy 11:24 that night in New Jersey, "*Every place the soles of your feet tread shall be yours...*" After the message and having laid hands on over 500 people, he suddenly realized he was preaching to himself. At the end of the service, he grabbed his Bible and asked some of his preacher friends to come with him to pray. "Come with me," he said. "We're going to walk around the building and lay some footprints down. I am going to claim this thing." He wanted to buy the building; yet, he never owned a bank account or had written a bank check, but he had faith in God. His friends refused to be involved in such crazy faith, "We'll wait in the car. You go ahead and walk." Evangelist Schambach went and marched around that building alone. At the time, he was renting the building, and it was not for sale.

The next day, they put a sign on the lawn—'FOR SALE!' He uprooted the sign and took it to the realtor's office. "Who put this on my property?" he asked. The realtor laughed and said, "What do you want to offer me for that building?" Schambach replied, "Nothing!" He told him to go and come back when he had money. Someone had already offered him $265,000. Just then, the Holy Spirit said to him, "Offer them $75,000." So he did. The realtor was very upset, but Schambach demanded that he informs the owner right away. When he refused, Schambach insisted on his right to have his offer be communicated to the owner.

The property belonged to an insurance company. The realtor reluctantly called the chairman of the insurance company and told him the offer. At the other end of the phone, the man said, "Sell it to him." The board of directors of that company had such a great year that they didn't mind taking a loss and paying less tax by selling it to a preacher. The realtor had no choice. Now, he had no money for the $35,000 dollar down payment, but God provided it miraculously.

When there was only a $10,000 dollar balance, and there was only 10 minutes remaining for the deal to be closed, the man of God was waiting in his office, expectantly. When a lady ran up to him, and he said to her, "Give it to me. Give it to me!" She said, "How do you know I have something for you?" He told her he would tell her later. She took the $10,000 dollars from her purse and gave it to him. Brother Schambach ran with it to the realtor and paid the balance in time. God provided the remaining money, and he bought that building.

One of Schambach's preacher friends who had stayed in the car while he marched around his building later called him (after having heard the testimony), telling him that they had found a building for his church. He wanted Brother Schambach to come and walk around it. The man of God replied, "Well, I am about 28 minutes from you, but I will make it in 20. Wait for me. But remember, brother, if I use my feet, it's going to be my building." He was probably joking.

Miracles are for specific times and situations, but we cannot expect God to do it every day for everything we need. That would be the 'manna' type of Christianity. There are times when God will feed us with daily manna, but His main purpose is that we possess the land and work it for our food. The manna will ultimately stop at some point![174] Don't expect to live on manna. Move up! Move on! Take the land, cultivate it, and eat the harvest.

Story 7. The Rarest Financial Miracle I Have Ever Heard
In another astounding testimony, Brother R.W. Schambach described how a man was saving up to buy a truck, but it was hard. He had only $500. Yet, God told him to give that $500 to R.W. Schambach and that He would buy him a new truck.[175] He simply obeyed and gave the money.

The next night, he returned to that meeting with one of the most amazing testimonies of all time: As he drove his old car down a Brooklyn Street in New York, the Lord spoke to him, "Stop the truck. Get out of the truck and lift up the hood." The man knew car parts. God will speak to you in the language you understand and at your own level.

As he opened the car bonnet, God said, "Look down at the carburetor. Feel it with your hand." He found a roll the size of an oil filter, all covered with grease. God said, "That's it. Break it off."

When he did, he found $26,000 dollars inside that baked grease roll. It was all in $100 dollar bills. That night, he presented an envelope of $2,600 dollars to R.W. Schambach for his tithe. That was when Schambach gave him the microphone at that meeting to tell the audience what had happened. He still had enough to buy a brand new truck. Praise the Lord!

Now, many folks who heard his story went to check the carburetor in their cars to see if there was any money there. God doesn't act that way. He won't use the same method to meet everyone's needs, but the principle is the same: God can supply all our needs according to His riches in glory through Christ.[176] Let Him do it in His way, but you do your part. Expect miracles, but be faithful and work hard.

Living By Faith
It is fashionable for missionaries and Christian workers of today to claim that they live by faith, but only very few qualify to use that phraseology. How do people generally do fundraising? They figure out the fundraising strategies—how many people are needed to pay the bills. Sometimes, they even suggest how much is expected from each person (indirect levy.) Even though God may permit the events to work in our favor because that is the level of our faith, it is still not appropriate to call it living by faith.

The modern fundraising approach is not qualified as living by faith because the object of faith here is not solely being dependent upon God—it is both God and people, and in most cases, the eyes are more on flesh and blood than on God. To live by faith is to depend wholly on God, without telling any man about those needs. When the needs are met that way, we know that only God can be responsible for it. Once we have disclosed the needs to anyone, we are not just trusting God, but we are sending an emotional appeal to men, as well. I am not saying this is a crime, but it is not really living by faith.

Those who had truly lived by faith in the past, such as George Muller, Smith Wigglesworth, John G. Lake, Maria Woodworth-Etter, and others, did not communicate their needs to people, but they expected God to use people to meet the needs and He did.

George F. Müller (1805-1898,) a German-born evangelist, built a huge orphanage in Bristol, England, and cared for 10,024 orphans, providing a home and an education for them. He established 117 schools and provided Christian education to 120,000 children, mostly orphans. He received over £180 million in today's worth, without ever mentioning his needs to anyone but God.[177] Müller never made requests for financial support, nor did he go into debt, even though the five homes cost him over £100,000 to build.[178] Muller received all the provisions through prayer, faith in the Word of God, and the Holy Spirit's guidance—without asking any individual. He proved that God is unchangeably the same, faithful, and able to meet the needs of those who can take God at His Word and trust Him completely. He also traveled and preached around the world.

Financial miracles can be a creative miracle, in rare cases
There was one case in the Bible where Jesus performed a financial miracle without anything. It was because no one in His team had money, and they needed to pay the temple tax. He told Peter to go and cast his net, and the first fish that came to him, he should open its mouth and take out a coin.[179] That was a creative financial miracle. It was a rare one, and it was never repeated, so it cannot be expected as the norm. This was the reason the apostles never expected it.

- The apostles also did not operate their faith to get free money in miraculous ways. They were not expecting a strange-looking fellow to bring money to them. Paul said he knew what it was to lack and how to abound. He had to work sometimes.

- Where did we get the envelope-burning miracle for debt-cancellation and anointing palms for the breakthrough we see in today's church? We must avoid any magical man-made formulas. They have no biblical precedence, so believers should be wary of them.

- We know God can do anything, even beyond the biblical records, but we must go by the word of God to judge anything. We must not encourage believers into laziness and wishful thinking.

- There is no promise in the Bible not to work or to expect a financial miracle as a means of living.

Financial Miracles Start with What You Have

God will normally work with what you have and what you do. Let us see how this works in the Bible:

- God created Adam from the clay He had already made.
- God asked Moses, *"What do you have in your hands?"* He said it was a rod—a shepherd's rod. With it, God delivered Israel from bondage in Egypt.
- Elisha asked the woman in 2 Kings 4 what she had in order for him to help her. She had to have at least a little oil for the miracle to start. Elisha said, *"Go around and ask all your neighbors for empty jars. Don't ask for just a few. Then go inside, shut the door behind you and your sons. Pour oil into all the jars, and as each is filled, put it to one side"* (2 Kings 4:3). The oil was multiplied!
- The widow of Zarephath had a little flour and oil. Her oil and flour multiplied.
- When Jesus multiplied the fish and bread, He asked for what the disciples had, and they brought the little boy's lunch, and He worked with that. Similarly, when He turned water into wine, He asked them to fill the jars with water first. He started with what they had.

This is what a financial miracle is all about. It starts with what you have. What do you have?

What do you have that God can work with? Your talent, resources, faith, time…? What do you have? The best financial miracle will come from your job, business, or investment. Financial miracles can operate when you critically lack and decide to partner with God and depend on Him. You can partner with God for finances by working hard and by trusting Him to supply your needs in any way He chooses.

What Lessons Can We Learn From All of These?

- Faith in God still works today as it did in Bible times, not just for healing but also for financial miracles. We must engage all the resources God has given us when we can, while using faith to go beyond them for results.

- Obedience and faith are keys to financial miracles.

- The ministry is God's work, so He knows how and where to bring money to do it. We must not rely only on the arm of flesh but become a hearer of His instruction and a doer in manifesting them.

- God expects us to take our provisions—our money, talent, abilities, time, and opportunities we have—and use it for the work of the Kingdom. Then He can partner with us and create a powerful synergy with our efforts and faith.

- When you invest into the Kingdom your resources, abilities, talents, time, and money, God is able to bring both earthly and eternal dividends to you in a greater measure than you can think or imagine.

- God will not work miracles when we can do the work alone. But He will leverage our efforts for tasks that are too huge for us, using financial miracles or other means.

- We need to know God's will about our situation, as what we receive is based on what we believe and how we act on God's Word.

- God can provide all that a minister needs to accomplish His work by Divine means if one is able to trust Him for our finances.[180] Our relationship with God, and our faith, coupled with prayer, is what matters here. When we partner with God, He supplies the resources for His business.

Chapter 9 Overview

Fundraising For Ministry

Ministry Issue
Is fundraising supported by the Scriptures?

Ministry Lesson
Fundraising is particularly important for expanded ministry, but not as the first option; this we will learn.

CHAPTER 9

FUNDRAISING FOR MINISTRY

Inviting Partners to Join Hands

"There isn't a single person in the world that can make a pencil. The wood may have come from Washington, the graphite from a mine in South America, and the eraser from a Malayan rubber plantation. Thousands of people cooperate to make a pencil."[181] Milton Friedman

Pastor Kennon Kallahan stated, "Effective church finances advance your mission. Effective practices in church finances will strengthen the health of your congregation. These practices will grow by your giving and the giving of your people. Congregations who practice effective church finances have a stronger mission, help more people, and raise more money. Their mission is increased. Congregations that do not practice effective church finances find that their mission is weaker, they help fewer people, and they raise less money. Their mission is diminished."[182]

Historically, missionaries received their support from denominational mission boards for all their needs. Today, the practice has changed: 70% of all missionaries are expected to raise their own financial support, and many have to wait for years to make that happen. So, how do we change this?

Dr. Edmund Haggai, the founder of the Haggai Institute, narrated a story of how the multi-millionaire and iconic giver to Christian centered missions, Paul Meyer, had learned his secret to life from his father's bicycle workshop:[183]

One incident particularly sticks in Paul's mind. He was in the garage one day, hammering on an old bike. His father intervened and said,

"Hold it; hold it! Take it apart the way the manufacturer put it together. There's an exact way it was assembled—Part A, Part B, Part C, and Part D. If it has twenty-six parts, you start with Z, and then Y, X, and go backward. You can take it apart, put it together, take it apart, and put it together." So Paul carefully dismantled the bicycle, laying the pieces out one at a time. When he'd finished, his father pointed at the last piece and said, "Do it again."

By the time he'd stripped and reassembled the bike twice, Paul Meyer knew a lot about bicycles. His father looked at the re-constructed bike and said, "Listen. You can do the same now with an automobile engine or an aircraft engine. You can do the same with your day. You'd better remember that all your life. Don't force things, don't force life, and don't force change. If you have a problem, remember, you've just taken a wrong turn in the road".

Jesus has a Blue Print for finance
Applying that concept to the Great Commission, particularly raising finances for missions, we can learn from the Manufacturer of Souls—the Giver of the Great Commission Himself. He has a definite way He has put the plan together and wants it done.

Jesus Himself presented this to us in His teachings and commands as we have already seen.

- You can earn and pay your own bills through earning a living and still have money to fund your ministry—as a *Bi-vocational Minister*. This gives greater self-esteem and facilitates frugality in handling finances. Accountability is focused on God rather than men. It is a method increasingly being despised by the missionary fundraising gurus of our time, but which had proved effective in the hands of the Holy Spirit through the ministry of Paul and through the ages. Reinhard Bonnke, in referring to evangelism, said, "I would rather use a method despised by man, but approved by God, than a method approved by man that gets no results."[184]

- You can live by anchoring your faith in God for your finances—*faith-for-finances*. However, we have been taught that this is supposed to be in times of need. Jesus did not multiply bread as the expected way to live or to do ministry. He did not get money from the fish every day as a source of money for the treasurer. The manna given in the wilderness did not last forever, and it stopped as soon as the people could work. So also, we must not starve and claim to live by faith unless God has instructed us not to work or raise finances. We should be sensible and use other approaches God has given in His Word.

- It is also legitimate for ministers to be supported by the local church, either by a salary or by providing and meeting all his needs. The worker deserves his wages, and the ox is not to be muzzled while it treads out the grain. This is the 'cultivators-shepherd-vine dressers' privilege as Christian workers that we have coined "*wagers approach*" in this book.[185]

- You can enlist motivated partners in the art of mobilizing or garnering financial support for the vision by using your Sword of the Spirit effectively—*fundraising* based on partnership. Although this is most common today, I believe it is more appropriate when a ministry has matured and requires the involvement of others to succeed. Here we have realized that the Master Himself never worked alone. He has designed the missionary and Christian worker to work in a partnership. The time of the Christian worker at this stage is more important than the income he could make from bi-vocational work. For example, when a new church plant has grown to a level where the minister's income could be fully afforded. At this stage, relational fundraising is critical to generate the needed finances as the ministry has expanded.

However, financial partners are not just 'donors,' but they're Kingdom investors, who want as much bang-for-the-buck as they can get. They also want an opportunity to participate in what the Lord is doing through your ministry.

A good investor will want to put their money where it bears fruit—where there are proven results. This is why many partner with individuals who have seen results in their ministry. People want to be part of what is working and making an impact. Whether it is ministry or development, fundraising has the same principle. Showing evidence of what has worked is better than hypothetical concepts of what can be done. This is the challenge for starters in ministry who want to send envelopes to get money and live by that alone. I suggest you start with Bi-vocational Ministry, grow your faith there, and produce some results. Then your anointing and the results of what God is doing will attract partners to you. Don't run to people to fund your ministry when all you have is a dream, and "Just trust me." When people see what God is doing, they will want to partner with you. That requires effective communication of the vision.

John C. Maxwell said, "Couple a vision with a leader willing to implement that dream, and a movement begins. People do not follow a dream in itself. They follow the leader who has that dream and ability to communicate it effectively."[186] To convince anyone as a visionary, people want to see how you have taken responsibility for the vision God has given you. There is no better way to do that than results from what you have achieved on your own with the help of the Holy Spirit. That is where starting with yourself and with what you have, become so important in recruiting partners to join hands with your vision. Why should anyone support your vision of a church plant when they have not seen evidence of conversion and how your ministry has transformed lives, even in a small but concrete way? If you want to be a shepherd (pastor), people want evidence that you really 'smell like the sheep.' They look for the fruits.

There's Provision—both for the Vision and in the Vision
God never expects us to live on a 24-hour miracle of provisions. That has its place in times of dire need when there is no other option, especially during times of financial wilderness. It was the reason manna was only available in the wilderness but stopped in Gilgal after people ate from the land. The people had been eating manna for 40 years—getting provisions in the vision until it was time to start getting their provisions for the bigger vision when they would enter the Promised Land. Manna provision was a means to an end, not an end in itself. In the Promised Land, they ate fruit from vineyards they did not plant and lived in houses they did not build, but there was a time they had to plan and built, and expand. That is how we should see ministry provisions also.

Your earning through investment and/or bi-vocational ministry can start the realization of the vision. It can provide the purse and the provisions you need to get going and realize the vision. But there's a point your savings, investment, and bi-vocational ministry earnings and resources will be insufficient to fully finance matured and expanded vision that can impact the Kingdom in the way God has revealed it to you or that your heart desires. That is where the vision must be turbocharged by the anointing of provision through others—financial Kingdom partners. There is provision in the vision itself because God is All-sufficient – Jehovah Jireh. The vision will be as a magnet that draws people to it. It was where Paul preached in Corinth when he stopped working.[187] He did not have to work in Ephesus because the vision had blossomed there.[188] That was the lesson Jesus was teaching the apostles on financing mission in Luke 9 and 10—provision in the vision, and Luke 22:35-36—provision for the vision. He expected them to start with the latter, and that was why He deferred that last instruction to the last day before His arrest. Where the provision was not sufficient, He had already demonstrated He was able to meet all their needs. They should know that in whichever way, there is provision *for* and *in* the vision. Peter and Jerusalem apostles generally follow the provision in the vision, and Paul and Barnabas and their team generally followed both options as the opportunity presented itself. We have discussed these at length.

Where is the Money to Fundraise?
Gordon Lindsay said, "Money is a necessary commodity in today's civilization…The day of self-sufficiency is a distant memory." Today, all products and services needed for an ordinary lifestyle must be purchased. Going through a single day without a cost or spending money for something is difficult, if not impossible. This dependence on money affects the way most people live their lives; it also has a major impact on the way churches and ministries carry out their work. Fundraising has therefore become a fact of life—a necessary part of an effective Christian organization, if it is to survive."[189] In many societies, every day has a cost, even the very water we drink. The only thing we do not pay for is the air we breathe, but people can pay a health cost if they live in a highly polluted, congested, or contaminated air space.

The total annual income of Christian churchgoers in the United States was estimated to between 5 to 10 trillion dollars![190] (this is only 55% of all Christians). According to the Richard Sterns estimate of how much is needed to help lift the poor of the world out of poverty, it would require a little over 1% of the income of American Christians' income.[191] With that wealth, the U.S. Christian Church's wealth is one-half of the wealth of all Christians in the world, and it is higher than the GDP of all countries of the Group of Seven (G7), except the United States.[192] However, most of the money is consumed internally. Reports show that the average American gives only 2% of his income to God's work, as "tithes and offerings", and the richer ones give less proportionately than poor Christians. Nonetheless, the United States of America is still the largest giver to world missions.

In general, in the United States, Christian workers have less difficulty in raising money from the network of other Christians who can give them money in exchange for tax-deductible benefits. (This means they can deduct the money they give to God's work from the income taxes they owe on their IRS Tax Returns). Therefore, fundraising is one of the most used approaches to fund a ministry. This should be used as much as possible to support the Great Commission. In other words, if 'Caesar' allows part of its share for God's work, there's no harm in it. However, this is not the situation in most of the other nations of the world.

The reality is that a European, Asian, African, or Arab Christian cannot rely on money from tax-deductible donations in the same way. Even in the United States, an alien, a non-American, and those who have no network of working-class friends or generations of Christian families, relatives, and friends, will find it challenging to raise funds on a regular basis. When this is possible, it may not be enough all the time.

As I have shared, missionaries have generally been advised to do fundraising for at least one full year before embarking on their intended mission field—that is, one year networking, developing, and presenting budgets to boards, individuals, sending out hundreds of letters to known and unknown people, and waiting for the 10% who might respond. They anxiously expect positive feedback from the 5% who will actually send in the checks or fill in the tax-deductible form. Imagine if that one year is spent on earning in a bi-vocational ministry; what a difference that would make.

How Did the Apostle Paul Finance His Vision?
The best model of fundraising from ministry work was exemplified by the Apostle Paul. This is what made him more successful in his ministry than any other Christian worker. He had declared the Gospel with signs and wonders—having preached the Gospel where it was not known previously, from Jerusalem to Illyricum,[193] including Syria, Galatia, Asia Minor, Macedonia, Achaia, and Europe—Greece, Spain,

and Rome. This effort spread all over Asia Minor, Europe, and to the rest of the world.

We should ask ourselves: what made Paul so effective and successful? I believe the reason is that he was not boxed in on the issue of starting with first raising finances for his personal ministry. Instead, he preferred fundraising to help other churches. He understood the heart of Jesus on raising finances for ministry. He was also very flexible in his approach; he used whatever approach the Holy Spirit led him to employ at any time. When he needed to work as a bi-vocational minister, he did. When he needed to live by faith and enjoy the hospitality of others or even ask his close co-ministers or trusted individuals, he did. When he needed to fundraise he also did, without apologies. He used holistic approaches, and that is the main emphasis of this book.

Paul had skills in raising finances for ministry. He was a missional fundraiser in a sense—raising money purely for the purpose of the mission. Notably, most of Paul's fundraising was to help the poor in Jerusalem; it was not for personal finances. The truth is that the idea of raising funds for personal finances was not popular in the New Testament Church. Let's look at this more closely.

1. Relational—Paul lived off the Gospel when necessary
First, Paul knew that every resource for God's business comes from God and that Jesus could meet our needs when we do not have the finances or are in circumstances where we cannot access funds. Just imagine how he started to preach the Gospel right away, as soon as he was converted.[194] He did not wait to worry about finances. He stayed with the disciples and began his ministry, even though he was not initially successful and had to escape to Jerusalem and back to Tarsus.[195] When Barnabas went to fetch him in Tarsus to return to Antioch, he did not hesitate for lack of finance. In such situations, he learned to be humble and depend on whatever others provided for him. He had no problem staying in the houses of other ministers—and he did that

in many places. He actually had a permanent or regular guest house with some of his minister friends where he could lodge any time he visited. We will later see how having valuable relationships with other believers is part of our most valued financial net worth.

Paul was a relational fundraiser. He had developed relationships with so many people wherever he went that he was able to tap into those resources—both financial and non-financial. To Philemon, he said, *"Prepare a guest room for me because I hope to be restored to you in answer to your prayers"* (Philippians 1:22). He also left his books in the house of Carpas.[196] It is not every friend you know who will be willing to give you financial support, host you in their homes, or be in a position to do so. There are those who will gladly host your stay, providing food and accommodation, transportation, and others may be willing to buy a ticket, pray for you, or just keep your company. Paul had tapped into all these sources, and also, he linked ministers in his team to his friends and recommended them for similar assistance.

He rallied support for his associates through his relational or social capital. He instructed Titus, "Do everything you can to help Zena, the lawyer, and Apollos on their way, and see that they have everything they need."[197] He actually trusted Philemon enough to ask him for personal support, *"I do wish, brother, that I may have some benefit from you in the Lord; refresh my heart in Christ. Confident of your obedience, I write to you, knowing that you will do even more than I ask."* (Philippians 1:20-21). Paul was in need, and one of his most trusted friends who could meet that need without a reproach was Philemon. It was a rare thing for him, but he trusted Philemon. He had left his books and his coat at the house of Carpus in Troas.[198] The Philippians often sent him some gifts, even when he was at other cities such as the Macedonia region.[199] He was very thankful—a gracious receiver when he needed to. He was also a giver himself. He told the Corinthians that he would rather give and spend himself than receive from them because they lacked in generosity. He did not want to be a burden to them.[200]

He did not apply his pastoral and apostolic privilege to demand financial support from them.[201]

2. Bi-vocational—Paul worked with his skills, talents, and abilities
Paul knew that the success of his ministry would depend on finances. But there were situations when such finances were not forthcoming, so he had to work to support his ministry, otherwise what was Paul doing in Tarsus? What was he doing in Arabia for three years?[202] We have no clue, but most likely, he was preparing himself for ministry—theologically, spiritually, and financially. He knew how to work and earn a living while doing God's work and preaching the Gospel. He demonstrated that flexibility as a creative avenue to support his ministry and his team in Corinth and Thessalonica.[203] He actually worked day and night alongside co-workers like Barnabas, Aquila, and Priscilla.

This suggests that the Pauline ministry was predominantly bi-vocational. That was why it was not strange to have a medical doctor (Luke), a lawyer (Zena), tent makers (Aquila and Priscilla), businessmen and women (Lydia), and other professionals and/or artisans on his team. He appointed elders, overseers, and deacons over churches who didn't need to leave their jobs. He himself worked with some of his co-workers in the ministry of tentmaking. Everyone probably had to use their talents and abilities when necessary, yet they also received support from the brethren. He also knew how to teach the believers about work ethics and financial stewardship—so that believers should live productive lives and work to earn for their living in order to provide for their daily necessities.[204]

3. Interchurch—Paul mobilized churches in constructive fundraising
Paul did not just rely on an *ad hoc* supply of funds from his friends, nor could he work to earn all the money he needed to do ministry work and help the poor. There were times when he had to appeal to the churches to give, especially to support another church—mainly the Jerusalem church. He implored the believers to be generous, cheerful,

and to give as they determined in their hearts.[205] For the Corinthian church, Paul had to write extensive letters, exhorting, encouraging, and motivating them to give proportionately, so the Macedonians who were generous givers would not be discouraged.

Paul's teaching in 2 Corinthians chapters 8 and 9 is the best classic teaching on the theology of financial stewardship. Yet this fundraising was occasional, and it should not be seen as a regular thing in Paul's ministry. It was directed at helping the poor and needy in the Jerusalem church. Thomas Jeavon, in Doug Carter's book, said, "When givers' hearts are fully attuned to God's heart and His priorities, giving becomes an exciting act of worship."[206]

Here, the Church in Jerusalem was undergoing famine, and Paul as a father to a child, wanted to help them. But knowing that the Corinthians were not generous givers, he had to explain all the basics for his personal fundraising appeal. They were to take the collection every Sunday.[207] He also insisted that an ethical standard be ensured in handling the funds.[208]

Paul succeeded because he first recognized that money is important in ministry, both for personal and ministry needs. He fully recognized that all money comes from God, regardless of whether it is given to us by others or is earned. He did not exploit his partners, churches, or new converts in regard to finances; he engaged and leveraged his gifts, talents, and abilities.[209] He knew that people could not give if there was no money in their pockets.

Chapter 10 Overview
Developing a Fundraising Campaign

Ministry Issue
What are key prerequisites of a successful fundraising campaign?

Ministry Lesson
We look at trust, partnership, stewardship, and unction in ministry. It begins with a compelling vision, its effective communication of how the vision has been tried and tested, and the stewardship in staying on track and without reproach.

CHAPTER 10

DEVELOPING A FUNDRAISING CAMPAIGN

Five Prerequisites to Developing a Successful Fundraising Campaign

Why are so many Christian workers that rely on fundraising unable to raise enough money? Why are many young missionaries and ministry workers unable to meet their needs? But what are the secrets of successful ministries that depend on fundraising? How did those ministers we discussed in the previous chapters meet their needs? The answer is simple: they have paid the price for the fundraising they receive. Unless we are ready to pay the price, fundraising is an uphill task, and I am not talking about fasting and prayer.

Today Christian workers want to join the Lord in soul harvesting without sowing. Some want to partake in His inheritance without sonship. Others want to join Him in receiving the prize without joining Him in His suffering. Many like to see the Lord as the ready room service meals from the chef at all times. But there is no eternal life without the Cross. Jesus said, *"Take up your cross and follow me."* Jesus came as a wounded healer, a peace-giver who suffered, and a life-giver who has tasted death for us. He came to us with the bread, fish, and wine in one hand and healing and health in the other. We tend to grab one of His hands, but we must choose neither of these above what matters most: His Cross. When we seek His Cross, we find true peace, prosperity, and eternal life. Using Paul as an example, let us reflect on some key fundraising principles.

Key Truths from Paul's Approach
   1. Explore personal resources first for personal ministry before asking for financial support from others. Paul did not ask others

for money until he had no other choice, especially when he was in confinement where he could not work or in places where his skills could not be deployed for income-generating work. The teaching that Christian workers should not use their own money, even if they have large saving accounts, is unbiblical. It negates Jesus' teaching on hoarding. All money belongs to God, including the savings. God's money should be spent for God's work when necessary.

It reminds me of a story of when the great servant of God, Dr. Uzo Obed, was praying along with his church leaders for finance on a project the church had just embarked on and needed money to complete. He himself had resigned from his career job as a university professor and was now a full-time General Pastor of a large congregation—of several thousand, with a membership of mostly university students and a large number of middle and high-income people in the city. Drs. U and Chy Obed (both former University Professors) had decided not to receive a monthly salary from the church or elsewhere, except voluntary gifts, until they retired from pastoring. They also did not receive tithes given to the church by members. They operated the true and rare *faith for finances* model—trusting only God for their finances. They never asked nor complained to anyone. When they were in need, they relied on God for the solution. They had amazing testimonies of God's faithfulness in all aspects of life and ministry, including finances. Such ministers who wholly depend on God and that trust God completely are rare in our generation.

That day, as they started the prayer, God spoke to him right there that he already had the money he was praying for in his bank account. It was a cumulative royalty of his book he had just received: a relatively large payment. So he stopped immediately and told his wife what the Lord had said, and they both agreed there was no need for further prayers. It was meant to be his personal reward for his labor on the book and a means of sustenance, but the Lord needed the money, and they gave joyfully. They totally released the money for God's use. Yet, they never lacked.

Christian workers in the marketplace should be able to use part of their own money to support bi-vocational ministry, depending on their income level. Why should missionaries or Christian workers stock hundreds of thousands of dollars in private savings and investment accounts, just because he or she wants to buy a home at retirement, and then keep asking people to give? It is the reason many people probably don't give generously because their money doesn't go for missions; instead, it goes for savings, investment, and life insurance, and personal needs of ministers. Missionaries can save and can invest, but there must be a point when we are willing to use our own money to meet personal needs and focus fundraising more for the ministry. There must also be a clear dividing line in how we manage and use both ministry and personal funds. It is a matter of ethics.

2. Personal fundraising should be targeted to close friends whom we can trust and as a last resort. Paul did not circulate 'appeal letters' to everyone he had ever met to ask for personal funds. He targeted his personal appeal to only a few close friends and longtime partners. Those friends knew his quality of life and ministry, his circumstances, limitations, plans, and vision. He wrote to them in confidence so that they would not fail. Several authors and fundraising leaders have identified that "giving should be a relational experience."[210] Personal fundraising cannot be done on Facebook and public social media as we increasingly see today. I am not talking of ministry needs, but personal finances should not be an open appeal, such as, "I want to spend a vacation in Disney World this summer, and I am believing God for $5,000. Let me know if God is speaking to someone." Or "I need school fees for my daughter in college. It is only $32,000. Can anyone help?" (Bank account given). I consider that approach an abuse of fundraising ethics.

3. Fundraising should be directed only to the vision. People are generally not attuned to funding a personal agenda or piecemeal activities of ministry. People want to see your vision and what God is telling you to do. Unless you can demonstrate that the vision is urgent and compelling, it has little appeal. The leader needs to create a compelling vision and rally support around the vision, not around his personality or personal needs. Doug M. Carter said, "If you can achieve your vision all alone, your dream is very likely not from God."[211] I would say the vision is either small or you have not explored its full extent. Remember that God also gives us talents according to our ability. There is a time when a vision becomes large enough so that no single person or group can accomplish it alone, without external help. That is the best time for extended fundraising.

4. Fundraising is more about trust than money. Can people trust you for the money you are asking them to give? How did you handle what you collected in the past? Do your lifestyle, ministry taste, and personal choices exhibit prodigality or frugality? For instance, why will anyone give you money to buy a personal helicopter or to buy a 2-million-dollar vacation home in the name of soul-winning? No matter how that appeal sounds, those who know your lifestyle will ask themselves why they are the right people to give such money. Doug Carter indicated that it must be about raising the level of every giver's relationship with God."[212] Pastor Callahan said, "Giving development is people development. Some share their generosity in steadfast, regular ways. Some give generously in short-term, highly intensive ways. Some are solid marathon runners in their giving. Some are excellent sprinters. God blesses the giving of all."[213] Some givers do not fancy fundraising that puts them under a long commitment. They prefer voluntary giving rather than doing it out of duty. Others prefer one-off moderate or large giving. Fundraisers need to know the preference of their givers and appreciate them.

5. *Fundraising is not a matter of do or die.* Fundraisers need to avoid fundraising harassment or exploitation.[214] There are ways fundraising is done that appear to harass the audience or target, whether group or individual. It is unethical to solicit funds from people you do not know unless your vision is big enough that anyone can buy into it. Can people find their calling in your vision? Because of the availability of mass media today, ministers appeal for money, even from unbelievers and those who have rejected God! Armed robbers, kidnappers, and terrorists donate money online to solicit prayers from some self-seeking ministers or ministries. This is because every message ends with one magic word, "DONATE." New converts are not spared frequent pleas for money. There should be a more dignified way of raising funds. Every message doesn't always have to end with pleas for money. Fundraising needs to be occasional rather than taking the central position in every event. The ministry of Jesus, the apostles, including Paul, had no such precedence. According to Doug M. Carter, the one making the appeal on God's behalf must first build relationships, cast the vision, teach biblical stewardship, ask for personal commitment, thank givers consistently, and report honestly and faithfully.[215] And I will add, must first be a giver. If you cannot give, how do you expect others to give to you? A good ministry leader does not just spend time asking people to give. She or he simply demonstrates how to do it.

6. *Fundraising should be seen as a partnership.* Fundraising should not be one-sided. You must ask yourself: what do my partners expect from me? What can I do for them? Partners want, first of all, to ensure that the fundraiser, i) is committed to God in consecration before they can give cheerfully; ii) is focused on the mission and not the nonessential stuff; iii) communicate the vision efficiently; iv) committed to investing in the relationship and learning to serve one another; v) has a heart to sincerely rejoice in the achievement, and iv) will celebrate, appreciate, and share credits with those who support your efforts. According to Doug Carter, it is only in committing to these five essentials that both the minister and their partners can begin to engage in a world-impacting ministry.[216]

7. Fundraising should not try to arm-twist the givers. New Age fundraising may have gone too far in many respects. We often hear of fundraisers specifying the exact amounts one should give by dividing their total needs by the number of people they expect to give. In some cases, letters are written to those we think have been giving the same amount regularly, asking them to consider increasing their giving to a certain amount each month. This has no biblical basis. It is also unethical in some cultures to make such demands on those who give to you willingly. Fundraisers often argue that we are only giving people an opportunity to be a part of what God is doing. We must remember that many Christian givers also have their own vision, calling, ministry, and other compelling Kingdom agendas that are important to them and that they want to support. Their giving should be voluntary rather than by compulsion.[217] We must avoid a situation when we are seen as being too pushy. Vision is what motivates constructive giving, not emotion or persuasion. The more compelling your vision is, the more generously people are willing to support it.

Prerequisites for Fundraising Campaign
A constructive fund-raising campaign involves five steps:

Vision—Articulating the vision, goal, strategic opportunities, and objectives; vision involves trust, so there must be no exaggeration. A vision is more than paper, showing photographs or building a castle in the air. It is a convincing strategy of what you aim to achieve in the long term.

Communication—Intimating to potential givers the action plan—compelling but honest communicating how the vision will be accomplished and/or how the money will be spent. The key here is concrete products—people want to see results. How will you impact people's lives and the Kingdom? How prepared are you, and are you equal to the task? Can people trust you with that task and their money? A showcase of what has worked is an important hook. Do you have a track record of success or an indication of potential, not just some emotional testimony of how life is hard for you in the mission field? Financial prudence and accountability are also essential, and partners expect a good financial report showcasing what has worked and what hasn't and how the minister has innovated or plans to address such emerging challenges in the near future.

Motivation—pouring coal on the scriptural basis, the felt need. This includes the rationale and the urgency. What will suffer if this goal is not realized at this time is the question every investor or financial partner would like to ask. This has to come with the necessary passion and with facts and figures, not emotions. This also is where previous or current results would be useful. It is more than simply saying, "God is telling me to do so. Just trust me." Experienced givers know that there have been many who claimed to have received visions from God but ended in the opposite direction. So don't assume everyone will buy into what you say out of emotion or claim you heard/saw in your dreams.

Recruitment—Inviting potential partners to support the vision is as important as making appeals for salvation after a message has been preached. If you stop at just the presentation, it becomes information, and no action will be taken. This is where the vision-caster invites others to participate in what the Lord is doing.

Follow-up to fundraising campaigns—Many participants do not make up their minds immediately, and some of those who had once been inspired may have waned in their enthusiasm about the vision if their expectation is not met. There has to be a forum or means of following up on their interests. For those who are interested, instant communication is important. For churches, this is normally done by the finance committee members and their representatives. For individuals, the task is more hectic, but it has to be done. This is why fundraising is better done as a team and at a mature stage of ministry rather than at the beginning.

Investor nurturing—Donors would be better referred to as investors or financial partners here because they are investing in a vision and the Kingdom. There is a return for them in Heaven. Unless we see givers as investors, we will not learn to use their money wisely. We have to nurture the relationship nicely, as appropriate, e.g., through personal contacts (meetings, phone calls, emails), website, Facebook, Twitter, text messaging, and other social media they use; meetings, video conferencing, worship services, personal notes or letters, sharing flyers, newsletters, CD, DVDs, books, booklets, personal gifts, and of course prayer support. Everyone likes to know that a prayerful person is willing to pray for him or her personally in times of need.

Paul's approach was clear: Operating as a bi-vocational minister when an opportunity avails itself; making limited personal fundraising, targeted to close friends; and limited public fundraising, targeted to a few churches to support other churches or the ministry of others. This is the biblically balanced approach to fundraising for the Great Commission that should be embraced.

We must teach believers to give and to be good stewards, but we must first teach them how to work hard and earn a good income, and even grow and multiply their money, so they can have plenty to share. When Christians have enough and plenty to give, the Church will not lack. If it does, it is because we have not taught a balanced Gospel on giving and receiving. We have mastered only the giving part and not the receiving: making the money. Many churches are shy to teach believers to invest their money for fear that their income or giving would shrink. This is selfish and myopic. Faithful christian investors are the best givers I know. When they make a huge profit, the first point of call is the Church. They are also not worried about not having enough for themselves or their future.

Fundraising Multiplier Requires Social Capital
There are those who are gifted with the skills and motivational ability to raise funds for a cause. What is often needed is a compelling vision and a feasible plan that Kingdom investors and financial partners can buy into and contribute to. One such gifted fundraiser was the Methodist layman and evangelist, Dr. John R. Mott, the CEO of Young Men's Christian Association (YMCA), who in this capacity, cast a vision of expanding the YMCA to many nations—to set up 49 YCMA centers in "China, Japan, Korea, India, the Philippines, Russia, parts of Latin America, and the Turkish empire..."[218] Dr. Mott estimated the required amount to be $1.08 million and requested $540,000 from John D. Rockefeller, who gave the money after a satisfactory independent assessment by his assistant, Dr. Burton (who later became the President of the University of Chicago).

In 1910, Dr. Mott took his appeal to a higher level: He went to William Howard Taff, who was the President of the United States, and asked if he could give an address at the "Worldwide Expansion of the YMCA. Jesus said, *"Ask, and it will be given to you; seek, and you will find; knock, and the door will be opened to you"* (Matthew 7:7). The President did not just agree to give a presentation but also hosted the whole event at the White

House.[219] The response was overwhelming. Mott received $2 million within months—much more than he needed. In a further expansion, he also garnered support and raised another $6 million. According to Dr. John Haggai, "Mott's gift of communicating this excitement in all its depths and richness motivated these people of great capacity to release the necessary funds."[220] Mott had, no doubt, combined three things—his powerful motivational and communicational gifts with compelling vision and relational social capital, to accomplish God's purpose. I also believe the Holy Spirit empowered him and gave favor.

In another instance, he went to the steel magnate and multi-millionaire Andrew Carnegie, who was once the richest man in the United States, and who was said to be in a bad mood when Mott arrived. Carnegie said, "Why are you giving your life to such a work? You are wasting your time. What is your plan?" By the time Mott outlined his plan and stimulating ideas and told Carnegie that he needed to contribute $10,000 to make it happen, Carnegie said, "I'll do it if Dodge does."[221] Both Dodge and Carnegie contributed to the vision promptly. He shared the outcome of his meeting with Carnegie with two other big shots: they were also motivated and gave $10,000 and $8,000 promptly, saying, "If Carnegie could buy into such a proposition, we would be happy to be part of it." Giving can be fun. It is also relational. People like to support what has worked, and each partner wants to know who else is contributing. But a compelling vision and feasible plan are important.

Whether the resource is being mobilized for a ministry, mission, development work or research, or charity, the same principles apply. The key is having appealing ideas, a plan, and a concrete product to market, a compelling way to communicate it, and having the right partners.

Unction for Fundraising
There is some fundraising today that leaves the hearers with guilt, doubts, and regrets they have ever heard such fundraisers speak

because it coaxed people and asserted biblical authority unduly. It makes people feel guilty and that if they don't give, God will punish them. However, there are genuine fundraising tactics that God would occasionally use to bless those who respond to it. The responses are usually unexpectedly overwhelming and instant. The fundraiser doesn't need to look at people's financial ability, but to God's, who is the giver. She or he will just state the need and watch the Holy Spirit stir peoples' hearts to respond.

One example of such a fundraiser was Freda Lindsay, the co-founder of the Christ For The Nations Institute (CFNI), whom God had used to take up the mantle from her late husband just three years after they started a Bible School in 1973. On one occasion, as she stepped up and announced the needs of the Student Center during an annual seminar, a missionary veteran, Wayne Myer, who had served in Mexico most of his life, and without a home or car of his own, came up and said, "The Lord has told Martha and me to pledge $100,000 over the next two years on the Center." Freda was almost sorry for him. But the Holy Spirit said to her, "Leave him to Me. Continue with the service." She obeyed, and $400,000 was raised.

Apostle Wayne Myer paid the pledge six months before the scheduled due date—in 18 months instead of 24 months.[222] The Student Center was completed on schedule. Having sat under Wayne Myer's teaching as a guest speaker at the Christ for the Nation, I can attest that he is a man who truly has committed his whole heart—body, soul, and spirit to the Great Commission. When God is in the fundraising, no matter how big the amount is, He sees to it that the budgets are met. All fundraisers must first check with God to be sure it is His will and, if possible, receive His word for what to do. Mott said, "A Christ-sent man, no empty board treasury can stop."[223] On the part of this veteran missionary—Wayne Myer, he understood that if God tells or leads you to make a pledge, He will see to it that you get the money. That is a veteran of faith for finances and a lifelong giver.

God Can Initiate the Fundraising

In the Bible, leaders rarely asked people to bring money or gifts for their own personal use. They received what they were voluntarily given. On the other hand, when needs arose for the work of the ministry, the trend was that over and above the normal offerings, the people were expected to provide. Moses received freewill offerings from the people for the construction of the Tent of Meeting. The people gave until they had to be told to stop bringing.[224] After David had given generously for the construction of the temple, the leaders and the people responded and gave generously, and the people rejoiced.[225] Likewise, it was recorded that the people and their leaders gave generously when Nehemiah, the governor of Judah, gave to the treasury.[226] Leaders who champion fundraising need a good track record of personal giving and integrity.

In all fundraising activities, we must recognize that God is the best fundraiser. Where relationships do not exist, He establishes them and connects the funder with the field that needs them. Pastor Henry Blackaby was pastoring a church in Canada that had just started its first mission outreach. They needed Jack Conner as the new mission pastor, knowing it was God's will to ask him. However, they had a problem with how to pay his salary and moving costs. Pastor Blackaby asked himself, "How in the world will God make this provision?"[227]

Meanwhile, Jack had started his move by faith to Canada. A letter arrived from a church in Lafayetteville, Arkansas, that said, "God has laid it on our hearts to send one percent of our mission giving to Saskatchewan missions. We are sending a check for you to use however you choose." That check contained Cd $1,100. Nobody had discussed this with them or known about this sending church.

Later, just as Pastor Blackaby finished with a phone call with someone else who pledged to pay Jack's salary, Pastor Jack pulled up into his driveway unannounced. When he asked him how much the moving had cost him, he said, "Well, Henry, as best I can tell, it cost me

$1,100" No one needs an angelic interpretation to know that God had arranged everything here.

Stewardship of Church Finances
Much has been said about individual investment, fundraising, and stewardship. In general, churches are good at raising money from members and partners through motivating and asserting biblical authority on giving, especially tithes and offering. However, the aspect of accountability is generally weak and non-existent in many cases. This has led to scandals that bring reproach to the Body of Christ. Areas that churches should pay special attention to include:

- Developing a God-honoring budget
- Spending church money wisely
- Financial management and transparency (including auditing)
- Church financing and taking out loans
- Can the local church engage in direct investments

A very good book on church budgeting is written by Kennon L. Callahan.[228] In conclusion, remember this statement from the Lord: *"Whoever can be trusted with little can also be trusted with much, and whoever is dishonest with very little will also be dishonest with much. So if you have not been trustworthy in handling worldly wealth, who will trust you with true riches? ... You cannot serve God and Money"* (Luke 16:10-13).

Jesus wants us to 'handle' wealth or money faithfully and use it, not to be its slave. Don't serve Mammon (money). Don't let it rule you. Make money your servant—let it serve you.

Avoid Excesses in Fundraising
Gordon Lindsay said, "But this revival can be greatly retarded if there is a continual auctioneering for money in the campaigns. There are some who are short-sighted enough to have destroyed their usefulness

to the Kingdom of God by an offensive handling of finances." Donald Gee also condemned the increasing commercialism of the Church in fundraising. "Good and faithful preaching of the full Gospel has been weakened by unscriptural appeals for money, to the stumbling of many."[229] Instead of treating fundraising as a partnership and as a relationship-building opportunity, they have used it as an opportunity for exploitation.

You Can Grow the Money for Ministry
No matter how good a fundraiser you are, there are times your budget will not be met. Paul said he knew what it meant to abound and to lack. Pastors also know that giving in churches fluctuates. Missionaries are not shielded from fluctuation in giving and support. Some of the fellows that have vouched support may pull out for various reasons. For instance, many churches are threatening to close due to financial decline attributable to the COVID-19 pandemic in 2020. How do we escape the devastating effects of this on the ministry? A sure way is to integrate personal investment as a part of our holistic ministry funding strategy.

The popular fundraising method employed in the Church today is asking believers to give joyously, but we have not explored other means of raising effective finances, nor did we teach believers how to generate the wealth they are supposed to share. Secondly, operating on 100% living by *faith for finances* may be sometimes stressful, as we have discussed, and ministers should not blame God during those times of seemingly unanswered prayers. God never promised an all-time free manna for ministry. Jesus has given us options for funding ministry at such times. Thirdly, bi-vocational ministry can generate finances for personal ministry, but there is a limit to what earnings from a regular income alone can support in ministry. The income sources need to be expanded and auto-piloted for effective and expanded vision. This is what we want to learn about in the next chapters.

As we can see in this and the next chapters, no single approach in funding a ministry is the best, nor can it provide a sufficient answer. We need to apply a holistic approach as Paul did, depending on the Holy Spirit's guidance, our financial circumstances, and the specific vision God has given us. We will examine three approaches to funding ministry: i) Faith-for-finances, which includes a paid salary from the church or ministries, ii) Bi-vocational ministry (tentmaking), and iii) the Partnership approach (constructive fundraising). A combination of these approaches are recommended in this book. Regardless of which approach is adopted, as long as it is God-honoring and the money is available for ministry, God is pleased.

Chapter 11 Overview
Earning to Finance Ministry

Ministry Issue
Was the bi-vocational model of ministry practiced
in the New Testament?

Ministry Lesson
Pauline-led ministries generally modeled bi-vocational ministry.

CHAPTER 11

EARNING TO FINANCE MINISTRY

Bi-vocational Model as God's Plan for Missions

"For you yourselves know how you ought to follow our example. We were not idle when we were with you... we worked night and day, ...so that we would not be a burden to any of you"
2 Thessalonians 3:7-8.

"Where there are no oxen, the manger is empty, but from the strength of an ox come abundant harvests"
Proverbs 14:4.

Bi-vocational ministry is an umbrella word coined for what is often called "Tentmaking,"—which in general refers to the dual modalities of working by any Christian worker who receives little or no pay for their ministry work and supports him or herself from a non-ministry related work while functioning as a minister or missionary. Or can also refer to a method of international Christian evangelism in which missionaries support themselves by working full-time in the marketplace with their skills, talents, and education, instead of receiving financial support from a church or fundraising event."[230] Some prefer to call it marketplace ministry or work as a business. It is usually this job that provides them their principal of source income or means of living, just as Paul did with tentmaking and Luke did with medicinal profession. Except for the 18 months of full-time ministry, I have been operating this way for the whole of my ministry experience in the last 23 years.

Unfortunately, the bi-vocational missionary model has been pushed to the sideline in the 21st Century mainline missionary work, even though it is a sound biblical model that is both effective and well-proven. As a result, the largest contingency of Kingdom warriors, successful church planters, unconventional missionaries, and potential Christian workers and soul-winners—those who are burning with the calling and passion for advancing into the kingdom of satan with the power of the Holy Spirit by using their own money—are shut out or discouraged by the dichotomous missionary structure that prioritized full-time over other forms of ministry. But the term full-time itself is subjective. It tends to assume that any worker not paid by a home church or missionary organization is less important than one whose salary is paid. But that is seeing things from human eyes, as we will soon realize.

A Shining Example of Bi-vocational Ministry
William Carey (1761-1834), who is known as the father of modern evangelical Christian missions—a Baptist minister, was a pioneer "tentmaker" in India.[231] He had a burning zeal and sense of responsibility for millions who had never heard about Jesus Christ. He was working as a factory owner and university professor while fulfilling his ministry as a missionary. In his over forty-one years of missionary work in India, he had translated the Scriptures, and his exemplary "tentmaking" work had inspired thousands of Christian missionaries to support themselves while ministering overseas.

Some of William Carey's missionary associates in India were Joshua Marshman and William Ward. Mr. William Ward's journal gave us a more detailed glimpse of their itineraries as a missionary team based in Serampore, India. I encourage you to read it online.[232] A more succinct glimpse is given as follows:

> "Up at 5:45, reading a chapter in the Hebrew Bible, "private addresses to God, "family prayers with the Bengali servants, reading Persian till tea, translating Scriptures in Hindustani from Sanskrit, teaching at the college from ten to two. Correcting proof sheets of Begali translating of Jeremiah, translating

Matthew into Sanskrit, spending over one hour with a pundit on Telinga, at seven collecting thoughts for a sermon, preaching at 7:30 to forty persons, translating Bengali till eleven, writing a letter home, reading a chapter from the Greek New Testament and commending himself to God as he lay down to sleep, is a sample of one day's work."—Galen B. Royer.[233]

We clearly see in the midst of this customized schedule and time management that these missionaries did not separate their ministry from outside work to earn their income. At one time, while in England, a neighbor complained to him for spending so much time preaching and neglecting his shoe business. Carey replied, "My real business is to preach the Gospel, and win lost souls. I cobble shoes to pay expenses." This is the heart of a true tentmaker—a bi-vocational missionary, the primary is the great commission, and the work pays the expenses. He devoted much of his income as a professor at Sanskrit and Bengali Forth William College, Calcutta to the work, and a small portion to the personal necessities.

In 1801, he became a Professor of Bengali at Fort William College in Calcutta. That same year he completed the New Testament in Bengali. His publishing business flourished. He was the first to bring the printing press to India. By the time he died at 73-years of age (1834), he had translated the Scriptures and printed them into 44 local languages, with over 200,000 copies.

By the time he died, there were over 30 missionaries throughout India, 40 native teachers, and 600 church members.[234] He had seen India open its doors to missionaries. He developed many dictionaries and produced the Hindu epic poem *Ramayana*. In all, he started 26 churches and 126 schools. The Trio also started medical missions, savings banks, a seminary, a girl's school, and a Bengali-language newspaper.[235] He had seen the edict passed, which prohibited *sati* (burning widows on the funeral pyres of their dead husbands). As a college professor, he had also founded a college at Serampore and organized the Agricultural and Horticultural Society of India. Dr. William Carey loved gardening and agriculture. All these he did as a bi-vocational missionary or tentmaker.

Earn All You Can
In his memorable sermon on "The Use of Money," the great preacher John Wesley offered a three-fold point of instruction on money and ministry, which applies to today's Church. It is summarized as follows: 1) Earn all you can, 2) Save all you can, and 3) Give all you can.[236]

Wesley said, "Gain all you can: It is the bounden duty of all who are engaged in worldly business to observe that the first and great rule of Christian wisdom with respect to money is, "Gain all you can." Gain all you can by honest industry. Use all possible diligence in your calling… Gain all you can, by common sense, by using in your business all the understanding God has given you."[237] He actually indicates how to gain the money by saying, "We ought to gain all we can, without buying too dear, without paying more than it is worth."[238] And you will find that in any modern best seller books on the subject of money, whether it is written by a Christian or non-Christian authors. Pick any book on wealth creation: if it is a well-written book, it will instruct on how to increase your financial flow by reducing your spending (frugality), paying your debts, earning income, and growing it by multiple streams of income until your income surpasses your financial needs. That was what the great John Wesley taught, and has been adopted by many, since the 18th century!

As long as your employment is not harmful to yourself or to others, or to God's creation or will, it is God-honoring and holy. Some try to argue away what Wesley meant on saving, as not referring to investing or saving large reserves. This reveals the sense of insecurity that keeps traditional church leaders from teaching on investment. The instruction "Save All You Can," and "Gain All You Can," by Wesley, I believe, includes frugality, saving extras and investing.

Lamenting the excessiveness of riches and how it has reduced the fervency of Christian revival, he said, "Religion must necessarily produce both industry and frugality, and these cannot but produce riches. But as riches increase, so will pride, and anger, and the love of the world in all its branches."[239] This is the same reason Paul has said the love of money is the root of all evils, but not money itself. The key is how to be humble and generous with money and use it for God's glory.

James Harnish pointed out that the acquisition of money will serve a biblical mandate on stewardship and generosity. According to him, "Ethical acquisition should lead to lavish generosity as a distinctive Gospel discipline."[240] In our day, Christian leaders teach and exhort folks in the Church mainly on the *giving* part but hide the *receiving* part through saving, earning and investment, from people. Saving is also a part of investing.

Wesley was teaching the complete Gospel of the need to earn money, invest money, and give money generously—all of which Paul also taught and practiced—he earned money, saved money, and gave money. In other words, what Wesley was teaching is this: save and earn all you can, invest wisely in order that you can have the ability to give—all you earn, generously.

Did the NT Ministers Have Any Prior Skills Before Starting Their Ministry?
In the Old Testament, Abraham, Isaac, and Jacob were wealthy shepherds, farmers, livestock breeders, and pilgrims; Moses was trained in the best education of Egypt, and later in how to be a good shepherd; David was a shepherd, musician, soldier, and king; Solomon was a pioneer investor; Joseph was a prime minister and Minister of agriculture and food security in Egypt; Queen Esther was a beauty regent and a prayer warrior in a heathen palace; Nehemiah was a cupbearer, and later, the governor of Jerusalem; Daniel was a

prime minister; Shadrach, Meshach, and Abednego were advisers to the king; Elisha was a commercial farmer; Amos was a tree breeder, etc. All had other professions that enabled them to function in their calling. They were Old Testament bi-vocational missionaries in a sense.

The Church has rarely asked the question about how the Early Church leaders started their ministries. When we hear of a minister working or doing business, we feel she/he has sinned or is secular. We send out missionaries and tell them not to pursue any profession or career because we consider them to be distractions to the ministry. This is faulty advice.

Let's look at the Early Church, starting with Jesus, Himself. We will discover that most of the ministers called to ministry had either worked or were working and had some skills by the time they started their ministries. Jesus did not call any clergy as His disciples, but He turned artisans like Peter, John and Philip, and professionals like Matthew and Levi into clergies. Many of Paul's associates like Barnabas, Luke, Aquila, and Priscilla and many others were Tentmakers in the New Testament. Those who were not had previously worked before they entered into the ministry.

Jesus was a Carpenter and self-taught theologian. Jesus was working with his earthly father, Joseph, and learned a trade as a practicing carpenter. Imagine that He had to buy His own wood, saw it, buy nails, and get His brothers to hold the ends of the wood for Him, then He made furniture and made money from the carpentry business. They were not built just for free. Jesus also learned theology at the same time through self-education and debating rabbi, as did all faithful Jewish men of the time.

Paul was a tentmaker/theologian. The only person many ministers think of in the New Testament Church was Paul because he was a tentmaker. He was a businessman. He would have to buy all the materials needed for making the tent, and build them, and make money from the tent business. He was also a rabbi.

Timothy had worked with Paul in his tentmaking business. We do not know if Timothy had any skill as a young man, but we are aware that he worked with his hands like Paul and was not a burden to the churches.[241] He was probably assisting Paul in his business.

Aquila and Priscilla were tentmakers—they operated a small-scale enterprise. Like Paul, this couple worked as tentmakers, and Paul actually worked with them for some time. They were fellow-workers with Paul.[242]

Barnabas was a 'tentmaker.' Barnabas was probably not a maker of tents, in the literal sense, but he had probably worked as a businessman. He may have engaged in a different trade than Paul. We know that he had worked using his skills.[243]

Luke was a physician. He was a medical doctor. He probably had practiced his profession as a medical missionary.[244]

Demas was likely a businessman. He actually deserted Paul later in preference for a business in Thessalonica.[245] Paul was upset with his disloyalty because of his love of the world—possibly an excessive craving for money. He had been useful to Paul in ministry in the past. Paul mentioned him, along with Luke, *"Our dear friend, Luke the doctor, and Demas send greetings"* (Colossians 4:14). He was an example of those that the apostles had warned about so as not to be greedy for money.

Peter, Andrew, John and James, Thomas, Philip, and Nathanael (also known as Bartholomew) were all fishermen. They learned and practiced fishing as a business. For John and James, it was a family business, along with their father. John, in particular, seemed to be skilled in writing. Anyone who has read the Book of Revelation knows that John was a seasoned scribe or stenographer, even though he was thought to be unschooled at the level of the Pharisees.[246]

Matthew (also known as Levi) was a professional tax collector. He was a professional, civil servant, earning his living from the tax office. He had some skills. That was why he could write one of the gospels.

Judas was an accountant. He betrayed the confidence reposed on him because of greed.[247]

Simon was a tanner. This was the minister Paul had stayed with in Joppa. He was described as Simon the tanner. Peter stayed in the house of Simon the tanner—he was making leather from animal skin.[248]

Lydia of Thyatira was a business tycoon. She was a merchant of purple cloth in the city of Philippi—normally patronized by kings and the rich in those days. Before she met Paul, she was already a worshipper of God.[249] She became important in Paul's ministry not only as his host, but also as a pillar in the church of Philippi.

Silas was a skilled writer or stenographer. At least he was a scribe for Peter, and he wrote one of the gospels.[250]

Zenas was a lawyer and missionary. Paul told Titus to do everything he could to support Zenas, the lawyer, and Apollos.[251]

Erastus was a city director. This was probably like the city mayor or administrator, and he was a co-worker with Paul.[252]

These were those who we at least have an indication of in the Scriptures who had some occupation or profession either prior to or as they did ministry work. The case I am making here is that Christian workers and missionaries are better off if they have a trade, skill, profession, or business that they can exploit as an alternative income source to support their ministry or as an entry to the mission fields.

The missionary model of the 21st century advocates for mainly full-time ministry, and in some churches, at least one to two years is spent in raising funds before any attempt can be made to go to the mission field. We did not see this approach in the Scriptures, where evangelists and missionaries had to first spend an equal amount of time in soliciting funds as the amount of time they actually spend doing the mission. If they had to work to save money, they did. I am not saying fundraising is not biblical, but our modern approach of shunning tentmaking altogether and looking down on this effective ministry approach is counterproductive and theologically flawed.

If we consider that doing ministry is enough of a sacrifice and that we deserve to be salaried in this way, then we must consider that working hard to earn a living to support the ministry as a tentmaker is a double-sacrifice to the Lord's cause and is God-honoring.

This doesn't mean everyone has to be a tentmaker, but there are those who will have no better way of doing ministry. If you are skilled, talented, and have the abilities for certain professions or have business skills, they can be deployed for ministry as bi-vocational ministers at home or as a missionary. There are many countries where a mission certificate does not guarantee an entry, but a surgeon, a pilot, an engineer, a nurse, a mechanic, an entrepreneur, a professor, a researcher, an expatriate, or diplomat will be joyfully ushered in. This is true of many of the countries in the 10/40 window, where most of the unreached people groups reside.

Let me be clear; there are those God has called to do ministry only as a bi-vocational ministry. I am a life testimony to this cohort of bi-vocational ministers, and every attempt to break out into full time has never received a nod from the Lord. I could tell of numerous own testimonies of how God has called, has been leading and working through both vocations in concrete terms, has been awesome, and deserves a separate volume someday. This includes being led to specific countries and jobs, with advanced notice of "the next place of assignment," and everything else must fall in place by His divine arrangement. We need to ask ourselves the following questions: How does God want me to operate—full-time or bi-vocational? How best can I reach those God is calling me to? Can I easily have regular home support for ministry? Is there another biblically sound approach to meeting personal expenses in the mission field? Do I have any talent, skill, or abilities that God can use to fully or partially meet both my family needs and ministry expenses?

Why are retirees, professionals, businessmen, and expatriates so few in the ministry and mission field? It is because we have let them think they are not suitable for the mission or ministry work because they are earning a living. They can only pay our bills, so we do missions for them. Listen, there are no longer Levites calling for this dispensation. We are all royal priests. We can both minister and work for our living when necessary. It is God-honoring if that is how He wants us to work, for that is the most effective way we can do ministry.

The Front-line and Supply-line Armies

The great missionary veteran, Dr. Oswald J. Smith, puts it this way:

> "But now for God's plan for the establishment of the local churches. How is it to be done? That is to say, how is it to be done without foreign funds? What is the scriptural method? Paul, you remember, evangelized, won converts, formed them into little churches and appointed elders. Herein lies the secret. He took two or three men and placed them as elders over the flock. Now, these men did not give up their daily occupations. But they became overseers of the church."[253]

That is, the church overseers, bishops (pastors), and elders had operated as bi-vocational leaders. Dr. Oswald J. Smith continued, "The fact is that we have built "up" instead of building "out." In organizing, we have gone from homes and halls to cathedrals… And so, today, we are over-burdened with property and top-heavy with machinery and organization. Whereas had we followed the Pauline method; we would have found the burden light. It solves the financial problem. Large gifts for educational and medical buildings are unnecessary."[254] That, in my opinion, is the greatest secret that can bring faster, global evangelization in the future.

Although Christian literature is so rich in the financial stewardship aspect of the Great Commission in terms of being *an inspired giver*, it is woefully weak in how to generate the finances that believers are expected to give—the Church is missing out on teaching Christians and workers how to become *an empowered earner*. The money for the mission can be earned, can be grown, and be deployed by the Christian worker without constraints through tentmaking.

Every genuine Christian is called to evangelize. We can do this either as a front-line missionary or as a supply-line soldier of the Cross. Let me explain what I mean. A missionary pursues the vision of the Great Commission, seeing the nations as the mission field by actually doing the work of evangelizing and discipling the world as a *front-line* soldier. The missional Christian, on the other hand, champions the world evangelization as a *supply-line* soldier, sending out and supporting combatants and captains into the warzone or battlefield. In response to the question, "Who will go down?" William Carey was known for saying, "I will go, but remember to hold the line." Someone has to hold the line while the other goes down.

The bottom line is that Christians need money if they are to have enough for themselves and plenty left over to give to mission work. How can we achieve this?

First, is to sensitize and teach believers on their commitment to the Great Commission, for both the clergy and laity—since we are all combatants in the Lord's battle. How then will the Lord's troops be ready on the day of the battle if we have no provisions?[255] Nothing is worse than for the troops of Jesus to be beaten down for having insufficient supplies of ammunition and provisions and not to be ready on the day of the battle. It is said that His armies are willing on the day of the battle.

Second, is to teach the Church, or believers in general, how to be more entrepreneurial in their thinking and actions. By this, I mean we need to teach believers how to create wealth by using their talents, abilities, and gifts and capture opportunities that are available and unique to them. God has given each of us uniquely natural and acquired talents that could be used for ministry.

Earning To Support Mission
There is a strong and progressive movement promoting the concept of "Business As A Mission" as a plausible example of this bi-vocational model for this century.[256] A lot of constructive arguments were presented at the Lausanne Conference in Cape Town in 2010 on Business As A Mission.[257] Joao Mordomo beautifully presented its application to the Brazilian missionary movement.[258]

In a sense, this concept is also a bi-vocational missionary. However, the phraseology, 'Business As A Mission" may send the signal that "business" *per se* is the main thing, especially when we do not hear much about the ministry aspect. There are many that God will lead to use their businesses to enter a new missionary frontier or country. The only concern I have is that there is the tendency to overgeneralize the concept to include nearly everything that could be done to earn money, including jobs that leave no time or money for preaching the Gospel and those that negate essential Christian ethics. The "business" component should only exist for the purpose of ensuring that world evangelization is accomplished. That is why I want to stick to bi-vocational ministry so that the ministry aspect is not lost or marginalized by business.

There are many believers who have received the calling or an inner conviction to make a greater difference to the Great Commission than they can make working a full-time, secular job, but they do not know how to do it. Some even resign their jobs and go to seminary only to realize they cannot move forward because of finances. I have seen many ministers really suffer financially in ministry when they could have avoided it. Being a bi-vocational missionary provides an excellent balance and channel for engaging in God's work without financial limitations. This can be in terms of salaried jobs, self-employment, or investment routes. It is also not all about finance; opportunities and access to the mission field are also important.

Bi-vocational versus Full-time Ministry

In 2003, I was attending the Camp Meeting of Brother Kenneth Hagin in Tulsa, Oklahoma. During the two hours we had between sessions, I spent some time with two pastors; one of the pastors was based in the United Kingdom, and the other was based in the United States. I met both of them for the first time at the Camp Meeting. One of the pastors told me he had a daughter still at school. He complained about what he was facing in ministry and vowed that his children would never be pastors or married to pastors. Jokingly—but prophetically, I looked at him in the face and smiled, then said, "Pastor, note this down. Your son will be a pastor, and your daughter will be a great woman of God. She too will be married to a pastor." He was so upset; he warned me not to repeat that declaration. He said it was a *curse* to him. He said if I knew what he had experienced in ministry, I would not have said that to him. I thought it was a joke, but he was really serious and upset with me.

When I refused to retract my statement, despite his experiences, he said, "Please, pray that they will be ministers, like you. You have come to the United States, paid the tickets for your whole family for a vacation, and have also paid your way to attend this camp meeting. Knowing the number in your family, I have an idea of how much your tickets cost."[259]

For years, I cannot afford to buy tickets and go to my own country. I have been here for many years as a full-time pastor. If they must be pastors or be in ministry, they must also have their profession like you. They must not experience what I have experienced." Yet, with the short time I spent with him, I knew he was a seasoned, well-educated, and down-to-earth minister. It dawned on me he had experienced protracted financial challenges in ministry. We prayed together.

Theologically, bi-vocational ministry is biblical, but it is largely underutilized and ignored by the mainstream Church as a workable model because of many man-made theologies that have conspired to alienate the *lay and tent ministry,* and Holy Spirit-trained and ordained bi-vocational workers from ministry—those who work for a living while they fulfill the Great Commission. We think they are having their cake and eating it, too, or that they may not have enough time for ministry. But this is very wrong. Tentmakers probably sacrifice a lot more of their personal time, energy, and money for ministry than many full-time workers. They only need to be committed, focused, and be an efficient user of their time.

I know a bi-vocational missional pastor, who was leading a large car rental company in Lusaka, Zambia, about a decade ago. He starts his day from the church office in the morning with a prayer and sets the ministry work in order. He goes to work as the CEO of that company and returns to his office at the church in the evening. He puts in some hours of work in administrative and spiritual oversight meetings, teaching, or doing visitation and prayers. He was instrumental in overseeing several dozens of parishes of the Redeemed Christian Church of God, along with other ministers and co-workers, mostly bi-vocational. I had dinner at his house one day and had an excellent time of fellowship with his family. I was amazed at how effective he has been in his ministry in Zambia, despite the success of the business he manages as a tentmaker.

One of the major flaws in ministers of the Gospel today is their one-sided interpretation of the Gospel and how to apply it to the work of God. Many think it is not proper to do God's work and work to earn income. We then separate the work of God into spiritual and secular. That is dichotomous thinking. We are an integral being with a spirit and a soul that lives in a body. Our spiritual and secular lives cannot be separated; they must be integrated. That is why we can be working and be singing or meditating in our hearts at the same time. Personally, I have experienced many spiritual manifestations at workplace ministries as well as in church environments.

I know several great ministers who had started ministries as bi-vocational. The first, of course, was my mentor and pastor, Dr. Uzo Obed,[260] the pioneer General Pastor of the Glory Tabernacle Ministry. Both he and his wife were Professors and senior faculty members at the University of Ibadan. Dr. Uzo Obed lectured Physics, and Dr. Chy Obed lectured Agricultural Extension. They were both successful pastors for many years as bi-vocational ministers before they felt led into full-time ministry. Within a few years, the church they planted had become a mega-church of several thousand members. It is one of the most spiritually vibrant churches in that part of Africa, with extensive and intensive outreach discipleship work across the continent. Even after they moved into full-time ministry, both of them refused to take salaries from this church until after their retirements,[261] even though the church could afford and repeatedly offered to pay them. Yet, they never lack. They fully practiced faith-for-finances and never ask anyone for finances. Anytime they ask the church to give, it is because there a need in the church, not for their own needs.

All the elders, and hundreds of neighborhood pastors, and deacons, and other workers at this megachurch have full-time jobs in all walks of life, and many are at the top in their careers. Many of them have been assigned permanent offices at the church, where they return after work and spend most of their evenings and weekends ministering and providing leadership and administrative oversights. The choice of working bi-vocationally for them was not due to limited finance; on the contrary, the financial health of this church is robust. They choose to direct all the resources to God's work rather than salaries. This vision of the founding leaders, the Obeds, has become contagious, such that from the Glory Tabernacle Ministry, hundreds of ministers have been sent out by the Holy Spirit, pastoring, serving as missionaries, and ministry leaders around the world. Amazing testimonies of what the Lord is doing through this predominantly bi-vocational ministry around the world is countless.

Pastor Enoch A. Adeboye is renowned worldwide as the General Overseer of the Redeem Christian Church of God (RCCG). He started as a Senior Faculty and professor of Mathematics at the University of Lagos, Nigeria. Today, he is an institution in Christendom whose impact cannot be accurately estimated because he is too humble to talk about his unparalleled ministry success in this generation. He started ministry as the overseer of a growing ministry of about 300 parishes; the ministry was handed over to him by the Holy Spirit after the death of Pa Akindayomi—an uneducated but highly anointed servant of God, who founded the church. Pastor Adeboye later resigned from the University to full-time ministry, and today the RCCG has grown to a global phenomenon. It is one of the fastest-growing churches in the world. It has a permanent meeting arena of 2 x 1 kilometers square where more than two million people meet every month, at one seating, and with more than 20,000 parishes in 165 countries as of 2015, and 850 in the United Kingdom alone. The RCCG Church has tens of millions of members worldwide. This ministry probably has more bi-vocational ministers and missionaries than any other Pentecostal Church in the world, at least that I am aware of—one of the reasons for its exponential growth.

Bishop Dag Heward-Mills in Ghana, a great teacher of the Word of God, started his ministry as a bi-vocational pastor and as a practicing surgeon. As a medical student, Pastor Dag-Mills founded and pastored a church for many years until the demand from the ministry and his intense heart for his calling compelled him to relinquish his high-paying job as a medical doctor. Today, the Lighthouse Ministry International he founded, flourishes with more than 2,000 church branches in 98 countries and he works with many professionals—doctors, lawyers, bankers, engineers, architects, business tycoons, professors, and other professionals in all walks of life—bi-vocational and full-time, as his ministers around the world.

Bishop Heward-Mills has defined bi-vocational ministry in terms of dual vocations as follows, "A layperson or minister is someone who maintains his secular job, and yet, is active in the ministry of the Lord. A full-time minister is someone who has abandoned his secular job to concentrate fully on the ministry."[262] However, not all 'bi-vocational ministers' can be said to be lay. The Oxford dictionary defines the word *lay* as someone "not ordained into the clergy; a non-professional." With that definition, we know that a bi-vocational minister can be either lay or clergy, depending on whether they are trained, ordained, or not. Just as it is possible for a full-time minister not to be trained in a seminary or bible institute, but just learn in the field. It is only a matter of whether they work full-time or work for a living while they do God's work.

In Bishop Heward-Mill's words, "Lay (bi-vocational) ministry is the key to the church." He provided excellent insights into both bi-vocational and full-time ministries, especially with his vast experience in both.[263] He alluded to the fact that many full-time ministers are more inclined to maintain their 'lay' ministers as mere financial supporters but are not comfortable involving them in the ministry. They feel that makes them more special than those they consider are 'having their cake and eating it, too!'[264]

In many mainstream church denominations, clergy must have a theological certificate, be ordained, and be in full-time before she or he can be accepted. That is not only true for the orthodox or many evangelical denominations but also true of many Pentecostal and Charismatic churches, as well. I ministered in the Assemblies of God in both Brazil and Malawi for nearly fifteen years altogether. Full-time ministry is the predominant or norm in both countries.

For more than two decades as a bi-vocational minister, there was a burning zeal in me, as with Paul saying, *"Woe is me if I do not preach the gospel"* (1 Corinthians 9:16). It was a burning zeal that was more than just ministerial titles or positions. My desire was to have the opportunity to do God's work without any hindrance. I never considered benefits as a motivation in ministry; I just followed my heart and the Spirit's leading. I actually avoided receiving any form of financial compensation. In 2011, I resigned from my career job, proceeded to bible college and was ordained at CFNI in Dallas for about two years, not for the certificate or to be called Reverend (even though I was ordained as a minister by the Presbyters of the CFNI.), but to further sharpen my battle-ax for the Great Commission. I also wanted to be wholly devoted to the things of God at the time. With a family of seven to support while I was at CFNI, I paid my school fees and fully covered all my costs of living, school, and family expenses for the two-year period. It was a spiritually refreshing and fruitful period in my life.

In a sense, Paul and Barnabas were bi-vocational ministers. Paul was obviously an ordained minister, so he was not a *lay minister*—he was ordained by the Holy Spirit, Who had first called him and commanded both he and Barnabas to be set apart for Him for the work He had called them to do. He studied under Gamaliel as a Pharisee.[265] The ordination was ceremonially attested through the laying on of hands from the elders of the Antioch church.[266] He was already a traditional Judaist clergy, but by his calling and ordination and his personal studies, he was a Pentecostal clergyman, as well; but he also worked for a living, when necessary, as a bi-vocational missionary.[266] He also taught the believers to work.

According to Paul, he had to work to avoid being a burden and to be a model for the believers. He said, "*...For even when we were with you, we gave you this rule: "If a man will not work, he shall not eat"* (2 Thessalonians 3:6-10).

Ministry is not a matter of whether you work full-time or part-time as a layperson or clergy; it is about undertaking and obeying the Great Commission in the most effective way for your calling. It is possible to achieve the Great Commission as a bi-vocational minister and be just as effective working full-time—Paul outperformed many full-time ministers of his day. There are those God may instruct directly to go full-time, but unless He tells you in specific terms, there is no harm in working while you do ministry. It is scriptural to work full-time, as well as part-time in ministry. Paul's ministry was fully directed by the Holy Spirit just as it was for Peter, James, and John.[268]

Who Is A Missionary?

One day, my claim to being a bi-vocational missionary was challenged by an elderly man in Malawi, who was a believing headmaster of a Christian Academy—an international school that was mainly for children of missionaries. He himself had volunteered as a retiree to work as a "missionary" in his capacity as a headmaster. That was the only 'mission' work he was doing at the time that I knew about, and God bless his soul, he may have impacted the kids. Now I wanted to move my kids to this school because the International School where they were studying was being over secularized—with the influx of many atheist and occult teachers; the children were forbidden to talk about Jesus, to preach, or be religious.

To have your child admitted to the Christian Academy, one of the parents must be a missionary. As an expatriate—working with an International Organization, the school fees for my children were not an issue because it was mostly paid by my employer, regardless of the International School they attended and regardless of the cost. But for this Christian Academy, having the money to pay or the academic standing of your child was not considered as important as being a missionary for your child to have a place at the school.

The headmaster said to me, "Sir, we only have space for children of missionaries. How can you prove that you are a missionary?" At the time, I was a Regional Director of an International Research Organization, and I was responsible for the Southern Africa region. (Twice, the Lord had let me know my next place of assignment, including my specific employer, several years, sometimes up a decade ahead). I then tried to explain how I was being called and being sent by the Holy Spirit from Brazil to Malawi as a bi-vocational missionary, with the Lord sending me off to the place of assignment saying, "Go and do the work I have sent you."

I laid my ministry work before this elderly man, including showing him two of my Christian books and telling him about the church plants, crusades, preaching in several dozens of churches and meetings, role in hosting and supporting other ministers, and other ministry works. He then asked whether I was earning a salary and support from a home-based church or missionary organization. I told him I wasn't. I told him; instead, I am the one that funds my ministry, supports other ministers, supports churches and people's needs as the Lord enables me.

He looked at me in the eye and said, "In our definition of a missionary, you must be financially supported by a missionary organization or by your home-based church—you must be receiving a paid salary from your home country or missionary agency to qualify. Are you still a missionary with that definition?"

"Well, I believe I am a bi-vocational missionary. (Explained what I have already shared with you and continued) I don't receive financial support from my home church, but I do have their full blessing in my work. In addition, instead of receiving financial support, God has placed me in a position to be the one giving for His work here in Malawi." I showed him a photograph of a medium-sized church plant the Lord was using me to fully support in the villages. I shared with him an amazing story of how the Holy Spirit went ahead and commanded me to build it, following a mass conversion, during one of my travels as a professional. as a professional. This happened after I had a flat tyre and preached to two men in a predominantly muslim village; when I sent a few bibles to the converts over 50 adults accepted Christ, and the number grew quickly. The village chief offered a temporary meeting place, until a church was built.

He responded, "Sorry, it doesn't fit our definition of a missionary. It was not my decision, but a decision by our board. I can't do anything about that." He was not convinced I was *a missionary* because I was not receiving financial support from a home church as a 'missionary'.

That conversation had opened my curiosity to how man-made theology has replaced biblical truths. There were many missionaries in that school who were not preaching the Gospel or engaging in any other mission-related work apart from teaching children science, mathematics, economics, health, sports, history, etc. They simply received home support and were qualified as missionaries. Or did they evangelize in their free time? However, many other teachers are quite effective in the ministry as Christian workers, working as missionaries at the school. I mentored a young man at our home cell who later became a teacher at that school. From a young age, he was on fire for the Lord and loved His word. He went to bible college afterward and planted and is pastoring a thriving church. I preached at his church a number of times while I was in Malawi. Today he is an executive in his workplace, and he still pastors. These are the ones I call bi-vocational missionaries.

In Heaven, the measure of missionary work is soul-winning, no matter how we argue it. If all you do is play the guitar or teach at a school, work at the hospital, or military, without evangelizing to win souls for Christ, you are not a missionary. You are probably missional if that effort contributes to other people's missionary work, whether it's financially or spiritually.

The next year, I went back to the same school when I heard that another headmaster had replaced the elderly man in his retirement. This new headmaster had listened attentively to my story. He was amazed and had commended the good work the Lord was doing through me and offered an immediate admission for my daughter to the school. He said, "I am convinced you are a missionary. You are doing great work. Can we keep your book in our library?" Later, that school actually invited me to come and speak to their students on agriculture, which I gladly did.

No matter what title you carry, if you work for a living as a minister of the Gospel or as a Christian worker, you are a bi-vocational minister. If you have been sent out by the Holy Spirit, like Paul, outside of your city or nation to another, you qualify as a bi-vocational missionary. With that explanation, it is important to note: It is one of the most effective ways of financing the Great Commission work because a larger number of Kingdom armies can be easily deployed to the field without any financial hindrance.

It is sad that today's ecclesiastical institutions would have denied Jesus the opportunity of preaching if He were to apply to their closed system. They would have also denied Peter and John the right to preach at the synagogues because they weren't rabbis, even though they had followed Jesus for three years. They would not have allowed Paul because he had no financial support from his home church.

While this chapter is not a discourse on bi-vocational or full-time ministry, it is to point out the importance of supporting God's work with income-generating ventures during certain periods in ministry. In the next chapter, we will learn more about how to earn money from our vocation to support bi-vocational ministry calling—how to move from simply earning money to making a difference in the Kingdom.

Chapter 12 Overview
Making a Difference

Ministry Issue
Are there benefits for scaling up a bi-vocational model of ministry today?

Ministry Lesson
Bi-vocational ministry offers an opportunity for overcoming financial challenges to the Great Commission and help meet family needs. It enables a larger number of Christians and leaders to participate in the ministry.

CHAPTER 12

MAKING A DIFFERENCE

Beyond Business As Usual in Bi-vocational Ministry
"On the contrary, we worked night and day... We did this, not because we do not have the right to such help, but in order for us to make ourselves for you a model to follow" 2 Thessalonians 3:8-9.

"If you desire to quit what you've been doing and do something else, that's fine. If you have enough money to be able to quit, that's great." [269]

As discussed in the previous chapter, bi-vocational ministry is an effective vehicle of mission and evangelization of the world since the early church time until today. Funding mission through earning from our vocation was a major approach in the New Testament church. Tim Dary compiled the top 25 books on 'Business As Mission,' and there is strong consensus that business—a broad term that reflects the many ways of making money—all profit-making enterprises—could be the beacon of hope for missions in the 21st century.[270]

Bill Peel and Walt Larimore discussed how to take evangelism out of the religious box and weave it into your life at work because people are looking for spiritual answers and resources as never before, in every part of the world, "Our proposition is simple: For most Christians these days, the workplace—not the church or a foreign mission field—is the primary setting for effective Kingdom work. We believe this is both biblically and historically true. When the churches have allowed people to set their focus inside the four walls, it has tended to dwindle in size...The early church is a prime example. It grew from a handful of disciples in the 30 ADs to over half a million people by the end of the first century. This growth didn't occur as a result of proliferation of full-time missionaries; it happened because ordinary Christians took their faith to the workplace and lived it out in their ordinary everyday encounters."[271]

Dr. Tony Merida said, "One of the blessings of Protestant Reformation was a renewed emphasis on this concept—living out one's vocation to the glory of God. For the reformers, there was no separation between the secular world and the spiritual world."[272] Today, Christian workers are embracing the 'clergy-lay' paradigm rather than the priesthood of believers and the responsibility on the shoulder of every believer to participate in the Great Commission.

I don't write this book from any other avenue than experiences lived through the Word of God as a bi-vocational minister. Having lived in six countries on four continents and have visited nearly 40 countries as a professional, earning my living, but I was also doing effective ministry work at the same time and funding God's work. When I am unable to do effective ministry, I advance my ministry with the keyboards in my private times.

In May, 1997, I moved to Brazil to take up a position with the State University of Maranhão, São Luis, Brazil, as a Visiting Professor and Researcher. I did not understand a single word, nor how to say "good morning," in Portuguese when I arrived, but within six months, I had started to speak fluently. The Holy Spirit led me to preach my first pulpit message at a small church by the end of that year without an interpreter. Later, I became a member of a larger church, the Assemblies of God, at Joao de Deus. Immediately, I started to assist in teaching men during Sunday school and was soon asked to join the eldership of that church. Since then, doors of opportunity to preach began to open, starting from my base church and also in the neighboring churches. In less than three years, I had preached in more than ten churches in São Luis city, in addition to regular preaching and teaching at our local church.

By the end of 1999, the Holy Spirit told me I was going to work with an International Research Organization headquartered in Nairobi, Kenya, and would be based in Malawi. He then said, "Go and do the work the Lord has sent you to do." I checked the website of that International Organization regularly until my exact position was advertised, and I was invited for interviews in both Nairobi and Malawi. Against all odds, the Lord gave me that job initially as a ten-year contract from the start. I knew I was going to Malawi as a bi-vocational missionary and was certain that the Lord had prepared the work ahead. I worked as country director of that organization in Malawi and later became the regional director for the whole region of southern Africa.

Tentmaking As A Professional
I spent about 12 years in Malawi in that job and traveled widely around the world. I also served the Lord in work of the Kingdom—teaching intensively, evangelizing extensively, and engaging in village church planting and other activities, such as ministering to the sick and writing Christian books. On a normal weekend, especially Sundays, I sometimes had to minister about 3-4 times a day in three different locations. Starting with Sunday school in the morning (8-9 a.m.), preaching at the main service at our local church—around 12:00-1:00 pm,[273] as the speaker for the main service (I was allocated about 25-30% of all Sunday preaching in 2009-2011 by the senior pastor), or going out to another church within the city to preach on invitations; in the afternoon, I often taught at a church and drove to the University campus to preach or teach the word of God to Christian students fellowship in the evenings.

Many weekends were also completely engaged in crusades, conventions, and similar meetings organized by the churches from different cities, towns, and villages. Four church plants were planted in predominantly Muslim areas, where there were no churches—by the leading of the Holy Spirit; the building of those churches was also financially supported by the Lord (through my income), including building the parsonage and paying the salary of the overseeing pastor for about ten years.

On some occasions, I was led to organize a week-long evangelistic crusade in a large hall or to preach in others organized by some churches, or hold several rounds of week-long lunch-hour open-air preaching at the city center, where middle-class leave their offices to come and hear the gospel for 30 minutes everyday during the week. From 2010 to 2011, I ministered at about 35-40 events each year, and my schedule was filled several months in advance. In all of these, I saw myself as a bivocational tentmaker.

During this period, signs and wonders followed my ministry as the Holy Spirit confirmed the Gospel with several astounding healings, deliverances and amazing miracles including the miracle of mass conversions. I have documented some of these in two previous books.[274] (Although the book you are holding is my fourth published book, I have also completed several other manuscripts written mostly during my free time, especially during weekends and annual leave or annual vacation over the years.)

Some of the documented healing and miracle cases include kidney disorders, ulcers, tumors, malaria, prolapses, three cases of fibroid of the womb, two cases of blind eyes, convulsion, the yoke of barrenness broken, paralysis and bedridden for 18 months, demonic-caused sicknesses, and several demons cast out, including cases of people delivered from mental disorders. These occur in churches, homes, hospitals (including a mental hospital), and in my own home, and remotely through phone calls. Some of these healings and miracles involved relatives of some of my workplace colleagues (at their homes, churches, or remotely). There were many other miracles not remembered and much more in mass healing crusades and meetings that were not being documented or reported. To God be the glory. Did God just heal others and not my own family? Several times myself and members of my family has been healed of various sicknesses.

More importantly, I have seen thousands impacted—saved, edified, equipped, and lives transformed in my various teaching, preaching, and counseling. Could I have done much more if I were a full-time minister? Possibly, but I doubt it, especially knowing absolutely that this was how God wanted me to operate. In all these, I did not receive any financial support and avoided financial compensation and gifts from anyone or church for ministering God's words and grace. I also covered my own expenses and those that travelled with me.. The Lord was meeting my needs from my professional job. Did I lag behind in my work because of these things? Far from it. I actually excelled at work and was awarded annually with first prize as the top published scientist in the entire organization for many years.

In 2009, my employer decided to offer me a rare opportunity to undertake a six-month fully paid sabbatical in a Belgian University to compensate for my hardwork and to rest. I was allowed to determine whatever I wanted to do during the period. I returned with high-quality publications and a new financial grant for my work in Malawi by a new donor. I also wrote a Christian manuscript during this period during my private time. I remained the best-published scientist until I decided to resign in 2011 from that Organization by the leading of the Holy Spirit. I went to undertake further ministry training for two years at the Christ for the Nations Institute—a bible institute in Dallas, United States. The very day I graduated from that programme at CFNI the Lord opened a new door of my professional job, better than what I left.

From Making Money to Making a Difference
The abundance of life does not just consist of earning paychecks, and earning air mileage, and earning people's respect as being wealthy, but in discovering God's purpose for endowing us with resources, abilities, gifts, and talents. There is a reason we exist and have been endowed by God with things\ other than money. There is a reason we make money for more than just the money, and other than for ourselves.

Larry Julian's book, "God Is My CEO," provides tremendous insight into how we define success as Christians. He crystallizes the need to move from success to significance, based on an analogy of Bob Bufford.[275] According to Larry, Bob likens a business career to a football game: "In the first half of our life, we pursue success. We work hard, sacrifice, and expend energy to become financially successful. In the second half, we focus on significance, giving our experience, time, talent, and energy toward making a difference in people's lives and leaving a legacy."[276]

We need to know what is more important to us in life. We all struggle between balancing a paradigm that has demanded that we operate in two worlds: a deeply competitive corporate world and a personally, fulfilling spiritual world.[277] Many times, Christian workers are caught in a financial treadmill of the nine-to-five, Monday-to-Saturday, and the Sunday-Sunday service routine, so that we forget the very purpose for earning money. We have to be fully engaged in the greater purpose of Jesus, even though we make money. Some call money or fundraising a ministry in itself. No, fundraising in itself is not a ministry. Money is not an *end* in itself, but a *means* to do ministry. Struggling to find purpose and meaning to working, bi-vocational, and missionary life stops when we balance between earning and living a purpose that is greater than life itself—obeying Jesus by evangelizing the lost and discipling them.

In order to succeed in your calling as a Christian, you need to fully understand God's Word on money—how to make money and how to use it for His purpose and glory. We must integrate the two. This book is designed to help you make two important connections. Whatever we have belongs to Him anyway. First, we must understand that Jesus expects 'money and mission' to go hand-in-hand if we are to obey Acts 1:8 and Matthew 28:18-19. We will be more successful if we do not forget His command in Luke 22:35-36. Second, we must understand that anchoring our faith in 'financial miracles,' fundraising, and earning directly, are God's ways of financing the Great Commission, and He is not limited to any of these.

Table1. The clash of two world views on money or wealth

The World/Religious View	*Kingdom View*
Based on human methods and rules	God's unchanging principles
Success is measured in dollars or crowd size, a number of cathedral seats.	Success is measured in faithfulness
Money is the goal (end)	Money is the means to an end or a tool
Seek after 'things'—wealth dreams	Seek the Kingdom and its righteousness, and "these things" come after us [278]
Money is an enemy of the Gospel—hate money	Money is a partner with the Gospel—use money
Money is an object of worship—love money	Money is a dutiful servant—ride on money
How much to keep is the main focus—keep all you can	How much to give away to God's work is the main focus—get all you can and give all you can
Money talks, everyone keeps quiet—money is the king	Money is dumb and a slave; God talks, everything else listens
Accumulating until you die and leaving it behind	Transferring money to Heaven ahead [279] by financing God's work while you live
Use money to win the world	Use money to win souls and help the needy
The "Universe" is credited for bringing wealth anyhow	God is the Source of all holy wealth, not the Universe, and (God is not man)
Poverty is a curse	Poverty is ignorance and can be remedied
"Prosperity" is unbiblical, "Adversity is better."	"Prosperity" is God's idea, but its hoarding, greed, and extreme is satan's [280]
Enjoy your money while you are here on earth	Defer your reward to Heaven and enjoy eternity
Use money to gratify your soul and flesh	Use money to serve God and to do good
Richness is to accumulate until you don't know how much you have	Richness is to have enough and plenty to share; be generous [281]
Giving is by compulsion and duty	Giving is joyful—the grace of generosity
Wealth feeds your pride, selfishness, greed, and corruption	Divine wealth produces humility, generosity, goodness, and dependence on God [282]
Working for money to live, as running on a treadmill	Earning to free up time for serving God
Money is a measure of spirituality and faith	The love of money can corrupt spirituality—character, faith, and purity
Money is the root of all evil, and wealth is evil.	The love of money is the root of all evil, not money itself [283]
Godliness is for financial gain	Godliness with contentment is gain
Desiring to be rich ends in a trap, harm, and backsliding	The blessing of the Lord brings wealth, and He adds no trouble or sorrow to it [284]
Put your hope in wealth	Put your hope in God [285]

Financial Miracles in the Workplace

I have not narrated the following story to draw attention to myself but to let you know that tentmaking is not just about the secular-spiritual dichotomy, but it is all about God. He who is interested in how to sustain the tentmaker.

When I joined the International Research Organization, I was working with at the time. The major donor of my program, a funding agency on development work in a North American country, who had funded my Organization for ten years, wanted to stop funding. I was on the job at that time just less than a year. Miraculously, the decision changed in favor of granting another phase as the Minister of Foreign Affairs from that donor country suddenly visited my program in Malawi in the year 2000, and another five-year funding of 13 million dollars was granted immediately.

One other time I had submitted a proposal to another funding agency in a European country, DBZ (not its actual name). All 15 of the International Research Centers around the world competed for the grants. The chance of our center getting it was slim. Each organization could submit as many as three proposals. Within our center, three other proposals had even competed with mine. I had earnestly prayed-in that money for our organization and my project.

That morning, I was in Tabora in Tanzania, on an official mission. I asked the Lord in the spirit, "Lord, what about my DBZ proposal?"

The Holy Spirit responded, "The DBZ Board has met twice. The first time the decision was not conclusive. The second meeting has just been held, and your proposal has been approved. It was 30/70" (meaning 30% of all seven of the proposals that were granted were in my category of proposals). He further said, "They respect your proposal." The Lord also told me about the need to intercede that morning for healing of a colleagues' two sons by revelation and the

Lord healed them [the two sons were suddenly hospitalized but were discharged that same day.] and He answered.[286] I worshipped and thanked Him that morning and left my hotel for the country office.

The same day, in the afternoon, I had just returned from lunch with my host (the country director), then the telephone rang, "Festus, Congratulations! Your DBZ proposal has been approved. The grant letter has been sent to Nairobi. A copy will be sent to you by fax." My colleague who was with me during the call said, "That is telepathy!" This is because I had told him in the morning that the Lord told me the proposal would be granted. I said, "Friend, that is not telepathy. I have just told you this morning that God told me." He believed. Resources came in and saved our program from a further downsizing. God answers prayers at the workplace.

Then sometimes later, I was appointed as the Regional Director, late in 2006. My program had inherited a financial crisis, and my regional budget went down to 30% of its former level, which led to massive downsizing. It was my responsibility to bring the region back up to speed, including resource mobilization. I had traveled to Rome, Washington, and to other places to meet donors and had written a number of proposals, but the funds were just not coming in. I cried out to the Lord. Suddenly, the Lord intervened, and a new donor became interested in my work. I had to urgently submit a proposal of 1 million Euro per year for four years, and it was granted within a week. This was a result of prayers.

The real headache was that although we had done all the work plans with partners and were set for implementation, the projected inception couldn't start because the money didn't arrive, and there was no news from the donor. One day, I received an email from my supervisor suggesting the need to further downsize if the funding didn't arrive. I didn't want to downsize my already lean team. I was worried for my staff. That afternoon, after I received the communication, I picked up my car key and drove out some distance—I had no destination; I simply wanted to talk to the Lord. I started praying at my steering wheel and poured out my heart to the Lord. Then, I returned to the office. At exactly six o'clock the same day, a phone rang from the Deputy Director-General, informing me they had just received a fax from the donor, signed by the Foreign Affairs Minister of that European country. The money was released the same week. This is to show how the Lord is also interested in our vocation in what we would have thought were secular, just as He does for the spiritual matters. I have experienced several financial miracles at the workplace over the last two decades, and each is unique.

By 2011, at the peak of my career at this International Research Organization, I felt led to resign from one of the most prestigious and well-paying jobs in my professional field. It was where I had built a career and reputation for being the top published scientist of the Organization—for four straight years, and had received prizes, awards and bonuses on an annual basis until I left (including a $5,000 cash award in 2009), and I also had just received a renewed contract for three years (after my initial ten-year contract). But I was led to move to the Christ For The Nations in Dallas, Texas, to undertake some training in the Advanced School of Ministry. The Lord had already let me know about this several years earlier, so the decision to relinquish my job was quite simple.

If we will be sensitive, the Holy Spirit Himself is the One Who will send the tentmaker to the right mission field of His choice. Before I moved from Brazil to the international job I have just described, based in Malawi, the Lord had let me know I would work in that country and with that same employer nearly a year before the job was advertised. Ten years before I got my current job, the Holy Spirit had revealed the country and my future employer and said, "That is your next place of assignment from here." That is, while still in Malawi and ten years ahead, I knew who my next employer would be and in which country

I would be based. It came to pass. CFNI was an interim plan of God for me, and I knew it before I resigned from my job at the International Research Organization where I was working and excelling. On the day I completed my training at CFNI, I got my current job—a dream job for top people in my career, which I would probably never have been able to get on my own had God not provided it. The Lord be praised. He also helped handle job-related challenges over the years, and when I look back, the testimonies are too many.

On the career front, I had a real breakthrough in my job, and I rose to the peak of my professional career in my previous job. My work became the flagship for the international research and development organization where I was working—having risen from the bottom, and I had received yearly outstanding scientist awards, along with my team for five straight years (2007-2011). This is to say that my job was not affected in any way by my devotion to ministry. All I had to do was to master my time management and rely on the Lord to grant me His grace and guidance as I commit my ways to Him.

Teach Believers to Work
Paul commanded that every believer in the Thessalonian church should work for a living, and there must be no idleness. Those who refuse to work were to be treated as unbelievers![287] He, himself, and his team demonstrated how to work and earn a decent living among them. He also taught Timothy and Titus the need to teach Christians to work and earn.

Paul's last words to the leaders of the Ephesian church were on work and money. He said, "*You yourselves know that these hands of mine have supplied my own needs and the needs of my companions. In everything I did, I showed you that by this kind of hard work, we must help the weak, remembering what the words of the Lord Jesus Himself said: "It is more blessed to give than to receive"* (Acts 20:32-35).

Today, we have reversed the Lord's saying to mean that we are more blessed if we receive than give and more blessed if we don't work or earn from a non-church source than if we do. Who is deceiving whom? Are we more righteous than Jesus, who said so, or more than Paul who put it into practice? Sometimes, some leaders try to explain away why Paul had to work. But he, himself, said he deliberately had to work in order to set this as a model for Christians. How much more for Christian workers?

Pauline Bi-vocational Ministry
According to Mark L. Russell, Paul was a missional entrepreneur who was on a mission for God.[288] In addition, Paul did not tell Timothy to excommunicate the rich Christians from the local church. Instead, he exhorted them to be generous and humble and to put their hope in God, who richly provided everything for us to enjoy and to share.[289]

We must not bully or look down on the wealthy in Church by our faulty attitude towards money. Rather, we must embrace the full counsel of God and exhort them to be generous and to be humble. We know people who have financial means and are yet humble and kind. One of the richest men in the world in our time was quoted for having said he doesn't really know whether God exists but that he has more important things to do on Sunday mornings. That is nothing but sheer pride and arrogance. It is also foolishness. John Flavel said, "To see a man humble under prosperity is one of the greatest rarities in the world."

If there is anything like a "Bank in Heaven" and you do nothing to put anything in that bank, and all you do is sit in the pew and praise the Lord on Sundays, then your account will be empty. The widow's mite story is often used to perpetuate passivity in God's work. Now, face it, if we teach that everyone should become poor and give a widow's mite, then we will have a church full of people with only a widow's mite to give. How then will the Great Commission be fulfilled? Everyone will still go to Heaven in that church, and they may even have a spiritual reward, but the Great Commission will still remain undone.

Work and Ministry

The Holy Spirit spent some time teaching the Church on the subject of work and ministry. If we believe the ministry of Paul was Spirit-led, then his bi-vocational ministry was also Spirit-led. Apart from Jesus, Paul was indisputably the greatest evangelist, a church planter, and teacher of the New Testament. He wrote a third of all the epistles in the New Testament.

As a tentmaker/bi-vocational minister, Paul did not just work at the Church of Corinth because they were not givers, but he also worked in Ephesus, in Thessalonica, and in Rome—evidently, he had worked in three cities, and probably also in most of the places he stayed for a long time, where the opportunity permitted.[290]

He must have worked in Arabia full-time too. He also taught the Church to do the same. One reason Paul was able to accomplish so much in soul-winning, church planting, and New Testament literature was due to his ability to support himself and his large teams through the tentmaking business.

Bishop Dag Heward-Mills, whom I have already introduced in a previous chapter, said: "One of the greatest keys to extensive church planting is the tent ministry—the tent ministry is the sacrifice of pastors and evangelists who labor without being paid for their services. The immensity of the work is such that, without the strategy of tent ministry, very few churches will be planted. Almost every ministry I know has ground to a halt because of mounting bills and the high cost of maintaining staff. It is virtually impossible for the Church to employ the people who are needed for the work of God."[291]

He lamented how, in some circles, everyone wants to be paid—the guitarist, organist, sound controller, and pastors constantly seek a higher salary for his or her services. This is especially so in the western nations. But if the command of Jesus for world evangelization must be realized, bi-vocational ministry is the key. Bi-vocational ministers often don't need or expect to be paid; they actually give more. I must mention that, in my opinion, one of the probable reasons church growth is shrinking in the northern hemisphere, and 4,000 churches are closing in the United States annually, is that the overheads are too high—yet pastors are underpaid, the finance structure is rigid, and the budget for missions has been cut to the bone or does not exist in many churches. Ministers want to be paid as competitively as those who are in the corporate world. If this is the case, then why work in ministry? If we still want to have everything and the same luxury as the other fellow, whom we think is not serving God, then why be in full-time ministry?

In appraising business done to the glory of God, Bill Peel pointed to seven key significances as follows:

Six Key Significance of Bivocational Ministry?
i) Morally significant, providing an opportunity to demonstrate personal character, thereby ethically enabling us to honor God.
ii) Economically significant—earning money allows us to invest in God's work, provide financial support to one's family, the church, and support missionaries;
iii) Relational significance—provides an opportunity to care about people;
iv) evangelistically significant—provides a platform for evangelism;
v) Social significance—open doors to address spiritual issues and do good in the community;
vi) Cultural significance—provides avenues for making the world a better place.

Seven Considerations for Bivocational Ministry.
Let us look at seven key advantages of Bivocational Ministry below:

1. *The best way to start a church plant is through Bi-vocational Ministry.*
In the United States and parts of Europe, it is easy to obtain mortgage loans on a church. This is non-existent in most of the other parts of the world, especially the developing nations. But Jesus wants to reach people in these places. Most of the world's population resides in these poor nations. A bi-vocational minister, who is able to take care of his/her personal financial needs, will be able to achieve greater success in difficult situations. They are also able to support the church. It takes time before a small church can pay salaries in poor nations. Even in developed nations, small churches struggle at the beginning. That is the time to work as a bi-vocational minister.

2. *Full-time ministry may pose unnecessary financial burdens on small churches.*
Being a full-term pastor, evangelist, or teacher, or any of the five-fold ministries without resources, may be a huge burden to small churches. Normally, there are many new converts who initially go to a church to 'enjoy' some comforts. They do not want to be bothered with too many financial requests. Any observed financial strain on members is a good excuse for them to leave the church and 'shop' for another. This is true of new believers, who still don't know the teaching of the Word of God on giving, but a church can lose them too early if all we do is sing the same old chorus of Malachi chapter ten and requesting money multiple times. Some of these will become wonderful and committed believers if we are patient with them and will be more sensitive in the fundraising methods in the Church.

When church finances are strained, building projects, equipment, expansion, and operational expenses, and more importantly, budget for missions or outreaches also suffer. The best way is to avoid being a burden to the small church. Family expenses could be huge if the minister has school-age children. In some countries, college students cannot obtain grants, loans, or scholarships for education; the parent is responsible for them. It may be too high for small churches. How will the new church be able to pay enough salary to guarantee good schools for your children when public schools are not adequate, and private schools are so expensive, as in many third world countries? Several times, Paul reminded people he was not a burden to them: Corinth, Ephesus, Thessalonica—he did not covet their money, or cloth, or eat their food for free![292] Rather, he said, *"We work hard with our own hands"* (1 Corinthians 4:12). Meanwhile, Paul was single. Imagine if he had also had a family?

3. Missionaries gain double advantage through Bi-vocational ministry.

In many nations, rules and regulations make it difficult to relocate to a new nation. Professionals overcome such problems legitimately by virtue of their employment. How can a missionary get a permanent residence in a nation where Christianity is persecuted or missionaries are not allowed? There are times and places where bivocational ministry is actually the only option for living in certain countries. In addition, the job supports the missionary. The reason the long-term missionary is becoming smaller is because of budget considerations. Missionaries can get over this problem by working as bi-vocational ministers. Few missionary agencies provide financial support, except for managing fund receipts and backup to the missionary. There are also nations where bank transfers are difficult or suspicious. Earning would be the most appropriate source of income in such places.

4. Support to the local church can come from bivocational ministry

The major income of the local church comes from the members who are mostly working in the secular world. Often, many bi-vocational ministers earn good income from their jobs or businesses, and because they are also committed leaders, they tend to contribute financially to the local church through their tithes, offerings, and other pledges. Bishop Dag Heward-Mills alluded to the fact that the top givers in his ministry were his bi-vocational (lay) pastors or tent ministers because they were involved in ministry, and they knew the needs and are committed to obeying God's words on tithing and giving.[293]

A larger portion of the pastors and leaders of the over 20,000 parishes of the Redeemed Christian Church of God (RCCG) are bi-vocational leaders.

When my childhood friend Dr. Olu and his family moved to Arnhem in the Netherlands, the RCCG parish there was looking for a pastor. For months, the leaders had been praying for God to send an appropriate pastor family to shepherd this church. Dr. Ajayi is an international policy scientist and global development expert. Dr. Olu and Mrs. Deola Ajayi and their family have worked and lived in at least seven countries around the world as bi-vocational ministers. They are mature and faithful Christian leaders, and they have impacted many as amazing vessels of God wherever they go. Immediately they arrived, the Holy Spirit confirmed to the leaders who felt led to put them in charge of this church as the pastors. Although Dr. Ajayi and his wife Deola had been elders in several countries where they had lived over the years, they had been prepared for this assignment all their lives, yet it was their first assignment as pastors. The couple prayed and accepted the challenge. The Lord honored their faithfulness and obedience. In 2017, I was privileged to preach at this wonderful church in Arnhem, together with my wife and children. What I consider more remarkable was the way the leaders of that church and members serve God sacrificially out of love. Leaders can model ministry for the lay and members and enable them to participate in the great commission.

5. Bi-vocational ministry makes a believer more productive and committed.

Working as a bi-vocational minister deserves a double honor because the ministry work is placed on top of a normal paid job—which many only do as full-time and still complain of being busy. They forsake their rights to earn from the 'altar' and work for their living by combining secular jobs with ministry, thus forsaking their free time and vacations in order to use it for ministry. This is the reason bi-vocational ministry is not for those who love much pleasure, sleep, and worldly comforts. This explains in part why many don't want to recommend or pursue it.

The tentmaker is one of the most effective "salesmen" for the Kingdom that can enter places most full-timers cannot imagine. Bi-vocational ministers meet and minister to people that you cannot find in church. Bill Peel and Walt Larimore illustrated this with the networking required in marketing, "Basic economic principles revolve around supply, and demand, and distribution. A business enterprise may have abundant capital, solid management, and a worthy product, but none of these will matter if the enterprise cannot address the challenge of distribution. No matter how strong the demand or how abundant the supply in the warehouse, if the enterprise cannot get the product into the hands of the consumer, its demise is inevitable."[294]

If the Gospel cannot get into places where the people are, keeping it within the church walls will be like a warehouse.

6. Some church leaders and members accept a bi-vocational minister more readily than a full-time minister because it costs them nothing.

If a missionary is interested in serving with a church, the first area of their reluctance is how to get the money to pay him or her. But if they realize the missionary is self-funding or bi-vocational, they open up because it has little or no financial implication to them. The church actually benefits from their giving.

One day I was having lunch with senior pastors of two churches in two cities that are located about 200 miles apart. I was moving from one of the two churches to the other church due to relocation by my employer's offices within that country. Both pastors were jokingly telling me about their reactions when they first heard I was about to relocate. We were all friends, so they knew it all depended on my employer's final decision. I only tried to give both of them a head-start should the move be confirmed. While the three of us were together, the originating church pastor said he was *binding*, so I would not move—praying that God should not let me leave his church at that time. (in other words, praying so my employer can change their mind to keep me in the city). The receiving pastor said he too was doing a prayer to "*loose*" the move—asking God to release me to his church (praying so my employer should proceed with their decision). One was *binding*, and the other was *loosing*, then God decided who won. We really had a laugh that day. The point is: a church will be happy to receive a bi-vocational minister who brings a ministry and does not bring a financial burden. The majority of bi-vocational ministers are also cheerful givers.

When a church knows they don't need to pay for expenses, such as relocation, transportation, children's education, and rental bills, they tend to invite you to minister to them more frequently. They are also aware that bi-vocational ministers will financially support their vision. It is a win-win opportunity for the Church and for the bi-vocational minister.

7. Bureaucracies are bypassed when a missionary or minister is self-funding.
As bi-vocational ministers, with your own funding, you will be able

to get things done faster. You will not need to wait for too many approvals when you are convinced that God has called you to do something. Many of the great revivalists God used had problems with their denominations' bureaucracy — trying to restrict them; for example, Evangelist Aza Alonzo Allen.[295] He was pastoring a church, but he felt called to the evangelistic ministry. But his denomination would not support that vision. He had to quit. No matter how spiritual you are, when you do not have enough money, you will have moments of anxiety, and you cannot plan clearly. Your mind will be engaged with how the money will come. If you must be proactive in making independent plans and execute your plans as God has given them to you, you will need to be financially independent, too.

When I felt led to build the first church in a village in Malawi and to support a pastor there, I did not seek to raise funds. God, too, was not expecting me to ask anyone else. When I organized a 7-day indoor crusade in a relatively large and expensive hall, and hosted and supported three other ministers to preach along, I did not solicit help—paid for the ads, the campaigns, the hall and the crusade equipment and instruments, paid singers, provision of entertainments and love gifts to ministers. If you have to raise funds or depend on others, it should be to complement what you already have. Unless financial freedom in ministry is your goal, and you make every effort to prioritize it and pursue it, you cannot attain it.

In some countries where a traditional missionary full-timer cannot be allowed or accepted, tentmakers with the needed skills are often being welcomed. Patrick Lai demonstrated this aspect as a church planter in the 10/40 window.[296] According to him, "tentmaking" provides many advantages, but the most important is giving the lost a good look, and often a first look, at who Jesus is. "Tentmaking" is using daily life strategies to tell people about Jesus. The model and methods vary, but the goal is to glorify Jesus among the unreached.[297]

In this, we have a unique opportunity to lift up the name of Jesus in the marketplaces—at industries and factories, shops and transport systems, courtrooms, laboratories, at the corner offices, at conferences and meetings, the citadel of learning, and among politicians, senators and parliamentarians, and top government officials.

Christianity is for people, and it must penetrate every facet of humanity, without exception. George Macleod said, "I simply argue that the Cross must be raised again at the center of the marketplace as well as the steeple of the church. I am recovering the claim that Christ was not crucified in a Cathedral, but between two thieves; on the town garbage..."[298] However, the level of tolerance depends on the nature of the employer organization. Even when marketplace ministry is not accepted, the bi-vocational minister can still minister outside the marketplace, such as in the church, home-cells, or elsewhere.

Where Do We Go From Here?
Advocating bi-vocational ministry is not to open Christian workers to the trap of pursuing money and wealth, which can easily entangle immature Christian workers and get them out of God's will.[299]

Rather, it is to help build some financial resilience to hardships and the discouragement the enemy uses as weapons to wear out committed or motivated Christian workers, who are trying to obey their calling and the Great Commission, without using money as an excuse.

In bi-vocational ministry, it is easy to become distracted from the preaching of the Gospel as the only hope for sinners and from the core of our calling—as ambassadors of Christ. We can drift to a place where everything is measured by our own happiness rather than our mission. As money flows in and we get entangled into the excuse of 'busyness,' the sense of our serving as a missionary or worker becomes secondary, if not offensive. This is a trap for bi-vocational ministers who are not fully committed to the Lord.

We must not be like the story of Alice wandering in Wonderland, who asks for directions from the Cat, with nothing in particular in mind. Todd Ahrend puts the conversations this way:³⁰⁰

"Would you tell me, please, which way I ought to go from here?" asked Alice.

"That depends a good deal on where you want to get to," said the Cat.

"I don't much care where…" said Alice.

"Then it doesn't matter which way you go," said the Cat.

Every potential bi-vocational minister needs to settle it in his/her mind that the overriding goal is to generate sufficient income to support themselves or their families, and have enough resources to use for the ministry, and even to share with others when necessary.

We must know where we are going. We must know the purpose of bi-vocational ministry. The Apostle Paul did not see the tentmaking as the money-maker or a job, but as *a means to an end*—not an end in itself. The end was the mission.

Read this carefully about Paul's tentmaking ministry: *"There, he met a Jew named Aquila, a native of Pontus, who had recently come from Italy with his wife, Priscilla. Paul went to see them, and because he was a tentmaker, as they were, he stayed and worked with them. Every Sabbath, he reasoned in the synagogue, trying to persuade Jews and Greeks. When Silas and Timothy came from Macedonia, Paul devoted himself exclusively to preaching, testifying to the Jews that Jesus was the Christ"* (Acts 18:2-5).

First, Paul began to work with his Jewish acquaintances, Aquila and Priscilla and earned some money along with them. Second, he did not neglect his ministry—his main focus, so he preached and taught every Sabbath in the synagogue. Third, when his companions, Silas and Timothy, came, "Paul devoted himself exclusively to preaching." He must have now saved enough money of his own, or his friends might have brought money with them from their own businesses. He knew when to stop working, so he could accomplish God's purpose.

The best bi-vocational job is the one that can enable a minister to devote himself exclusively to God's work whenever he or she wants. This is where private business is excellent for bi-vocational ministry. Paul's style was not as an employee but as a business owner.

Better still, business or investments can be auto-piloted at certain points in bi-vocational ministry without adversely affecting the financial flow—that is, when our investment becomes more important than our hard work. We will spend a part of this book on that aspect of creating finances for ministry.

Fourth, Paul eventually co-opted his hosts into ministry in Corinth and elsewhere. They might have been mature Christians before Paul joined them. It was not evident whether they had engaged in proactive bi-vocational ministry before Paul joined them in Corinth. Later, we realize that they became part of Paul's missionary traveling team and "fellow-workers in Christ."[301]

The point here is that Paul had deployed the bi-vocational ministry as a means to fulfill his mission. In addition to not wanting to be a burden, he had used it to build relationships, networks and to support his team financially. He also set a good ministry example for his followers and co-workers. This is how we must see bi-vocational ministry and all the knowledge about money creation that we will gain from this book.

Chapter 13 Overview
Marketing Your Skills and Talents

Ministry Lesson
Successful People Position Themselves as Entrepreneurs, and Apply Business Principles to Improve Their Earnings.

CHAPTER 13

MARKETING YOUR SKILLS AND TALENTS

When Your Business is Your Service

"Do you see a man who is skilled in his work? He will serve before kings; he will not serve before obscure men" Proverbs 22:29.

> *"When a person with experience meets a person with money, the person with experience will get the money, and the person with the money will get some experience."* [302] Anonymous

Business in the twenty-first century has become far too complex to describe. It has defied conventional rules, and new entrepreneurs must look at themselves through a new lens. The "information-technology" era has changed the entire business landscape, and all its characteristic paraphernalia—the speed, distance, cost, service, and marketplace ambiance have all changed. Instead of face-to-face and endless chains of command, it is now virtual business. It is nanoseconds instead of transactions that take hours, weeks, months, and even years. It is paperless, instead of files, certificates, receipts, handouts, and notepads. It is cyber-money instead of cash, checkbooks, and traveler's check, etc. It is online transactions rather than face-to-face transactions. Conferences, meetings, seminars, and webinars, are now popular on Zoom, Microsoft Teams, Skype, and others, with faster and interactive presentation features. Zoom, in particular, can accommodate hundreds and thousands of people on the same platform, connecting people around the world and cutting costs by as much as 90% compared with face-to-face conference meetings.

Business today is digital, multi-currency, instead of paper dollars, euros, and pounds sterling. It is decentralized networks of 'produce-on-demand,' rather than tons of goods in the warehouse and garage stores. For instance, ninety percent of books are largely sold as print on demand, eBooks, audiobooks; and distribution is vast and rapid through many outlets. Film-making is now increasingly relying on digital technology rather than reality. Business is more successful through partnerships, alliances, and coalitions to build synergies rather than competition and individualism. Corporations and businesses are rewarding servant-leadership and inclusive leadership rather than the all-important boss. To make the most income, it is about the quality of service and ideas rather than industry. And I'm afraid globalization and digitalization have also messed up real business etiquette.

On Wall Street, there are two categories of millionaires who make money, and the two are interdependent. They cannot make money without each other: First, are the investors or entrepreneurs who engage in the market to grow their wealth. Second, are the investment experts who help the rich manage, protect, keep, transform, and grow their wealth—they are partners.

The entertainment industry is not any different. In Hollywood, there are two types of millionaires. First, is the star who is gifted, talented, or has trained for thousands of hours to acquire the needed skills to make money. Second, is the promoter who identifies talents, creates, or adds value to the stars and gives them the exposure and platform to make money, and more money. In the sports industry, both the coach or manager and the star athlete are money makers, and they cannot do without each other.

Regardless of the industry, there are those who make money because they are talented, gifted, and skilled. There are the other groups who make money by making the talented become 'stars,' by imparting skills, professional advice, or providing them with a platform, exposure, needed resources or link them to the marketplace of success. Politics is not any different.

One often wonders what makes a football star or Hollywood star earn as much as or even more than a CEO of a company, or more than the President of the United States, the Secretary General of the United Nations, the World Bank President, or a senator or a university professor, a neurosurgeon, a pilot, an architect, or a U.S. Army general? It is because she or he has captured the opportunity to leverage his/her talents to benefit their many fans, sponsors, and investors. The rule is this: the more people your work affects or impacts, the more the potential income you are likely to make.

None of these have products to sell, but they simply market their skills, ideas, and talents in the 'innovation market' that consumers pay for with hard-earned money. The promoters, coaches, chief advisers, and mentors have simply mastered the art of creating a leader, a star, or celebrity out of an obscure but talented artist or athlete and market these to build wealth. They first find, develop, create, or add value; then they apply four marketing skills to capture the market and the profits:

i) Create market awareness,
ii) Interest the market, and trigger the decision to support, adopt, or buy,
iii) Maintain streams of pipeline buyers or financial partners through *branding*, and
iv) Invest in visibility and advertisements.

Unfortunately, most professionals and experts rarely knows how to position or rebrand themselves to earn more money in this way. Traditionally, professionals often think working harder is the only way to make money, and there is truth in that, but it is not an innovative way of thinking. Two out of ten employees have to wait until the end of the month to make some payments, and most retirees have no reserve in most countries of the world. It was once said that 9 out of 10 have to wait for a paycheck every month in Great Britain to pay their bills.[303] What would be the case in developing and poor countries?

The Bible encourages a good man to leave an inheritance for his children.[304] Working hard alone will not make you rich or create a surplus for the ministry; you need to find value, add value, or create value with your talents, skills, or abilities to attain financial freedom. The future generation will laugh at our educational curriculum that does not train people to succeed through entrepreneurial value addition and efficient marketing of the individual services, skills, and ideas we offer to the marketplace. However, things are beginning to change; at least in the United States, high school kids are beginning to be taught leadership, dollar sense, arts, digital photography and film making, business skills, computers, and more innovative ways of learning, even in the public schools. This is the future.

Tradable products and services

Tradable products are those that can be exchanged for money. They can be sold in a formal or informal marketplace. Only these are the products most people think qualify as businesses. You will be producing them, selling them, or buying them. That is conventional business. Conventional products refer to tradable commodities that could be seen, e.g., real estate, toys, cars, aircraft, food pens, CDs, lumber, iPads, cellphones, computers, books, etc. Most business ideas were developed around these items in the past, and that is the reason there is advancement in the product market, and stiff competition, too. Today, products could be a model, tools, methods, digital solutions, packages, even ideas, etc. But to attain a breakthrough in product business, you need innovation.

Tradable services comprise any kind of service that could be traded for money. All professional jobs, services, and consultancies are based on this—services offered in exchange for money. A CEO, an Engineer, an ICT specialist, a messenger, a dishwasher, taxi driver, professor, coach, police officer, lawyer, sportsman, etc., all sell their services in exchange for money. These are also referred to as the knowledge and innovation market. If you are a professor, your success depends on how many people you offered quality education to and the level of their success. If you are a lawyer, what is at stake for those you represent, and what is their realm of social, political, and economic influence? If you are CEO of a company of 200 people whose services are demanded only by a single town or tribe of 1000 people, you will earn less than a CEO whose influence is global or who serves a niche market of people whose service affects more people. That is the reason car brands such as Ferrari, Bugatti, Koenigsegg, Rolls-Royce, Lamborghini, Mercedes are all time-expensive. People who provide services to those companies also make more money than their peers in average car companies. Why is golf a highly paying sport? It is not the level of training required, its entertainment value or how many people watch it, but the wealth status of those who value it as their sport. It is a brand for the wealthy class in society.

The same principle applies. Money-making is all about how many people we affect in life. What made the one-of-a-kind Patek Phillippe wristwatch sell for $31 million at a charity auction market in Geneva in 2017?[305]

That wristwatch was not sold because of its quality and great features, but because of the charity angle—it helped boost charity for Duchenne muscular dystrophy held by Christie's. Again, it's about how it affects people's wellbeing. Do not build your income generation around yourself, but around how many lives will be touched. Think global but act local.

When Eric Yuan, CEO of Zoom, came out of WebEx after it was acquired by Cisco (a video conferencing company), he had a vision of the future digital video conferencing, but it was not attractive to his new employer for sponsorship. He left and founded Zoom in 2011, along with some 40 engineers. After two years, they built the product and put it on the market. The sudden nature of the Covid-19 pandemic catapulted Zoom to a global phenomenon, as it rapidly shifted from an obscure platform to become the face of the "work-from-home" or teleworking model. Users of Zoom jumped by 30-fold from an average of about 10 million daily meeting users or participants in December 2019 to 300 million daily participants in April 2020.[306]

Its stock reached $450 on 1st September 2020 compared to about $100 in March, $70 in January, and $65 when it went public in April 2019.[307] Its reliability, stability, flexibility, and user-friendliness attracted many investors. As of January 2020, the net profit of Zoom in July 2020 increased by over 3,000% compared to a year earlier.[308]

Besides the COVID-19 pandemic, the reason Zoom is seeing this phenomenal increase is because its product is easier, more user-friendly, and more robust than its peers, such as Hangout, WhatsApp, Facetime and Skype, etc.; it is available when people really need it most; like the others, it's free to access, except for companies. The result is an exponential increase in patronage, a situation its CEO never envisaged would develop. The fact that it was free did not jeopardize their chance of making money because that opened up the capital market space for them. Sometimes the quest to make money by setting too high a price jeopardizes growth of many companies.

Today, it is more about how many use your products than the price. However, Zoom was ready before its time came. How can we be ready before our time in the workplace, in politics, in businesses, and technology—more importantly, in the ministry?

A CEO is paid for her brainpower in decision-making that generates returns for the company. His or her pay depends on the number of people and the quality of influence. Similarly, a lawyer, a professor, a medical doctor, an engineer, a pilot, etc., are also paid for their knowledge, quality, and extent of influence. These are a result of experience, ideas, and training (education, self-development, or on-the-job skills), also the right timing and opportunities. The difference between someone earning $500,000 and another earning $50,000 per year may not be really great in their qualification, except for three things: first, self-worth or actual brainpower; second, extent and quality of influence; third is the right time and opportunity. If President Obama had contested five years before and five years after his first election, he would never have got to the White House, just as President Donald Trump could never have won if he had contested earlier than 2016. Although Senator Hillary Clinton was prepared and ready. She had all the qualities and what it takes to be a very successful president. From the outside, we knew the United States America was not yet ready for a woman president. Although the timing was right, but her opportunity did not come. President Joe Biden had contested for Presidency twice and lost, but when his time and opportunity synchronized, he won. This is where right timing and opportunity play an important role. There will come a time when a man would find it hard to win an election in the United States—Democrats or Republic no matter how well prepared. That will be the time for women, and it is very near. It is already happening in the corporate world. Women need to get ready at all levels. Do we take advantage of the time and opportunity we have? They are part of our talents, both in life and ministry. There is a time to work full-time, and there is a time to work bi-vocational. One size doesn't fit all.

One person may think she or he needs to work more hours to make money, and another may be smarter to know how to make money with just a few hours, but leveraging the efforts, experience, resources, talents and skills of others with his own in a win-win manner. This also benefits other people throughout the investment chain because it allows more money to exchange hands.

Financial self-worth—this calls for a proper understanding of one's financial self-worth when it comes to taking offers. If your employer doesn't value your qualification, experience and knowledge, do you know your own worth? Eric Yuan quitted Cisco because he knew his self-worth. For instance, an insurance company had advertised a job and listed it at $120,000 U.S. dollars per year; fewer than five people applied. A few days after the closing date for applications, the CEO decided to change the salary to $60,000 U.S. dollars per year and re-advertised without changing the requirements. This time more than 250 applications were received. When the interviewees were asked why they did not apply the first time, they all said they had thought the job was for a higher executive than themselves.[309] Sadly, they did not know their self-worth. Amanda Gorman, the 22-year-old poet, who stunned the listeners, and the world at large, at the Inauguration ceremony of President Biden and Kamala Harris on 20 January, knows her self-worth. According to her she is motivated by words. Words matter; she sees words as a way to revitalize the power of poems. Each time she performs, she says to herself the following mantra, "I am the daughter of black slave writers. We are descended from freedom fighters who broke their chains and changed the world." In other words, she did not deny the challenges she faces as a black person, but she sees great possibilities. Her self-assertion reminds me of President Obama's world-changing mantra, "Yes, we can!" Of Amanda, Hillary Clinton tweeted the same day, "Wasn't @TheAmandaGorman just stunning? She's promised too for president in 2036, and I, for one, can't wait." Know your self-worth and trust God to achieve your dreams.

Risk-bearing capacity—our ability to take risks differs, and some people are paid more because of their ability to take more risk with their life, business, money, health, time, reputation, etc. Such are people in the military, the police, or security-related jobs, pilots, airline hostesses, and flight attendants, medical doctors, astronauts, etc. The United States spends nearly one million dollars to keep a soldier in Afghanistan for one year.[310] That is due to the risk-bearing aspect of the job. Pilots and airline hostesses also earn higher wages because of the risks involved, in addition to the training and experience. The travel agent who sits at the office undertakes less risk than an airline hostess, for instance, or a pilot. The astronaut who makes it to the moon is recognized more because of the great risks involved. Business itself is about risk-bearing. In the business world, the greater the risk, the more the financial returns. If you want to make more money, you must be prepared to take more intelligent risks. The ministry is also not different. Many do not succeed because they do not want to take a leap of faith. They are too risk averse.

Knowledge is power. It is a well-known fact that most of the greatest achievers are not necessarily the most intelligent, smart or educated. Some did not even finish college. They have knowledge and skills that have made them stand out among their peers. Often they have invested in knowledge, in studies, and in reading books. According to Sandra Wu,[311] the Billionaire Warren Buffet is said to have spent 80% of his daytime reading, sometimes reading 600-1000 pages per day. Bill Gates was said to be reading about 50 books a year at certain times! In 2007, an 84-year-old Charlie Munger said, "I constantly see people in life who are not the smartest, sometimes not even the most intelligent, but they are learning machines. They go to bed every night a little wiser than they were when they got up, and, boy, does that help, particularly when you have a long run ahead of you."

Social capital—how do we bear fruit? Our relevance to God is the key. We are also profitable to society if we become relevant. Everyone works for relevance or significance. How profitable we are is determined by how relevant we are to God's purpose and the vision He has given us, how relevant we are to our nation or our employer, and to people. We are paid accordingly. If we want to increase our profit or money-earning potential, we have to increase our relevance.

John Rockefeller said he would pay for a man who is able to make and nurture relationships. Networking is about creating relationships, not gathering business cards—those who connect with people in conversation.[312] This is social capital that is rare in many. Usually, there are some folks who repel others at work, and also customers are repelled by their behaviour. The company loses because of their inadequate social capital; they become a liability rather than an asset to the company. Yet, they wonder why they did not get a raise, bonus, or recognition.

Such people are unable to keep a job for long, and they get the same or lower pay or job level each time they move because they did not develop their skillset to be ready for their next job. The reverse is the case for someone with robust and positive social capital. So if you have worked for a company for some time, they will know how relevant you are, regardless of your qualification. You can then market the social capital asset better to them or to other employers—their competitors will soon discover you. It involves excelling in what you do now rather than shopping for new jobs when you have not yet proved your worth

As a regional director with an International Research Organization where I worked for about 12 years, I was responsible to lead and manage and to get the vision of the organization realized. It was a job that involved hiring, mentoring new scientists, and building and nurturing partnerships with other organizations. There were employees that I was ready to give raises to—well above their peers— in order to keep them. There were others I waited to hear from when they would eventually tell me they were about to move on. In rare cases, there were one or two people I had to help out as they had become liabilities in their posts, in case they failed to make that decision before they could sabotage the Organization. Some were involved in frauds, thefts, other incompetence and displayed a bad attitude to their work—such as playing truant. Unfortunately, there were Christians among them—the most disappointing. It is about being an asset or a liability to your employer. Yet some of my most loyal employees were Christians.

Knowledge, Skills, and Service Markets
Only a few are aware of knowledge innovation being the great business revolution in the twenty-first century. The best knowledge marketers determine their own pay. They have met the 'ownership and control' criteria for wealth building.[313]

As long as someone else determines your worth and your pay, you cannot easily attain financial freedom. You can be a wage earner, salary earner, or fees-earning consultant, and yet, determine your pay and be in control of your energy, time, and value.

If you do not know how to increase your self-worth and cannot negotiate your earnings or income, your chances of becoming financially independent or getting rich are limited. Many, who are in this category, will always complain about their job—of their being underpaid, undervalued, and are dissatisfied with their employment; yet they cannot leave. They are chained to that job because they are not easily marketable elsewhere. They are at their employers' mercy. They are just like the men in the parable of Jesus who complained of having been given equal pay with those who came later.[314]

The CEO of Facebook and perhaps the world's youngest billionaire, Mark Elliot Zuckerberg, founded Facebook, along with his classmates (Dustin Mokosvitz, Eduardo Saverin, and Chris Hughes) while they were students at Harvard University. They broke into social networking based on internet entrepreneurship, and Mark became a billionaire. Mark's financial net worth was

$17.8 billion in early 2012, on an annual salary of $600,000,[315] and he was 18th on the Forbes List of billionaires in 2012.[316] Today, the 36-year-old is worth $86.5 billion and has become the fourth-richest person in the world on Forbes 2020 list of the World's Billionaires, published in early April. He was named four times in *Time Magazine* as the most influential person in the world, and in 2012 he was "The All-Time TIME 100."[317] This is not to encourage Christians to seek to become billionaires with excessive wealth and hoard money, while billions are suffering. However, it is not a sin to be a billionaire, if God is at the center of our wealth and we use it to glorify Him. That's not the point, but to show us some possibilities for those who would dare use what talent God has already given them. Let's face it, the brains of Christians are not different from non-Christians. With the help of the Holy Spirit we even have access to divine resources beyond our ability—not by might nor by power but by His Spirit.[318]

What did Mark Zuckerberg do? He earnestly invested his time into knowledge. He marketed his skills and talents—creating values in computer programming and becoming an internet entrepreneur. He also maintains a firm grip on *ownership* and *control*, essential for wealth creation. It was the same knowledge investment that catapulted Bill Gates to fame and wealth. The same magic has worked for Eric Yuan, CEO of Zoom, Jeff Bezos, the billionaire founder, president, and former CEO of Amazon, the largest e-commerce company in the world. That's the key to financial success in the knowledge economy. Recently, he attained his dream by a monumental launching of a rocket into the suborbital space on 20 July 2021—through the New Shepherd developed by his newly founded spaceflight company, Blue Origin. Knowledge is power.

We do not all have to be billionaires, but if you are a billionaire or millionaire and you are sure you have acquired the money in a God-honoring way and are willing to be generous and humble, there's nothing bad about being one. Imagine what a billion dollars can do in the mission field. However, we really do not need to aspire to be a billionaire to impact in the Kingdom. We must avoid the snares of wealth.[319]

Do you know that money was never a problem for King Solomon? It was his lust for women that ensnared him. God said to him, *"And I have also given you what you have not asked: both riches and honor so that there shall not be anyone like you among the kings all your days. So if you walk in My ways, to keep My statutes and My commandments, as your father David walked, then I will lengthen your days"* (1 Kings 3:13-14). If money was bad, God would not have made him rich in the first place. Otherwise, he would have blamed God for his moral sins. If Solomon had obeyed the command to keep God's statutes and not loved foreign women, he would have had a testimony of a righteous and wealthy king, like his father. God did not rebuke him for having money, but for having been lured away into idolatry by his so many pagan wives.

Our goal in this book remains to inspire Christians and Christian leaders in the art of creating finance for the ministry and to provide the knowledge needed for Christians and workers to have enough and plenty more to share—to use for the work of the Kingdom and to help the poor. What idea, knowledge, or ability can you harness to increase your income or earnings? Just think about it. If you think well enough, you will find one.

It is About Teamwork
It was not just the 'brain power' alone that did wonders for the Facebook co-founders; likewise, Zoom was not simply the brainpower of only Eric Yuan; there are also 40 engineers that leveraged his vision. It is about the power of synergy—interdependency among the co-founders that created massive wealth for them. It follows that you can strengthen or leverage your creative power and increase the results when the unique skills of others are pooled to work together in a mutually beneficial way. Teamwork is actually the game for twenty-first century success.

The ability to attract a powerful team, where each member brings in new skills, gifts, and abilities, is what sums up to be an explosive combination and is one of the greatest attributes of a good leader. In the investment or business world, key levers that could be harnessed by leveraging through other people include investment money, knowledge, ideas, temperament, passion, energy, principles, experience, systems, tools, talents, skills, networks, leadership, time, team, and a mentor/coach, which can result in astonishingly high performance. The success of great companies, and many of those on the Fortune 500 list of companies, hinges on this type of leveraging peoples' knowledge power to create wealth.

The next question to ask yourself is whether or not there is anything or anyone you could team up with to create a synergy. John C. Maxwell simply puts it like this, "One is too great a number to achieve greatness."[320]

He also said you become more valuable to a team if your values are the same as those of the team. While other levers may be different, the team members have to be on the same page on the main values of the business—share the same values to work together. Can two work together unless they agree?

John Maxwell articulated the compelling attributes of each of his team members, which summarizes the returns on his investment in his team this way:[321]

- My team makes me better than I am.
- My team multiplies my values to others.
- My team enables me to do what I want to do.
- My team gives me more time.
- My team represents me where I cannot go.
- My team provides community for our enjoyment.
- My team fulfills the desires of my heart.

He considers building a team as like developing a financial nest egg, "Investing in the team compounds overtime."[322] Whose knowledge, abilities, attitudes, finance, and partnership can you leverage to achieve success?

Gifts, Abilities, and Talents
There are differences between gifts, talents, and abilities: talents and abilities can be learned, but gifts are only given; they can't be learned. The integration of both gifts and talents can become our skills and abilities. Generally, God gives us talents and gifts according to His grace and our abilities—He gave them *"to each according to his ability"* (Matthew 25:15). He expects us to develop and use them. If you focus only on your gifts and neglect to develop them, you cannot reach your optimal success.

Spiritual gifts are special or divine abilities given to believers by God through the Holy Spirit as listed by Paul: *"Now about spiritual gifts, brothers, I do not want you to be ignorant...There are different kinds of gifts but the same Spirit. There are different kinds of service, but the same Lord...All these are the work of One and the same Spirit, and He gives them to each one, just as He determines."* (1 Corinthians 12:1-11). The Holy Spirit gave these *"for the common good"* (1 Corinthians 12:7). Those in ministry were told by Jesus not to go unless they had received power from on high and that the Sword of the Spirit—the Spirit's authority and power of the Word of God—is not negotiable.[323] Those are gifts. Yet, they were told to go with the Word of God (Gospel) and their finances (talents). The anointing is a gift. Gospel needs to be studied and understood. So the Gospel and finances are talents, and they go together.

Ministry gifts are five-fold ministerial gifts that are given to the Church by Jesus—God the Son, "But to each one of us grace has been given as Christ apportioned it. This is why it says: *'When He has ascended on high He led captives in His train and gave gifts to men'*"

(Ephesians 4:8-13). This is to build the Church for service until we have grown to the measure of the fullness of Christ.

Natural gifts (***Talents***)—special abilities are given to every person by God the Father, regardless of whether he or she is a believer. Talents are natural to us, but they are "gifts" from God the Father to everyone—believers and non-believers alike; and they can be at the level of unskilled, a semi-unskilled artisan, professional, or the leader—each person has something he or she can do better than most other people around. Natural ability is what makes some people better in science and mathematics, while others are better in social sciences and arts. Or some are very good in certain sports, while others are good in language learning or singing.

In terms of gifts and talents, Paul said, *"We have different gifts, according to the grace given us. If a man's gift is prophesying, let him use it in proportion to his faith. If it is serving, let him serve…; if it is leadership, let him do it diligently; if showing mercy, let him do it cheerfully"* (Romans 12:6-8). Here Paul has mixed the natural with spiritual gifts: Serving, encouraging, helping, generosity, leadership, mercy—these are natural talents that both believers and unbelievers can have. The gifts of prophecy and faith belong to us because only believers can have the gift of prophesy and faith in Jesus. They are the gifts of the Holy Spirit. But Paul was writing to believers, so it was in order.

Pastor Zacharias T. Fomum said, "God, the creator of Man, has given every member of the human race a talent or talents with which to function in His universe—every human being has a talent."[324] He listed 66 examples of talents.[325] Therefore, discovering and honing your God-given talents and learning to effectively use it to serve God, serve your society, and yourself can create wealth you have not yet realized. This is the reason "talented" individuals are sometimes in their own class and can set their own income.

Chapter 14 Overview

Repositioning Yourself to Earn More

Ministry Lesson
You have to reinvent and rebrand yourself to earn more and move up the earning pyramid.

CHAPTER 14

REPOSITIONING YOURSELF TO EARN MORE

Reinventing and Rebranding Your Services At The Market Place
"A wise man will hear, and will increase learning, and a man of understanding shall attain unto wise counsels" Proverbs 1:5.

"There is no substitute for work. It is the price for success." [326] Earl Blaik

The Pyramid of Capitalist System refers to an American cartoon caricature in 1911, which was a critique of capitalism.[327] It was based on a Russian flyer of 1901, focusing on social stratification into social class and economic inequality. The picture is of a social pyramid depicting the hierarchy of power and wealth: first, is the ruling class, political leaders, and royalty at the very top of the pyramid—*we rule you;* second, is the privileged clergies associated with the upper class—*we pray for you;* third, is the military elite class—*we protect you.* Fourth, is the bourgeoisie, representing the middle class and city dwellers in the society obsessed with materialism and consumerism—*we eat for you.* Their social, political, and economic views are based on concern for property values and respectability. They are in their position based on their level of education, income, and employment. Fifth, the masses at the bottom of the pyramid comprised of workers and peasants represent the large majority, doing all the hard work and supporting all the others but barely making ends meet—*we work for you all.*

The main message was that if the workers and peasants carrying the pyramid withdrew their support from the system, it would collapse and overthrow the existing social order because they are the main pillars. But it rarely happens. Each social class tends to hold tight to its own territory. Earning power also follows this social pyramid in any capitalistic society of today. In any society, there are different categories of citizens or residents, and these are associated with the levels of their quality of life, income level, respect, voice, and authority they command. The most important factor is related to what they offer in the marketplace.

Unfortunately, peoples' quality of life is also closely related to these factors; even in most of the cities of the world, people are still classed and locate their residence according to their wealth or income levels, especially in the major cities. The ruling or wealthy class tends to live in the best settlements, the middle-class lives in moderately good areas, and the workers and peasants with low-income live in high-density areas or even slums; they are often exposed to insecurity of all forms. Just mention where anyone lives in any city, and you have an idea of their wealth class without having to ask. There are still gaps everywhere, including developed nations that advocate democracy, equality, and inclusivity at international levels. That is the reason $1.5 dollars a day is considered the poverty line. Which person with decent living conditions can depend on 2 dollars a day? But that is where the majority of the people in the world spend their entire life. Sadly, the majority of Christians (especially in poor nations) form part of this category, and the church tends to encourage them to stay there and to accept that the stereotype that poverty is good and wealth is evil; yet we expect them to give generously to the church. In this chapter, we want to learn why it is important to get out of this poverty trap, whether as a minister, missionary, or a Christian working for a living.

Pyramid of Income Earnings
1. Unskilled worker
At the bottom of the pyramid is the unskilled worker and peasants who mainly depend on their sweat and long hours of hard labor to earn a living, yet they wait until the end of the month to pay their bills. They bear the brunt of dysfunctional governance and leadership, economic and market fluctuations, and failures. Unskilled workers are

the majority of workers all over the world. They apply great strength to earn their living. Although, if the amount of energy, sweat, and time spent on a job were to be tallied, they deserve the most decent income. If they stopped working, everyone else would suffer, but they dare not do so because it also means starvation for them.

Unfortunately, business life does not follow that rule, except in socialist societies. It is the opposite in capitalistic states. Instead, the unskilled do most of the dirty and tedious work but earn the least in a factory, company, or any set-up. Most live from paycheck to paycheck, and the majority live in debt and are unable to meet their basic livelihood needs. The majority of small-scale farmers also belong here. They sleep less, eat less nutritious food—save the best of their produce for sale to the wealthy, and have less time for pleasure.

The worst houses in town are inhabited by the unskilled. They live under the threat of crime, insecurity, natural hazards, diseases, and abuse. Most have no insurance or social security or access to social protection. The unskilled take the most risks in life in any work. It is even worse in rural communities. Life seems to be generally unfair to people in this class, and sadly, no one seems to really care. Society feels comfortable to keep them there as if they don't deserve more. The children of people here need more effort to escape the poverty trap. This is familiar ground to me.

To be in this group is not a crime. However, it is not a cause to be complacent about and put the blame on others or the state alone. I was once there. By God's grace, I deliberately spent a substantial part of my life from age 14 to 31 moving up and getting out of extreme poverty. Life is tough to those at the bottom of the social pyramid, yet anyone can move to the next level. Anyone in this group should determine not to remain there for long; she or he should never dream of their children remaining there. It is not a place to pitch your tent. It is a passage for those who have to pass through it. It is more fun when you tell your children how you have passed through it than seeing them follow that route. If you are in this class, spend all efforts to educate your children as best as possible, and train them in the way of the Lord.

2. Skilled and semi-skilled (artisans)
Skilled people are in two categories: skilled workers or semi-skilled (artisans). It is possible to attain financial freedom, even as a semi-skilled artisan. The artisan combines his skill with labor or strength, e.g., a carpenter, mechanic, bicycle or watch repairer, driver, tailor, shoemaker, painter, etc. These are skills that do not require specialized and prolonged college training. You do not need five years of college training to be a taxi driver, road-side mechanic, carpenter, copy typist, or telephone operator. Even if you have an advanced degree—that would mean underemployment. You only need some hands-on training. In some countries, only well-skilled people can engage in these jobs. It's either due to unemployment or underemployment or for reason of their residential status.

Whether skilled or semi-skilled artisans, it is possible to achieve financial freedom by doing what you know how to do best. A good example of this is the Wright Brothers; they were skilled artisans. They were not engineers, nor had they any university training. They applied their skills in bicycle repairing and later became professional pilots and aircraft builders through self-learning. They attained financial freedom with the skills they had. How did they achieve that? They took charge of two things: control and ownership of their inventions—although they nearly overprotected it, to create wealth.

3. Talented people
The naturally talented individual is one who outperforms others in a particular skill, with little or no training. They are skilled, but much of the skill is not due to training but to their innate or natural talents. Bill Gates, Mark Zuckerberg, Elon Musk or Eric Yuan trusted their gifting. In the world sense - they were each talented, and they recognized how to apply the talent.

God has given each person unique giftings/talents so that if we are able to identify them and develop them, we will realize there is something each person can do better than many other people, with less educational training or effort. They can easily bring out ingenuity with very little training and mentorship. The "utility delta" of whatever you do and how many people it affects determines success. In other words, the more people your work can touch and improve their lives, the more success you get.

Nicholas J. Vujici turned deficiency into a great talent and financial success. He has no legs and no hands, just the head and body up to his stomach. He was born with *tetra-amelia* syndrome but has become a celebrity and a well-sought international Christian evangelist and motivational speaker, encouraging young people. He has a Bachelor of Commerce degree from Griffith University and has a foundation. He has addressed over three million people in 24 countries![328]

He is an author. He has acted in Award-winning films. In the short film "The Butterfly Circus," he was selected as the Best Actor in 2010. He has a loving family. Isn't that amazing what one can do when you discover your gift and work it?

I have seen a single-legged woman who has no hands but finds the ability to use her mouth to perfect painting with exemplary fine artwork, which was displayed at CNN. It earns thousands of dollars for her. There was a man that was a cripple, but he developed his hands and became the best shoemaker in my home city. Eventually, this man employed many able-bodied people and trained them in his company, and he created wealth for himself.

All these are natural talents or handicaps that have been cleverly turned into wealth. When we see life through this positive lens, we will realize that there is virtually nothing that could not be used to our advantage.

Gifted preachers fall into this category. There are those who are gifted with the power of communication, relationship building, empathy, counseling ability, and teaching ability that no college or seminary could have offered. Some authors are also gifted, and they produce classical works that become best-sellers. Healing evangelists are gifted and anointed individuals, and many of them in history had limited education. In many cases, the power they use has nothing to do with their hard work, education, knowledge of the Bible, or their prayer life. It is the gift of God—the anointing of the Holy Spirit. All the nine-fold gifts of the Holy Spirit are talents from God. You cannot earn them through certificates.

President Barack Obama became prominent, not because he made any spectacular mark in the history of the United States before he was elected, nor has he surpassed many other lawyers or senators who were his peers, but his talent with 'oratorical brain-power' is phenomenal. Some will argue that his success was because Obama is black, but far from it; many good African-Americans have attempted to contest high offices before he did, without success. It is a talent, combined with extensive education and self-development, that has helped him hone his compelling, political, motivational speeches. That doesn't mean he would be a good preacher or counselor unless he is anointed by the Holy Spirit and committed himself to the Gospel. He may not even be a good professor in the classroom. In the ministry, we must identify where we excel, and in the vocation, we must also identify our talents, skills, and natural abilities that can be turned into a steady income source.

4. *Professional (experts)*
The next class of employees or income-earners are those known as professionals. Professionals are experts who earn their living through their intensive college educations—usually advanced learning, with substantial experience and quality of service delivery. The length of their training and experience is often related to their income, compared

to someone with similar qualifications. Many professionals trade their intellectual capital—innovation, strategies, models, copyrights, royalties, and ideas. The service they market is knowledge or ideas—they are knowledge providers or purveyors. They have mastery of the knowledge, and they commercialize it. These are the pillars that hold any worthy enterprise. It is not surprising that their income could also be astronomically high compared to the unskilled or semi-skilled worker. Astronauts, medical doctors, surgeons, lawyers, professors, architects, consultants, policymakers, lawmakers, pilots, engineers, astronomers, and scientists, etc., are in this category. Generally, professionals are also leaders in their fields of expertise. Nonetheless, they are not top in the pyramid.

5. Leadership (governance)

Leaders are those talented individuals who learn the skills of steering, coordinating, and using available talents and skills of others to achieve greater goals for the community or organization. Leaders are not necessarily managers or professionals, although they may be. Some do not even have advanced education, but they must have leadership qualities to succeed. John C. Maxwell says, "Everything rises and falls on leadership."[329]

They emphasize vision, values, and motivation. Leadership is the ability to enthuse and sustain others to follow. That explains why leaders are sought after. The leadership gap is so easy to detect, even by those who have no leadership skills or attributes.

Richard Barker, a professor at the University of Cambridge, made it clear when he said, "Management is not a profession at all and can never be one. The professional is an expert, whereas the manager is a jack-of-all-trades and a master of none. Good management, then, relies on the smart integration of knowledge, skills, and experience—a competence that cannot be taught and must be learned on the job."[330]

A manager doesn't need to know everything but must know the right professional who has the needed skills.

Leaders of an organization or nation do not need to be professionals, but they must be able to integrate knowledge, skills, and experience to make decisions. It is not surprising that leader managers often top the pyramid for income and benefits in any organization or setting. It is possible to achieve a breakthrough by becoming a leader in your field and organization. But this is not for everyone, except those who are determined to pay the price to make a difference, and integrity is key. However, leadership opportunities are plentiful and within reach of most people.[331]

The truth is there is hardly a recipe that works for everyone. I know a friend and schoolmate who started off as an insurance broker, and he became the CEO in less than 15 years. In addition, he owns five other companies, has several dozens of real estate properties, and is a multi-millionaire. He did not go to college before he joined the company but later had earned an MBA through correspondence and also an honorary doctorate. The leader does not always have to be an expert. What really counts for a leader is the ability to lead by integrating all the other skills, talents, and abilities of others and make them work in a seamless fashion to achieve the goal of the organization, enterprise, or nation.

Now there is a difference between a manager and a leader. Managers are generally professionals, but top leaders who constitute the overall management (governing) of an organization are not administrative-managers, but leader managers. Some organizations differentiate this by lower, middle, and top managers.

John C. Maxwell defines leadership as having to do with vision and motivating people, while management is the process of ensuring that the program and objectives of the organization are implemented. People want to be led, not managed. True leaders lead rather than manage their people.

A CEO is not a manager but a leader. A university registrar is a manager, but the Vice-Chancellor or President is not. He is a leader. Board members are not managers; they are oversight leaders. Managers manage and ensure that things are done right and procedures followed. But leaders do the right things, sometimes outside of conventional procedures. Leaders are known by what they do: they make decisions. This is why they are risk-takers. Managers do not take or like risks and must safeguard against risks in their work.

Many organizations have problems because they have managers as their leaders and vice versa. The manager who becomes a CEO will likely get bogged down with micro-management issues, while a natural leader who serves as a manager may become tired with the routine or day-to-day nitty-gritty and overlook important issues.

The leader is also an innovator, even if she doesn't do the nitty-gritty experimentation. Bill Gates revolutionized and transformed the computer industry from a machine once requiring specialized skills in programming to simple software that is not only affordable but available for low-income people with limited skills. Today, the computer has become a virtual necessity of life for digital data storage and sharing, music, communication, video, photography and metaverse products. In the process, he also earned billions of dollars in return for his leadership in the digital technology and innovation market. Many others have also innovated and developed other important products that have created wealth for them. No one has a monopoly on knowledge. Knowledge will never stop with one leader, company, or generation.

Increase Your Net Worth Per Hour
In this section, we want to look at a specific aspect of net worth—the human asset, in terms of how much you are worth per hour. What is the worth of your sweat while you are sleeping and undertaking other non-job-related activities? This depends on how much income you make. Every Christian must understand this well.

Each of us has 24-hours per day, yet we do not have the same worth in dollars. Why? We differ in what we bring to the market in terms of knowledge, abilities, skills, talents, social capital and personalities.

Assuming that you earn $60,000 per annum, and your income after tax, insurance, other deductions leaves you with about $38,225. The gross number of hours in a year is 8,760 hrs. If you work 40 hours per week, you only spend 1,920 hrs. i.e., 22% of your available time for normal work.

Of this, you have about 160 to 250 hours for work each week (depending on whether you work 8 or 10 hours per day). If you work 8 hours a day, your effective return on your labor is $19 per hour worked (1920 as the divisor of your net annual income). If all your available hours are to be accounted for because they also contribute to your income, then you are worth $6.64 for every hour wasted, worked, or used for other activities (8760 hrs. as the divisor of your net annual income).

Every hour of sleep, chatting, watching TV, bathing, dressing, eating, or spent playing videos, at the market, in the car, on picnics, or exercise, and everything you do, is costing you $6.64 an hour. Since time does not wait, you can well imagine that someone is dropping $6.64 to your account every hour or removing it, depending on whether you are investing that time or wasting it. You could spend or try to earn an extra $6.64 to your income for every hour you are able to create out of your schedule or double your time investment in other ways. This is key to your success.

Your net worth per hour will further show you whether that amount is increasing or not. We will discuss more on this later. Your strategy is to create productive time out of the remaining 16 hours that you are not working to earn additional income. You can create just one hour every day by sleeping a little later or getting up a little earlier, or by cutting out some of your leisure time.

The time spent watching television, going to the stadium to watch matches, theatre, cinema, or playing video games, dinner out, tourism, can give you what you need to achieve financial freedom if you reduce it by half or more. Now, devote that time to the investment route you have found more appropriate to your situation. You can invest 2-3 hours a week in studying, finding information, and actually investing or writing books. Ask yourself what you can do to increase your income per hour, and invest in that. Likewise, investing more time in your current job or business can also increase your earnings over a few years. Many people do not invest in knowledge and understanding of how they can be more effective and impactful in their current jobs. But your next job depends on your performance in the current one unless you are nearing a retirement.

Positioning Yourself to Earn More

Why do skilled people working in air-conditioned offices seem to be more financially successful than those who work under the hot sun? They have positioned themselves as entrepreneurs rather than mere participants as 'employees' in the labor market. They have moved from 'price-takers' to 'price-givers.' They determine their own pay through their significance. A salaried job is a business with a guaranteed income. Everyone loves guaranteed employment—whether you are a salaried executive or factory worker, the key motivation is *financial security*—when things get tough, you still get your paycheck at the end of the month. Whether you are working for wages, salaries, or fees, you can increase your earnings. Different ways of increasing your earnings are:

1. Develop new skills.

The rule of the game is to acquire uncommon skills that set you apart from average employees or competitors—you must excel in knowledge delivery. The key is to study, study, study, and keep studying. Acquiring more knowledge may entail undertaking more training, advancing your education in the same field or in other fields, and there is no substitute for self-learning. If you want to earn more on your job, you must command more in-depth knowledge in your chosen career. For more than a decade in my leadership position as Country Director of a global research organization, and later its Regional Director for Southern Africa, I have come to learn that there are some employees you cannot push aside—you cherish them, and they are nearly indispensable. But there are those who leaders or managers are ready to let go from the organization at the earliest opportunity. That usually happens after much encouragement, mentoring, or coaching, and investment in them does not seem to be working.

The difference in successful people is not because of their academic background, smartness, or eloquence, but they have mastered what they do and excel in it, delivering a quality service. Their employer is happy to overpay them. As their manager, you do not feel ashamed to put them up as outstanding for their performance evaluation and corporate *bonus* every year, again and again. Some of them can actually be smarter than their leader in their fields and areas of expertise. Your leader will have great respect for you if you can *complete* him by possessing or acquiring the skill he hasn't got. That's the key. On the other hand, there are those you are unable to rank above average, except for empathic reasons.

Developing new skills is not an easy thing. It is a hard process. This is why many do not pass through it. Important pre-requisites in the knowledge economy are talent, passion, zeal, persistence, and determination.

> *Talent*—Everyone is talented. Identify what you are good at and develop supremacy. Acquire knowledge and skills, if needed. You can increase your ability to earn by developing your talent beyond ordinary to extraordinary.
>
> *Passion*—Love what you do, and be ready to do it even without being paid. A lukewarm person cannot succeed beyond average performance. Passion is what makes anyone do more than what is expected of him or her.

Zeal—Value your goal and pursue it. Self-motivation is the key to great achievement. Be zealous. When you love what you do and cherish your goal, the fulfillment that accompanies it is like fuel.

Determination—Every worthy goal will face repeated failures, mistakes, and attacks from pessimists, opponents, critics or competitors. Determination is what carries you on when the going gets tougher. Be resolute in your determination to succeed. Don't compromise with setbacks.

Delayed gratification—Be willing to risk or sacrifice today's short-lived enjoyment or benefit for future rewards. With regard to teamwork, John Maxwell said; "If everyone doesn't pay the price to win, then everyone will pay the price by losing."[332]

2. Set a standard that is above the market standard

To increase your earnings through your professional, career, expertise, skills, or talents, you need to set a high standard for yourself. Carve out a niche for excellence, and be determined to break the conventional records of the number one in your field of endeavor. There is a saying that, *"If you cannot be a mountain, be a hill; if you cannot be the sea, be a river; if you cannot be the Sun or the Moon, be one of the stars, but be the best of whatever you are."* (Anonymous).

Be determined to be one of the best in your field. You can achieve this by creating synergies through teamwork; build a truly unique and compelling value of what you do. You need a common sense radar for knowledge and also command insider's knowledge about your field, your organization's business, mission, and value.

One way to stand out is to look for loopholes and weaknesses in the existing products that can be improved, such as services—strategies, ideas, models, and innovations that your organization or its competitor has been espousing, and improve it developing a better and more cost-efficient option, system, process, or product. If you are able to develop a hard-hitting and superior alternative that is different from your organization's competitor and save millions of dollars or attract a greater share of the market, you are sure to receive attention from the top. A value proposition that resonates well with clients, superiors, and peers are sure to make it. It needs to convey scholarship, distinction, and it should be defendable.

In 2006, a scientist from a competitor, an international research organization, had attempted to discredit the flagship research by our organization and had sent his publication to the attention of the Chair of the Board of Trustees. The Board Chair shared it in an Annual Science Meeting—where scientists had gathered from all regions of the world where we worked—to alert our center of the development. The criticism was a cold bath. The research had originated from my region and had positively impacted more than half a million smallholder farmers. At least 50 million dollars had gone into this work in our region for nearly two decades. It had become the flagship of the organization.

Fortunately, I had read this work before that meeting and had already started to work with the two top scientists on my team to review that article. Although the criticism had no sound basis, I quickly realized there's a need for more research to be able to respond constructively. At the meeting, I stood up and pointed out some flaws in the article. I assured the Science Forum of my intention to produce a superior evidence-based meta-analysis and policy-oriented publication that would bring the matter to rest. I had world-class scientists on my core team, each with unique skills and talents. My leadership role was to create synergies and make the team interdependent so that the whole was more than the sum of its parts.

We assembled 100 high-quality research publications across sub-Saharan Africa in the area and subjected the data to advanced meta-analysis. Our research was built on the empirical weaknesses of that alarmist publication by our competitor. We produced a high-impact publication with compelling empirical evidence that demonstrated superior results and confirmed our nearly two decades of extensive research for development work. We got that publication published in one of the most respected scientific journals in our field.

The Board Chair was so excited that he shared that publication with our competitor directly, and he also forwarded his communication to us, where he had humbly admitted that our approach was superior to his. We did not just get the attention of the CEO, but we also got that of the entire Board and the entire center. My team became rising stars. This work had attracted donor investors and interest from policymakers and development partners at high levels. In 2009, I was invited by the United States AID Administrator to give a presentation on that work at a UN General Assembly Side Event on Food Security in New York, along with three other global leaders in Research for Development. In 2012, part of the work was on the front cover page of the *American Society of Agronomy Journal*, as well, and more than five different media sources sought an interview with my team.

In addition, the team had been fired up and maintained first place in our center for five straight years (2007-2011), as the "Most Productive Team," "Top Published Region," and three of the scientists (I was in the first place) had been awarded annually as the "Top-Published Scientist" in our Organization for five straight years. Whereas, in 2005, none of my team members was among the top 10 or had even dreamt of getting closer, until a major turn-around began after I took over the regional leadership in January 2007. I had set my eyes on the first place and was determined to remain there until I left the Organization, and God granted it to be so. It goes without saying that my experience on that job had prepared me for the next (my current job). My colleagues, who were my top deputies, also consistently maintained the 2nd and 3rd positions each year. According to Al Ries and Jack Trout, "The law of opposites says: if you are shooting for the second place, your strategy is determined by the leader."[333]

We are still talking about setting a high standard for ourselves.

3. Create Awareness by Doing, Not Just Talking

Reinvent yourself by improving your delivery efficiency and quality—a sort of 'quality that thrusts itself to attention.' You can rediscover yourself by engaging in quality thinking and be motivated by significance rather than performance.[334]

Make yourself an indispensable asset to your employer, and let your work speak for you. You can also work on your personal behaviors and attitude to work in a more positive way. Organize your work and your time. Create synergies and develop more people skills. All these have a way of increasing your income.

You can *rebrand* yourself and your services through packaging and the assembling of intellectual capital in ways that resonate with your management, client, and peers. With strategic focus and a thorough command of details and quality, you will begin to shine as a rising star in your organization. Schulz and Doerr described eight pillars of intellectual capital as follows: distinction, salience, relevance, consequences, defensibility, realism, elegance, and presentation.[335]

Simply put: what makes you unique or distinct from your peers or competitors? What is the importance of having you? Who will miss you if you are fired, or you resigned? How important is your position, your skills, your personality? How relevant is your job to the employer? What would be the consequence of having or not having you? No one is indispensable, but some employees are more dispensable than others. Can your absence defend your presence? Can your output justify your pay—remuneration? Napoleon Hill indicated that your income should be 6% of what you contribute to your employer's goal.[336]

How real is your contribution? Before you complain that your employer is underpaying you, try to estimate your actual contribution.

If all emotions, personality, or your certificate were to be torn off, would you still be needed by your employer? Will you still be able to earn a decent income? Do people, your client, and your employers see you as being real, or do they feel you have too much covering your true identity? Do you convey some aura of confidence and elegance? What is your general presentation like? Are you a team builder or team destroyer? Are you a finisher, have a flair, or a taste for truth, quality, integrity, and excellence? All these will contribute to your ability to commercialize your services. I recommend you read leadership books and acquire new skills. Jeffrey J. Fox wrote a simple but excellent book on *"How to Become CEO—The Rules of Rising to the Top of Any Organization."*[337]

It is an insightful book to read on some dos and don'ts of the corporate ambient for those aspiring to get ahead in today's business world.

4. Negotiate your position
The fear of job insecurity is the number one reason many employees do not request a raise when they have stayed on their job for a long time without a promotion. Each delay in your promotion will affect your pay at your next job unless you are nearing retirement or you have a reason for staying on that job beyond your pay. As a rule, do not tolerate it for too long if you are good at what you do. How do you know if you are good at what you do? The competitors of your company will be interested in poaching you at any opportunity. Such interests may be put as offers to you informally or indirectly. For some fields, the poaching ground for the posts of the CEO are the outstanding deputies or second-level senior managers in competitor organizations.

One way the hiring agencies place the bait for you to apply is by asking you if you know any qualified people or if you are interested. I have been receiving many of this type of head-hunted invitations for top jobs several times in the last decade. They sometimes customize the job to your interests and sometimes tell you which of them they think you are most suited for. They assure you of the confidentiality and opportunities that you may not be aware of. They offer to set up interviews if you are interested. If you are being passed over or ignored despite your high performance, changing jobs might be the best option. It is also one way to move up in some professions, but every move must be carefully weighed in terms of how it affects your personal life (family well-being, education, jobs, etc.) and your ministry or calling if you are a bi-vocational minister. Ask yourself this question, "Is this where God wants me to be at this time?"

Sometimes your employer even values you more when you notify him of a possible move to their competitor organization or if they cannot afford to lose you at the time. Oftentimes they will give you a counter-offer to keep you, putting you in an advantageous position to negotiate for a higher position or a substantial raise. Rebranding your specialization, selling your value to your employer, and honing a compelling camera-ready résumé for your next job may be necessary.

Never wait till you need a job before you update your résumé—keep updating it regularly. You can steadily aim for the top without giving yourself away.

5. *Know when to move on.*
Except God calls you to a particular place of assignment, then never stay in one single job or position until you retire. It could be boring, counterproductive, and economically unwise to do so. It can also be evident that you are not very marketable and have been working in survival mode. As a rule, when you move from one paying job to another, there is a steady increase in your income. There is also

excitement and confidence that comes with it. You should never accept a job that pays less than your current job; ask for at least 10-20% above, or even more. Negotiate your benefits before you accept an offer. Your argument to yourself should be that if you stay in your current job, you will likely get that raise within the next two years, and that is a reality for top performers. However, if you do not have leverage, do not make frivolous demands at an offer. Don't take advantage of an offer. Know your self-worth. There's the right timing for everything, too, so be wise.

To ensure that you are not disadvantaged, try not to leave a job until another contract is signed elsewhere. A jobless person will often get a lower salary than someone who has a contract and is well valued by his current employer. If you are not currently in a job, you have low negotiating power. Also, moving too frequently can backfire and reduce your value to that of 'hoppers.' It is better to work for a minimum of 3-5 years on a job or longer before moving to another unless it is beyond your control. The more you rise to the top and have a position of higher responsibility, the longer you should normally stay on a job to be able to make a meaningful impact.

6. Plan to work for yourself as the ultimate goal.
Plan to work for yourself as the ultimate goal. Being your own boss, if you can, has several advantages. Never work until you reach the last retirement age without planning on your retirement life well ahead. Retire early—voluntarily, or partially and gradually, if you can. Leave when you are still useful to yourself; the half-life concept applies here. That is why it is important to plan. Seek your passion or calling and pursue it. For those called to the ministry, this is where thoughtful planning on when to devote more time to your calling becomes relevant. This book is about preparing you for how to earn and grow your income, so you can be financially independent and do God's work, and spend your resources and time for the Kingdom.

7. Keep reinventing and 'rebranding' yourself in your field

The reason many high-paid professionals retain their jobs or have very attractive job mobility is because they have mastered the art of re-inventing and rebranding themselves on the job. They need to always have "*new bait*" that keeps their employers and competitors on their toes. Once you get a new job, don't mark time until you retire and just keep the status quo—innovate, re-invent, and rebrand yourself. Do something worthwhile. Do something new.

Chapter 15 Overview

Blooming in a Financial Wilderness

Ministry Issue
Are there biblical financial blueprints that can be learned?

Ministry Lesson
The Scriptures have very rich financial models exemplified by the example of King Solomon, Joseph, Jacob, Paul and teachings of Jesus that have been mined by many wealthy people of all ages.

CHAPTER 15

BLOOMING IN A FINANCIAL WILDERNESS

Joseph's Investment Formula

"Let Pharaoh appoint commissioners over the land to take a fifth of the harvest of Egypt during the seven years of abundance. They should collect all the food of these good years...and store up the corn..., to be kept in the cities for food.

*The food should be held in reserve...,
to be used during the seven years of famine..."* Genesis 41:34-36.

Anytime, and anywhere in the world, Joseph's wealth-creation formula wins. It is based on the biblical lesson that King Solomon would later teach in his proverbs when he said, *"Ants are creatures of little strength, yet they store their food in the summer"* (Proverbs 30:25). He further said, *"Go to the ant, you sluggard; consider its ways and be wise. It has no commander, no overseer or ruler; yet it stores its provisions in summer and gathers its food at harvest"* (Proverbs 6:8). This was the key investment secret that made Joseph become a champion ruler in Egypt. In this chapter, let's explore the stories of Joseph, Jacob, and Isaac, in terms of investments.

Joseph had a vision of greatness when he was a young boy, but he didn't know how that was going to happen. However, he believed his was a God-given vision. He simply was resolute in his determination to succeed. He trusted that since his vision came from God, He would be able to lead him to his breakthrough. From then on, everything else began to turn, but it wasn't toward his vision. It was contrary to his vision, and yet he held on to it. The more the enemy tried to stop his destiny, the more he advanced toward it. Joseph was a real fighter—he had the will to persevere in the midst of multiple miseries and trials. He was thrown into the pit, sold into slavery, lied against by a wayward woman, and thrown into jail, but his dream could not be destroyed or stopped. One day he stood before the king, and his dreams came to pass. He became the Prime Minister of the land where he had been sold as a slave.

After Joseph interpreted the vision to Pharaoh—the king's dream of seven years of plenty and seven years of want; he also gave the king some wise *investment principles* and said: *"Now, therefore, let Pharaoh select a discerning and wise man, and set him over the land of Egypt. Let Pharaoh do this, and let him appoint officers over the land, to collect* **one-fifth of the produce** *of the land of Egypt the seven plentiful years. And let them gather all the food of those good years that are coming, and* **store up grain** *under the authority of Pharaoh, and let them keep food in the cities. That food shall be* **as reserve** *for the land for the seven years of famine which shall be in the land of Egypt that the land may not perish during the famine"* (Genesis 41:33-36).

Many people are good at advising but are bad at implementing. Joseph was an excellent counselor and implementer as well. The king said no one is better than Joseph to implement these investment ideas. It was a vote of confidence, but Joseph did not disappoint. From that point on, he became the Prime Minister of Egypt and CEO for the National Food Reserve Bureau of Egypt. He became greater than Potiphar and everyone he had ever met in his life, except Pharaoh. What was the secret of Joseph? He walked with God and had an entrepreneurial or investment mindset.

What key investment principles can we learn from Joseph?
1. Recognize God as the giver of the power to make wealth. The secret of Joseph is that he had recognized that wisdom comes from God, and if he had to succeed, he must partner with Him. When Pharaoh wanted to make him feel that he had a special wisdom for interpreting dreams, Joseph immediately answered, *"I cannot do it, but God will give Pharaoh the answer he desires"* (Genesis 41:16). He knew God was in charge.

Let us look at Joseph's interpretation of the dreams:
"The seven good cows are seven years, and the seven good heads of grain are seven years; it is one and the same dream...Seven years of great abundance are coming throughout the land of Egypt, but seven years of famine will follow them. Then all the abundance in Egypt will be forgotten, and famine will ravage the land...And now let Pharaoh look for a discerning and wise man and put him in charge of the land of Egypt" (Genesis 41:26-33).

Whether in ministry or a secular job, there are times God will allow you to have abundance that you cannot explain. It will be more than you can normally consume, but that is the time our ego rises and our flesh demands better compensation. It tells us we deserve to live like a king, and now is the time. Before long, the money vanishes.

You can create your own job
Joseph continued, and he had smartly spelled out the job description and terms of reference to the king for the new position—a wise and discerning man. Are you still waiting for a job advertisement? You can create your own job if you can partner with God. Joseph created a position that never existed before in Egypt. It was a customized position that was greater than a Minister, and no one else could fill that position but him. The king created the office of the Prime Minister according to Joseph's job description, and no one else was eligible to apply or contest the unilateral appointment of the man who was in partnership with God. Joseph's nationality, age, and tribe became unimportant. His educational background became non-essential for the job God was giving him. His social status as a slave in a foreign land was no longer relevant. God had lifted him up.

Supposing God had given you such a revelation: seven years of plenty and seven years of lack in your life, what would you do? Maybe you are doing well today, but if you lose your job today or next year, and you do not get another one for one year or five years, how will you fare during those years of lean, without an income?

Learning from Joseph:
Joseph said, *"Let Pharaoh appoint commissioners over the land to **take a fifth of the harvest** of Egypt during the seven years of abundance. They should collect all the food of these good years that are coming and store up the grains under the authority of Pharaoh, to be kept in the cities for food. This food should be held in reserve for the country to be used during the seven years of famine that will come upon Egypt so that the country may not be ruined by famine"* (Genesis 41:34-36).

The plan seemed good to Pharaoh and to all his officials. Pharaoh immediately recognized something: The king knew that if God had revealed the secret through Joseph, God's Spirit is needed to see it through. He said, *"Can we find anyone like this man, who has the Spirit of God?"* The rest is history.

Joseph's wisdom was simple. He had a vision of greatness, and he pursued it. He knew God's plan for his life. Do you know God's plan and purpose for your life? Are you in the right place and doing the right thing at the right time? The investment principle of Joseph is still being used in most countries today: nearly every country has a 'national grain reserve'—Israel, the United States, China, India, Italy, Angola, Malawi, etc. It has been a solution to both famine and price instability.

The Egyptians were eating and sowing in the years of plenty, and they were putting all the *extras* into the grain reserve. The savings became so large they were immeasurable.[338] What do you do in your year of plenty? Every *season* of plenty or financial surplus has an end, except for the wise.[339] King Solomon said there is time and season for everything under the sun.

Joseph turned the seven years of plenty and seven years of famine into a vibrant global business for Egypt. We read that, *"All countries came to Joseph in Egypt to buy grain, because the famine was severe in all the lands"* (Genesis 42:56-57).

Joseph could even afford to sell to other countries and make more money for the treasury. He sold grain to the Egyptians. He bought all the wealth of the people of Egypt and their lands for the king,[332] and bought the wealth of the neighboring countries—their livestock, gold, and silver, lands…for the king of Egypt.[333]

He established an income for the king from the land rent payments of 20% from all the proceeds of every man since the king (the state) now owned all the lands.[334] In many countries today, the land belongs to the state. Many millionaires have proved Joseph's formula of wealth-making without being conscious of it. If anyone would save and invest 20% of his or her income every month, that could create a huge wealth within a few years.

2. Save as much as possible in the time of plenty and maintain a financial reserve

Joseph instituted that 20% of all the proceeds should be held in reserve.[335] It translated to saving at least 20% of your income every month. This was the principle Joseph applied. Expenses naturally grow to the level of your income unless you are able to control them. It is when you start to save that you will know that you can actually live on less than your current expenditure. Have you ever thought of how savings in those seven fat years was able to meet the need of the seven lean years and still leave a surplus to sell to their neighboring countries?

Assuming that the harvests during those seven years were three times the normal years and people ate one part, the mandatory food reserve expected by Joseph was 60% of the normal years of food produced previously to be stored each year. In addition, they still had 240% for themselves. The Egyptians could consume all the 100% of normal harvest and sell back 140% to Joseph for cash. Indirectly, Joseph would have collected back 200% of the food produced of a normal year, in which the government only paid for 140%. With that, Egypt would have gained enough food reserve for an extra 14 years!

Since they were also harvesting during the famine years, assuming they produced only 20% of their normal harvests, Egypt would still only need 80% from the reserve and still feed as normal. They would then have an extra seven years' worth of grain to sell to their neighbors at high prices and make huge wealth in those years. Grain prices could be as high as five times the normal because of global scarcity and inflation in the neighboring nations.

In the story of how Isaac sojourned in the land of Gerar, we learn that God can bless the produce of the land, and the 100-fold could be harvested.[344] If the Egyptians had harvested five times their normal harvest, it means they had so much surplus; they could even continue to sell after the famine.

The key to Joseph's investment was to have Egypt accumulate enough food reserves for the future or lean years.[345] This might appear contradictory to what the Bible says about a man who tried to accumulate reserves in his store and said, "I will enlarge my store, and O my soul, now you can rest." That man did not know God; he was probably a wicked, stingy man. For a blessed man, the Lord says whatever he touches prospers.[346] His house and store will never lack food. He has enough for him or herself and plenty more to give for God's work, to share with the poor and to needy, and his storehouse will still be full.[347]

Joseph's investment model encourages us to put all the excesses of the years of plenty in reserve (Investments) as much as possible.[348] Many believers are wasteful when we have more than enough. Because our income flows in regularly and easily, we rarely envision any possible days of financial famine. This is true when we live on money that is given freely to us by others. We didn't think there might be a time when "the brook could be dried up" as it did for Elijah.

In summary, you need to save as much as possible in the time of plenty. As shared previously, John Wesley said, "Gain all the money you can, save all the money you can, and give all the money you can." Unless you first learn to make and save money, you will have nothing to give away. You will always have seasons of good and bad times; what you do during the good times are more important. Save a fifth (20%) of your income each month in a safe reserve (account). Joseph did not focus on the bad years to come but on how to maximize the good years.

3. *You can help others as you help yourself through investments*
You can save many people from famine: financial stress; or provide jobs and opportunities for progress for them and also make good money yourself.[349] John Rockefeller said he would rather make money through 1% of 100 people than 100% of his own time or effort alone. Immediately, believers will think about Luke 18:22—the story of the rich youngman that Jesus told to sell all he had. Rockefeller was talking pure business here. He talking about the power of leveraging other people's talents to create wealth for both himself and those worked for him.. Did the Scriptures say we should not expect anything back from those we help?

Joseph started to sell grain to the people of Egypt until their lands were turned over to the king's control. Yet, they were very grateful because they would otherwise have died of famine.[350] With this act, he was able to get their attention and create loyalty to their king. He got them engaged when they could have been without work and food. It may appear a 'win-lose' situation to us now because it is a story, but the Egyptians who were facing the threat of death by famine didn't see it that way. They saw it as a win-win situation. He also created a lot of jobs and means of livelihoods for many people during a period the 14-year people of plenty and famine. More importantly, he also preserved a whole nation of Israel—his ultimate grande mission in Egypt.

We have to look for a *win-win* situation always. Joseph saved the situation, and he became wealthy, but he first helped the nation of Israel and its people: he prevented the Egyptian people from experiencing a devastating famine, when many could have died as was the case in other nations. In the process, he saved many lives, and he enriched the king and the nation, as well. The wealth of the land still belonged to the people of Egypt, but now it was in the king's custody. He raised the GDP and per capita income.

4. You can have multiple streams of income from your initial savings
Joseph started with the grain reserve; then, he introduced livestock, lands, money, and continued to accumulate wealth for the king. It means that we can actually start with one business and diversify to another as the wealth grows. Your initial capital may come from your salary, inheritance, or from selling a car, then to stocks; then, you can buy your house. This was the secret of Solomon's wealth that we have learned, as well.

Joseph started to sell the grain…

in exchange for their money
- in exchange for their livestock
- in exchange for their land
- in exchange for their labor

He put the land under the king introducing the people paying rent (tax). That was the beginning of collecting a tax for the lands in the nations.

5. Developing a Partnership with God is wisdom
Because Joseph partnered with God, abundant wisdom was given to him to fulfill God's purpose. The king himself recognized that partnership was the key to success for the nation of Egypt. He said, "Who else can we find such a spirit of God?" Joseph knew that the seven years of plenty was short and would soon be out-surpassed by the seven years

of famine. It is wisdom to know that we have a limited number of days on earth and that we must spend the shortest time being profitable—by investing on earth and in eternity.

6. Revisit your financial blueprints

Harv Eker asserted that the difference between the rich and the poor is simply in their financial mindset. This is what tailors their lives to their long-held blueprints. If your blueprint is set for low net worth, there is a chance you will be attracted to a lifestyle, and that's what will keep you there.

To change your outcome, you simply need to work and adjust your blueprint to success and create a wealth mindset. This has nothing to do with the power of positive thinking. Harv believes that those who are rich have a certain pattern of life and attitude that can be learned. Joseph never spoke small. He spoke big and with confidence. He spoke like a seasoned professional, a politician, and an astute businessman.

Perseverance wins

A good example of this is a story of a man who, while digging for a well, found gold.[351] He had burst into a gold mine accidentally. He realized for him to recover the gold that he needed a machine to bring it up. He decided to fill up the hole with dirt so no one else would come across it until he would return. For the next few days, he sold all that he had, borrowed from his relatives, and bought the machine. He returned there with the machine and with his uncle digging up where he thought the pit was. In digging, they could not find the gold. They had left in frustration and sold the machine at a low price.

The man who bought the machine heard about his dilemma and decided to try his own luck. He consulted an engineer to work out the depth of that gold. The calculations revealed the gold to be at just three meters away from where the man had stopped. He went out and started to dig and found gold; he became very rich.

Perseverance is the key to success for those who want to partner with God. This is the reason Jesus asked, *"Which man will build a tower without first a plan and knowing the cost,"* so he will know that he can complete it? Always finish a project you embark upon. Don't abandon your dream because of flimsy excuses.

There is no better example of perseverance that I know of than the compelling story of the young Sofia Pedro. She was a Mozambican woman in her twenties who gave birth in a tree in 2000 before she was airlifted by a helicopter out of the worst floods her country had seen in decades.[352] She was pregnant, but the only way to survive was to climb a tree. Getting there, her labor pains started. She delivered the baby in the tree while holding on to it until she was rescued by the helicopter.

If you seek to achieve financial freedom, you need perseverance and delayed gratification.

Jacob's Entrepreneurial Model
Another interesting biblical model of wealth-creation that was based on a partnership with God was that of Jacob. He had fled from his brother Esau and was living with his uncle. By his father's instruction, he married from there. He served fourteen years for the two daughters of Laban—Leah and Rachel. While he was working for the dowry of his two wives, he tended the livestock of Laban, and God prospered the man because of Jacob. His small livestock herds multiplied and became large. Jacob was very hard-working, and the Lord was with him. But Laban was a shrewd man. He was determined to exploit his son-in-law to build great wealth for himself.

Jacob became tired of his situation. After he had fully served for his dowry, he told Laban of his intention to move on with his family. Laban did not want him to go. He had consulted diviners and knew that God was blessing him because of Jacob.

Then they reached an agreement that all the speckled animals would be Jacob's wages for the work he had done and would be doing for his father-in-law.[353] Jacob's choice of speckled animals was based on revelation from the Lord. When Laban saw that all the animals that gave birth to young ones had speckles, he changed the wage to those that were streaked and spotted, but the animals also gave birth to those with streaks and spots. Whatever he changed to, the animals responded accordingly, until all the animals became Jacob's,[354] and he became exceedingly prosperous.[355] Laban became envious.

What Laban did not know was the fact that God had just revealed to Jacob the key to his breakthrough in a dream.[356] The Lord had seen the injustice of Laban and wanted to take Jacob to his next level. God partnered with Jacob to transfer the wealth into his hands.

Lesson 1: Diligence, endurance, and dependence on God
The investment lesson here is 100% dependence on God and hard work. Jacob did his work with all his strength. Skills and hard work are important in making wealth,[357] but without partnering with God, it is in vain. Promotion does not come from the east nor the west but from God. His employer prospered, and Jacob negotiated to be a shareholder as payment for his services. Laban had no choice because Jacob was a valued service provider. The Lord made him indispensable to Laban's business. We need the spirit of wisdom and revelation to achieve success in Jacob's situation.

Lesson 2: God can reveal our financial investment pathway to us.
Mark Victor Hansen and Robert Allen relate the power of synergy with God's 'spiritual math." According to them, "You are either multiplied by infinity with God; or multiplied by zero without God. One times infinity equals infinity. But a million times zero still equals zero. That's why I tithe. I want God on my side."[358] It is even more than tithing. Also, tithing simply by donating a tenth to a charity cause, as is the practice of some investors, is not legitimate tithing—a biblical tithe

is given to God. It is about knowing your God, doing His will, and walking with Him so intimately, that we are filled with His fullness. Do not labor in vain by doing it without God. Jesus said, *"Everyone who is heavy laden or burdened should come to Him"* (Matthew 11:28-30). He wants to share the burden with you to make it light and easy. Put God first and let Him lead you.

Lesson 3: Isaac's Wealth Model
Isaac was carrying a Covenant of Divine Blessing, but he was not aware that it included his prosperity. When the famine started in the land he was sojourning in, he started to contemplate relocating to Egypt with his family. God saw his heart and told Isaac not to leave the land of Gerar in the land of the Philistines. He told him to remain and dwell in the land, and He would prosper him there.[359]

Isaac obeyed God, and he sowed in the land and reaped a 100-fold return because God blessed him. Let me remind the reader that 100-fold increase is not same as 100% as some teach. Because 100% is simply a doubling of your investment, which is nothing extraordinary. A hundred-fold gain means 100 times your investment—that is 10,000% profit! Isaac reaped 10,000 profit! Let that sink in for a moment.

When God blesses you, whatever you do will prosper, regardless of where you are based. It was recorded that *"The man became rich, and his wealth continued to grow. He had so many flocks and herds and servants that the Philistines envied him"* (Genesis 26:12-14).

God knows your wealth-formula
Isaac became so wealthy that the people of the land started to envy him until the king himself begged him to leave the land because he had become so powerful.[360] This was because God had shown Isaac what his financial prosperity formula was. When God partners with you, nothing can stop your breakthrough.

A friend once told me the story of a believer who was shown some land while he was inside an airplane. According to the story, the Holy Spirit asked if he knew the place well. He answered affirmatively. Holy Spirit then told him to go and buy that piece of land of which he obeyed. Years later, wells of oil were found on the land. Now he receives millions of dollars as royalty from the land. God showed him where the gold was, and He can show you where yours is also. Just look around you for your treasure; God will show you.

Acres of Diamond
There was a man in the ancient Persia kingdom by the name of Ali Hafed. He had deserted his own productive field and spent most of his life searching for a mythical *'Field of Diamonds.'* He traveled far and wide, climbed mountains, and searched valleys, looking for diamond fields. After many years of toil, he ended up dying a poor man in the process. A few years after his death, an incredibly rich mine of diamonds was discovered in his own abandoned land in his backyard. That story was said to have been repeatedly told by Dr. Russell H. Conwell—the pastor of Grace Baptist Church and founder of Temple College, the author of the book titled *Acres of Diamonds*.[361]

God knows where your diamonds and gold are. You may not need to travel far and wide like Ali, for your gold may be just under your tent—just in your backyard, your city, or your country. Dr. Russell Conwell himself discovered his own 'acres of diamonds' from this poor man's story and dug it deep. He had mined the story and sold the diamonds in thousands of teachings and seminars. He became the most sought-after motivational speaker in America for his time, with over 6,000 lectures delivered in diverse forms in the late 1880s.[362] The money from his speeches on the "acres of diamonds," along with the turnover from the famous *"57 Cents"* story, had built the Temple University in Pennsylvania, Philadelphia.

God knows the location of your goldfield. You need God to be able to locate the gold, and you have to dig it out. He knows the route that can take us to a breakthrough—which investment stream will yield the most profit. He knows which real estate or stock option will skyrocket in a few months or years. *"It is God who gives us the power to make wealth"* (Deuteronomy 8:18). Ask Him to help you discover it. It may be right in your backyard. *"Silver and gold are Mine," says the Lord"* (Haggai 2:8).

A wise investor must partner with God, Who is the Owner of all wealth. Financial freedom (prosperity) follows those who fear the Lord.[363] Our faith and action must agree if we want to see results. The point I am making is that the starting point for financial freedom is not reading a book or attending seminars, but to first pray to the Lord and ask for His direction. He gave Solomon his investment wisdom and how knowledge on how to create wealth. He gave Joseph the winning dream. He told Isaac to remain where he was. He knew where and how each of them would attain a breakthrough for their financial freedom. He can do the same for you. After that, you may attend any seminar, read books, and acquire knowledge on how to make it happen as He will guide your steps.

Chapter 16 Overview
Developing Your Financial Plan

Ministry Issue
Can financial success be achieved without a plan and discipline?

Ministry Lesson
In order to achieve your financial dream, you need to set clear goals for your dream to happen.

CHAPTER 16

DEVELOPING YOUR FINANCIAL PLAN

Turning Your Dream Into a Reality
*"Suppose one of you wants to build a tower.
Will he not first sit down and estimate the cost to see
if he has enough money to complete it?"* Luke 14:28-30.

*"You know farming looks mighty easy when your plow is a pencil,
and you're a thousand miles from the corn field."*[364]

The importance of money cannot be ignored or brushed aside by believers or ministers, regardless of the level of anointing they possess. Money is not just a want that we "wish to have," but a "need to have," or even a "must-have,"—it is a necessity for all Christians. No matter how much some try to demonize money, it is a can't-do-without commodity.

According to Dr. Jerry L. Williamson: "Until the issue of money is sorted out in someone's life, they feel incomplete and uncomfortable. Poor financial management has hindered and even stopped many otherwise qualified and gifted persons from pursuing their missions call or ministry effectively."[365] Therefore, it is important for ministers to plan for those finances if we must avoid experiencing financial headaches later in life. Pastor Matthew Ashimolowo wrote in his book, "Money is like food; when you have enough of it, you do not think about it. Until you are financially satisfied, you will have to meditate on the subject of finance no matter how spiritual you are."[366]

Can you imagine spending most of the night thinking about how to pay the bills that are due for payment the next day? Sad to say, a high percentage of the Church does just that.

There are those who consider planning for finances a secular effort or even lack of faith. Yet, they do not mind freely asking others for money to do ministry and highlighting their need. That is why there are many starters in ministry that do not have a plan on how to earn money. If you want to avoid headaches in ministry, listen carefully - plan for finances. Don't just engage in futile daydreaming about someone donating a house, car, monthly income, and education for your kids and free everything else. You, too, can plan to be a giver instead of a taker and bless others.

Paul quoted Jesus as saying, *"It is more blessed to give than to receive"* (Acts 20:35). It was in the same breath he also said, "I have not coveted anyone's silver or gold or clothing. You yourselves know that these hands of mine have supplied my own needs and the needs of my companions. In everything I did, I showed you that by this kind of hard work, we must help the weak." Plan for your finances in ministry, but before planning to receive, be determined to be a faithful giver.

Roger Smith wrote an article in Fortune Magazine in 1989: "If you plan, you can greatly influence your own future. I think everyone needs a vision. A lot of people just wander mindlessly through this world, thinking one or maybe two days ahead. They don't have a vision for themselves or where or what they want to be." Failing to plan is planning to fail. Jesus even said that if you want to build a house, you will have to have a plan and know the costs in order to be sure that you will be able to finish it.[367]

King Solomon said, *"In his heart, a man plans his course, but the Lord determines his steps"* (Proverbs 16:9). You cannot become financially independent or be financially sufficient by chance; just as you did not become poor or become broke by chance, everything has a process. Maybe you find yourself poor; it could be due to lack of wisdom, change of circumstances, poor opportunities, etc. But that doesn't need to be your eternal dilemma; your future can change.

I know many great people who were not very well educated but who have achieved financial success: some didn't attend college. Some had dropped out of high school. The list of billionaires and multi-millionaires who didn't finish college is long.[368] Education is important, but it is not the most important guarantee of financial freedom.

Although these wealthy men may not have completed formal education, they had developed a workable plan on how to achieve financial success. They are men who have taken their world and their generation by surprise. They became forces to be reckoned with. Many of them became more knowledgeable than outstanding university professors. Acquire education as much as you can, but acquire skills in the art of making money also—which you can do mostly by self-learning.

Solomon said, *"To man belongs the plans of the heart, but from the Lord comes the reply of the tongue...Commit to the Lord whatever you do, and your plan will succeed"* (Proverbs 16:1-3). Everyone wants to be rich, but there is a proverb that if wishes were horses, beggars would ride; even beggars would like to ride in a luxurious limousine car. It will be a mere wish unless there is action.

Remember this, *"No one who puts his hands to the plow and looks back is fit for service in the Kingdom of God"* (Luke 9:62). It is the same reason why some whose wish was to be a medical doctor end up becoming a taxi driver or a biology teacher at a High School. By the way, none of these are a lesser or less worthy job than a medical doctor, but I am only contrasting dreams and outcomes here.

Ben Okri said, "We plan our lives according to a dream that came to us in our childhood, and we find that life alters our plans. And yet, at the end, from a rare height, we also see that our dream was our fate. It's just that providence had other ideas as to how we would get there. Destiny plans a different route, or turns the dream around, as if it were a riddle, and fulfills the dream in ways we couldn't have expected."[369]

This is nearly correct, except that what Ben has called providence is what I understand to be God's will and purpose for each person's life.

The life of Joseph is a good example of this as, I have already shared.

Financial Acquisition Precedes Investment
Many Christian leaders use the words 'investments' and 'giving' interchangeably; thereby, giving the impression that when you give, you should think you have invested, and that's it. Well, that is right in the spiritual sense only. In this book, I define giving as a Heavenly investment and the act of literally putting money to work in order to have enough money for your family needs, for giving away to the work of God, the needy, and for multiplying it as a 'Financial Investment.' There must be no confusion; when you give, you are investing in the Kingdom—spiritual investment, but when you leverage your effort by multiplying the money, that is financial investment. Therefore, we will refer to giving specifically as giving and the process of creating wealth as investing.

Steps to Getting Started
A financial plan is a projection of your cash inflow and your cash outflow for a certain time period that represents the steps a person is taking in every area of his or her life.[370] A comprehensive method of designing a personal financial plan is given by Ron Blue and Jeremy White.[371]

Five basic steps are important in planning to achieve financial freedom or financial success:
> *Step 1. Estimate your present and future financial requirement.* This is a picture of where you are currently in your financial status.

> *Step 2. Develop your long-term financial goals.* This is to determine where you really would like to be in the future (future goals);

Step 3. Assess your financial net worth sincerely. This involves your inventory—listing and estimating value of all your liquid and non-liquid assets, your liabilities, and determining the differences. We will explain this in detail in the next chapter;

Step 4. Prayerfully develop a feasible financial plan. These are your actions to achieve the long-term goals (through increasing your asset value, cash-flow margin, and ultimately, your financial net worth). In other words, determine how additional streams of income can flow to you in a legitimate manner to grow your financial net worth over time;

Step 5. Follow your plan diligently. Commit it to the Lord and be tenacious.[372] Planning is encouraged by God's Word, "The plans of the diligent lead to profit as surely as haste leads to poverty."[373]

Setting Your Financial Goals
Goal-setting starts with a vision of what you want to become in the future—what you see yourself to be. A *vision* is what God has called us to do. It is like visualizing your pre-determined destination in a lifetime. It is thinking the end from the beginning—using the part of God's nature that is in us.[374] He declares the end from the beginning. *"Where there is no vision, the people perish"* (Proverbs 29:18). When your vision is with commitment, it becomes a mission. Your vision requires faith, plus the appropriate action in order to materialize it. You won't achieve your vision until you do something about it.

You may have a vision to plant a church, establish a bible school for training credentialed leaders, create a Christian publishing house, a parachurch ministry to help poor Christians or generate finances for supporting missionaries in the field. Such vision requires a commitment to act, which is called a *mission*—a statement of reality articulating why we exist. That is, what we are anointed or recruited to accomplish in God's business—'His mission.' Jesus stated His five-fold mission statement as follows:[375] i) To preach the Gospel to the poor, ii) proclaim freedom for the prisoners, iii) To bring about the recovery of sight for the blind, iv) To release the oppressed, and v) To proclaim the year of the Lord's favor.

To achieve these, Jesus had to build His invisible, living, and universal church—that the gates of hell cannot overcome. He had to preach, teach, heal the sick, and develop faithful leaders who would carry out the vision and pass on the baton at all cost. The five-goal mission statement of the Lord was further broken down into concrete outcomes designed to accomplish the vision in three years, while some of them were long range and short-term goals. In pursuing these goals, Jesus had a plan of how to achieve each objective on daily basis. Every day, minute and second was important for His three-year ministry. For us as Christians, we need to develop our vision into an action plan. This simply involves writing down clear goals, objectives, and your expected results—long-term (outcomes) and short-term (outputs). Then develop the steps that are required to achieve these results—known as milestones, based on where you are now to what you want to achieve at progressive periods, with a timeline for attainment.

The vision is important, but it will never be realized unless a goal-driven program is put in place and followed faithfully. Without goals, the vision is merely wishful thinking.[376] What are your goals in life?

Financial Goal
The first step is to ask yourself—what is your vision in life? That is: What do you see yourself being? What has God laid on your heart? The next is: What are your goals to achieve the vision? Unless you know what your goals are, you cannot know how to get the money you need to achieve them. The key to your financial freedom is when you focus on your life's goals, prioritize them, and allocate your time, finances, and effort to them accordingly.

A financial goal is not an end in itself, but a means to an end. If your goal is just to be rich, you will never make it, or you will become rich in the wrong way. Put God first in all your planning. The time you spend on your intellectual goals in life—acquiring skills, knowledge, and developing yourself are important. Time spent studying new things can pay off. Your spiritual goals depend on your relationship with God, service, and eternal destiny. The time you spend with those who are important in your life counts and can also affect your financial goals.

What do you really want in life?
Everyone wants to have money, but what amount of wealth is enough for you? John D. Rockefeller pursued his goal to be a billionaire and live a long life. He did just that. I am not encouraging Christians to desire to be a billionaire. I am simply advocating that a believer should have a concrete plan. Henry Kaiser said, "Determine what you want more than anything else in life, write down the means by which you intend to attain it, and permit nothing to deter you from pursuing it."[377] Do you want to see yourself funding missionaries using your own financial means? Do you want to support the building of churches in a developing world, among the unreached people groups of the world? Do you want to fund world evangelism in a burdened nation or nations of the world?

Someone's goal may be to own a car in two years or own a house that is free of a mortgage payment in 5 or 10 years; another may be to have enough provisions and money—food, shelter, and upkeep, for five years of missionary work in Cambodia, Liberia, or Bhutan. Do you want to help give scholarships to the children of 5, 10, 50, 100, even 1,000 missionaries or full-time Christian workers who have insufficient financial means and establish a foundation to support that vision beyond your lifetime? Someone once said, "If your aim is to just be comfortable, you will never have enough."[378] Your income will always level up to your needs and commitments—no matter how much you earn.

Do you need money for God's work? Are you a minister, or have you been called to reach out to the lost? There is no revival without plenty of costs. Are you a Christian who would like to have enough for your family upkeep and enough to give to God's work and to others? Many want to have a financial surplus at one moment, but in another breath, they lament about their inability and impotency in their failure to know how to make it happen. I encourage you to read on and finish reading this book.

Ask yourself, "If you become what you dream, what will change in anyone else's life? If God makes you who you want to be, what will change in the Kingdom of God?" If your interest is to consume it on your own pleasures and lusts, then this book cannot help you because God's Spirit has breathed through it for His glory.

Be sincere to yourself: Why do you need money? Roughly, how much money do you need to realize your goals? How are you going to get it? When your WHY you want to have money is big enough, your HOW to generate finances will fall into place.

Define Your Goals in Life
Assuming God gives you 500%, 400%, 300%, 200%, 150%, 100%, 75%, 50%, or 25% of the years you have already spent, or He gives back all the money you have ever earned in your life in 100-fold, what would you like to achieve during that period? What would you like to do better in order to achieve your main goal?

List your goals and arrange them in order of their priority to you—the main one, and secondary, and so on. Remember, Jesus only spent three years of ministry and a total of 33 years on Earth. But He achieved what no other person has ever achieved. It is because He knew His goals and pursued them meticulously. Each of these goals affects the other.

Why do you need money? John D. Rockefeller said, "If your only goal is to become rich, you will never achieve it." Life is more than just earning paychecks and accumulating air mileage from frequent fliers. Life is more than just buying stuff, storing and displaying jewelry, and changing your wardrobes frequently. Life is more than buying the expensive wristwatch, fleets of cars, boats, or owning private jets. What common sense is there in buying a Rolex wristwatch for thousands of dollars when a $50 or $150 wristwatch gives you the same time? If we have a choice in spending for show or sowing into the Kingdom – Kingdom must be always prioritized. Whenever we are tempted to squander we must keep this Scripture in mind, *"But God said to him, 'Fool! This night your soul will be required of you; then whose will those things be which you have provided?"* (Luke 12:16-20). You will say that's not a Christian, but it is no worse than when ministry leaders hunger for private jets, just as unbelievers do. There is nothing wrong with living comfortably, but extremes are dangerous. Focus on God's purpose in your life, and you will discover your vision. The Lord admonished us to seek first His kingdom and His righteousness, and "all these things" will be given you us as well.[379]

Your Goals must be SMART!
Goal-setting is not a one-time thing that is cast in stone, rather it requires constant review and changes, according to how the situation changes as you go to fulfill the vision. In the corporate world, every goal is validated when they meet the following criteria: they must be **s**pecific, **m**easurable, **a**ttainable, **r**ealistic, and **t**ime-bound. This is acronym known as **SMART**.

Specific—Your goal should not be ambiguous or complex. It should be specific. For instance, you may have a goal that says, "I want to plant a missional church that caters for the unchurched Hispanics, Africans, or Arabs in my district, or county, or city, in the next five years." It cannot be that "I want to find ways of helping Christians enjoy better fellowship in America. Or all over the world"

Measurable—Your goals should be easy to measure. If you cannot measure it, then how will you know you have reached that goal? Jesus knew when He had finished His work on Earth—He had achieved all the goals set for Himself when He prayed to His Father, *"I have brought you glory on earth by completing the work you gave Me to do. And now, Father, glorify me in your presence with the glory I had with you before the world began"* (John 17:4-5). Paul knew when he had attained his… he had set his eyes on the goals.[380] When he completed them, he said, *"For I am already being poured out like a drink offering, and the time has come for my departure. I have fought the good fight; I have finished the race. I have kept the faith…"* (2 Timothy 4:6-8). How do you know you have achieved your goals? They must be measurable.

Since the purpose of goal-setting is to establish a set of steps for your vision, it is important that your goal is defined with measurable, achievement steps. For instance, a goal of planting a missional church with a 500-membership capacity in Arlington, Dallas County, United States, within the next five years, seems measurable. To be "measurable," the *what, when,* and *how* of the goal needs to be able to be measured and must be clearly defined.

Attainable—It is good to set high goals, but they must be attainable. If someone is illiterate, and their goal is to become a motivational speaker on Stem Cells technology within six months, or he or she wants to teach the 'End-Time' prophecies in Madison Square, in New York within a year, that is a laughable goal or a hungry man's dream at best. Make your financial goals attainable while you build your faith in God. If you have never traveled outside your city, and you set goals of shuttling the world in one year, that is unattainable, and you do not know what you are setting as a goal. You have never preached to two people, but you want to fill a stadium—it is a daydream. Some people want to fund the Great Commission and send missionaries all over the world, but they've never held more than $500 in their account and they have never paid a tithe or give offering.

Realistic—Just as the goal has to be attainable, your goal must be realistic. It must consider what can be possible within the available resources and opportunities you have. It could be expanded later as the vision expands, but do not set a goal of building churches around the world, when you do not even have the resources for building one where you are yet. No one will buy into your goal if it is a 'white elephant' goal or a pie in the air. Start small, and grow. Dwight D. Eisenhower, the 34th U.S. President on September 11, 1956, said, "You know, farming looks mighty easy when your plow is a pencil, and you're a thousand miles from the corn field." Be realistic with your goal setting.

Make Your Goal-setting Holistic

You cannot set goals financially or physically for your life without considering your spiritual well-being. What are your goals in each of the different areas of your life? List your goals for each of these:

1. *Spiritual goal*—Your relationship with God and spiritual maturity may be set as a goal. Sometimes there is a cost to your spiritual goal, as well. For instance, if you are committed to attending certain revival meetings, prayer commitments, studying the Bible, etc., this will include the time you need to spend in prayers and in studying God's Word. Apply the SMART rule as a check;

2. *Ministry goal*—Ministry goals depend on what God has called you to do. That should be the heart of your goal, and every other goal should revolve around it. Has God called you into the ministry—full-time or bi-vocational, lay or ordained; how will you answer that calling? Who will pay the bills and how? We all know that if God has called you, He has provided the provisions required, but it is our responsibility to discover and access that provision. How do you want God to support you? Understanding what you want will help you to know how to direct your prayers;

3. *Family goal*—It is important to have a clear goal for your family. Paul said whoever does not take care of his family is worse than an unbeliever. What do you want your family to be like now and in the future?

Current goals include ensuring proper welfare for your family. What type of old person would you like to be? Do you want your children to go to private schools or to college? In many poor countries, the difference between public and private can be miles apart. Do you want to leave an inheritance of a house or other properties for your children?

Your spouse is part of your goal here. How will your spouse grow with you? Perhaps, the best way is to jointly define the family, ministry and financial goals with your spouse. If you jointly plan and own assets together, the journey will be easier. Cost-cutting can never be achieved unless the goals are mutually agreed upon and worked out. Your family values will to a large extent, determine your goals, and they will affect your financial goals. Apply the SMART rule as a check.

4. *Intellectual goal*—To what extent and how do you want to develop and apply your brainpower? What skill, training, or education do you need to achieve your vision in life? A leader keeps learning, for the surroundings will keep changing. The knowledge you desire has a cost, so it must be included in your financial goal—short-term or long-term. What would be the cost of your investment in knowledge through books, CDs, seminars, conferences, etc.? How many books do you read to expand knowledge in what God has called you to? Do you need to attend a bible college and pay your own tuition fees and other expenses?

5. *Physical goal*—What is your state of health, and how do you foresee your health in relationship to your goal. How will you

maintain a healthy life—diet, exercise, food, etc.? Do you have health and or life insurance? If you are 75 years old and your goal is to evangelize the world in 20 nations per year, it is not impossible, but unless you already have been in the field as an evangelist, you may have an unrealistic goal that can negatively impact your health and life. The cost of raising the finances can have a toll on your health, as well. How will you maintain your health? Goals for rest, exercise, and diet are important. These have financial implications.

6. *Financial goal*—Money is not an end in itself; it is a means to an end. Unless you need money for something, it becomes a useless pursuit. You need to determine your goal for your current expenses and future expenses. What do you need to achieve all your stated goals above in terms of the finances involved?

You will realize that there are just too many important things to do when setting goals for your life. However, you will need to list all the goals and prioritize them according to their *importance*—to your vision and *urgency* of its implementation. There are some goals that are more urgent than others, and some are more important than others.

Ask yourself: what, why, when, and how and with whom will you achieve this goal? Develop them into long-term and short-term goals, and prioritize within each of them. Start with the short-term goals.

Now, select 5-6 of your top priority goals from your list and pour coals on them—put all your energy, time, and resources into them. Obviously, you also have the top three most important goals. Your financial plan is simply to put money value into what you are planning to achieve. Put your energy into your goals, and you will achieve them when you learn the investment skills you will acquire in this book.

If you ask many ministers and Christian workers how much they are worth today, financially, they have no idea. The next chapter will teach you how to determine your current financial net-worth—this is how much you are worth financially, that is, the value of all your current assets minus all your liabilities. Knowing your *financial net-worth* will help fuel your determination and ability to achieve financial success.

Chapter 17 Overview
Building Your Financial Net Worth

Ministry Issue
How Do I Achieve My Dream of Financial Success?

Ministry Solution
Know where you stand and plan your investment systems prayerfully. You need to know your financial net worth. Nothing comes by chance.

CHAPTER 17

BUILDING YOUR FINANCIAL NET WORTH

Charting The Road Map To Financial Freedom

"Commit to the Lord whatever you do, and your plans will succeed" Proverbs 16:3.

"Failing to plan is planning to fail." [381]

The former president of the United States, Jimmy Carter, received a proposal from Mr. Millard Fullard inviting him to help promote a new vision, "Habitat for Humanity." Mr. Millard Fullard was the founder and former president of Habitat for Humanity International (HFHI), which started in 1976. HFHI is a worldwide Christian housing ministry, building 200,000 homes with projects in 100 countries.[382] Mr. Fullard had listed several areas the President could help in: serving on the board, media contacts, helping to raise money, doing a 30-minute video, and working with a building crew for a day. Mr. Carter did not just agree to do one or two of the items on the list; but instead, he agreed to do everything.

At first, people thought Carter would just stop by for a brief photo up for publicity, but the former President put together a work crew, traveled by bus to the Brooklyn, New York, building site, worked tenaciously every day for a week; slept in a church basement along with everyone else, and swung a hammer to help construct a house! Since the first time, in 1984, Carter has done similar tasks every year: a servant leadership spirit that has transformed the mindset of many towards serving.[383] What would prompt a former U.S. President to go that far in pursuing what he believes in? To go cross-country by bus, sleep in a church basement, and do manual labor for a week? It is the Law of the Big Picture, according to John C. Maxwell. The goal is more important than the role.

When we talk about knowing your financial net-worth and turning that to wealth, it is for everyone, but few will actually tap into the power it unleashes. For about two decades that I have been teaching on Financial Freedom in Christian settings, one thing I realize is that those who have been able to go beyond the excitement of learning about money—have, after the discovery of actually analyzing their financial net worth, taken the steps that brought them out of poverty into financial freedom. Those go-getters have been able to run with the vision and share amazing financial testimonies with me.

How To Determine Your Financial Net-Worth

The purpose for determining your goals, and specifically your financial goals, is to help you work out your needs—in order to design your personal financial plan. Assuming you have an idea of what amount of money you need in the short and long-term, you can set your goals around that.

Your "Financial Net Worth" is your starting point—it is the estimate of what you are actually worth at a point in time financially if all your assets and income (wealth) were to be quantified monetarily.

The best starting point for wealth creation is when you know where you are now. It's only in knowing where you are now to where you are going that will help you get there. Similarly, you really need to know what your net worth is before you start your investment plan.

Take an inventory of all your assets and income

The first step is taking an inventory of all that you currently and legitimately own—your financial and non-financial assets, including your home or other real estate properties, your automobile, if you have a self-owned business, and all that you own that could be converted to liquid income. To do this, it is advisable to draw a table of all your financial assets and all your financial liabilities. List all your tangible assets that have a market value on the left column and put the estimated values in the right.

Do you have monthly salary, pension, insurance, or any other cash income earnings? Do you have a real estate property in your name, an automobile, electronics, stocks, bonds, treasury bills, money due from debtors, treasures like diamonds, gold, or silver; do you have a warehouse, a franchise, businesses, or any other tangible or intangible assets that can be easily liquidated? List them and sum them up as in the table below. The sum of all your assets, minus all your liabilities, equals your financial net worth.

Your Financial Net Worth

Financial Assets	Financial Liabilities
List of all your assets, e.g., cash, pension scheme, real estate, income on rents, automobile, stocks, bonds, promissory notes, treasures such as gold, diamonds, antiques, furniture, or other tangible and intangible assets that can be easily liquidated.	List of all your liabilities, e.g., debts, mortgages, rent, car lease, school fees, commitments, employment bonds, insurance, loans, etc.
Total Assets = TA	Total Liabilities = TL
Financial Net Worth = Total Assets – Total Liabilities	

There are important questions to ask yourself about your financial worth. How easily can you liquidate them into cash?

FNW = TA – TL
Where:
FNW= Financial Net Worth
TA= Total Assets
TL= Total Liabilities

When FNW is zero, it means you are debt-free. When it is negative, you are in debt or in the *red*, and when it's positive, that means you have a surplus or a measure of wealth that you probably did not take notice of before now. You may actually be living in debt and thinking everything is okay, especially if you have been buying many consumables with your credit cards and don't pay off your monthly bills.

This is the most important exercise I have found that many of those I have taught in seminars or training sessions always enjoy the most. This exercise will help you impose some caution on your lifestyle that will ultimately help you to create wealth. You will get a warning signal on where you have been negligent and a green light on where you could take even more advantages. It can be so interesting when you do it with your spouse, or adult children, with the goal of improving your financial worth. However, you must not allow the position of your current financial net-worth to be a discouragement to you. Do not force the data to enable you to look good. You are not doing it for anyone but yourself. Be true to yourself.

The results should spur you into deliberate actions to improve your situation. It should form the basis for making some adjustments in your lifestyle and for planning for your future and those of your family. For some people, because the exercise has allowed them to discover money that they were not conscious of, they might be tempted to be complacent. The choice is yours. The purpose is to help you know your starting point on your way to your financial freedom, and you should see it only in that light. That will help you make the right decision on the investment path to take.

The financial net worth is positive for those who have enough earnings or real estate assets or other investments already. But for most people, the net financial worth is often negative, even for those who earn a good income. It is not really whether it is positive or negative that matters; what matters is to know where you are and how you can get to the next level. In planning, it is important to determine your timeline to make the money you need. When are you going to need more money than you have now? Having an idea of what it will cost you in time, effort, and the resources you need to deploy can help to keep you better focused. Then you will need to ask yourself the Big Question of "How am I going to accomplish this?" It will help you to know how to channel your prayers and efforts.

Set a financial net worth target for yourself and give yourself a timeline. Do this prayerfully. Update your record regularly, e.g., every three months, bi-annually, or annually. If it remains the same after a year or two, then you are not making progress. Your strategy is to move from a negative position to a positive one and to move up in your net worth.

Let me illustrate the concept with three employees working in the same company: James is the Production Manager, Laura is the Accountant, and Julie is the Sales Manager.

Financial Net Worth

Liquid Assets	James	Laura	Julie
• Cash available (balance)	4,560	6,580	3,345
• Annual income (salary, fees, rent, etc.)	65,653	55,114	43,266
• Savings account (@1.5% interest)	0	3,000	0
• Certificate of Deposits (CD) @ 3%	0	0	6,000
• Securities (Stocks, bonds, bills)	23,667	35,321	0
• Life Insurance (cash values)[384]	0	6,190	4,887
• Retirement dues (pension, IRAs, etc.)	16,000	12,765	5,349
Total Liquid Assets	**109,880**	**118,970**	**62,847**
Non-Liquid Assets			
• Treasures (gold, silver, coins, diamonds, etc.)	0	0	15,895
• Furniture & other household assets	9,568	3,450	4,000
• Automobiles (cars, motorbikes, etc.)	36,997	4,587	11,055
• Real estate properties (Land, home)	263,774	66,322	76,324
• Real estate properties (Rental properties)	0	120,000	0
• Business value (revenue, products, assets, etc.)	0	34,611	56,345
• Intellectual assets (Inventions, franchises, royalties, etc.)	15,000	0	0
Total Non-Liquid Assets	**325,339**	**228,970**	**163,619**

Liabilities

Debt	James	Laura	Julie
• Car loan (auto loan)	28,000	0	6,000
• Bank loan (for business or any reasons)	10,000	5,000	20,000
• Life insurance premium	8,000	6,000	4,000
• Mortgage loan (on real estate properties)	234,000	25,000	0
• Credit card (debts on credit card)	9800	4500	1200
• Health (insurance, fitness & other costs)	6000	500	1000
• School fees (children, training, etc.)	26,500	11,296	0
• Living expenses (groceries,)	14,789	10,341	8467
• Auto insurance and maintenance	6850	3205	2460
• Vacation & travels	5000	2000	500
• Others (gifts, tithes, etc.)	0	7489	6432
Total Liabilities	**348,939**	**75,331**	**50,059**

Financial Net Worth Analysis[385]

Net worth Indicators	James	Laura	Julie
1. Assets			
• Liquid assets	109,880	118,970	62,847
• Non-liquid assets	325,339	228,970	163,619
Total Assets	435,219	347,940	226,466
2. Liabilities			
Total Liabilities	348,939	75,331	50,059
Total Net Worth[386]	**87,000**	**272,609**	**176,407**
Productive assets[387]	**15,000**	**154,611**	**56,345**
• Real estate (rental)	0	120,000	0
• Business	0	34,611	56,345
• Intellectual assets	15,000	0	0
Liquidity assets[388]	**28,227**	**44,901**	**9,345**
Propensity to Borrow (Liabilities divided by Assets, multiplied by 100) [389]	80.2%	21.7%	22.1%
Propensity to accumulate wealth[390]	3,400	15,145	19,601

Although James is the highest earner of the three employees and has a higher total in his assets, his lifestyle does not support him in growing his income. He has the highest liabilities and the highest propensity to borrow (80.2%). This is because much of his assets are in borrowed money (automobile and mortgage). Laura has the lowest propensity to borrow (22%) and a reasonable propensity to grow her income and achieve financial success. Although Julie has a low income, she has a very low propensity for borrowing and the highest propensity to accumulate wealth. This is due to the relatively short period she has worked, relative to the wealth she has built up. Her loans were directed to productive assets rather than consumption. She does not owe money on her home or credit card. She can easily buy a second house and rent out her home. Her loan was directed towards business. She also has treasures—diversified investment. She spends less on vacations and has no school fees to pay. In the long-term, she will likely be better off.

Indicative Non-financial Assets and Liabilities

A smart investor must consider some key personal human assets and liabilities that can directly or indirectly impact them on their ability to make wealth. Like DNA, most of these are innate attributes, but they could be developed and learned. The bottom line is to eliminate liabilities and acquire positive behaviors that are assets.

Personal Assets	Personal Liabilities
Integrity (honest, sincere, truthful, dependable)	Lack of integrity (dishonest, fraudulent, greedy, insincere, deceptive, undependable, bad reputation)
People-oriented (friendly, relational, Loves and respects diversity, kind, loving, forgiving)	Hostile to people (quarrelsome, enjoying conflicts, strife, lone ranger, discriminating, hateful, embittered, cruel, love criticism, unforgiving)
Polite (Meekness, humility)	Pride (Arrogance, full of ego)
Cheerfulness (happy, joy, motivated, zeal)	Melancholy (depressed, empty, discouraged)
Generous (tither, giver, can easily let go, likes to give rather than receive)	Miser (stingy, hates giving, petty-minded, cannot afford to lose money to others, likes to receive more than to give)
Organized (pragmatic, self-disciplined, hardworking, result-oriented, time-conscious)	Disorganized (scattered, lazy, undisciplined, squanders time, complacent)
Faithful to God, love God; put God first	Unfaithful, hypocritical faith; seeks God for himself
Willing (balanced or an open mind set on money, optimistic, open to new opportunities)	Unwilling (conservative, pessimistic, closed to opportunities, skeptic, extremist—has poverty mindset)
Spirit-led and can apply wisdom	Led only by logic

The greatest asset you have is yourself. You are the most important capital asset. The challenge for you, the investor, is to constantly find ways of increasing your net worth. Your vision, creativity, imagination, time management, time availability, courage to take risks, determination, persistence, knowledge, skills, hard work, self-discipline, result-oriented, and your love of excellence are a few of these ways. Your ability to nurture useful relationships also matters. It is often said that those who crown the king or queen do not always look like the king or queen. Your net worth also includes the real worth or the value of your relationships. People of integrity and impeccable character, wisdom, knowledge, and experience are assets to your net worth. Here I am not only talking about Christians.

On the other hand, someone who is narrow-minded, fearful, disorganized, and lazy, has a bad reputation, is dishonest, arrogant, unreliable, pessimistic, a perfectionist, complacent, etc., is a liability to himself and his potential to create wealth. Each of these can also be prayerfully worked on as you develop your wealth-creation skills. Solomon said, *"If an ax is dull and its edge unsharpened, more strength is needed, but skill will bring success"* (Ecclesiastes 10:10). You can sharpen your skills and behaviors in a positive way that will help you achieve your goals. You may ask yourself, "Who do I know that has these qualities or attributes?" The next is, what is it that imbues those exemplars with such enviable qualities? How can I adopt such qualities?

Increasing Your Cash Flow Margin
Your goal is to increase your financial net worth from where it is, using different approaches. Let us use the examples of a couple, Richard and Caroline, in the table below.

The first action, after knowing your financial net-worth, is to develop a financial plan with a more efficient and frugal budget, as above. The result is an increased cash flow. For instance, consider Richard and Caroline (fictitious names), whose gross income is only $53,000.

Before their financial plan, they had a negative cash flow of $1,414—their income could not last until the next month. They needed to put more debt on their credit cards or borrow. After the financial plan, they carefully identified where they could cut expenditures. They were able to reduce their charges and taxes slightly. They were committed to paying their full tithe. They were committed to paying their debts off within a year, so they could do investments in the next year. If they used their credit card from that time on, they would pay before the due date, so it did not attract a new interest rate. Otherwise, they will use a debit card or cash. They minimize buying from convenience stores as much as possible.

Their vacation, clothing, transportation, education costs, and expenses on the kids were all reduced. They were determined to stay within their budget and be disciplined. For instance, they reduced dinning out. Their household watchword is frugality. In summary, they have managed to pay their debt of $1,414 and have an extra $8,963 cash flow which they could plan to use for constructive investments after a year. Their cash flow will increase dramatically in year three due to being debt-free and having an increased income. The extra cash flow will be directed to investments, such as real estate, business, or stocks.

Financial Cash flow for Richard and Caroline

Item	Before Planning	After Planning	Action Plan
Annual Income	53,688	53,688	
Less tithe	1500	5,369	Shift from non-tithing to tithing regularly; the tithing should be 10% or more.
All taxes (Income tax and charges)[391]	16,109	14,451	Reduce taxes by paying your taxes, avoiding charges by paying promptly.
All debts ($14,256 at 18%)	0	6000	Plan for debt payment as indicated
Other giving (offering, etc.)	1500	1500	Maintain as it is, but increase later
Net Spendable Income	34,579	31,768	**Consider this as your actual income**

Living Expenses			
Food (monthly)	5200	4500	Reduce eating out; shop for your groceries, avoid convenience shops
Rent (monthly)	17,400	13,500	Reduce rent by moving to a cheaper but convenient house, not too far from work if you take public transport, and to cut down on gas; Plan to buy your home and pay off the mortgage
Clothing	1045	800	Buy value, not brand names; choice of good schools with uniform may reduce clothing needs for kids.
Children's school fees, plus other expenses	5800	5300	Reduce extra costs as much as possible
Transport	2674	1855	Negotiate and pay insurance in advance to reduce interest; if necessary, change your car, or reduce fuel cost with the location of residence.
Vacation and entertainments	3000	1350	Reduce frequency and look for lower costs
Medical Insurance	1600	1600	Non-negotiable except where there are better providers. Most employers deduct directly.
Miscellaneous	1000	500	Reduce general expenses
Total Expenses	**35,993**	**22,805**	
Cash flow[392]	(1414)	8,963	

What is Required to Work Your Financial Plan?

Once you know where you are at present (current net worth) and where you want to be with your future goals (expected net worth), the next step is to design your financial plan (Step 3 above).

1. Desire and be determined to increase your financial net-worth

Transforming your desires to financial freedom requires money, creative thinking, and being bathed in prayer. Since wealth-creation is a mindset, it is important to desire to be financially independent. (Christians may hate to hear that anyone desires to be wealthy, but they are happy to hear "financial freedom" or "debt-free.")

You have to admit; you need to be better off financially. Prepare your heart to be greatly blessed by God as you follow your plan.[393]

2. Make a definite action plan!
Stop dreaming, stop wishing, stop procrastinating and start planning. Make plans that are faultless, but don't wait until you have a perfect plan. Start from where you are.

Be realistic and honest with yourself. The Bible encourages us to commit our ways to the Lord in prayer.[394] Do not just daydream, be proactive in your plans. The Scripture says, *"A man's heart plans his way, but the Lord directs his steps"* (Proverbs 16:9). Make the plans God will decide.[395]

Seek good counsel, but be wise.[396] Prepare yourself for what you need. Abraham Lincoln said, "If I had eight hours to chop down a tree, I'd spend six hours sharpening my ax."[397]

3. Be a Doer
President Dwight D. Eisenhower said, "In preparing for battle, I have always found that plans are useless, but planning is indispensable."[398]

Start implementing your plans with definite actions. Get your act together. Stop planning too much; make firm decisions. To be successful, an investor needs to be able to reach definite decisions quickly and firmly, and change things slowly. Don't be easily influenced by the opinions of everyone else, but listen, act, and talk less.

Chapter 18 Overview
Pathways to Financial Freedom

Ministry Issue
How can a minister generate finances without altering God's plan for his life?

Ministry Lesson
Explore one or a combination the three investment routes.

CHAPTER 18

PATHWAYS TO FINANCIAL FREEDOM

Definite Wealth-Creation Routes

"The investment industry considers the perfect customer to be the one who meekly and gratefully hands over his wallet, asks no questions, and goes away, praying for good luck." [399] President Dwight D. Eisenhower

Larry Julian noted, "Jesus didn't say money or financial success is wrong. There is a greater purpose in our work beyond just making money, whether it is for ourselves or for our corporations."[400]

As a matter of fact, you can't be a generous giver if you have nothing to give. Jesus Himself expects us to be a giver. He said the measure you use—that includes the money you give, spend, and invest—is the measure you will receive back.[401] But you can only give what you have, and God doesn't expect us to give what we do not have. For instance, God doesn't not expects us to go borrow or give off our credit cards when we don't have the money. You can only continue to give when there is a means of replacing what you have spent or used up.

Unless we deliberately teach believers how to make money and manage their finances wisely, they cannot contribute to God's work meaningfully, without complaints. God wants the Kingdom to expand on earth, and it will certainly need money to take cities, nations, and Kingdoms for Christ.

In Paul's letter, he indicated that God could provide the means for us for our own well-being and enough to do His work, plus give to others. We do not always have to depend on others to survive, and ministers do not have to compromise their calling and integrity for the sake of meeting their daily provisions.

The majority of ministers suffer from financial hazards. Recently, Dean Hoge and Jacqueline Wenger published the results of their findings on why Pastors leave the local church ministry.[402]

Among other reasons, finance featured very high. This was for Pastors whose annual income ranged from $31,000 to $46,000—which is considered too low in the United States, but a fortune in most parts of the world. Recent data also corroborates this fact as we have already seen in the earlier chapter.

But must this be so in the Kingdom? Are ministers superhuman, and do they not have a right to the essentials of life? Like Paul, don't ministry leaders and Christian workers have a right to food and drink, and can't we have a family in the ministry?[403]

Are spouses of pastors, ministry leaders, missionaries, and other Christian workers being unspiritual to expect a reasonable level of the necessities of life? I don't think so.

The solution is to understand the principles of acquiring, using, sustaining, and multiplying God-given money by investing money that has already been earned, either in ministry or in tentmaking.

Get Rid of The Midas Mentality about Money

The vast majority of Christian churches face challenges on how to finance God's work and accomplish His last command. God has the money we need to do His work. Whether it's corporate, individual, or for the local church, every worthwhile way of generating finances must answer the following questions: purpose or rationale (why), importance (what), urgency (when), and action (how).

Why do you need to have money or attain financial freedom?

Assuming money is not an object, what are your desires or ambition in your life and ministry? If God endows you with more than enough finances, what will you do with the money? Do you have the Great Commission in mind, or is it just for your lustful pleasures? James says it is the reason many who want to have money never get what they need—because of their wrong motives, *"When you ask you do not receive, because you ask with wrong motives, that you may spend what you get on your pleasures"* (James 4:3). Again, I must say that if that is your attitude, then you need to change and get your priorities right and in order.

What importance do you attach to money?
What is money to you? Our attitude must be like those of God's friends who had the money and were sold out to His work and purpose. David was one of the richest kings of his time, and he saved up his entire wealth just to build the Temple of God. Just imagine the huge treasures of gold and silver that David had personally provided for God.[404]

The people gave because he himself was a giver and had given generously. This was David's mindset to money, *"Wealth and honor come from You; You are the ruler of all things."* He believed whatever he had or gave belonged to the Lord; it was one and the same—He was ready to use God's money for God's business. That should be our mindset in the Kingdom, also. Daniel was wealthy, yet he would not forsake his integrity and spirituality. He prayed and fasted to his God three times a day, even when it became a threat to his life.[405]

How urgently do you need money?
Can your financial plan wait for 2, 5, 15, 20, 30, 40, or more years? If your situation doesn't change during this period, what would happen? What and who would suffer because of your financial lack?

Now turn the question around: supposing things work out for you in those years, what will improve? How many lives will that touch, save, or affect positively? How many souls can be won to the Lord? How long can they wait for you? How determined are your decisions to make money? What are your goals? What actions do you want to put into place to make your goals happen? The choices are yours, and how best and sincere you answer these questions will determine how you achieve your dream. Let your plans, actions, and decisions be anchored on your goals.

The great Bible teacher, Rev. Kenneth E. Hagin, in his book, "The Midas Touch," told the story of how many Christians behave when they want to acquire money.[406]

Let me paraphrase the story as follows (emphasis mine):

According to Greek Mythology, King Midas lived in Phrygia in 8 BC. Midas was very rich, but he was not satisfied with his wealth, and he wanted more gold. He spent most of his time counting and storing his gold. One day, a stranger (possibly it was an angelic demon) visited him and asked him for his wish—only one. He requested that he wanted whatever he touched to turn to gold. His wish was granted, and Midas had the mysterious power to turn things into gold.

He woke up to find his bed and cover cloth had become gold. He touched the wall, it turned to gold, and he went to touch almost everything he could see within his sight, dancing—they all turned to gold. As he was about to eat his food, the plates, spoons, and the food itself all became gold. He danced to the garden and turned all the fruit trees and vegetables to gold. The rock turned to gold. He was so happy; his house, his robes, shoes, and turban were glittering. Finally, as he returned home, his only daughter was just awake and came out to embrace him, and she turned into a golden statue. His wife became gold. He got more than he bargained for. He had to go beg the angelic demon to restore his family back to him. He didn't want the power or gold anymore. It is only God's wealth that doesn't bring sorrow! (Proverbs 10:22)

Many believers behave like Midas. They want every 'man of God' to lay his hand on them so they can prosper and be wealthy. They take their envelopes to "Anointed Debt-Cancelers" to burn them and 'cancel' their debt by the laying on of hands, so they could find a miraculous way of making their debt payments. Show me one Scripture where anyone had ever laid hands on envelopes to have debts canceled. You can spend the whole night searching; you won't find one. Not a single one. If that was possible, Elisha could have made it a lot easier for the poor widow—so she wouldn't need to borrow vessels, multiply her oil, and trade to pay her debts.[407] The 'name it and claim it' to create unlimited wealth is a magical path of financial freedom. The envelope burning ritual is unbiblical. It can only further enslave and bring disappointment. No matter how they keep on naming and claiming everything in sight, they have not been able to possess anything yet. The only beneficiary is the preacher, who deceives them to enrich himself further.

Secret 1: You must master wise ways of acquiring money

Many people come out of investments with casualties, and some are ruined, simply as the Bible says, *"My people perish for lack of knowledge"* (Hosea 4:6). Understanding and mastering investment routes that best suit you are crucial. Learning how to manage your investments, and maneuvering your way through thick and thin in financial cycles, has no substitute. You cannot attain financial success without acquiring this knowledge. If you have read this book this far, then you are already acquiring knowledge, and more will come as you read further.

Secret 2: There is no best investment route

Just open any newspaper in the last five years, and you get the most discouraging hype on investment possibilities: the global economic meltdown, bringing down longstanding financial investment empires,' federal debt, inflation, capital market volatility and 'bubbles, and business woes. These are enough reasons to keep your money under the pillow or at least in a locked safety box underground. Now the Covid-19 pandemic has complicated the situation for many aspiring investors.

I have read several books on investment, and have noticed that there is a general tendency to present one investment route as superior to others, mostly due to the areas each so-called investment guru, millionaire, or expert was more knowledgeable in—their 'comfort zone'; but I think that is a misleading approach. For instance, a real estate guru would often put down stocks, put down businesses, put down insurance, and vice versa. Stock gurus would consider real-estate as a money-tying investment effort; they often tend to exaggerate the 'real estate bubble' and state that investing in bonds, certificates of deposit, or insurance vehicles is a waste of time. Commodity market investors would argue against the volatility of stock and cryptocurrencies.[408] And the list goes on. These faulty advisors often leave the newcomer in more confusion with narrow options.

No investment route is superior to another, whether it's real estate, businesses or financial capital market. All that matters is understanding the area of investment before dabbling into it. You don't need to be a guru to make money in any investment area; however, you do need to understand the key principles that control the profits and losses and how to turn them to your advantage. Also, we must teach that diversification wins, most of the time when it's done with knowledge.

The richest folks in the world are entrepreneurs—businessmen and women, but that doesn't mean they can assert that business alone is superior to other investment routes. Most investors actually combine different routes to accumulate wealth. Yet it is not everyone who is cut out for every investment route, and some are more gifted or have the time, the heart, and energy, and are able to take risks for certain investment routes than others. The important thing is to know which area you want to explore to grow your income. I will endeavor to provide you with a cocktail of available options.

Secret 3: Explore all available opportunities where you reside
On 'Why the United States of America is so Rich,' T.C.A. Srinivasa-

Raghavan said, "From time to time, everyone wonders why America is so rich. Mostly, the reasons are traced to its spirit of competition, attitude to risk, and its ability to pursue innovation with almost demoniac zeal. In the end, however, how rich anyone is—individual, company, or country—depends on how well the resources at hand are used. Endowments play a role, but it is how you use them that eventually decides the outcome."[409] An article in The Economist also alluded to the "economic freedom and business optimism" as important factors.[410] In that article, Karl Smith pinned them down to a combination of three factors: i) The Common Law, ii) The Massive Immigration, and iii) The Great Scientific Exodus during World War II. What opportunities do you have where you live?

To be financially successful, it is important to understand the available opportunity in your country and the place you live. If you are going to invest in a business, the nearer it is to you, the better. Despite the digital and electronic technology, there are still limitations to being far away from where you have invested your money. Opportunities for making money often open within a short time. Sometimes, it requires making a good assessment before making the final decision. You can't buy a property or business you have not seen and then think you have made a good decision.

Timeless Financial Wealth-Building Strategies
Wealth is a relative term. It measures the value of all the assets of worth owned by a person. According to AnthonyRobins, there are three paths of wealth, and he advised that money be allocated to these three buckets: i) Financial security, ii) Financial independence, and iii) Financial freedom. Let me explain these.

> **Financial security:** All investments that are directed toward the future security of the family. This involves ensuring that the investment money is not lost. Insurance, pension, and buying a

home as an asset are considered financial security. Such money is normally in less risk or risk-free investments.

Financial independence: Financial independence starts when you are living free of debts or financial commitments. This includes paying off your mortgages, education, health costs, and livelihood, etc.

Financial freedom: Investment made to create profits. This is growth investment, such as those in stocks, real estate, and growth businesses. According to Tony Robbins, this bucket is for enjoying your life, e.g., vacation, etc.

I will come back to a proper guide to financial allocation for Christians in the next chapter.

The Concept of Income Streams

To understand this concept, just imagine what a *tributary* is. It is a stream flowing to a larger stream, river, or lake. The ocean is replenished because of many sources of water that flow into it. When a water pool is not replenished, it dries up. When the streams and brooks dry up, the larger water bodies such as the lakes, rivers, and even the sea, also recede in their levels. The Dead Sea is dead because living waters don't flow into and out of it—living waters do not dry up; when they flow, the water will become refreshed.[411] Incomes need to be replenished, or they will be exhausted. They must also be used wisely. Unless money flows in and out of your account you cannot achieve financial success.

The reason folks are broke before the end of the month is not only because their limited income is being spent, but it is not being replenished through investment inflow. Have you ever seen a dam overflowing above its abutment or threshold? It is because it is receiving more water than can flow out of it. The more volume and speed of the waters that are flowing into the pool, the easier it will overflow. Likewise, money can flow into your income pool at an accelerated rate, replenishing more than you can reasonably spend once you learn how to create diverse income streams for yourself.

Diversify your income inflow by generating income from multiple streams (diverse sources of income flow). In the miracle of multiplying the fish, Jesus demonstrated a powerful principle: bread and fish went out from the basket, and they were being replaced back at a rate that was more than the disciples took out and could distribute. They gathered 12 full baskets as leftovers after 5,000 people had eaten and were full.[412] The reason they had an excess of 12 baskets as left-overs was because the inflow was more than the outflow—the receiving was more than the giving out; otherwise, they would have only had five small barley loaves of bread and two small fish the entire time.[413]

The hand that gives out is normally wider than the one that receives. Unless money flows in at a rate that is higher than it is spent, there will be debt. The replacement of what was used or spent is normal, but bringing the replacements at a rate that is higher than what was spent is the key to getting out of debt and achieving financial success.

Your motivation in wealth-creation will be to develop and perfect the art of replenishing your income pool or gross profits or earnings from investments at a rate that is much more than you are spending. Generating passive income and active income is the key to winning the money game. Several wealth-creation and investment gurus agree on this.[414]

You need the recurrent income that flows into your account, whether you are physically there or not. Earn enough passive income—whatever you can get on top of your present income—this is your liquidity for wealth creation. This can only come through investment.

Can the money flow without your physical presence?
Now that you understand what I mean by streams of income, the next question to ask yourself is, "Can the money flow to you without your being physically present?" Many folks undertake multiple jobs in order to meet their budgets. That is not what we are talking about here. That is not a healthy strategy for financial freedom. It is not about meeting budgets but having a surplus to invest in, in order to make more money. There are two forms of income: Active and passive.

Active income—is income you earn through your hard work. This comes to you as compensation for your services when you are physically present at work. Your prolonged physical absence would mean a loss of income if you were paid weekly or paid based on the hours you worked. For some people, just one week off would reduce their income substantially. Your active income is your normal job. For about 18 months, I resigned from my career job and all its benefits and undertook full-time training at the Christ for the Nations (CFNI) in Dallas, United States. I did not just forfeit the monthly income and employment benefits but also had to cover all my own tuition, educational and other related living expenses, and those of my family members in the States, but I still maintained my financial commitments to others and maintained my giving to God's work. I also made passive investments in stock and real estate during this period to create opportunities for passive incomes. All those came outside active income. They were mainly benefits from my previous employment. If the money finished unless I got another job or had earnings from passive income, I would have been in debt.

Passive income—is the income you earn without your physical presence. Rather than your physical presence, it is the presence of your investment money that will work for you. Your passive income is the profits earned from your investments. There are several sources of passive income. We will discuss these under "auto-piloting" your wealth creation.

The key to your financial freedom starts to open the door of wealth as soon your passive income exceeds your active income. The more you grow that difference, the more financially free you become. A Christian worker can increase passive income until the active income is no longer critical for her livelihood and ministry. That is the time to move full-time. That should be your primary goal as a minister. As a Christian, that opens the opportunity for you to participate in funding the Great Commission with ease.

Start from Where You Are
- Stop the blame game: nobody is responsible for your financial predicament, and no one will get you out of it except yourself.
- You are not where you are because you earn too little money. Earning more than you currently earn to meet your needs is not the long-term solution to your financial situation; it is learning how to manage what you are currently earning, so it can earn more money for you. You are there because of your spending habits and negative investing habits. As said earlier, the practice of frugality—reducing expenses—is the first step in obtaining extra money for investments.
- Don't ever procrastinate and say, "I'll start next year." Start now, and start where you are. It is not by mere wish but by action.

Common Systems for Investing
For all ages, basic investment systems are the same, everywhere in the world and throughout the ages. No matter which book you read on financial investments or wealth creation, the principles are the same. As a matter of fact, if they do not include these basic principles in this section, they are incomplete. Now we are talking of principles, not methods. Methods can vary, but principles cannot change. Don't fight principles, but work the methods, so that they can work for you.

So far, you have repeatedly read many of the principles of wealth-creation from the biblical models of Jesus, Joseph, or Solomon. We want to start applying these to modern investment opportunities. George S. Clason stated in his ancient Babylonian Parable of Wealth-Creation, "Lo, money is plentiful for those who understand the simple rule of its acquisition:

1. Start thy purse to fattening;
2. Control thy expenditures,
3. Make thy gold multiply,
4. Guard thy treasures from loss,
5. Make thy dwelling a profitable investment,
6. Insure a future income,
7. Increase thy ability to earn."[415]

To put this into our modern-day English:
i) start to grow your income through investments
ii) reduce your expenditure by spending less than you earn
iii) invest your money (the difference between your income and expenditures, extra savings)
iv) invest wisely to avoid loss
v) buy or build a home as part of your investment
vi) build a future income from your investment,
vii) acquire knowledge to enhance your ability to earn more money.[416]

David Bach puts it in five imperative phrases:
1) Spend less
2) Save more
3) Make more
4) Give more
5) Live more.

As you can see, all of these ideas have been discussed in the previous chapters, one way or the other. Let us put them into perspective and call them *Financial Laws* governing wealth creation, for the purpose of understanding their relative importance.

1. Reduce your expenditure (indirect savings)
2. Save all your extras (savings)
3. Pay your debts (owe no one)
4. Invest your savings in profitable ventures (multiply your money)
5. Plow back your gains (re-invest your profits)
6. Diversify and grow your income portfolio (secure your money and explore different avenues to make more)
7. Invest in the Kingdom
   (give more and excel in financial stewardship)

Before we go into the heart of money-making, we need to first understand our financial goals and how to acquire the start-up investment capital. If you practice the seven rules outlined above, you will be home-free and on dry ground. Moreover, soon you will be swimming in surplus.

In the whole world of money, there are only *three* major ways of becoming wealthy—money systems:[417]

1. Capital market—Financial Investment Instruments: business of investing in stocks, accumulating shares, bonds, money market, certificate of Deposits (CDs); investing or trading in digital or cryptocurrencies, e.g. bitcoin, altcoins, and Exchange Traded Fund (ETFs),[418] commodity market, insurance or other financial products, etc.;
2. Business or entrepreneurship: marketing products, services, or ideas, employment, including digital products;
3. Real estate investment: owning, buying, and selling real estate properties.

Most wealthy people of all ages-from the richest man who has ever lived, the biblical, King Solomon, to the "Richest man in Babylon," Arkad,[419] the richest man in modern times, John D. Rockefeller, and all the current 500 World Billionaires on the Forbes List, have made their money in one or more of these three routes. These are considered the heart of this book.

Although our objective in this book is not to become a multimillionaire or billionaire in the worldly sense, but to be financially endowed with enough money 'Provisions for the Vision.'

The aim is to have plenty more for the worker and the work in the Kingdom (see 2 Corinthians 9:8-11). Yet, the principle of wealth creation is the same, whether you want to make one million, five million, ten million, hundred million, or even billions of dollars.

Don't let the zeros intimidate you or discourage you from investing, but never let the zeros enchant you to do financially or biblically foolish things, either. Start small and focus on your life goals and what God has called you to do.

Chapter 19 Overview
Financial Decision Guide

Ministry Issue
What is the most important decision needed to create and increase your financial flow?

Ministry Lesson
The most important decision is how you allocate, spend and invest your income. The decision guide provided in this chapter consists of five cardinal income allocation boxes. (This is not financial advice)

CHAPTER 19

FINANCIAL DECISION GUIDE

Three of the Five Investment Allocation Guides for Achieving Financial Independence

"Cast your bread upon the waters; after many days, you find it again. Give portions to seven, yes to eight, for you do not know what disaster may come upon the land...He that observes the wind shall not sow, and he that regarded the cloud shall not reap" Ecclesiastes 11:1-2.

No one will attain financial freedom without knowing how to earn, save, spend and invest money wisely. God created mankind and expected us to work for our living. However, human strength has a limit; it gradually wears off until we can no longer work. This is where the saying applies, "The pride of the youth is his strength." To be old and poor is the evidence of having made poor financial decisions at certain stages of life. It means we have missed opportunities to achieve financial freedom for our whole life. However, most people will not admit that, but rather prefer to blame the rich or the government for their situation. That is the coward's choice: blame game. Sometimes, it is due to lack of knowledge on how to harness opportunities until they slip away. Inability to delay gratification is also a culprit to young people's financial predicaments—they do not know how to say no to their self-addictions. Pleasure limits their ability to take control of their situation. It is important to work hard while one is young to avoid having to work harder when we're aging and to ensure that we continue to earn income after our retirement when we do not need to work hard. I do not mean just pension payments, (because it is not everyone that earns pension at old age). I mean when our investment can work in our place and continue to generate income we need. God's Word expects us to leave an estate or financial legacy for our children too. Have you considered that?

Many people think having a good income and a good life is what breakthrough means. What if you lost that job? Would you still be able to live a normal life and function in God's work while you are waiting to get another one, without creating a financial burden or becoming a liability to someone else?

As long as we are still tied to our regular, salaried jobs and unable to break from them without experiencing a financial crisis, we have not yet attained financial independence. If you depend on credit cards or loans to meet your basic needs every month and are in debt, you are in no way financially independent. You are enslaved to your credit card companies or the bank. Financial independence is the threshold where your financial investment has attained a critical mass of capital which generates income that keeps flowing to you, whether you work or not. The point at which your expenses are less than the passive income generated from your investments, without your regular salary, is regarded as the beginning of financial independence. For some, it can reach a point where the income is no longer worth your full-time salary, and you can even live without it. Imagine if you can earn your income without working and can devote more time to what God has placed in your heart. Wouldn't that be something!

Financial independence does not mean you do not have to work; it means you have the freedom to decide how to use your time. You are no longer bound to your job. You can also choose to be self-employed, or work part-time, so you can be in full control of your time. You can use that time for more eternal purposes while your money works for you, with minimum management. This should be the goal of the twenty-first century minister, who wants to do great things for God. If you have achieved financial independence, you are able to give yourself more to God's service or the Great Commission without any fear of losing your job.

We must get our priorities right to allow God to equip us with financial independence. Jesus said, *"For the pagans run after these things, and your Heavenly Father knows that you need them. But seek first His Kingdom and His righteousness, and all these things will be given to you as well."* (Matthew 6:33). God knows you need certain things, but do His will first, and "all these things" will also be given to you. Don't run after them. Of course, I do enjoy a nice vacation once in a while, but I don't make them my financial goals; we must let God give them when and if He wants.

There are three mindsets on money (Table 1).[420] The first is the poverty mindset, which teaches that money is only to be used and spent. Keeping or investing money is evil; give everything away. Nearly 40% of all Christian books on financial stewardship focus on this. It is a fundraising mindset that teaches only on how to give away money and anything else is tantamount to hoarding and mammon worship. This is a poverty mindset. The second mindset is the middle-class mindset, which teaches that money is to be managed and spent so that we have no debt, our budget is met, and we can sustain monthly expenses.

Nearly 55% of Christian books focus on how to manage your money and be debt-free. It is a risk-averse mindset that is happy to be debt-free but will not invest in making more money. The third is the mindset of how to generate and invest money to become a stream with many tributaries that never dry up. This is the mindset that the Church has shunned so far because of fear of worshipping mammon. However, it is the mindset of the wealthy in any society. This is why the Church is struggling with finances, and most are unable to pay their bills. We have either majored in a poverty mindset or a middle-class mindset. We have discouraged Christians and ministers from investment mindset and called them worldly. It is the reason pastors and missionaries are quitting the ministry because they cannot pay their bills.

Table 1. Three money mindsets and classes of Christians

Mindset	Poverty-class (Lower-class)	Spender-class (Middle-class)	Investor-class (Upper-class)
Attitude to money	Money should be spent, used, or given away quickly.	Money should be managed to be debt-free.	Money should be invested to create more money.
Income flow	Daily or weekly wages from labor, or remittance, or from charity.	Salary from jobs, paychecks, honorariums, and fees.	Increases in net worth from investment.
Giving orientation	Widow's mite or nothing to give; expecting to receive.	Commitment to tithes and offerings, plus limited generosity.	Generous financier of churches, ministries, and missionaries.
Residence	Ghetto, slum, and welfare housing.	Apartments and small houses.	Custom house or a villa.
Life focus or obsession	Survival	Debt free	Financial surplus.
Investment priority	None, that's for the rich.	Financial security.	Financial growth and opportunity.
Worldview	Who to help me? Feels financially powerless.	How can I help myself? Feels self-empowered and motivated.	Who can I help? Looks for an opportunity to empower others.
Missionary interest	I need money	I need time	I need someone to send.
Employment level	Jobless to partial employment, underemployment	Fully employed, but no free time.	Self-employed and fully in control of use of time.
Impact	Local people around, e.g., friends or next-door neighbors.	Impacts local and/ or national church.	Impacts nations and the global Church.
Motivation	Prayer, fellowship	Service, teaching	Mission, evangelism, and even charity

If you have a financial net worth of a million dollars today, what will you do with it?

Wisdom in Financial Allocation

Many people fail and get into trouble not because they don't work hard or earn a good income but because of how they have spent their money. The decision on how to spend our income in this book is called '*financial allocation.*' Most people are unable to attain financial freedom because of the wrong financial decisions. You must remember the money you need to achieve your financial freedom will not come like a lottery, but from the income you are already earning. You need skills to allocate your income.

In this chapter, I want to teach you three of the five ways to allocate your income to achieve financial freedom as a believer. I want you to consider these five golden boxes as your *financial decision boxes* where you must allocate your income or investment capital on a regular basis. Here you will have to determine what percentage or fraction of your income you will allocate to each financial decision box yourself. The figures given are only suggestions, and you can use any rate or figure suitable to your situation.

Let us call these our five imaginary **Income Allocation Boxes** (IAB). The IAB financial decision guide consists of five cardinal income allocation boxes as follows:

Wealth Box 1. Financial Covenant
(Investment that is Heavenly-focused)

Wealth Box 2. Financial Obligations
(Investment that is Family and the Society-focused)

Wealth Box 3. Financial Security
(Investment that is Security-focused)

Wealth Box 4. Financial Growth
(Investment that is Growth-focused)

Wealth Box 5. Financial Opportunities
(Investment that is Opportunity-focused)

Wealth Box 1. Financial Covenant
The first rule is: *Pay God first.* Some investment gurus generally teach that after taxes, the first action is to "Pay yourself first." That teaching implies that if nothing is left, we must first satisfy our needs before considering any other thing or person. This is wrong for a believer, and I disagree with this from a biblical standpoint. Our first priority is to God. After we have received our income, we must first honor God.[421] God wants the first part, not the last, or if there is a remainder. It is recommended to allocate at least 10-15 percent of your income to this crucial Wealth Box. This rate is not a biblical command, but I take the liberty of suggesting a reasonable rate to start with to be a good steward to Jesus.

The beginning of every God-given wealth that leads to prosperity and financial freedom is when it operates within a covenant with God. I don't mean a legalistic requirement here but implying that we must first acknowledge God as the Giver and our Creator. Governments say they own you when their tax is automatically deducted, even before you get your check. Yet, if God owns us, then we must set aside the first priority portion to God. Don't postpone your tithing, but give it to your local church and not some charity cause. We will discuss tithing later in this book.

We must know that divine wealth-creation is 95% God and 5% effort, regardless of what formula we apply—it is God who gives the power to make wealth.[422] King Solomon received the anointing and power to make wealth, but he did not get blank checks. He worked God's plans for wealth, and it worked for him. God certainly wants all His children to prosper and escape poverty.[423] The Psalmist said, *"Blessed are all who fear the Lord, who walks in His ways. You will eat the fruit of your labor; blessings and prosperity will be yours"* (Psalms 128:1-2). He delights in the prosperity of His saints. His plan is not for us to live from hand to mouth, but He wants us to live and spend our days in prosperity.[424] He wants us to prosper in our body, soul, and our spirit.[425] That includes material or financial prosperity.

The only way to start unlocking the keys to a breakthrough is by giving back a voluntary, covenanted portion to God. In the Old Testament, this was known as mandatory *tithing* or ten percent of all your income. In Old Testament times, through tithing and offerings, God made a financial covenant between Himself and the Jewish people. If they fulfilled their part, He would bless them and prosper them beyond their expectation and watch over their income source.[426]

Although we are not required to obey the Law of Moses on tithing, in the New Testament, Paul did imply that we need to give generously, willingly, and a proportionate amount of our income so that we could excel in the grace of giving.[427] This means Paul probably expected more than ten percent here, which was the minimum under the Old Testament, but under grace, surely it should be more.

The Lord told the Pharisees to continue paying tithe and never stop doing so because it is good. *"Woe unto you, scribes and Pharisees, hypocrites! for ye pay tithe of mint and anise and cummin, and have omitted the weightier matters of the law, judgment, mercy, and faith: these ought ye to have done, and not to leave the other undone"* (Matthew 23:23).

When folks want to give an excuse for not paying a tithe, they like to quote Matthew 23:23. They are quick to talk about the rebuke of Jesus on their neglect of the *"weightier matter of the law."* They forgot the last part of Jesus' statement, which is equally important. *"These ought ye to have done, and not to leave the other undone."* Jesus only condemned the arrogant attitude of those who pay tithe yet disobey more important aspects of God's Word.

Let me paraphrase what Jesus was saying here:

You have done well by paying your tithes faithfully, but you have failed in other matters of the law that are more important—you are paying tithes, but you practice injustice, you have no mercy, and you are unfaithful and lack faith in God. You must keep paying your tithe faithfully and never stop doing so [because it pleases God]. But while you pay your tithe, you must obey the other more important laws of God on judgment, mercy, and faith.

Does that excuse us from paying tithes? Not at all, but manipulators and revisionists on tithing want you to believe that. Jesus also taught that our financial blessing by God is tied to giving.[428] This operates on the law of sowing and reaping.[429] Many folks have continually violated this covenant and failed to reach a financial breakthrough for this reason.[430] They put their money in pockets with large holes and their investment leaks like a broken cistern. Failing to give may stop your financial flow and usher in a financial decline.[431] It can close the door of Abrahamic blessing that we inherit through Christ.

When we obey the command of Jesus to give,[432] we are not obeying Mosaic Law but acknowledging that God is our Source. He has promised His blessings, His protection of our blessings by rebuking the devourer for our sake, and financial overflow by opening His windows of Heaven.[433] In New Testament times, regularly giving an amount of at least ten percent or more constitutes an investment in Heaven, and this yields dividends that connect us to financial breakthrough.[434]

Remember that the tithe is not the same as portions of money given for charity, as many financial gurus wrongly teach. A tithe is strictly defined as giving 10% of your income to God—through church leaders for God's work and in His house. Rather, for New Testament believers, the *tithe* is not commanded as a mandatory requirement. It should be seen as a gracious minimum, not to be given by compulsion of law, but by the grace of giving, and we are encouraged to excel.[435] The Law came through Moses, but grace and truth came through Christ.[436]

Personally, since the day I made up my mind to be faithful in my tithing and offerings to the Lord, the Lord never let me lack. I had actually added an increasing rate of financial commitment on top of my tithe as a token of my consecration for nearly 15 years, yet I have had enough to eat, to give, and to invest, both for my family and for the Kingdom.[437]

Although, as my children grew up and with high school fees for International Schools in Rome, and the cost of University education in both the United Kingdom and the United States, extra generosity beyond tithe and offerings reduced, yet we still tithe, give offerings and give to others. It has become a natural thing to us. When we give beyond normal tithes and offerings, it is an expression of gratitude to God, and always, the Lord reciprocates in allowing finances to flow. In difficult financial situations, He always makes a way.

The Lord called me to the ministry shortly after I moved to Brazil in 1997. In 1999, when my income was reduced by half there, firstly due to inflation to the local currency, the exchange rate had been reduced by half—from 1:1 to 1:2, *dollar* to *real*. Secondly, one of my two legitimate income sources had just stopped because the research Foundation was closed down by the state government. Until then, I was receiving a legitimate double salary both as a visiting professor at the host university and also as a visiting scientist by the State Research Foundation. It was an arrangement to attract expatriates as senior members of faculty to the MSc in Agroecology Program. My salary and savings lost value rapidly, so I was worried about my financial situation. It was then the Lord showed me He was giving me a new job with an International Research Organization (a dream job for my career), as shared earlier. The Lord specifically told me the name of the Employer and where it was based, and how many years I would spend there. it happened exactly as the Lord had revealed.

Therefore I was absolutely sure the Lord was sending me to Malawi as a bi-vocational minister. I kept checking the websites of my prospective employer regularly until the job was advertised. Within six months, it was advertised. Excited, I called to my wife, "Honey, come and see my job. It has been advertised." She came and said, "Yes, it is our job!" We took God's world seriously—*"God who gives life to the dead and calls things that are not as though were"* (Romans 4:17b, NIV). Paul said, *"It is written: "I believed; therefore I have spoken." Since we have that same spirit of faith, we also believe and therefore speak"* (2 Corinthians 4:13). Then I submitted my application online.

Sometime in September 1999, as I was getting ready to travel to the countryside to attend a one-week workshop with an NGO, as a resource person, the Lord spoke about the job.

"Someone named Samuel is looking for your fax address in Nairobi, Kenya," The Lord said. (Referring to the headquarters of my employer organization at the time where the interview was to take place).

Then I replied, "Lord, why is Samuel looking for my fax address in… (name of employer organization, and city), when I am here in Brazil?"

The Lord said, "Will I allow my son to suffer?" I was hired for this lucrative international job despite much competition. Within months, I was netting more than double my income from the previous job. I got an increase of about 20% of my monthly base salary just within two months on the job. God can search out a job or business opportunity for you and secure it by His mighty power.

If you want to attain financial freedom, then start by being faithful in your giving to God. Many people fail in this area because they consider everything as their money. If you acknowledge God, He will not let you suffer.

Wealth Box 2. Financial Personal Obligations
The second rule is: *Pay yourself second*. Allow yourself to spend. Depending on your income, 20-60% is appropriate. Money should

be allocated to meet your personal and family needs. Everyone has some form of personal financial obligation. It is needed for paying your mandatory levies, school bills for your children; paying your rent, automobile maintenance, mortgage, or loan financing (if applicable), utilities, medical, other bills, groceries; providing for your family and your other dependents, helping others, etc., are all personal financial obligations.

In reality, this is where a larger amount of most people's income is allocated. The higher the percentage you allocate here, the less money there will remain for your investments, and the more difficult it will be for you to achieve financial freedom. Your goal is to get to a point when this component is less than half of your income. The greater your income, the less this proportion should be. Most poor people spend more than 80% of their income on groceries (food-related), shelter (rent), and transportation. In developing countries, a large segment of society earns less than a dollar a day; thereby, spending nearly 100% on food and the basic necessities of life. Even if that is where you are at present, all hope is not lost on financial breakthrough if you can follow through in reading this book.

Your goal is to gradually decrease the percentage of your income that goes to personal obligations and increase the extra investment. If your goal is just to have enough to eat, wear good clothes, have a nice car and a good house, and be happy, your goal is small. Kingdom dreams are a lot bigger and take you out of yourself and into a place where you wish to help others. Money brings friends, gives a voice, and helps solve problems other than your own. Most marriages break up because folks are trying to save all their income or allocate them to the wrong things in the name of 'investing.' Investments should not destroy your family or your children's education. Investing is better when there is an agreement between couples on the allocation proportions. Also, never try to make investments at the expense of not giving to God (Rule #1 above). If you do, the investment will not bring expected returns.

Wealth Box 3. Financial security

The third rule is: *Protect your invested or seed money.* You must try to allocate money for both financial securities and growth investments, if you are to achieve financial freedom. Lock up a small part of your income in the Financial Security Wealth Box 3—saving for the future or for a longer-term, secured, and more stable growth investment instrument. It is called security because the risk is low or zero. Don't keep this money in the house. That's a risk. Keep it where your access is limited by the procedure you need to get it out, such as savings account, CD, money market, bond or mutual fund. Financial security is very useful in times of critical need without losing your premium.

Make it a compulsory decision to be an investor. Without investing, you cannot breakthrough, but have savings as well. It doesn't make any sense for you to have millions locked in assets and not have available, ready money in a security account that is not prone to risks. There are those who do not believe in saving. It is a sub-optimal lifestyle. No matter how small your income is, you can still save part of it. Put all the money for your savings account in this imaginary Wealth Box 3. Your first investment is like golden eggs, and you do not want to lose money from the start. So you have to put your golden eggs in baskets where you can watch over them.

Poverty is just a matter of mindset. The reason I say that is most people spend more because they think they are poor or have a poverty background, and they want to make up for their financial shortcomings by showing off. They buy the most expensive things like wristwatches, jewelry, shoes, clothes, cellphones, and drinks than the wealthy people do. They generally live above their means and are mortgaging their future. One way to ensure there is money for the security box is to start saving 2%, 3%, 5%, 10%, 15%, 20%...etc. of your income depending on your ability. If your income is so low, start investing with just 2%; put that money in the savings account where you do not spend it under any condition. That requires financial discipline, too.

Attempt to increase it to 3%, 5%, 10%...as time goes on. Once the money is substantial, it is advisable to move that money to a Fixed Deposit account, also known as a Certificate of Deposit (CD), and add to it every month. You could use a seven-day CD or money market account for this, as well. The advantage of a financial security investment vehicle is that you do not lose your capital. That is why it is called a Financial Security Box because you want your capital to be secured by all means and yet, receive some small returns on your investment capital, generally less than 5% per annum. It is higher in developing than developed economies. This is the starting point for most people. Do not attempt to put all your first income or your investment capital in more risky investments.

Unfortunately, this is the mistake most people often make. They will get advice to withdraw their money and put it where it will yield more, and they lose their entire investment capital because of inadequate experience. The effect of that loss could be devastating for a starter and may cripple their future interest in investing. Never climb a tree from its top. The excitement of saving itself can motivate you to increase your investment after some time when you know your balance. But don't also make the mistake of keeping large amounts of money into a security account; you will be losing money by doing so—especially through inflation and the opportunity cost of the profit you could have made on alternative investments. The next two boxes—**Financial Growth and Financial Opportunity** are your most practical and indispensable vehicles for financial freedom. Your investment seed money will have to be put to work in Box 4. [Boxes 4 and 5 are detailed in the Bonus Chapters 1-3 in the last section of this book)

Mark Hansen and Roberts Allen showed that saving one dollar a day ($30 a month), if invested in a venture that gives at least 10% returns, will amount to $1 million in 56 years. The number of years required to grow one dollar a day to a million dollars is as follows:

Table 1. Number of years required for the investment of one dollar a day to yield one million dollars.

% Interest	No. of years required to grow investment of $1/day into $1 million[438]	Method of investment
0%	Never	Kept in a Safe
3%	147 years	Savings accounts, Low-yielding CDs
5%	100 years	CD, Money Market, Low-yielding Mutual funds
10%	56 years	Home, Mutual funds, Low-yielding stocks
15%	40 years	Medium-yielding stock when bear market-dominant, Real estate, Business, Insurance
20%	32 years	High yielding stocks, Real estate, Business, Bull market-dominant

Although this seems a lengthy time, you do not need to wait for 30 or 52 years to succeed financially. It is possible to reduce this waiting period to a few months or a few years in today's fast-paced technology-driven investment environment with growth stocks and cryptos that are opening new and unprecedented opportunities. However, it also involves more risks and requires some skills to navigate. You must first master financial security; otherwise, you can lose your investment.

Chapter 20 Overview

The Grace of Giving

Ministry Issue
How can we please God with the way we give and spend our money?

Ministry Lesson
God is interested in our whole life. That includes how we spend our resources. There are four ways of spending money that pleases God, including i) our Heavenly responsibility; ii) family responsibility; neighborhood responsibility; and societal responsibility.

CHAPTER 20

THE GRACE OF GIVING

Giving that Pleases God

"Whoever can be trusted with very little can also be trusted with much, and whoever is dishonest with very little will also be dishonest with much.

So if you have not been trustworthy in handling worldly wealth, who will trust you with true riches?..." Luke 16:10-12.

"Giving is the mother of getting"—Anonymous

One of the common areas of controversy in the Church has been how money should be handled. The way we conduct business when it comes to handling money and fundraising in the Church reveals that the giving practice is mostly based on legalistic doctrines and unbiblical practices, rather than on God's Word and practice in the Old and New Testament. It is an area where the Church today seems to stumble the most, and it certainly deserves more attention.

According to Charles Swindoll, "Legalism is conforming to a code or system of deeds and observations in the power of the flesh, hoping to gain the blessings and favor of God by such acts. Legalism invariably denies the principle of grace and exalts the pride of man."[439] There are those who suggest that there can be no wealthy Christians, and all believers are expected to be paupers. On the one hand, there are those that promote money as indications of acceptance by God. Others are like the Pharisees and believe wealth was God's reward for their strict obedience to the law. They believed that anyone who was poor was under a curse for disobeying the law.

Interestingly, there are believers in today's Church who are worse than the Pharisees. They see the wealthy Christian as being blessed for His faithfulness but see the poor Christian as being punished for unfaithfulness. Those who know the heart of God will know that wealth has little to do with your relationship with God. What is esteemed highly by people are like filthy rags before God. Similarly, God does not hate anyone for having wealth. You do not become less spiritual for having financial means; it all depends on its place in your heart in relation to Jesus. God's Word actually teaches that money in the hand of believers can be a great blessing and that it is God Who gives the ability or power to make wealth.[440] Paul asserted that God wants us to have enough and plenty more, so we can share, and he commanded the rich to be generous.[441] He didn't say the rich will not enter Heaven, but by being humble, doing good, being willing to share, and being generous, they will be able to indirectly transfer their wealth to Heaven, "...*In this, they will 'lay up treasure' for themselves as a firm foundation for the coming age*" (1 Timothy 6:18-19). You must note that those who aren't generous will have nothing in the Heavenly bank account. I am not talking about the amount, but the heart of giving and actually doing it. The poor can be generous.[442] If you are poor and mean, how will you be blessed?

How Does God Expect Us to Spend Money?
The multi-millionaire, John D. Rockefeller (1839-1937), a major philanthropist, said, "Every right implies a responsibility; every opportunity, an obligation, every possession, a duty."[443] Another multi-millionaire and philanthropist, Andrew Carnegie, decided to stop acquiring more money and share what he already had even more. He actually gave away 90% of all he had before he died—liquidated $250 million of business interests (worth over 100 billion in today's money) in 1901 to devote himself to supervising his philanthropy.[444] He said, "That was why I resolved to stop accumulating and begin the infinitely more serious and difficult task of wise distribution."[445]

Now, I am not promoting the political correctness of mandatory philanthropism, although this is not a bad thing. However, it is not all acts of philanthropy that please God unless our heart pleases Him first, and we do it out of genuine love.[446]

Religion can make us think that God hates money and that if any Christian has money, they should just give it all away to charity in order to make God happy. This is simply legalism. Giving all your money away does not improve your relationship with God unless you already have a relationship. If you have a relationship with Him, then the question of giving will not be a problem to you but a blessing. Paul said, "*If I give all I possess to the poor and surrender my body to the flames, and have no love, I gain nothing*" (1 Corinthians 13:3). I will further add that without God, the act of philanthropy is nothing but giving out of pride, guilt, or emotion.

The first and most important part is the giving toward God—which is known as *vertical giving* toward God's Kingdom. We have emphasized this in the chapter on Financial Decision Guide. Vertical giving is important because God owns everything we have. Silver and gold, the earth, and its fullness, they all belong to Him.[447] He is the One Who gives us the power to make wealth. When we obey His commands to give, He has promised that the floodgates of Heaven will be opened and His blessings will be poured out on us immeasurably and beyond our expectation.[448] God also promised that He would rebuke the devourer over our income, life, and health.[449] The blessings aspect is what we should teach believers rather than the curse in Malachi 3. Read these blessings very carefully: "*Bring all the tithes into the storehouse, that there may be food in My house, and try Me now in this,*" Says the LORD *of hosts,* "*If I will not open for you the windows of Heaven and pour out for you such blessing that there will not be room enough to receive it. And I will rebuke the devourer for your sakes, so that he will not destroy the fruit of your ground, nor shall the vine fail to bear fruit for you in the field…*" (Malachi 3:10-12).

Firstly, God says He will open the windows or floodgate of Heaven. That means money will flow to you like a flood. When such blessings are poured out like this, they overflow whatever has been limiting you.

Secondly, God said He would rebuke every devourer for our sake. Many who refuse to tithe, spend the money on channels they cannot explain. They earn, and it is blown away. They kept the money, but it is in a pocket with many holes. Devourers include ill health, disasters, ill luck, and many things that stop progress and wellbeing.

Thirdly, He said, *"And all nations will call you blessed."* That means your blessing is no longer a local one, not just national but worldwide. It is not just about money, but your realm of influence, those who will be blessed through you. That's what Paul meant when he said that your generosity or blessing would lead others to give thanks to God.[450] Have you seen how there is no boundary between the blessings of the Old Testament and the grace of New Testament in giving?

Ten reasons why we give to God
1. Biblical Giving is a Command. Throughout the Scriptures, we are commanded, encouraged, and exhorted to give. God told Moses to command the children of Israel to give cheerfully. Jesus, our Lord, gave the law governing sowing and reaping—it is a command, with a promise: *"Give, and it will be given to you"* (Luke 6:38). The teaching of Jesus is loaded with multiple blessings—materials, finances, and eternal spiritual blessings. That single verse summarizes the need to give and to expect that God will bless us for doing so.

2. Giving honors God. Our first financial responsibility is toward God and His work. It is the reason God incorporated tithing and offerings in the Law. Tithing itself is an all-time God-honoring principle—it always pleases God, even before the Law and after the Law was given. It is an upward giving toward God—that is, investing in the Heavenly bank.[451] Our giving acknowledges God as the Giver and Owner of our wealth.[452] When we give generously and cheerfully, we are honoring God.[453] It is recognition of ownership to God of all we have.[454] That is why giving is commanded.

3. *We give to God to receive more.* Money begets money. We give because we also believe that giving is the mother of getting. Giving brings more money to us.[455] God gives us the power to make wealth. The Bible is full of the principles of sowing and reaping. To reap, you must sow—both materially and spiritually.[456] Paul said those who give generously receive bountifully, and those who give sparingly receive sparingly—what we receive from God always surpasses what we give.[457] When you are a generous giver, you also receive generously from the Lord.[458] You cannot out-give God. A giver is like a funnel that has a larger receiving end and a smaller dispensing channel. Our prayer should be that we will be a conduit or channel through whom God's blessings can flow to others.

4. *We give to advance God's work.* We give to ensure that there is food in God's house. Ministers and those who labor must have the strength and energy to serve God.[459] The Church can support the needy, e.g., an elderly widow.[460]

5. *Giving shows we are responsible.* Every faithful believer gives because we know it is our responsibility to support God's work. An irresponsible person doesn't give. Instead, he depends on others. He goes to church and likes to enjoy all the privileges provided by others. When you pay no tithe but you like to use the church bus, sit on the best seats, enjoy AC or fans, receive newsletters, and eat, you are abusing the church.

You expect your pastors to look nice and preach inspiring messages, yet you don't give. That's immaturity and lack of self-esteem. A proverb says, "Fools can make money, but it takes a wise man to know how to spend it."[461] Moffat also said, "A man's treatment of money is the most decisive test of his character—how he makes it and how he spends it."[462] Be a responsible Christian. There are four ways God expects us to spend God-given money and to use our finances:

First, *Heavenly responsibility*—fulfilling our mandatory giving toward pleasing God, as part of the family of God (Upward);

Second, *family responsibility*—fulfilling our required obligations toward our immediate family and relatives, as part of a family (Inward, central);

Third, *neighborhood responsibility*—fulfilling our obligations to our neighbors, people in contact with us who need help (Peripheral, lateral); and

Fourth, *societal responsibility*—fulfilling our extended obligations to society at large (Outreach).

6. We give as thanksgiving for our income and life. In the Old Testament, God promised that givers would be protected from devourers, plagues, and pests.[463] More importantly, giving brings more wealth and being ungenerous leads to poverty.[464] Scott Morton quoted an ancient poem in England that reflected the understanding of the early nineteenth-century church on tithing, "For lamb, pig, and calf. And other like, Tithe, so as thy cattle the Lord do not strike."[465] Giving protects our income, our life, and possessions.[466] It was the reason God told the Jews to give a half shekel, to protect them from the plague, which is the temple tax that Jesus also paid.[467] In the modern church, some leaders make folks believe that if they do not give or tithe, God is going to strike them with some diseases, or knock down their car, or kill their son. This is a wrong view of God. He is a loving God. Only satan brings evil, not God. God's love is unconditional and unfathomable.[468] In the Old Testament, the temple levy was used to atone for their souls. Our souls have been redeemed once and for all through the blood of the Lamb, so our giving is no longer to redeem our souls but as a thanksgiving unto the Lord. Giving brings more blessings. That means we give to be blessed, not to avoid a curse or evil.

7. We receive the power to eat of our labor. The Bible tells us that God gives the power to enjoy the fruit of our labor.[469] It is the gift of God.[470] God gives grace to givers.[471]

8. We receive power to abound in every good work. There is the grace of giving that follows a giver so that he doesn't lack anything good. In giving and sharing with others.[472] God wants us to excel in giving.[473] It should be a joy to have others share in our blessings. *"When goods increase, they increase also who eat of it."* (Ecclesiastes 5:11). Do you know the joy of being a giver? Paul said the rich in Christ should be taught to… *put their hope in God who richly provides us with everything for our enjoyment. …to do good, to be rich in good deeds, and to be generous and willing to share. In this way they will lay up treasure for themselves as a firm foundation for the coming age, so that they may take hold of the life that is truly life"* (1 Timothy 6:17-19). Givers abound in every good work. It means to prosper and be blessed in all that we do, and unusual blessings accompany us. We are positioned to be blessed everywhere we go and in everything we do—blessed in every way.[474]

9. The act of giving is the character of God Himself. God is the greatest giver. God expected His people to imitate Him, so He can surprise us with His abundance.[475] He expects us to give as a way of testing our obedience. Giving is a command both in the New and Old Testaments. Giving is a grace and attribute of God, and we ought to excel in it.[476]

10. We give to deepen our relationship with God. We do not give to fulfill the law, but we give to deepen our fellowship with God, express our love to Him, and because we expect blessings from Him.[477] By giving, we prove to God that we are good stewards and that we can be trusted with worldly wealth.[478] We give in acknowledgment that God owns everything, and we are only stewards. The financial ownership is transferred to God when we give back to God.[479]

The Law of Giving and Receiving

The Law of Sowing and Reaping is this: "*Give, and it will be given to you, good measure, pressed down, shaken together and running over, will be poured into your lap. For with the measure you use, it will be measured to you*" (Luke 6:38). Righteous giving follows the Law of Sowing and reaping. Let us break it down into its various parts for a proper understanding of this single verse.

> ***Give, and it will be given back to you (reciprocity)***—giving is reciprocal—as you give and you also receive. God does not expect anyone to give without receiving back. When you give, do so with faith and the expectation that God will give back to you. God actually said we could test Him with our giving.[480] Everywhere giving is commanded, receiving is also promised.[481]

> ***Good measure (sufficient or abundant)***—When He gives it back, it is God-sized. God's size is a good measure, and it is a much greater measure than we can think or imagine, according to His Spirit that works in us.[482] His thoughts and plan towards us are always good.[483] When the woman of Zarephath gave to Elijah, God responded by giving her a good measure—that could not be exhausted until the famine years ended. The woman who helped Elisha received a good measure back—God-sized blessings and the days of her barrenness were over within a year. She received her dead son back and also got back her lost estate. She was also deemed righteous.

> ***Pressed down (protected and stable)***—This means to make it more tangible and well protected, so it does not flow away. In order to have more space to receive more until it overflows, it is 'pressed down'. It means the blessings will be tangible and *solid*. This also implies financial security, stability, and assurance.

> ***Shaken together (concrete and integrated)***—When God shakes our blessings together, He is about to pour out more blessings in different forms. The shaking is to create more room and better

quality. There are times our blessings are 'shaken together,' and we don't seem to understand what is happening, but God has a better plan.

Running over (surplus)—This is overflow, and more than enough or expected. David gave us the picture of a surplus abundance when he said, *"You prepare a table before me at the presence of my enemies. You anoint my head with oil; my cup overflows"* (Psalms 23:5). The table refers to food and blessings, and the oil refers to the anointing of the Holy Spirit. Likewise, the flour runs over when it is full. Paul said God would give enough and plenty left over.[484] This is the reason Malachi said there would not be enough room to contain God's blessings.[485]

Men will put in your bosom (placed at your disposal, at your reach)—When God wants to bless someone, He rarely sends angels; He uses people. He gives favors to them, and resources flow to them supernaturally, without having to cry and beg for them. The blessings of God will flow to you and be within your reach. This is a promise of God's special favor.[486]

The same measure you use will be measured back to you. Good measure in God's standard is a generous measure. When we use God-honoring measures to give, God doesn't give back to us what we gave in terms of dollar for dollar, but He gives back what we have used up, according to His will. He replenishes our stock—our storehouse, our income, our purse, our bank account, our investments, as we use them for His glory. When you give to the work of God and spend for your family and for the needy, these things are all in His will, so He gives back everything you have spent in good measure.

By good measure, it means He not only gives back to us what we had given, but based on the measure we had used when we gave. On the one hand, this means the "measure" we "*use*" is *not* just what we gave, but that God will reward our heart of giving with, rather than the amount. What does that money cost you? What measure do you use for your giving—is it a mean and reluctant measure or a generous measure with a cheerful heart? We get back from God in good measure, pressed down, and running over. What measure do we get back from God? It is not arithmetical but multiplicative or even exponential. In other words, everything we have used up for a righteous cause we get back in greater measure because it is an investment, just like sowing seed. Some returns are 30-fold, some 60-fold, and some 100-fold.[487] Another interpretation is that God will give you back what you have used up as a giver—including your generosity towards His Kingdom in your tithes, offerings, donations (or even the pledges or vows to Him when you keep your part), and what you have spent for all other personal needs and your generosity towards meeting the needs of others. For that return to come back to you, you must first invest or sow into the Kingdom from what you have.

On December 11, 2012, at CFNI in Dallas, I sat under the teaching of the veteran missionary and generous giver Wayne Meyer when he said, "The real value of what you are worth is how you invest day-by-day. If you are living to give, you will always have your needs met." He says he gives every day, and someone said to him, "You can't live like that; you'll be broke." He replied, "I was broke when I started." That's amazing!

What are the Characteristics of the Grace of Giving?
The keywords for free will or liberal giving that Paul advocated are proportionate, willing, voluntary, generous, cheerful, and we are admonished to excel in the grace that abounds in every good work and expression of thanksgiving to God.[488] This can be a fraction, less, more, or even multiples of a tithe, or the whole amount, depending on grace, your relationship, and your heartfelt level of generosity. There is no fixed or mandatory limit to what we can give to God. That is why Paul said, "as we purpose in our heart"—that refers to offering.

- *It is a Heavenly investment.* The first thing we have to know in giving is that it is an investment in Heaven. We can get the dividend here on Earth and in Heaven. How do we get it on earth? I believe that when we are in need, God can look at our Heavenly account, and if there is credit there, we get a withdrawal. Paul alluded to this truth, *"Not that I desire your gifts, what I desire is that more be credited account"* (Philippians 4:17, NIV). Here Paul was not talking about a spiritual matter, but money. There is an account in Heaven where God credits our giving history, and which no moth and rust can destroy, and where thieves do not break in and steal."[489] What does your Heavenly account look like?

- *It is giving that is done by faith, not by our own ability.* The grace of giving implies that the ability to earn and to give was given to us by God beyond our own ability. It is done by faith. It is possible to ask God to give us the grace for giving, so we can give beyond our usual or normal ability. Paul talked about the Macedonian church that gave beyond their ability.[490] This is what Wayne Meyer did when he pledged a huge amount of money that was beyond his income. God gave him the grace to fulfill that promise. I am not teaching that anyone should make a public pledge or vow for an amount they do not have. It is a sin to make a vow and not fulfill it (Ecclesiastes 5:4-5). However, we tell God that if He gave us the ability, we would like to give. If God honors us with the money, we fulfill the pledge; if not, we have not broken any pledge because we didn't have the money anyway. God gives the ability to give. For instance, if you are a giver of coins, like the 'widow's mite,' you know that a widow's mite will not preach the Gospel today. You can ask God to give you the grace of giving, so you can give a certain substantial amount. God doesn't fail the righteous. In 1984, the great evangelist, Oral Roberts, was in need. He and his wife Evelyn sent $22,000 to Freda Lindsay, the CEO and President of Christ For The Nations, with a note as follows:

"Dear Sister Lindsey:

"For many years, Evelyn and I have appreciated Christ For The Nations—and all that God has done from the beginning with Brother Lindsey…We rejoice at the thousands of churches and other works, including the Bible Schools. The purpose of this letter is to plant a seed out of our need…into the 'good soil' of Christ For The Nations…to be the one percent of the cost of the Lindsey Tower dormitory you are purchasing by faith…Our seed is $22,000. We want it to help you…, also we focus this seed for a desired harvest in sending our first Healing Teams to the nations…I ask your prayers that we will be able to fulfill this…our calling."[491]—Oral and Evelyn Roberts

With this gift, Oral and Evelyn Roberts gave out of their own need, and God didn't fail them.

- *It is voluntary, free will and faith giving, not mandatory.* The New Covenant does not require nor expect us to operate legalistically, but as a *free-will* faith giving by grace. Under grace, we willingly decide how much we can give without a grudge, and that will please God. That is what the Bible teaches, and the apostles practiced.

- *It is based on willingness according to what one has.* God accepts our giving, and He doesn't judge us based on what we do not have. Paul said, *"For if the willingness is there, the gift is acceptable according to what one has, not according to what he doesn't have"* (2 Corinthians 8:12). Depending on our level of faith, it is safer to be willing from what we have. The grace of giving is a liberal or free gift.[492]

- *It is a generous gift not to do grudgingly.* Never give any gift that is out of duty to please people. Paul said, *"Each man should give what he has decided in his heart to give, not reluctantly or under compulsion, for God loves a cheerful giver"* (2 Corinthians 8:7).

- *It must be a generous giving.* The grace of giving is not a peanut giving; it has to be generous. Jesus said we will receive back good measure, pressed down, running over. Also, if it will be in our account in Heaven, then it has to be generous. Paul said, *"Remember this: Whoever sows sparingly will also reap sparingly, and whoever sows generously will also reap generously"* (2 Corinthians 8:6). The principle of sowing and reaping is a powerful one. The quality of a seed and its size can determine the vigor and health of the plant. The seed will sprout and grow all by itself. God gives grace to our giving, and it becomes an all by itself harvest. This is what Oral Roberts called "Seed-Faith" giving.[493] The key is to sow in good soil.

- *Lastly, it is something we must excel in doing.* Paul said, *"But just as you excel in everything—in faith, in speech, in knowledge… and in love for us—see that you also excel in this grace of giving"* (2 Corinthians 8:7). If we are to excel in the grace of giving, it means our giving should not only be a lifestyle but should exceed the norm as it relates to our tithes and offerings. It should be the grace of excellence in giving. To excel means giving more than is expected of you. You need to be outstanding as a giver. That was what placed Barnabas apart from the rest of his friends in the Jerusalem church to the extent that he was nicknamed Barnabas by the apostles, meaning "Son of Encouragement."[494] If giving an ordinary 10% is too difficult for you, how can you be an encourager like Barnabas, who gave 100% of the money he made from his property? He did not become poor because he gave it. Giving a tithe and offering and helping the poor will not be an issue to a generous giver. Let us be generous.

Chapter 21 Overview
Tithing in the Modern Church

Ministry Lesson
Should Christians tithe in today's Church when the New Testament is silent about it?

Ministry Solution
Tithing is an all-time valid means of pleasing God and maintaining a relationship with Him—it is a practice that existed before, during, and after the Law. It is part of the larger command of Jesus to give, and greater blessing is available to those who faithfully obey rather than a curse.

CHAPTER 21

TITHING IN THE MODERN CHURCH

Has Tithing Been Abolished in the Church?

"Woe to you, scribes and Pharisees, hypocrites! For you pay tithe of mint and anise and cummin, and have neglected the weightier matters of the law: justice and mercy and faith. These you ought to have done without leaving the others undone" Matthew 23:23.

"I never would have been able to tithe the first million dollars I ever made if I had not tithed my first salary, which was $1.50 per week." John D. Rockefeller

In the Old Testament, the tithes, offerings, "holy things," and voluntary giving by the people of Israel were required in order to support the Priesthood, the Levites, and the poor and for the maintenance of the house of God.[495] Abraham was the first to give a tithe to God on record, based on a vow he had made.[496] Tithe (*teogothian*, in old English) is the act of giving a tenth of one's income to God's work and has been adopted by the Church for hundreds of centuries. This was done by giving it to the Church directly or to a servant of God.[497] Tithing pre-existed the Mosaic Law. It was later introduced as part of God's financial laws to Israel. Levites were not given their own lands for farming because they were to receive the Lord's portion. God commanded that the tithes and offering be brought to the sanctuary so that there may be food in His house.[498] Today, the work of God is beyond the maintenance of the 'Levites and priests,' or just the in-house maintenance of the Temple in Israel. Yet, some Christians still ask whether or not we need to tithe today.

The answer is emphatically yes. Do we have a house of God inside and outside Israel today? Yes, God dwells in the Church—the body of believers. Do we still have priests and Levites today? Believers are royal priests—Jews and Gentiles, and there are those who serve at the altar and have the right to eat from the altar.[499] Giving in the New Testament is even more important with the commission to make disciples of all nations[500] If the Old Testament gave tithes and offerings, and other forms of giving—roughly 20-30%, to support the in-house ministry of the priests and Levites in only one central Jerusalem Temple, the New Testament Church needs more than tithes and offerings to achieve the Great Commission worldwide. This is all the more reason why Christians should give generously. Those who preach the Gospel are expected to eat from the giving of believers in this way.[501] However, leaders should not hoard the resources within the Church, as we see in many non-missional mega-churches today. Church budgeting must be a reflection of the will of God to reach the nations and for helping the poor. God's Word also encourages Christians to do both the giving and the preaching of the Gospel. Our example is Paul, in who I have explained his giving. He was a businessman, a generous giver, and a minister—church planter, preacher, and teacher of the Gospel. This deserves double honor.

Is Tithing a Command for the Church?

The issue of tithing is controversial as some critics are now advocating against tithing. But we must always view everything through the lens of the Scriptures, not by some social media and self-serving and revisionist ministry leaders and theologians trying to re-write the Scriptures.

In a cursory look of the New Testament, we are confronted with a stark reality of an utterly stunning indifference by Jesus and His apostles to the Mosaic Law on tithing, along with other mandatory sacrificial offerings. A deeper study reveals there is a reason for this, and I will come back to that. Although they did not condemn tithing, there was no evidence that they specifically practiced or taught tithing as a requirement for the Church. Jesus did not receive tithes, and He generally shunned anything having to do with asking people for money. One spiritual explanation is because the love of money had corrupted the religious leaders of His day. But that begs the question when we consider the call to evangelize the world.

The apostles were charged with the responsibility to teach the Church what they heard from Jesus or observed Him doing.[502] The Early Church followed His model—the Jerusalem church. Why was it that tithing did not feature in the practices and teachings of Jesus and the apostles? None of the Gospels or the Epistles mentions anything about tithing. The Book of Acts also did not mention the word 'tithe.' If we also take the Epistles, starting from Paul's letters—from Romans to Hebrews, the Epistles of James, Peter, John, and Jude, and the book of prophecy—Revelation, none has any documentation of practice or instruction on tithing. We must also understand the context because if Jesus and His apostles had received or put emphasis on tithing or money, their ministries could have been ruined by the Pharisees in a number of ways. Context matters in all things.

On the other hand, they also did not prevent or teach anyone from paying tithe and offering. They did not teach against tithing. So, why then is the New Testament completely silent on tithing? Does this silence mean they did not endorse tithing, or does it mean it was a norm, so they didn't even have to discuss it? No one seems to have any credible answer that has New Testament backing. But one thing is certain: they did not condemn tithing. Whether they practiced tithing is a different issue, and no one can be really sure. We have to look beyond just what the apostles said, wrote, or did. We need to see the Bible as the whole counsel of God. God is the same, yesterday, today, and forever. If we understand that Jesus existed in the Old Testament, and Abraham, Moses, and David had all enjoyed His presence, we will not have problems with tithing. The tithe is an all-time God-honoring practice.

Some arguments of the critics of tithing—a rebuttal

Anti-tithing movements are rising in the 21st century Church, and their teaching and campaign against tithing are increasingly appealing to folks who do not yet know the importance of gracious and generous giving. The outline here details their main arguments, and the brief explanations are the authors' rebuttal of each. Here are their claims:

i) That majority of Church lives outside Israel today. They believe tithing is irrelevant outside Israel. Tithing is not about Israel; it is about God. Abraham and Jacob paid tithes outside the Promised Land when Israel was not yet a nation, so tithing did not start in Israel. Each time Israel abandoned worship of God and His commandments, including in tithes and offerings, they suffered famines, defeats, and exiles.

ii) That Levitical tribe and priesthood has been discontinued. Critics point to Hebrews 8, claiming that the Levitical Priesthood no longer exists. That negates the promise of God that David will never cease to have Levites minister to Him—a covenant that cannot be broken.[503] The role of tithe to the Levites and the Priests is not about their tribe, but about the need in God's house and worship.[504] The reader should note that the Levitical system will be restored in the Millennium, including the sacrificial system of worship by Israel and the feast of the Tabernacle involving the whole world.[505] Today, the Church has more needs than did the Levites. The absence of tithing has always been replaced by more corrupt practices throughout the Church history.

iii) That there is no central temple anymore. They claim that tithe can only be received in the temple in Jerusalem. But the truth is that tithing existed before there was a temple, and it was never abolished with the Law. If it was, then all types of offering should also have been abolished. If temple worship has been abolished, why did God give in detail another temple design for the Millennium Kingdom era and Levitical system of worship? (Ezekiel 40-48).

iv) That tithing is only required for agricultural produce and not on wages or salary. The Old Testament worshippers paid "tithe of everything"[506]—all their earnings, whether it be produce and livestock for farmers or wages and other holy things. Critiques claim that only a few people in OT paid tithes and that artisans and salary earners did not pay the tithe, which is untrue. It makes no sense that God would have placed the burden of God's house on farmers and not on other workers. Abraham gave "a tithe of everything"—all the plunder, including gold, silver, treasures, and livestock.[507] King Asa took money from the treasures in the temple. That is evidence that money was tithed. Jacob also promised to give "a tithe of everything"—whatever God gave him.[508] David and his chiefs and the people of Israel gave generously toward the construction of God's temple—they gave gold, silver, and other treasures.[509] The people were allowed to give money equivalent to their gifts to God. Besides produce from the fields, the Levites also collected money from the people of Israel.[510]

v) That the poor were not required to tithe. God did not exempt the poor from paying temple tax, and there is no exception on tithing unless one has nothing to give. He actually commanded that no one should come to His presence empty-handed when the males appeared for feasts three times a year.[511] One anti-tithing advocate claims, "Tithing is not required from those who are living on welfare or who are living from their savings."[512] That's incorrect. Someone on welfare receives income, only it is a gift because she did not have to work for it. It is an indirect income. Whether it is small or not is a different thing, but every income qualifies for tithing unless it is a loan. Your savings come only after you have paid tithe on your income, so there is no need to re-tithe.

vi) That tithing is tax and was taken over by the King. Arguing against tithing in the Church, Dr. R.E. Kelly asserted that tithe is a tax and was given to kings.[513] This is clearly a faulty theology. He even cited that David took over the Levites and the tithes and all the contributions they were to receive under the Law.[514] Nothing is farther from the truth. To be clear, God never re-assign the tithing system to the purview of the king. The Lord only warned Israel of the danger of having asked for a king; that king would demand a tenth of their possessions and oppress them.[515] God only granted this as permissive will. That did not apply to righteous kings. King David never took tithes for himself. That would have violated the Law of God. On the contrary, he gave more than tithes of all his possessions and from his plunders of war.[516] He organized the Priests and Levites for the service of God. David separated the royal service from the service of the temple of God and treasury, and in assigning roles to the Levites and the others under a theocratic government system.[517] The same applies to all other righteous kings in Israel, such as Hezekiah and Jehoshaphat.[518] They all gave to God and commanded the people to give tithes.

King Hezekiah gave possessions and commanded the people to give the portion of the priests and Levites. The people gave a tithe of everything, and these were piled up in heaps.[519] King Asa took money and treasures from the temple that his father had dedicated to God.[520] That shows these were not in the royal treasury. They were not for the king. People gave tithes and all types of offerings to the Lord in the days of Nehemiah. Most reformer kings in Israel, such as David, Josiah, Hezekiah, and Jehoshaphat, actually led people back to God and to their commitment to His Law, and that included tithing. As a governor, Nehemiah did the same.[521] Generally, three types of reforms were dominant: (i) the removal of idolatry, (ii) restoration of the tithing system and related offerings and holy things to God to support the Levites and Priests; (iii) restoration of true worship of God. These three are still important in the temple of the New Testament—we are the temples of God.[522] We must remove *mammon* (god of money) from our hearts; we must give cheerfully to God beyond tithing; we must have a heart or gratitude to God and worship.

Three types of tithing were practiced in the Old Testament: firstly, the general tithing that was given annually to the Priests and the Levites, or when they have them as long as they live in the land.[523] Secondly, was a tithe that must be consumed before the Lord annually during the feast of the Tabernacle at a designated place;[524] and the third was given every third year for the widow and the poor.[525] Some argue that these three tithes should be given if the church wants to pay tithes, but that makes no sense. Tithing existed before, during, and after the Law as simply ten percent. The Word of God cannot be broken.

Collecting tithing was not feasible in the early Church

First, it could have been the easiest excuse for the legalistic Pharisees and Sadducees to charge Jesus as an impostor. Remember that Jesus was of the tribe of Judah. He was not a Levite, neither were most of the apostles—Peter, Philip, John, and James, were not Levites. Paul was a Benjamite. That means they were not entitled to receive tithes. Only the priests and Levites, descendants of Aaron, were entitled to receive tithes and the Levitical offerings. Jesus and the apostles could not have legitimately collected tithes without violating the Law or reproaching their ministries at a time when Judaism was the main religion. The eternal priesthood of Jesus was confirmed only after the Law has been changed after His death on the Cross—the New Covenant.[526] Remember that the Jews and their leaders did not accept Him at the time of His ministry and those of the disciples in the early church. Again, context matters. The Scriptures were silent about the tribes of the apostles. Some think they were chosen from each tribe, but that does not hold water because there were brothers like James and John, Peter, and Andrew. Even if any of them was a Levite, he would not be qualified to collect tithes directly. Tithing was a highly centralized system. It was not collected in the Synagogues or churches but only in the temples. That explained why Jesus and the disciples did not cross the red line of the Sanhedrin on tithing. But we are not living in the days of the apostles or the Sanhedrin. We are in the days of gracious worship with our substance in tithes and in offerings.

Second, tithing before the Law was given to a priest or high priest, such as Melchizedek, and to Aaron and his descendants, and for the Levites in the time of the Law. The tithe also was given at the Temple in the time of the Law. So if Jesus or His disciples were now seen to be collecting tithes from people elsewhere outside the Temple and Synagogues, it could have been a major scandal. That was why Jesus and His disciples did not receive tithes. The early church mainly met at the Upper Room, at the Solomon Colonnades in the Temple, and later at members' homes. So collecting tithes in such settings would be odd at the time. Those who want to use the early church as an excuse for not tithing should first think of the context of Jesus and the apostles' ministries. We do not know whether Jesus and His disciples gave tithes, but it is most likely because they also kept part of the Law anyway, including paying the mandatory Temple Tax. Jesus did pay the temple tax.[527] Paul also performed sacrificial rituals to prove that he kept the Law on the advice of James. We can argue that the apostles did not receive tithes but we cannot argue that they did not give tithes. That would be myopic. If they kept the Law including circumcision, then it is likely they paid the tithe without singing about it.[528]

Jesus had a positive view on tithing
If Jesus did not pay the tithe, the Pharisees, Sadducees scribes, and lawyers of the Law could have confronted Him with that question, as they did for other matters of the Law. It is most likely they paid, even though it was not recorded. They could have included that among the allegations they levied against Jesus before the Sanhedrin and Pilate. Instead, they said He taught people not to pay tax to Caesar[529] when He actually said the opposite.[530] "Give to Caesar what is Caesar's and to God what is God's." Jesus actually commended the Pharisees for their faithfulness in paying tithe. In other words, He was telling them to keep their obedience to God in tithing, but to add other deeds they had neglected, such as mercy, faithfulness, and justice.[531]

The Gospels were not supposed to be detailed minutes or records of everything Jesus did and said.[532] It was rather an *aide-memoire* of essential issues which the Holy Spirit wants to document for us. This is to say we must not simply use what the apostles did and didn't do as a yardstick—the context matters. Jesus Himself implied that tithing was an important aspect of the Law, even though it is less than faith, justice, and mercy—so He recommended paying the tithe only when we have obeyed the timeless will of God.

Tithing is timeless will of God. It applies before and after the law. Teaching against tithing on the ground that the New Testament did not practice or teach it is only a half-truth—a half gospel, and counterproductive to the work of the Holy Spirit on earth. We must not forget that the early Church was not centralized, but was based more as home cells—meeting at homes of members, at least for the first three centuries. Collecting tithes in such a setting was not only going to be problematic but would have set the early Christians against the predominantly antagonistic Jewish religion of the time and reproached their mission. So the apostles did not emphasize tithing or make it a requirement for the Church for both technical and legal reasons. This remained so until after the third century.

When did tithing become the main income of the Church?

Throughout the Scriptures—both the Old and New Testaments, we have seen that God expects His people to give back from what he has given to them as an acknowledgment of His provision and that He is the Owner of everything we own on earth and Heaven, including our wealth.[533] Many who argue against tithing have linked it to the Constantine Edict of 313 A.D. and how it has led to many changes in the Church practice and tradition. Scott Morton said, "The lack of teaching about tithes in the first 300 years after Christ is important because it sharply contrasts with many who strongly emphasize tithing today, 2000 years later."[534] Well said, but let us first look at what history tells us.

Historically, tithing seemed to have migrated to religious and civil law beyond Israel as early as 200 A.D.—about 1820 years ago, well before the Constantine Edit of 313 AD. According to Scott Morton, "For 300 years after Jesus, the church fathers did not advocate tithing."[535] According to Morton, Irenaeus (A.D. 120-202) had criticized tithing as being legalistic. However, as the Church spread and became more popular, money was needed. The fact that Irenaeus criticized tithing means it was being practiced in the second century, albeit it was not obligatory. That was well before Constantine's Edit.

As Christianity spread across Europe, tithing became obligatory for adherents. By the 4th century, as the Church became a politically important institution, the tithing system was re-enacted as a "Law of the Church." The prominent Church fathers of that era put their weight behind tithing. It was enforced as a secular law in Europe from the 8th century, and payment attracted ecclesiastical penalties. For example, in A.D. 585, those who failed to tithe in the church were to face ex-communication, and there were cases of imprisonment about half a century later.[536] According to the source, many of those who migrated to America from Europe were fed up with the tithing law and its handling by the church. However, the Colonists themselves reverted to 'compulsory tithing,' realizing it was a good way to finance the church and the clergies. In some nations, tithing was a requirement by Law in 16th and 17th centuries by both Protestants and Catholics.

However, opposition to tithing grew, and it was repelled in France (1789), Italy (1887), Ireland (1871), and it died out in Scotland. Nevertheless, Protestant churches in European countries continued to practice tithing as a voluntary system rather than a legal requirement.[537] In my opinion, the above is important to know, so the church will have a balanced attitude toward tithing and to avoid its abuse. But it is not enough reason to advocate the prohibition of tithing in the 21st century Church.

The New Testament shows that tithing has never been abolished in Scripture; on the contrary, Jesus said the Pharisees should continue to do it as a righteous practice as long as they kept the other weightier matters of the Law. Practices may change, but biblical principles remain unchanged. Jesus and the apostles practiced ministry in a different context to the modern church. Regardless of how we argue it, the reason for tithing far outweighs the argument for free-will giving, without a deliberate tithing. Human souls always want freedom and do not want to take responsibility or sacrifice. Giving is a sacrifice, but there is no crown without the Cross.

Some anti-tithing advocates claim it was introduced in the church after 200-300 A.D. If so, the fact that tithing was resurrected after 200 A.D. is not evidence that it is a bad thing but rather repatriation of a righteous practice that all the righteous people in the Old Testament Scriptures practiced—Abraham, Jacob, and David. Jacob received the blessings from God because he had vowed to God that he would give his tithe.[538] It is a practice that Jesus had endorsed and never criticized. We must not throw out the baby with the bathwater. There must be a good reason the apostles and the Reformation fathers did not protest against tithing. Martin Luther criticized the sale of indulgence as a means of raising income in the Catholic Church, yet he supported tithing in the Church. It is because they knew that it is a major way that the Great Commission can be fulfilled in modern times. Times have changed, but tithing existed before and beyond the Law.

The New Testament took a broader approach of free-will gifts, contributions, or collections, which were not tithes but free will giving—usually more than tithing.[539] The emphasis is more of an inward nature of the heart based on a relationship with God rather than an outward performance of duty or rule. However, if we want to use that model, we must also be prepared to sell all we possess and *"bring it to the apostles' feet"* as they did or give them to the poor as Jesus commanded the young rich man. But we know that is half-gospel.

In the New Testament, one of the reasons we see less emphasis on tithing and mandatory offerings is because giving in New Testament is by grace through faith, with a voluntary and cheerful heart. What that means is that there is no longer a curse anywhere in New Testament for not giving tithes. Jesus has redeemed us from the curse of the Law by becoming a curse for us on the Cross.[540] No one can keep the whole law. Paul said, *"The righteous will live by faith."* The law is not based on faith; on the contrary, *"The man who does these things will live by them"* (Galatians 3:11-12). However, the blessings of voluntarily giving to God's work, whether by tithes and offerings, and/or other substantial contributions to God's work, have continued to be valid for Christians. Jesus came to fulfill the Law but did He fulfill the tithing requirement for us, so we do not have to give? Not really, because tithing is not about imputing or removing sin. Jesus came to die for our sin; He did not die for our tithe or offering. The tithe is not about sin but about maintaining a relationship with God and pleasing Him. It is about receiving a blessing rather than avoiding a curse. Did Jesus die for that? Although Jesus has removed the curse associated with the law of tithing - Malachi 3:8-9. He did not remove the multiple blessings promised to those who give tithes. The reader should read both Scriptures and choose what is better—avoiding a curse (v.8-9) or seeking manifold blessings (v.10-11). If you tithe, you will always get the blessings. It is a promise.

Jesus Himself said it all, *"Give, and it will be given to you. A good measure, pressed down, shaken together, and running over, will be poured into your lap. For with the measure you use, it will be measured to you"* (Luke 6:38). This was superior to just tithing, but a broader giving that attracts exponential blessings of God, in ways that propel a believer to financial freedom and surplus so that we can continue to have enough for ourselves and plenty of extras to share.[541] I strongly believe that tithing pleases God, and it is part of that of the "good measure" reward that Jesus promised givers and the grace of giving that Paul taught. The most important thing to know is that God sees the heart. There are those who like to argue against tithe because they do not like to give more than voluntary offerings—usually less than 5% of their incomes. Ten percent is too high for them. If we are unable to give a tithe, it simply reveals our heart and how much we love money. Then using the New Testament to justify their error is a double guilt and trespass.

Some also argue against tithing because they would like believers to direct their giving to their own personal ministries. They want that money to be given to them freely, outside the church, and unless they condemn tithing, they know that an average Christian knows that a tithe is given in God's house or to Servant of God and not to some websites. There are preachers who have realized that the level of tithing is predictable, and their income may plateau at a low level unless they find ways of raising money. They first take tithes away from the picture, and they gradually find a way of bringing Christians to the Jerusalem church practice where people give all they have. I have heard a preacher say if you give a tithe, you are stingy. They now start to pump up believers' egos to giving 40-60% of their incomes and more. That is unscriptural, and it can lead to Ananias and Sapphira's type of hypocrisy, reluctance, and giving grudgingly. Although we are encouraged to excel in giving, prescribing what we should give apart from tithing is unscriptural. Paul said, *"Each man should give what he has decided in his heart to give, not reluctantly or under compulsion, for God loves a cheerful giver"* (2 Corinthians 8:7). Remember that tithing itself is a proportional giving that depends on your income. If you want to show more generosity, the offering above tithing is where to do so, but it must be done willingly and according to your faith.

Jesus' specific instruction in giving has integrated all the blessings that are superior to those who faithfully give tithes and offerings and other types of giving, including what we give to the poor. It simply remains to decide how you do it. Giving in the New Testament is no longer a matter of duty or law, but the grace of giving or generosity by faith in Jesus. That is, we give tithing, offerings, donations, alms, etc., because we love God as our Father through our salvation in Christ Jesus. He receives it, not as a legalistic sacrifice, but as a sweet-smelling aroma, pleasing to the Lord, which He invariably deposits in our Heavenly account.[542] If you give a tithe because you love Jesus, that is giving by grace because we give it by faith. That is the New Testament attitude to giving.

Jesus said although the Pharisees had paid their tithes—'spices, mint, dill, and cumin'—and had fasted twice a week, they had neglected the more important aspect of the Law, namely justice, mercy, and faithfulness.[543] The Pharisees did not give the tithe by faith; they had no mercy and were not just—they neglected more important aspects of the Law. He actually asserted that just tithing without obedience is insufficient to get them into Heaven. *"For I tell you that unless your righteousness surpasses that of the Pharisees and the teachers of the law, you will certainly not enter the Kingdom of Heaven"* (Matthew 5:20). Likewise, if you give a tithe without obeying God's words, it is of no benefit. But please don't misunderstand me: when we give to God out of faith in Him, when we show mercy to others, especially the poor, and are just, God receives it as a sweet-smelling aroma. It is not that we deserve to give God anything, but because of grace, we are His children, and He is able to give and receive from us graciously. We are acknowledging His ownership of all things that He has given us. That is why Paul said, *"God will meet all your needs according to His glorious riches in Christ Jesus"* (Philippians 4:19).

The Law, Grace, and Tithing
The practice of tithing and offering existed before the Levitical Law, was practiced as part of the Law, and continues to exist after the Law (New Testament). Tithing is an all-time blessing, and it is a gracious giving in the New Testament. Those who gave before, during, and after the Law, knew that it is God who gives the power to make wealth. That is grace.

We are not under any curse for not tithing, but whether it's from the Old or New Covenant, if we do not give generously, we may be preventing blessings from flowing as they ought. Jesus told the Pharisees that tithing was not the most important law but that they ought to keep tithing as guardians of the Law, while they should observe the more important matters of the Law—mercy, justice, and faithfulness.[544] He didn't say they should stop tithing. It is part of the Law that we have retained, just as voluntary offerings! So tithing is not wrong, but we must be careful not to be legalistic about it.

The right position still remains that unless there is a more robust way of funding the Church, the old method of tithing is still good, but giving more than tithing is even better. We must stay with the New and interpret the Old in the light of the latter, and not vice versa. God is pleased with all kinds of giving, but in the New Testament, giving is an act of grace that expresses thanksgiving to the Lord. However, we must not promote tithing as a legalistic requirement but rather as a voluntary and gracious giving by faith to the work of God. All the practices decisions of Jesus and His disciples were based on Old Testament Scriptures—they did not have New Testament Scriptures as we do today. We must not dichotomize or allow a polarizing rift to deprive us of God's blessings promised to faithful givers.

Let me summarize this in the following table below.

Focus	Before the Law (Pre-Mosaic era)	During the Law (Old Testament)	After the Law (New Testament)
Practice Tithing	Tithe and offering as a voluntary expression of gratitude to God	Tithing, offerings, first fruits, restitution, were mandatory requirements to maintain a relationship with God	Cheerful and voluntary giving to God (including tithing and offerings) as an expression of relationship and gratitude to God
Motive for tithing and giving offering	To appease or please God and to be blessed. It is a form of worship.	To please God; so there may be food in the house of God; to be blessed; It is a form of worship.	To please God; to ensure the Great Commission is fulfilled; to be blessed; It is a form of worship and to enjoy fellowship with Him.

Consequence of non-tithing	Neutral effect; but lack of a blessing;	Regarded as a punishable offense attracting an automatic curse as a robber.[545] It was regarded by tithers as a debt payment to the Lord. Appeals to fear of being punished.	Neutral; there is no more a curse,[546] but also no blessing expected. Any form of giving is investing in the Kingdom (Heaven). So non-giving and non-tithing has no reward. It is only evidence of no relationship and no true love of God.
Benefit of tithing	Blessings accrued.[547]	Abundant blessings as rewards and protection of income source and prosperity.[548]	Multiple blessings of Old Testament.[548] and New Testaments.[549]
Who has modeled this in the Scripture?	Abraham;[550] Jacob[551]	All the nation of Israel who obeyed the Law	Pharisees paid tithe, and it was endorsed by Jesus;[552] Barnabas, and all the faithful Christians in the early church who gave all they had paid more than a tithe, and those who continued to obey the Law;[553] many who gave at least 10% of their income in the church age, till today.
Who is the focus of giving?	Focus is the priest. It was voluntary. It existed before Israel.	Focus is the sanctuary, the priest, and Levites. Rights for the priests and Levites. It is limited to the temple and Israel.	Focus is the Great Commission, the Church and the Kingdom work. It is a privilege for Kingdom laborers. Use is voluntary.

In sum, we give tithes and offerings, not because we want to obey the Law, as these existed before and after the Law, but mainly i) to please God; ii) to be blessed, and to ensure the house of God has sufficient resources to fulfill the Great Commission. There is nowhere in the Scriptures where tithing is prohibited or abolished, just as there is nowhere in scripture where it says we should stop honoring God under the New Covenant. The key is faithfulness and attitude of our heart. When you have the right attitude to money, tithing becomes a matter of relationship and gratitude to God rather than the rule. If you have the wrong attitude, you will look for endless reasons why you do not need to tithe.

Notwithstanding, there are four types of tithing in the Bible:

i) Voluntary tithing. The first recorded tithing in the Scriptures was the free will tithe giving by Abraham to Melchizedek, the priest of Salem.[554] He gave it by faith, voluntarily, and out of a deep relationship with God. It was not a mandatory tithe, nor was it required, but a free-will voluntary tithe. Tithing was voluntary before the Law. The Lord integrated it in the Law given through Moses as a mandatory requirement. In the New Testament, it is no more a legalistic requirement but a timeless giving that pleases God. Tithing in the New Testament is voluntary, and it has blessings attached to it. However, it is a righteous expectation for those who know God and have an intimate relationship with Him. Jesus warned the Pharisees (and by extension, His disciples and us) not to neglect paying a tithe while we must also obey the weightier aspects of the law.[555] However, because human nature is generally not to give, the best position is to encourage believers in the whole counsel of God on the subject of giving and receiving money.

David had demonstrated voluntary giving in his provisions for the temple from his own provisions over and above his legalistic requirement of tithes and offerings.[556] What he gave was estimated to be worth $5.9 billion in today's money.[557] David gave it willingly when he said, *"But who am I, and who are my people that we should be able to offer so willingly as this? For all things come from You, and of Your own we have given You"* (1 Chronicles 29:14). That was not just a tenth, but more than that. If David understood voluntary giving above the tithes and offerings, then we should be able to model a better picture in the New Testament Church and know that God expects voluntary and gracious giving of tithes, offerings, and more, not by compulsion.[558] In the New Testament, Barnabas sold his possession and gave everything, and he was described as a good man, yet he never lacked.[559] Many other believers did the same. Whether it is a tithe or offering, voluntary giving that is done by faith comes with joy and peace, and they should come with an expectation that God is pleased.

ii) Vowed tithing. The second form of tithing recorded in the Bible was Jacob's vow to give a tenth of all his income to God on the condition that He brought him back alive.[560] Although this was a voluntary tithe in a way, it was conditional and transactional. It was a vow that had to be fulfilled by Jacob because God fulfilled His part. This type of vow has two parts—God's part and our part. I actually started my tithing experience with a sincere vow in 1996 and said, "Lord, if you will make a way for me to get this job I have applied for, I will not only start tithing, but I will also add X% to my tithe, and increase it as you bless me." Before that time, I had never paid a tithe nor believed it was necessary. A religious Christian Elder had told me much earlier that tithing was not in the Ten Commandments. Today, I know better: that person had no adequate knowledge of the Scriptures.

The Ten Commandments are only a part of God's word, not the whole counsel. Also, if we love God with all our hearts, we should not have a problem with tithing or giving more than tithes. Later the Lord led me to open an account for that extra—over and above tithes and offering, for the purpose of ministry expenses. That account has provided the basis for funding my various ministry expenses directly. Several times, the Lord also has directed me on what to use the money for in the ministry. With that money, the Lord led me to organize crusades, plant and build churches in rural areas, and support ministers and brethren and over the years. I was able to attend ministry-related conferences, travel for preaching commitments and ministry work overseas and nationally, and paid the cost of publishing books without fundraising using that account. Nonetheless, I still covered most of my family expenses at bible college from family income after tithing, except those that related to ministry. The Lord also never disappoints.

This type of vow giving is not arm-twisting—using God's hand to get what we want. It is an acknowledgment that God can do all things, and evidence that it is He Who has elevated us, sustained us, or given us the power to make wealth. For me, it is the relationship that I treasure most, when God can rely on us to address other people's problems or execute His plans and priorities that money could have easily limited without having to ask anyone.

iii) Compulsory tithing. The third form of tithing was mandatory. The law of tithing was instituted by God Himself in the Old Testament times. After the Israelites crossed the Red Sea, God gave them laws and ordinances to follow. This was necessary to direct the Jews back to Him on a regular basis. They did not yet know how to worship the God of their fathers. As part of worship and allegiance to God, He gave them a set of rules and laws to obey. Tithing was one of them. It was compulsory, and the failure to tithe was a sin in the Old Testament.[561] Failure to pay a tithe was tantamount to owing or robbing God—a debt that needed to be dutifully paid. Does it mean that tithing is not compulsory today? Biblically speaking, yes, because it is not a legalistic requirement, but in principle, God still expects us to give our tithes and offering. Tithes still serve the same purpose of providing for God's laborers and keeping food in His house, *"Bring the tithe into the storehouse that there may be food in My house"* (Malachi 3:10). Today, no one is bound to the law to pay a tithe. I don't know of any church that arrests or excommunicates anyone for not tithing today, but we are bound by expectation of obedience and love of God.

Let me assert this: tithing has never been abolished with the Law. It remains valid today as it was before, during, and after the law as a voluntary act of worship and expression of thanksgiving to God. Jesus said He did not come to abolish the Law but to fulfill it. What did He fulfill? It is the sacrificial Levitical system—in place of the blood of pigeons, goats, and bulls, not the tithe and offering to the house of God. Barnabas could have said there was no need to sell his property and bring it to the apostles because he was under grace. However, no one is cursed for failing to give tithes. I believe that whoever gives tithes faithfully will be abundantly blessed by God for the heart of giving, not for obeying a law but as a gracious giving and sweet-smelling aroma. Teaching against tithing is a rebellion against God's will and His righteous timeless principles. There is no biblical argument against tithing anywhere, except those manufactured by those who still need to deal with their heart and attachment to *mammon*. Whoever does not give tithes deprives himself or herself of blessings associated with tithing as well. So, we have a choice—to give tithing and be blessed or not to give and not to be blessed. We have a choice, not compulsion.

iv) Gracious giving—A liberal proportion of monetary gifts to God, regardless of whether it is 'tithes' and 'offerings,' or vows, not based on the law, but based on a voluntary heart and awareness that God is the Giver. This is generous and voluntary giving by grace—that is, by faith. A gracious giver doesn't think in times of legalistic tithes or what she or he gets back but as a voluntary, sweet-smelling, faithful appreciation and thanksgiving to God. The early church Christians had a way of giving that was even more generous than tithing and offering that we are talking about. *"*Unless you are able to give tithe faithfully when your earning is low, you will find excuses for not tithing when your earning is high. This is where many who argue against tithing hide their challenge. Because they have not been able to tithe when they earned small amounts, they see tithing as a big challenge. The Billionaire John D. Rockefeller said, *"I never would have been able to tithe the first million dollars I ever made if I had not* *tithed my first salary, which was $1.5 per week."* It takes a heart of generosity to tithe 100 million or a billion dollars.

Firstly, there were those who gave everything they had in the Jerusalem Church—that's 100%. The grace of giving was taught by Paul extensively.[562] There is not yet a better way of getting believers to give freely today. Neither Jesus nor Paul or any disciple taught against tithing. Without it, the house of God will be empty, so churches need tithes and offering to do the Great Commission to disciple the nations. Without tithing, church planting dwindles, churches will close their doors in many countries, and the Great Commission will be jeopardized. This is why anyone recommending that tithing be terminated in the Church or not to be paid by Christians is doing God a disservice and is not faithful to the Word. However, I want to assert that tithing should not be treated as a legalistic practice. Likewise, we must stop seeing people who don't tithe regularly as sinners or criminals. Instead, we must teach them how to be generous givers and build their faith.

Secondly, the apostle Paul's teaching on "The Grace of Giving," implies that giving should be done in proportion to your income or wealth, generously, cheerfully, and excelling through grace. Tithing itself is a type of proportionate giving—10% of each person's income depends on how much they earn. Government tax is also a proportionate giving according to your earning. If we have no problem giving a proportionate tax to Caesar (Government), then why is it difficult to give to God what is God's? Paul said those who sow sparingly will reap sparingly. How much is sparingly? Jesus used the widow who gave her only coin as an example of how God values our giving—how much it means to you.[563] If we have to excel in giving, we will give tithes faithfully and offerings generously. What we are expected to give is not just a tithe because giving in the New Testament is more than tithing. Even the Old Testament people did not just give a tithe; they gave different types of both mandatory and free-will offerings as well. The Old

Testament gave first fruits, temple tax, and other types of offerings that are no longer practiced or required today.

Tithing should be seen in the Church as an investment in Heaven by faith, rather than paying a debt we owe to God or avoiding a curse from Him. It is rather a pleasant aroma to God.[564]

Regardless of whatever argument anyone may have, tithing is always pleasing to God. Revd. Billy Graham once said, "We have found in our own home that God's blessing upon the nine-tenths, when we tithe, helps it to go farther than the ten-tenths without His blessing." I prefer to get to Heaven, and God tells me that tithing was no longer needed on earth. I will tell Him that "Lord, since I did not see where you have abolished tithing in the Bible, and even if there was, I am glad to have been able to give tithe and offering to express my gratitude and to help carry out your work."

Tithing is not a debt, because there is no reward for paying a debt, except to avoid punishment or a curse, but when we invest in the Kingdom, we reap bountiful harvests of both earthly and Heavenly rewards, as promised by Jesus.[565]

You don't become rich for paying debts. You don't even get a thank you for that. Paul said, "You will be made rich in every way, so that you can be generous on every occasion, and your generosity will result in thanksgiving to God."[566]

Tithing fits well with the local church structure and makes it easy to keep the income flow steady if everyone complies. It is easy to remember and easy to collect. Since the New Testament did not command that we should not tithe, tithing should be seen as pleasing to God. However, we must teach believers the whole counsel of God on giving and present the giving instruction in terms of enjoying the art of giving—aiming to develop a culture of generosity giving rather than religious giving by compulsion.

Chapter 22 Overview
Financial Reforms for the Twenty-First Century Church

Ministry Issue
Why should 95% of Christians sit in the pews without being engaged in the Great Commission?

Ministry Lesson
Leaders must teach believers and Christian workers on the whole counsel of God in finances. We must put money on what is needed. There is need for more financial accountability in the Church. We must inspire believers to participate in the Great Commission.

CHAPTER 22

FINANCIAL REFORMS FOR THE TWENTY-FIRST CENTURY CHURCH

Getting Back On Track With Finances
"But now if you have a purse, take it, and also a bag; and if you don't have a sword, sell your cloak and buy one"
Luke 22:35-36.

"God's gift to me is my potential. My gift back to God is what I do with that potential "[567] John C. Maxwell

The phenomenon of many non-evangelizing Christians spending all their lives sitting on the pew without preaching the Gospel is pathetic. Why? Lack of finance is the major problem. The Christian church has become disfigured and distorted in our desperate attempt to return to its true form and original Gospel, but has done more damage in two areas: firstly, the loss of Spirit power and crucial tool of finances, both vital for fulfilling the great commission. The latter is the key problem at the moment. This is due to historical financial ignorance in the apostolic church; financial abuse in the pre-reformation Church; and the loss of balanced financial theology in the post-reformation era, resulting in cycles of recovery and abuse of finances as one of the principal catalysts for preaching the Gospel in the modern church; and the confusion and corrupt handling of finances in the church history—characterized by the eras of reason, revival, progress, and ideologies that followed.[568]

Christianity is rooted in Jewish history and religion that had existed long before the birth of Jesus Christ. It was He who challenged the clergies of His day, the Pharisees and the Sadducee's teachers of the Law for their financial corruption—greed, hypocrisy, distortion of God's words, and bad theologies on money. They had taught that prosperity was a sign of righteousness and God's favor, while poverty was despised as a generational curse or sin. Jesus Himself did not model an extreme 'austere preacher' nor "wealthy preacher," but He had authority over provisions, just as over nature, the devil, sin, and diseases. He performed miracles on financial and provisions, though not as a norm for living. He taught or gave instructions based on the financial principle in terms of investment wisdom, sacrificial giving, reward on giving, and the role of finances in preaching the Gospel.[569] His enlarged vision and last instruction on money and provisions for world evangelization is contained in Luke 22:35-36 and has been well discussed in this book.

The Jerusalem church never fully understood what Jesus meant by "When you go preaching the Gospel, if you have money and provisions, take it…" Instead, they resorted to a socialistic approach to raising finances—those that have wealth brought it, and those that had properties sold them and brought the proceeds.[570]

Some that violated the practice were severely punished, even by instant death.[571] Nevertheless, this practice was probably necessary at the infant stage of this rapidly growing church, without any deliberate preparation for church planting. The practice led to hypocrisy, corruption and conflicts, and the impoverishment of the Jerusalem church before and after the persecution of Stephen. Later, the Gentile churches had to come to their aid at the time of famine.[572]

Nevertheless, we must know that this pleased the Lord at the time, but it was probably in the realm of His permissive will. The practice could not be sustained, nor can it be modeled by the rapidly growing Gentile church under the ministry of Paul, nor can today's Church consider it a sustainable way of ensuring finances.

On the other hand, the Pauline style of ministry had diversified means of raising finances that seemed to be closer to the Lord's command on the subject than the Jerusalem Church. Paul practiced the whole counsel of God. Support was raised from voluntary offerings among churches, from individual givers through networking, and through earning from bi-vocational work when the opportunity had permitted, and teaching believers not to be idle—to be diligent in their work and see themselves investor givers.[573]

He also enjoyed the generosity of believers and ministers, and did fundraising when the opportunity warranted that.

Following the end of the apostolic era and the first three centuries, the church drastically became so corrupt in theology, power, position, influence, and in attitude to finances.

Let's Return to the Score Board
When footballers know the scoreboard, they spend hours studying the game and devise a detailed game plan for the next match. As the game begins, the game plan is more important than the scoreboard, but the scoreboard increases in importance as the game draws to the finish.

Likewise, today's Christians, Ministry, and Church leaders must start with the scoreboard to know where we are in the Great Commission. What progress have we made, and how do we accomplish the remaining task of global evangelization? What is our winning game plan? What would Jesus do? Indeed, He is amidst us; but how long shall we continue to handcuff His hands in the area of finances? The Church does not want to talk about how to reform this area. The Medieval Church empire era had veiled the Scriptures on disciplined ways of raising finances. The reformation church leaders would rather not discuss finances. The great awakening and revival also despised finances in the extreme; that is, many had embraced the "Adversity Gospel" and celebrated financial misery as a virtue. The modern Church on the other hand, embraces a mix of the "Prosperity-Adversity" and "Consumerism" Gospel, also in their extremes. Currently, there is an unhealthy dichotomy in our theology, rooted mainly in traditions, on the subject of finances for the Gospel, which is generally faulty. The church needs a financial theology reform.

An average Christian, and even a leader, is not literate on the subject of money and likes to spiritualize it or make it a no-go area—for fear of being tagged a "Prosperity Preacher" or the guilt of taking a wrong leap. If we must reform the financial theology, we need a balanced mindset.

Fundamental Lessons on Finances for the Gospel
As Woodrow Wilson said, "We should not only use all the brains we have but all that we can borrow."[574] We must be prepared to learn the wisdom which was stolen from the Bible and repatriate it back to the church to raise needed provisions and finances for the mission. In this book, we have learned great lessons on wealth creation pathways. More importantly, we have studied the teachings, parables, and instructions of Jesus—in particular, Luke 9, 10, and 22, on how to finance the great commission.

Since we have already reviewed these in previous chapters, my purpose at this point is to first to bring us to where we are—the scoreboard, and then chart the way forward on solutions that the church needs. I have come to the conclusion that the Church needs urgent financial reforms to fulfill the Great Commission. Where do we go from here? Here are fundamental points for the Church to consider going forward.

Truth 1. The whole counsel is needed on finances.
The New Testament Gospel, especially the teaching of Jesus about money, is poorly understood and taught by the church. Two extremes are promoted—swinging between "Prosperity Gospel" and "Adversity Gospel," as an 'either-or" attitude among Charismatic and Pentecostal Christians. Neither of these honors God. Each camp considers itself

"radical," but is dominated by faulty and misleading advisors and teachers with non-biblically sound ideas that are rooted in traditions, cultures or sheer religious spirit; but often with hypocritical motives. As a result, an average Christian is uneducated on how to handle finances. The Church needs a shift in mindset and must return to the scoreboard and the word of Jesus and His apostles, especially those of Paul on the subject of money for the Great Commission. We must embrace the whole counsel of God on finances if we must fulfill the great commission.

Truth 2. *The last instruction of Jesus on money must be revisited and applied.*
Obedience to the issue of finances is as important as the command to go and preach the Gospel. Jesus commanded that we take money and provisions if we have them. He implied that He could supply provisions for those who do not have, but Christians would do better if they deliberately invest and manage their money in the service of the Gospel. He commanded those who have talents, provisions, and financial means to take it for preaching the Gospel. Here, bi-vocational ministry, entrepreneurship, and investment, including auto-piloting investments, must be fully harnessed for the Kingdom.

Truth 3. *The church must recognize that money is the single most limiting factor to the Great Commission.*
Evangelism is on the decline in North America and Europe. The support and zeal for mission are declining likewise. In 2012, I was part of a class of the pastoral school of the bible college where people have come from nearly 40 nations. The church planting class was given an assignment in eleven groups. Instructions were given on church planting. Only one of the eleven teams was keen and actually developed a project on Church planting. The rest were "para-church ministries," another Christian word for charity-focused engagement. This interested me, so I started to ask questions from members of each group and discovered that the decisions were influenced by the state of the Church in the United

States of America. To qualify for support from the US Government, which most ministries tap into—and thank God for such opportunity, there are conditions attached in recent times: it must not reflect 'church' terminologies, e.g., church, prayer, pastors, mission, evangelism, etc. As a result, these para-church ministries tend to tailor their activities to what could be eligible for funding by the Government. In other words, a development activity. The dilemma here is that the church is eyeing 'secular' money for doing God's work, even if it alienates us from preaching the Gospel. This needs to change. God's money can and should be used for God's work. And where we must use "Caesar's money," there must be no condition attached.

Truth 4. Missionary support is ridiculously too low, and it receives a low priority or no place in the Church budgets.
Many churches do not prioritize mission in their plan and budget, and this has to change.

The estimated cost of post-9/11 wars has been estimated at over 4 trillion US dollars.[575] Between $1.09 - 1.41 trillion was budgeted in 2012.[576] Over $1 trillion was spent in Afghanistan alone between 2001 to 2020[577], and the cost of an average soldier was about $1 million.

This is not about raising any sentiment on the costs of US troops. Anyone knows it is a life-and-death job, and no amount of pay can compensate for the soldiers' own lives. These are heroes in their right. The real point I want to make is to ask, how much does it take to send a missionary to the field, and how much is really being paid to missionaries? How much do we spend on each soldier of the Cross, especially the missionary in the front-line and fiercest battle against Satan and his 24-hour battle-ready cohorts of demons fighting Christian workers and believers on all fronts and all the time? Think about it.

The monthly cost of a missionary worker ranges from $1,500 for a single person to $5,000 or more for a family, depending on location and lifestyle, ministry type, and other benefits.[578]

How much is the average income actually received by missionaries? Generally, it is less than $100 a month for most missionaries from third-world nationals and $1,000 for developed nations. The majority are actually self-funded—raising finance from retirement benefits, from family, friends, and church supports, and many are volunteers. Paid positions are difficult to come by, especially for developing nations. Giving to missionaries is meager, and irregular and becoming less prioritized by churches. Only a few are fortunate to work and support themselves in the mission field. There is 'giving fatigue' for the Great Commission, in general.

The question is: If the world considers it appropriate to station a soldier in a fierce war zone, how much should be provided for the Kingdom soldiers? The American Church, which is considered the major provider of missionary funds, gives only 2% of its income to foreign missionary work, and that money is largely spent on supporting American missionaries in the field. There is increasingly less motivation to go and preach the Gospel to all nations by most Christians. A large army, supposedly the army of Christ, is sitting in the pew, waiting for finances to be able to go. Some have laid down their armor on the battlefield, and others are just barely hanging on.

With these scenarios, how will the Gospel be heard by everyone? The general apathy in providing the great commission finance should be a concern to every Christian, not just those called into mission or mission-minded Christians. A bigger question is: if you have the money to support missionary work, which agency is really doing God's will out there? How many sending churches do we have, and how strong is the finance? What proportion of the mission fund goes to overheads, and how much goes to the soldier in the field?

Financial reform is needed in the mission-sending sector *per se*. Here is what is needed: the action is not just to wait endlessly for a philanthropist, but for Christians to be financially empowered and be taught how to create God-honoring financial flow and to institute financial ethics and stewardship. For too long, the Church has been on the *asking side*. We need to major on the *giving side* for the purpose of God's work. We need to equip and deploy more troops and supply the needed finances and provisions for these troops whose hearts are inflamed by Jesus' ultimate command—the Great Commission.

Truth 5. *The church must strengthen its theology of work and vocation to create finance.*
All that some Christian leaders can do today is to gang up against the subject of money in all its forms, against earning to do ministry, and against the financial success of believers by demonizing businesses and vocational work as secular and distracting. Worse still, they demonize tithing. That is ludicrous. If all we can tell believers is to give all their money to us or not to give a tithe, but not how they can earn more and be better stewards, we are preparing the Body of Christ for another global famine that will take a toll on Christians and the rest of the world. The famine that hit the Jerusalem church harder than the rest of the churches could be chalked up to their misconception on finances. They claim Jesus didn't want Christians and ministers to work.[579]

Through his effective, self-supporting vocational-based ministry, Paul seems to have proved this to us indirectly to be counterproductive, as has already been discussed at length in this book.

We need to return to the theology of work. Dr. Dallas Willard said, "We have realized that the Bible did not start in Genesis 3, but in Genesis 1. The problem is not sin—work is not the cause of sin."[580] There is a tendency for Christians to view Sunday or Saturday as spiritual and Monday-Friday as secular, yet we are warned not to hold any day sacred. The popular governing view of the church is that those Christians standing in the pulpits (ministers) are spiritual, while those sitting in the pew (members) are secular people who have come to be blessed by the spiritual. This is a long historical background, according to Dr. C. William Pollard, "There is a reason we talk of clergy and laypeople. Both words are extinct from the language. Why is the platform elevated and the congregation at a lower level? It has a historical basis. I don't think it is biblical. The time will come when the pastor will say "Bob and Larry, come up here. We're going to pray for them. They are going to the mission field. Bob is going to start a business, and Larry is going to teach in the public school."[581]

The church paradigm that sees lay and clergy as different and that one is less spiritual is the reason for the current decline in church attendance in the west. Christians think we just come to church to get energized and refreshed by the sermon of the ordained minister, so we let him do his thing on Sunday mornings, and we do ours Monday to Friday. It doesn't bestow responsibility. This negates what William C. Pollard called the priesthood of the believers. Why should a Christian sit in church for 20 years, hear thousands of messages—teaching, preaching, exhortations, songs, seminars, read books but have no testimony of a single conversion witnessed to? The apostles only heard and witnessed Jesus preached, taught, and ministered to the sick and needy for three years. With that, they changed the world.

Most of them were not resource endowed, nor were they adequately educated. It is time we start to encourage and prepare every believer to participate in the Great Commission, not only by writing their checks on Sundays or dropping their money in the tithe and offering bags, but as ministers in the workplace, the marketplace, and across regional, and international frontiers as tentmakers or bi-vocational Christian workers, missionaries and ministers? That is the only way the 90% of churchgoers who do not participate in evangelization can obey the command to make disciples. Remember that the command is for every Christian, not just the apostles. Believers can make the best disciples through workplace ministry in their everyday life. Some of the amazing miracles of healing and deliverance, or financial miracles and spontaneous conversions I have witnessed, are mostly workplace-related.

The marketplace or workplace is the largest place we can reach people with the Gospel of peace and touch lives with the love of Christ, even more than in the churches. Why? The reason is that larger proportions of people do not go to church on Sunday morning, and majorities are non-Christians. However, they all converge at the marketplace.

Os Hillman recently writes in a daily devotional:

"Over 70% of our time is spent in a working environment, yet our training and teaching focuses on areas where we spend much less time. The workplace is the greatest mission field of our day, yet we do not train workplace believers how to effectively integrate their faith into their jobs. The Wall between Sunday and Monday still exists. Most believers do not understand that all of life is spiritual, not just life on Sunday. A recent study found that 50 percent of Christians have never heard a sermon on work. 70% have never been taught the theology of work, and 70% percent have never heard a sermon on vocation. Why do we focus on fringes rather than the center where most people spend most of their time? —the workplace?"[582]

Pastors and leaders who are balanced in the Word of God will not hesitate to appoint and ordain Christians they have once thought were *lay*, as "workplace ministers"—operating as marketplace or workplace apostles, prophets, evangelists, pastors, and teachers. While operating as a bi-vocational minister in Malawi, I used to teach at a "Lunch Hour Fellowship" meeting in an open place at the city center in Lilongwe, founded by a beloved *lay* pastor. The believers came from all directions from corporate offices to hear the 30-minute sermon, and on several occasions, I had an opportunity to teach them daily for a whole week between 12.30-1.00 pm—highly concise messages. I normally went there during my lunch break from my own office as a regional director of a global research organization and always returned to my work afterward.

Dr. Wayne Gruden discussed this intersection of workplace and ministry by explaining seven reasons why God creates us to work: [583]

i) Work gives us the privilege of creating something new—an attribute of God, thus allowing us to imitate God and show His glory in creativity.

ii) The privilege of creating value of things—materials and services in the world. He referred to research on what makes people happy indicates that "Earn success—having responsibility and doing it."

iii) The privilege of supporting oneself. Work gives dignity and independence.

iv) The privilege of enjoying the work of one's hand.

v) Privilege of doing good for one another. According to the speaker, the value of Christians doing business is not just donating money for missions by also doing good for society. I will add that also, ministering at the workplace, through both verbal and non-verbal communication, is a win-win for the Kingdom.

vi) Relational—God wants us to be relational. I believe that we can do a lot more relating at the workplace where we spend 40-60 hours every week than on 2-4 hours weekly meetings.

vii) We work to imitate God. God started the Bible by introducing us to how He had worked. Jesus also said, *"My Father has been working until now, and I have been working"* (John 5:17). God's work didn't stop on Sabbath rest.

Five financial reforms needed

1. The Church and ministry leaders need to teach and promote balanced teaching on the subject of finances. It is time we stopped making believers trust in frivolous "magical prosperity" in the name of anointing. Instead, we must teach them better financial planning, decision-making, and how to earn better and grow their income so they can become better financial stewards.

2. We need to empower and equip ministry leaders and Christian workers on how to create God-honoring income through businesses, tentmaking, investment, and inspire stewardship in handling finances. We must teach believers the theology of work and vocation.

3. Leaders should commit to channeling a significant proportion of church or ministry finances to sending missionaries, undertaking evangelism, and equipping believers for evangelism and mission, and helping the needy in church. Excessive consumerism that is dominating the modern-day church—spending on multi-million-dollar cathedrals, temples and satellites, and private jets and high overheads, can be reduced to finance mission. We must ask ourselves what Jesus would do if He were to be in our Board meeting.

4. Leaders need a high-level forum for discussing and agreeing on biblical ethics and accountability in finance and mainstream it into the entire Christendom. Financial malpractices need to be checked, exposed, and condemned.

5. The global Church needs to better explore and promote 'Missional Christianity and Bi-vocational Model' for mission. The Church needs to promote the Pauline model of bi-vocational ministry, tear down the artificial dichotomy of clergy and lay ministry, and embrace the priesthood of believers. We must inspire believers to do ministry with dignity and passion and to see it as a worthy cause.

Why Christians Should Embrace Financial Reform

- God's Word doesn't despise finance for the Gospel. If God doesn't despise money, and Jesus doesn't despise it, why should we? We only need a balance. We must interpret the Scriptures in the right context and be faithful to His commands.

- Whenever God gives a vision, He also gives provision, but how He does it may be different for each Christian work. One size doesn't fit all. There are those He will sustain by faith-living, financial miracles, and those He will endow with financial investment wisdom to have enough and plenty to give for God's work.

- It is God who gives the power to make wealth. The first trillionaire, King Solomon, was God's idea, not man's. Many close friends of God were men of means. God still has rich friends in church. We must teach them financial stewardship, not to love money, and to learn from their wisdom.

- The advocates of both adversity and prosperity gospels are counterproductive to the cause of Christ. They should consider reconciling their views, return to the Scriptures for guidance, and be faithful to God's word.

- It is a paradox that much of the knowledge used in the corporate business world to create wealth had originated from the Bible. There is no investor who has not used the Biblical investment wisdom of Solomon, Joseph, or Jesus. All of the Forbes List of 500 Billionaires have mined the Bible directly or indirectly to create wealth.

In studying many wealth-related books, materials, and documents, one shocking truth that I encountered is the fact that most of the world-wealthy writers on corporate wealth-making systems are not just unbelievers, but some have hidden occult beliefs behind their writings, including symbols, language that defames God and elevates man, or the god of this world. Some celebrate or hold immoral, blasphemous opinions and unwholesome languages. No wonder Jesus said it is easier for the camel to walk through the eye of the needle than for the rich to enter Heaven. It was the reason James was hard on the rich of this world. As believers, how can we create wealth and not serve mammon, as the world does? That is the hard part that we must master. God needs a wealthy Christian worker with a difference.

Put the Money on Getting the Message Out, Not on the Buildings. Putting the money where it belongs is the greatest challenge facing the twenty-first century church. Oswald Smith lamented that the Christian church had made the greatest mistake in putting money into buildings instead of the message. The Gospel is the power of God, not the building, philosophical entertainments, or musicals. There was no single building at the time of the apostles and early church of the first century, but they touched millions of souls around the Roman world. This is not to suggest that church buildings are not important, but the point is to avoid consumerism, excessiveness, and concentrating the resources to only a few people, buildings, or locations.

John Maxwell asked a very penetrating question: "If you had anything you wanted—unlimited time, unlimited money, unlimited information, unlimited staff—all resources you could ask for, what would you do? Your answer to that question is your dream. Make it worthwhile."[584]

Do you just want to mark time in church or ministry? Do you want to be successful? Or do you want to make a difference in the Kingdom? Make your life count for the Kingdom!

BONUS SECTION

Bonus 1 Overview

Financial Growth and Opportunities

*Last Two of the Five Investment Allocation Guides for
Achieving Financial Independence*

Ministry Issue
What is the most important decision needed to create and increase your financial flow?

Ministry Lesson
How you allocate your income, spend and invest it.

BONUS 1

FINANCIAL GROWTH AND OPPORTUNITIES

Last Two of the Five Investment Allocation Guides for Achieving Financial Independence

"And Hiram sent his men-sailors who knew the sea to serve in the fleet with Solomon's men. They sailed to Ophir and brought back 420 talents of gold, which they delivered to King Solomon" 1 Kings 27-28.

"Where no oxen are, the trough is clean; But much increase comes by the strength of an ox" Proverbs 14:4.

In chapter 19, we have learned about first three of the five Financial Decision Guide, known as the Income Allocation Boxes (IAB) for achieving financial freedom. The five boxes are as follows:

Wealth Box 1. Financial Covenant
(Heavenly-focused investment);

Wealth Box 2. Financial Obligations
(Investment that is Family and the Society-focused);

Wealth Box 3. Financial Security
(Investment that is Security-focused);

Wealth Box 4. Financial Growth
(Investment that is Growth-focused);

Wealth Box 5. Financial Opportunities
(Investment that is Opportunity-focused).

The reader will recall that the first box—Financial Covenant concerns our relationship with God; the second box—financial Obligations, is for ensuring a decent life and meeting our obligations to our family and neighbors, and the third box—financial security, takes care of the rainy day. The last three boxes are the most pertinent for financial freedom, yet they are not obligatory or compulsory, unlike the first two. unlike the first two. The last two boxes—Financial Growth and Financial Obligations, are what make the difference between the rich and the poor. You can hardly attain. You can hardly attain financial surplus or self-sufficiency without them. Most Christians ignore these, and they remain poor.

Wealth Box 4. Financial Growth
Financial growth (Box 4) is the investment vehicle that aims at multiplying your investment capital faster. With low-risk financial security vehicles, you will require decades to multiply your income because the rates are generally low (0.2-5%), but a few months or years can make the difference by using financial growth vehicles—which can earn dramatic returns. The only caveat is that the risk is also as high as the returns. The higher the potential of the return, the higher the potential risk. Never forget that rule. You can lose most or a part of your investment capital if the market turns sour. As I write, the stock market, cryptocurrencies, and commodity markets are reeling in losses. Some important growth stocks, especially tech, cryptos, and ETFs, are down by as much as 20-50% in the last three months. But do not let that scare you. There are safer ways of operating growth investment that I will teach you in the subsequent chapters.In reality, to experienced investors, these fluctuations—hikes and dips, create more opportunities to make a profit. For instance, I have also seen cryptos and stocks gaining 100% to 200% of invested amount in less than two months recently.

As a rule, do not make Wealth Box 4 your *first* or your main investment option until you have enough money to spare for a high-risk growth investment—do not invest money you cannot afford to lose in this Box. In Wealth Box 4, you are now an investor, and you want to go the *extra* mile with your investment capital. Becoming an entrepreneur requires real care and skills. *"A simple man believes everything, but a prudent man gives thought to his steps"* (Proverbs 14:15). Take a portion of your financial security that you have now accumulated, and devote a proportion of your income to this financial growth box.

You will now be splitting your income between the financial security box and the financial growth box in your monthly investments. Never invest in the financial growth when that is all the money you have—diversify your investments. There are generally two types of financial growth investments, depending on the returns and associated risks: 1) Moderately aggressive and 2) Highly aggressive.

Real estate can be a form of aggressive investment, depending on the market economy. Your home in a high-value location can become an investment when you rent it out. Also, there are aggressive business ventures with high risks but high profits, as well. The most phenomenal is the aggressive financial liquid capital market, such as growth stocks and cryptos, and wisdom and knowledge is always needed. We will discuss this in more detail in another chapter on Financial Investment. These three are growth investments: real estate, being an entrepreneur (business), and the stock market. We will devote the next two chapters to these areas and learn how to autopilot your investment.

The returns are indications of the risk, and in both cases, you may lose the capital. The highly aggressive investment is very risky but may also yield exponential growth within the short term. Although the risk is worth taking, many investors have had bad experiences, especially during a period of financial crisis. The poor are afraid of losing money; they do not want to lose anything, and so remain poor. Money-making involves taking a risk. Millionaires lose hundreds of thousands to make millions, while billionaires must lose millions to make their billions. Yet, good investors make their money irrespective of the financial seasons or crises. They see the crises as opportunity. Unfortunately, many investment coaches and gurus, who sell books and tapes and videos on the art of money-making, rarely reveal the real skill required in turning aggressive financial growth into a powerful money machine.

Many quick-fix product sellers will only bait you with how much you could make without telling you the intricacies of investing in the stock market at bad timing. They pump up and appeal to people's low-level emotions of greed by displaying historical performances of popular stocks or cryptocurrencies—100%, 200%, 500%, 1000%, 2000%, even 20,000% of the investment. These are possible, but no one can guarantee a repeat performance. Each of them will claim to be the first to have discovered these stocks ten years ago. They also claim to have names of secret penny stocks or cryptos that will be 5X, 10X, 20X their worth in one year. But these are not guaranteed of future performance. They need your money. Don't believe them; if they know the stocks that will multiply by ten or twenty times, why would they not investment themselves but instead ask for $50 to reveal the secret? If they knew, would they not have hidden them and sell their house or cars to invest in them? Be wise. There is no secret anywhere that will not be known.

They simply advise people to put their money in stocks, as if we must just put out the money and wait for sheer luck. If everyone was just putting their money into aggressive investment vehicles and losing them the way ordinary investors lose, then it would be only by chance that anyone could become millionaires. But far from it, financial markets have principles that govern them. If properly understood, even the uneducated person can make money from the financial growth market. I devoted myself to understanding the principles governing the financial market—stocks, crypto currencies, and commodities trading and investment, and have gained considerable skills and practical illustrations that I would be happy to share in another book in the near future.

Wealth Box 5. Financial Opportunities
Box 5 offers financial opportunities. Many had built their businesses to rely on the 'boom-and-bust,' often time-bound opportunities, but recession caught most businesses unaware, and they faced tough uncertainties that could not be easily maneuvered. Historically, every recession and every uncertain condition in the market—whether real estate, volatile financial capital market, or other investments, often also created unexpected opportunities to make wealth for smart investors, despite their known risks.[585] For instance, the Covid-19 pandemic boosted the Zoom stock to unprecedented levels recently, increasing from $68 on 02 January 2020 to $423 on 02 September 2020. The Covid-19 crisis, especially the lockdown forcing people to telework more, created opportunity in an unexpected manner. It means that an investment of $1000 could have yielded $5220 profit in nine months! That is how aggressive stock in a bull market can be when targeted at the right time, but it is also possible to lose all the investment capital when the market is bearish. A bear market can create opportunities for investment as well. This is where skills are important. Here it is not the amount of money you invest that really matters, but the right investment opportunity—right type and timing.

According to Donald Sull, "Shifting regulations generate unexpected sources of funding; changing consumer preferences create demands for new products and services; distressed competitors may sell their assets cheaply. More than ever, companies need agility—the capability to consistently spot and execute unexpected opportunities before rivals do."[586] This was also detailed in powerful advice to companies on how to survive during turbulent markets. That is how individual investors also must think. But you cannot capture unexpected opportunities if you lack the money to invest at such strategic times and the heart to take a leap into the dark. As many amateur investors withdraw their money from stock in turbulent market times, smart investors see it as the best time to make money—when the stock is low. Your readiness to effectively move fast when opportunities abound and take advantage of them is crucial to turbocharging your wealth-making.

To spot new opportunities, investors must break from their *silos*, reexamine the past opportunities they missed, which others spotted, and reflect on how to avoid that in the future. Wealth-making is not exactly about how much money you invested, but how you invest it and when. It is about how much you make out of your investment. You will maximize these opportunities when you have clearly set your financial goals and priorities. The opportunities that arise in your priorities will signal where to devote your attention at any time. You don't want to be like a hunter who aims at anything that dangles in the bush and fires randomly. The Opportunity Box provides the investment money, but it shouldn't be misapplied if priorities are not right and options are not carefully weighed. To achieve these, limit it to your few best-bet value investment options only.

Imagine that you are sitting with someone on an airplane, and you realize that person has paid half or even a third of what you paid for your ticket to the same destination. One person has made a good choice, and the other hasn't. At any point in time, you will always find that situation with stocks. In a bear market, you will find stocks, cryptos, ETFs, commodities, or real-estate assets that are a fraction of their real value. That is what I consider an opportunity to look for. Sometimes, you are the same person that has bought the overvalued stock at a high cost due to Fear Of Missing Out (FOMO). Another opportunity may present itself when the price drops substantially. If it is a good stock, you now have an opportunity to buy at a lower price to reduce your average cost, and you can repeat that cost averaging as it goes further down until it bounced back. That is called cost-averaging. You will reap the cumulative profit later. Sometimes, it comes back very quickly, and sometimes it takes a longer time. Patience is your best asset. For instance, I have bought shares of a stock that had dropped as much as 42% of its price, and I still made 85% profit within two months. If I had opened a new position instead of simply waiting to recover my loss, when it dropped to 42% of its price, I could have sold this second position at 127% and the first position at 85%.

Many salary earners do not make much profit on their investment because their income is regular. When they have money, so does everyone else, and when they lack, everyone else lacks, too. As a result, they often invest at the wrong time and in the wrong options—those available only when they have received their salary. Prices fluctuate a lot in the business world. For instance, in 2010-2011, for several months, I tried to get the best deals for some financial growth shares and stocks (buying shares at a low price), but by the time my salary came in, the prices were up again. After I bought my stocks, the prices went down. One way a good investor can deal with this is to have a fifth financial Wealth Box to be known as the "Financial Opportunity Box." In general, households that spend less than they earn and invest the difference smartly, by capturing opportunities, often experience financial surplus and become wealthy.

My advice is to allocate certain investment money to this box and only spend it to capture strategic investment opportunities every month or quarter. Opportunity often shows up a few times in a year, for short periods or a few days, and that time could be when you still have 10-15 days to the next payday. Wealthy investors always have available funds to capture rare or strategic opportunities, and that is why they are always richer. Everything works to their advantage. You, too, can operate like them if you have some of your money in this imaginary box. For the stock market, you could keep that money in the security account directly. If such opportunity takes months, you could even put it in a conservative account, e.g., CD or money market, and withdraw when you have the opportunity. You will only lose penalties on the interest, and it may still be better than zero gain for the waiting period.

To properly position yourself, along with the successful investors, so you can invest before, or when they invest and reap when they do, you too need to have what they have—financial opportunity money. This is purely an opportunity-driven investment. You can even be a bit smarter than they are by not waiting until they sell before you reap your own profit. That is the role of your strategic opportunity box. A financial opportunity box is a strategic allocation of income in readiness for unforeseen or strategic investment opportunities that maximize profits. From May to June 2021, many prices of tech stocks, commodities, and cryptos had fallen substantially—some as much as 20-70%. That is the best time to buy and make good profits. If you have already bought and have some shares or cryptos that have experienced such decline on your invested positions, the best approach is to do cost-averaging by buying more at cheaper prices. For instance, the price of Tesla shares has dropped from about $880 in early January to $560 in mid-May 2021. When I bought Tesla at $620 in February 2021, I considered it was cheap, it had dropped from over 800 per share, but on 19 May I bought some Tesla shares at $549 each. In late November Tesla sold at about $1235 per share—that is 125% gain in seven months!

Likewise, Bitcoin (BTC) cost over $63,000 in April 2021, but it has dropped to $35,000 in Mid-May 2021. BTC was only $200 per share in 2015! At its peak, the Ethereum Classic (ETC) I bought ETC at $45 per share in early May had gained 230% within a week, having reached over $160 per share, but it later dropped to 33% of its value. Some have dropped to a third of their original price in January, but have quickly bounced back again in August 2021. Ripple (XRP) that I bought at $0.53 per coin in 22 June 2021 rose to $1.29 as of 20 August, having gained as much as 143%. I also saw an increase of about 150% in Ada (Cardano) bought at the same time. That also happened last year, and many who defied the odds and invested when the financial capital market was generally low and have made a lot of profit. when the market bounced back on a bull run.

I recorded a screen shot of an anonymous retail investor who bought just $41 worth of Ada (Cardano) in late March 2020 and reaped $3270 when Ada reached about $2.5 per coin in August 2021—about 7989% profit! Ada was $0.04 per coin in early 2020 and has reached 2.5 to 2.9 in August. This person made a total investment of $1627 at an average of 0.07 per coin between 2018-2020, and may have reaped about $54,500 profits! That sounds crazy but it is an actual performance of an anonymous investor on the Etoro platform. Imagine what the investment of $10,000 by this investor could have yielded, with the same crypto and time. That is where the money you set aside for opportunity becomes important.

Stock investments are heavily time-bound and volatility is high for aggressive growth stocks. Waiting for a loan application or the next payday means missing a grand opportunity. It ensures that money is readily available for you to capture the best investment opportunity, anytime. This financial decision box helps you to explore financial opportunities at a financially odd time. It serves as your 'interest-free' auto-bank for investments without any condition. You can strategically apply this to portfolios that would yield diversified and multiple streams of income and passive income.

Your "auto-piloting" investment opportunity can be fast-tracked by this type of financial investment, i.e., directed to investments that do not require your presence. Auto-piloting investment will be discussed as a full chapter. The Financial opportunity box must be regularly replenished after its use. The more actively the money in the financial opportunity box is used, the more wealth is created if you are a smart investor. However, I must advise the reader first do its own due diligence and acquire knowledge on financial investment before making any decision. It is easy to lose money than gain it if you have no knowledge and investment skills.

Viking Investor
A smart investor cannot afford to be like the ancient *Nordic Viking* warriors who often scouted to spot unprotected territories and attacked to dispossess them.[587] When they realized their chance of winning was slim, they retreated with their long, big boats. The retraction is for pursuing the next opportunity. When they found one that they are able to overpower, they settled there, farming the land and building

protection around it. Their concern had shifted from adventures of pursuing new opportunities to protecting what they had captured.

That happened to me in 2006 when I invested in an aggressive stock—Zenith Bank Plc, Nigeria, during the bull market and had just watched my investment go up exponentially in 18 months; I reaped my profit which had quadrupled the investment. I still had four times the amount I invested unused in a low-yielding money market account for nearly a year instead of investing it in that stock or some other stocks. When I eventually invested it, I did it in less-yielding opportunities in real estate.[588] It was an opportunity lost. I was more protective. It is the reason I have not sold some of my stocks and Cryptos that yield more than 100% and 200%, but rather buy to accumulate more shares for higher prices in the future.

The lesson here is that I should have spotted the stock as an opportunity and invested more into it than I did or diversify into other similarly aggressive stocks the same way at the time. And there were other vehicles that could have multiplied 4- to 8-times their purchase value within the same period. Investors don't settle by just farming and walling around their money alone. They put it in some financial security but also pursue new opportunities and capture them when they open. You need to be more of a 'Viking' than a 'Farmer' in your investment adventures: think growth and take advantage of opportunities more than settling for security. Smart investors don't settle for farming; they keep on hunting and capturing opportunities.

The Financial Opportunity box can help you to achieve both financial security and opportunities. You secure what you had in the box, avoid losses, and wait for the next round of opportunities. It is the reason Warren Buffet said, "When you know the business…, you understand it, the price is right, the people are right…then you take your thumb out of your mouth and barrel in.

Managing Your Financial Portfolios

Your ability to make wealth and attain financial security will be fast or slow or never attained, depending on how well you manage your five financial portfolios. That is, it depends on how you have successfully allocated your income or investment funds to the five boxes described above and managed the levels in each. Personally, from the start, I decided the percentage to devote to my tithe as a vow, a variable amount in a separate personal ministry account, plus generous offerings, depending on the need and my conscience and willingness. I do not allow pressures from fundraisers to compel me to give when I do not believe it is right or necessary to do so. Nonetheless, I like to be a good steward of God's money as best as I can. I am also not impressed by excessive fund-raising campaigns that exploit givers. However, our giving can be a reflection of our level of relationship with God. Nevertheless, wisdom is needed.

Assuming you are an average giver, you will likely give a portion (e.g., 12-15% including tithe + offerings) of your net income for offering related expenses toward God. That is 15% of your net income after tax. You have an extra 85% of your disposable income to spend. How do you allocate the 85%? Your financial obligation box can be very demanding, and you need financial discipline to keep it moderate. An average person spends 75% of their income on financial obligations. At the upper end, you have only 10% to invest and to create wealth at the beginning. That is not bad.

For those who are in well-paid jobs, especially top professionals or executives, this percentage could be as high as 30-50% of their income or more that is available for investment. Assuming you have only 5-10% available after boxes 1 and 2 are met, you will realize that 5% of your income cannot quickly take you to financial freedom unless you plan on how to increase the amount you invest. Oftentimes, situations hijack this opportunity to invest the 5% from us, ranging from people borrowing to unexpected ill-health challenges by self or loved ones, or other expenses. You must keep those within the second box as much as possible and assume the remaining 5% is not available to you. It should not be money you can easily access. That is where you start your investment from. It is better to put the money in an account that is some effort to withdraw. There is no formula to it; you can gradually increase your percentage available for investment over time. All this is still about allocation, but managing it is even more important.

Do not let anyone deceive you that putting your money into Wealth Box 3 (Financial security) alone will make you rich. It won't. What it does is to save your money from losses at the initial period when you do not have much to invest. If you just leave your money there forever, your returns would be so small, and it can even be offset by "forex" depreciation (if the rate of inflation is higher than the return on your money). You must consider the money in that box as your 'seed money' for investments into financial growth—Wealth Growth Boxes 4, or even 5.

Apply part of the money to carefully chosen financial growth investments, e.g., real estate investment property (not home, because home is still security in a sense), financial capital market such as equity that could compound higher rates of returns for you. Here you need real skill, and we will discuss it at length in another chapter. You can also invest in entrepreneurial work (business) if you have some free time or extra labor to manage it, e.g., family support. Aim at applying 30-40% of your total investment in the financial growth box once you have reached a significant threshold. You may move money between Box 4 and 5—Growth and Opportunity, Wealth Boxes. Use that box strategically. You can shift the rates as opportunity opens but be disciplined in how you respond to the opportunities. Never deplete your financial security to zero, unless you have enough equity or assets that could be easily disposed of to generate cash without affecting your livelihood.

Bonus 2 Overview

Receiving Your Investment Capital

How to Acquire Your Investment Start-up Money

Ministry Issue
How do I get seed money to invest?

Ministry Lesson
Showing how to receive seed money.

BONUS 2

RECEIVING YOUR INVESTMENT CAPITAL

How to Acquire Your Investment Start-up Money
"Formal education will make you a living; self-education will make you a fortune."[589]

"Dishonest money dwindles away, but he who gathers money little by little makes it grow" Proverbs 13:11.

The most daunting reality faced by those whose hearts are willing to invest and create wealth is the question of how to get the start-up capital for investment. It is a question of the chicken and the egg. Which came first? Is it the financial surplus or the seed money to invest and generate wealth? Obviously, you need the seed money to make headway, but it is not usually as arduous as it seems. Many people think you need to have a lot of money before you can invest. The first secret is - you don't always need to acquire money first in order to make money. You can earn money, spend money, and grow your income while at the same time you are investing in your future and ministry. You can generate the start-up from what you save from cutting your expenses and from your direct earnings. We will learn how you can do this in this chapter.

Let us first review profitable ways of creating start-up capital for investments. The reason we have spent a large amount of time in the previous chapters is to help stimulate the reader's interest in investments once we have determined where we stand. By now, you must have become restless and are more knowledgeable on how to either get out of debt or how to increase your net-worth, so you can reach your financial goal in life and ministry. It is to get the brain charged with new possibilities. Andrew Carnegie said, "You cannot push anyone up the ladder unless he is willing to climb. You must capture and keep the heart of the original and supremely able man before his brain can do its best." before his brain can do its best." The reason the author has put the juicy part of the book to the bonus section is because a successful needs perseverance and must be keen to learn knowledge. A casual reader will not have reached these sections. But gold is not found on the surface of the seashore. You have to dig deeper. So I congratulate the reader.

Generally, there are many ways to obtain start-up capital for investments—that is, your investment seed money. This is the money you want to make work for you to generate more money. Here you need the money you can use as your slave to create more money for you. George S. Clason puts it this way, "Gold indeed is a willing worker." That is the secret of all wealth—money begets money.

Every innovative endeavor that brings financial success is unlikely to depend on a *hand-me-down* method that is not dynamic, malleable, or durable. Our challenge should be to discover unconventional principles that open up new streams of financial innovation or wisdom from God's perspective. To discover new principles we should start with asking ourselves two questions: What has challenged me so far in reading this book? Am I sufficiently motivated to start investing? What principles am I going to apply in my financial plans?

Based on your financial net worth, your nature, the type of job you currently have, and the investment skills you've acquired, the next step is to decide the investment route to take.

Different paths of obtaining investment money can be followed, and the list is endless. These include salaried jobs, contracts, fees, honorarium, consultancies, allowances, premiums, dividends, etc.), OPM— other people's money (loans, borrowing, mortgage, inheritance, gifts, partner's funds in a joint venture), business (marketing/selling products, services, and ideas). Also, self-employment (small, medium, large-scale businesses) can be a viable source. Others are returns from previous investments, etc. It is not advisable to start your investment with borrowed money. As a rule, you start with investing what you can afford to lose. However, with more skills borrowing to invest is not a taboo. Wealthy investors become rich with OPM (mainly from loans). Whereas, loans keep the middle class poorer. This requires skills.

The main headache for new investors is, "Where and how do I obtain the start-up capital for the investment in order to create wealth?" In any investment vehicle, you don't have to wait until you get the cash or have to build the investment capital before you decide to invest. The best is to first commit yourself to invest and then come up with ideas on how to get the money. This means you build that wealth first in your head and prayerfully work toward its reality. Once you have your financial net worth analysis done, you do not wait and stay, hoping that you will build wealth one day, but you plan on how to increase your net-worth right away.

In the following session, we will explore various ways to acquire investment capital.

How to Acquire Start-up Capital

One's financial net worth is a very good gauge of where you stand and how to begin implementing your money-making ideas. There are five plausible scenarios for most people who want to build financial wealth:

Scenario 1. Get out of bad debt, and build up your credit

One of the greatest barriers to creating wealth is debt—money owed to anyone for any reason. The very mentality of owing others money makes us think we are poor and we cannot invest. Our mind keeps telling us we are debtors all the time. Each time we think about the debt, fear grips our hearts. Hear me clearly: debt is not a sin. We are only discouraged from borrowing without paying back. Borrowing is not a bad thing on its own, especially if it is for investment purposes or a short-term project. It is when we owe, or we are not willing, or we don't have the ability to pay it back, that it becomes a trap. There are times when borrowing is inevitable, such as when buying a high-value real estate property or investing in a business that has a much higher return than the interest we are expected to pay on the loan. For instance, it is even wise to borrow at 5-10% interest and put it in an investment that yields 30% or more at the end of the year. That is a normal thing for investors. A real estate billionaire recently said, "debts makes the rich richer but the poor poorer. I loved debts!"

It is easier to get into debt than to get out of it. In my teaching, I am fond of using the photograph of a giraffe that fell into a big pothole in the middle of the paved road, with only its head and half of its neck being visible. The poor animal looked pitiful and helpless. It pictured how we feel when we find ourselves in deep financial debt. You may even be getting near to declaring bankruptcy. You can still come out of the pothole in good time.

We live in a generation where most people have long-standing debts and student loans. Modern civilization has enticed us into believing in living above our means and in debt. In some developed nations, you are more trusted than someone who pays cash if you can buy your purchases on credit and pay back later with interest. Many businesses in the United States and many other developed nations of the world prefer using credit cards to cash. All you need is to have a credit card and a good credit history—the ability to borrow and pay back the amounts due promptly. You could buy virtually anything without money if you have a good credit record. The danger of this is that many people cannot control their wants. There is a difference between needs and wants. There is a tendency to overspend on expenses by using free money rather than when it is your own earned money. Ron Blue identified five types of debt: i) credit card debt, ii) consumer debt, iii) mortgage debt, iv) investment debt, and v) business debt.[590]

However, the economy is hard, and there are many who are unable to adjust their living expenditure to stay within their means, especially when the facility to buy using credit is available everywhere with many attractions and promises of discounts. Because of this, many in the developed nations have been trapped into perpetual poverty without recognizing it. The notion that you can also build up some *credit* (ability to owe and pay) by paying regularly, is a big snare to draw people into debt.

The problem with borrowing, especially from corporate lenders that carry interests, e.g., credit cards or banks, is that borrowing compounds interests against you in the long term. Interest rates of some credit cards can be as high as 20% or more. You don't make that profit from most conventional investments. The compounding works in favor of the lender, but it works against the borrower—in a reverse way. The lender gains, and the borrower loses due to the compounding effect over a long time, except in times of high inflation. How can you turn that around?

As a rule, avoid unnecessary debts as much as possible, and pay your debts at all times. Paul warned Christians, *"Let no debt remain outstanding, except the continuing debt to love one another…"* (Romans 13:8). Owe no man. Debt can mortgage your future unless you get out of it as soon as possible. Remember that *"The borrower is a slave to the lender"* (Proverbs 22:7). It deprives you of your self-esteem, dignity, and financial freedom.

The story of Debasir, the Persian slave, was dramatically told in the famous book "The Richest Man in Babylon" by George S. Clason.[591] Because of bad debts, Debasir sent his wife back to her parents and ran away from his creditors, hoping to find quick wealth in a foreign land. He met his doom there and was sold into slavery; he suffered untold hardships.

One day, a rich noble woman who he worked for heard his story and confronted him about his cowardice in running away from his debtors. She told him he was a weakling and naturally had a *slave mindset*, even before he ever became a slave—because he ran away to avoid paying his debt. That statement haunted him, and he inquired what he needed to do. The woman let him know that his debts are his enemies, and he must fight them if he wanted to be a free man. After she helped him escape from slavery he waged lasting wars against this mindset of debt, and he did not only pay off his debt, but he also became very wealthy—he became the richest man in Babylon. It was like becoming a Rockefeller in the past, or a Jeff Bezos, Bernard Arnault, Bill Gates, Warren Buffet, Helu Slim, Mark Zuckerberg, Larry Page or the Elon Musk of our time.

How did Debasir do it? He returned to his wife and agreed with her about his determination to pay off all his debts: "My good wife hath supported my intentions to pay my creditors. Because of our wise determination, I have earned during the past moon…the sum of nineteen pieces. This I have divided according to the plan. One-tenth have I set aside to keep as my own, seven-tenths have I divided with my good wife to pay for our living. Two-tenths have I divided among my creditors as evenly as could be done in coppers."[592]

First, he separated 20% of his net income for debt repayment every month and shared it among his various creditors. This he paid off over two years. Your net income should be what you have after deducting the tax, your giving to God, and a portion of your debt, if any, have been paid. It is unethical to spend or invest all your money when you still owe others unless the investment is at a high rate of return that can help you pay the debt off more quickly; otherwise, you are preventing your creditor from creating wealth as well. Jesus said we should do to others what we would that they do to us. If it is a bank, you are incurring more interest on the loan.

Second, he set aside 10% of his income and kept it in savings as personal reserve. That money accumulated, and he later invested it through trusted money lenders to make more money. Third, he lived on 70% of all his income. In summary, after taxes and your giving to God (or tithe and offering) as a Financial Covenant, the formula for debt repayment is as follows: 20% Creditors (debt repayment, if owing), 10% Financial Security (Savings, money market or CD), and 70% Financial Obligation (family expenses). The percentage for family can be reduced, depending on your income. After paying off the debts, the proportion used for debt payment would be excellent to use as your start-up money for investments. Learning to pay off your debt can help you learn to invest. The discipline you applied in paying debt is the discipline needed for saving your investment start-up.

The borrower is always a slave to the lender, whether by credit card or by paperwork. Treat debts as an enemy that must be fought. You cannot be wealthy unless you change your mindset about frivolous debt accumulation. To live in debt is to mortgage your future wealth. If the land is dry when watered, the water will be gulped up and the land will not be wet. It will only become wet or flooded when more than the required water is continually poured onto it. Don't make yourself a dry land.

- You can pay your debt while making investments at the same time, but you may need to get approval from your creditor on the payment schedule.

- **The Rule of Thumb is this:** Honor God *first*; Pay yourself *second*; Pay others *third* (including your debts). Assuming you owe two credit card companies $5,000, $3,000, $1,250 each, and your monthly income after taxes is $3,800. Your strategy is to pay your tithe first and give some offering (about $400). Pay yourself second by putting $380 into a reserved account every month (preferably a CD, money market, bond, or short-term treasury bills, etc.). You still have $3,020 spendable money. You will have to tell your mind that your income is actually $3,020 and not $3,800.

- Be determined to spend 70% on all your living expenses ($2,114). The remaining 10% is for paying your creditors. Your best option is to start with the smallest debt or the one with the highest interest. This is the one you are losing more money on with time. During the period of paying the debts, you will have to adjust your expenditures to fit your available income.

The first investment gear is to owe less. Owing is a reverse gear. It can keep you many years behind your financial freedom. In general, owing is a *reverse gear* unless it is for investment purposes.

- Paying off your debt is a *neutral* gear—you are free, but you are not advancing forward. You have to engage your financial wealth-making gear by investing; if you have to move forward—*forward gear*. Many folks celebrate being debt-free, and they stop there, but that is supposed to be the starting point. You were in a hole; now you are on solid ground, so you can walk or run. You are better off escaping from the hungry lion if you're on solid ground than in a hole.

Leveraging from People's Money

- This is the most misunderstood concept by most eager investors. They understand it as an opportunity to borrow money from people and banks without having a plan for repayment. If you have a debt-owing syndrome, then this is not good for you. If you are too quick to borrow and find you're unwilling or slow at paying it back, my advice is that you should not borrow. I have had to write off debts for many brethren who refused to pay me back after they had borrowed. For many of them, they had borrowed to invest the money in a business, and some made profits from the business, yet they were unwilling to pay it back. Some took the money and disappeared. Others returned less than what they had borrowed.

- In my experience, many of those who do not pay back debts do not fail to pay them because they are too poor, but because they lacked financial self-discipline. If they had done that to unbelievers, they would have reproached the good Name of our Lord.

- Once you are sure that you are an honest and disciplined borrower, you will first have to weigh your options and be sure it is the last option you have. It is unethical to have your own money and go ahead and borrow from others, not even a bank. The reason is that there is a cost to every borrowing. If the money is from your friend or relative, and they choose not to charge any interest (usually without any interest), it is still not free money because they have an alternative way of using their money to earn for them. They have sacrificed their interest to you, and you must appreciate and recognize that by paying them back promptly.

- Some employers have loan facilities for their employees at zero or very low interest, and some can be repaid over time. You can invest such money and pay it back from your income on a schedule or from your profits. You can also borrow from the bank, especially if the interests are much lower than the profit you envisage. Remember that the longer you delay, the bigger the amount you pay in the long run. Borrowing from the bank to buy a house for 30 years costs you much more than at 15 or 5 years period. It is prudent to borrow from the bank when the interest rate is much lower than the return you get from investing the money. But be wise. Do not borrow at a high rate and put it in a low-yielding investment. Let me say this, borrowing, even from the bank is not always the best option, if you have your own money. unless you need additional leverage to capture a potential growth investment opportunity.

- Nonetheless, money from other sources can help in obtaining the start-up capital that we need to invest. Borrowing money requires as much wisdom as spending it. You need to learn about your risks, count your gains, and ensure you have the ability to pay them back. Even if you borrow from a relative, you have something at stake; if it's not paid back—your self-esteem, your relationship, your ability to go back and borrow again are diminished unless it is paid promptly. In addition, you also will be obliged to lend to that fellow one day if she/he is in need. So do not take it as free money.

• For mortgages and borrowing from the bank or other lenders, there is a cost. You pay high interest, and you stand to lose your collateral if it's not paid. Your credibility as a citizen is also at stake. You are even more vulnerable to reproach as a believer or minister, "A good name is more desirable than great riches; to be esteemed is better than silver and gold."[593] Investment experts assert that ideal money-making systems are those with zero cash, zero risks, zero time, zero management, and zero energy. But in ideal situations, you can hardly find such investments in reality, without a cost. There is no business without an element of risk, some cost, some input of time, management, and energy.

Scenario 2: Available money that can be invested
The second scenario is when you have money to invest. You do not owe any debt, and you are able to invest immediately. If that is you, congratulations! You can start investing right away. However, I advise that you read *Scenario 3* below well, to see how you could further increase the available money for investments. Unless an angel brings money to you, which is a rare thing, there are generally two sources of money for investment:

• First is *your own money* (YOM). This is to be seen as a very important investment opportunity. Such money could be from your income (salary, wages, fees, commissions, honorariums, awards, profits, gifts, withdrawals from insurance, pension, etc.).

- The second is *other people's money* (OPM). OPM includes inheritance and loans, especially low rate or soft loans. For instance, it makes sense to obtain a loan with 5% interest for an investment that could yield 18% annually. A mortgage at 4% is good where the rate of appreciation or rent goes up by 10% or more. There are also cases when relatives or friends are happy to loan out money to us without interest. As a rule, never borrow money for an investment you are not certain will make profits, or a business you do not understand. This also applies to leveraging stock purchases for investment. You can incur huge losses when leveraging is done at a higher rate (e.g., X5, X10, X20, ... X100) at a wrong time, stock, or market environment. Starters are not encouraged to use leveraging for that reason until they have mastered the art of investing.

Scenario 3. Discovering hidden money you never knew you had
Many people think that making money is all about acquiring new money. This is not true. As a matter of fact, the *first* step to making money is to reduce your expenses. The less you spend, the more money you have for investments. Learn to live on less than your income or earnings. To be rich, you must learn to curtail your lust and unnecessary expenses. It means that right away, you can start to make more money than you ever knew you had by working out feasible and practical ways of reducing your current expenses. If your income is not enough or just enough for you, it is most likely you have been living above your means. Someone said, 'what we consider as necessary expenses are *financial weeds*' which if unchecked, they will always outgrow or equal your income, no matter how much you are earning.'

Your ability to weed out your unnecessary expenditures and cut your spending is a key step to financial freedom. Curtail your expenditure, and live within your means. The amount of savings you can earn from wise spending and cutting your expenditures can be more than a quarter of your income. Imagine if you have 10-25% of your income available to you immediately? That could be accumulated and become part of your start-up capital.

The rule is this: *spend less*. Be frugal. The less you spend, the more money you have available for your investment pool. It is not easy; it requires determination and some discipline. This may involve considering other cheaper or cost-effective ways of living. Some examples are given below:

a) Reduce your rent. Our rent is often the biggest single expense from our income, especially for salary earners. The first place to look for an opportunity to cut is on rent if you are renting. For instance, single or newly wedded couples do not need to live in a big *villa* unless they are millionaires. They don't even need a 4-5 bedroom apartment for a start. Moving from an expensive house to a less expensive one can save you hundreds of dollars per month.

b) The second place to save money is your automobile. An automobile is another big spender of most people's income: the purchase, loan payment, insurance, fueling, and maintenance costs eat up resources. Explore possibilities for paying less on transport. This could be done easily by paying upfront, say six months, so you do not pay interest for that period. You may want to buy a good, used car instead of a new one and save more dollars for investments. You could buy a fuel-efficient car to save money on gasoline. Drive with care, so you don't spend on avoidable repairs. In many European cities, it is even smarter to go to work on a bicycle, metro or by train. Small cars are also considered smarter.

c) Third is reducing the frequency and costs of your purchases. This is where a lot of expenses could be reduced. To attain financial freedom, you must learn to curtail your habitual financial lusts and adjust by devising ways of cutting all your unnecessary expenses. It may involve changing your lifestyle: your diet from luxury and brand consumption to what your health really needs. Consider how much money people spend per month on simple things we become addicted to: coffee, eating out, hairstyling and products, pedicures, manicures, perfumes, driving uneconomic fuel usage cars, buying purchases on credit cards at high interest.

Many times people buy things because they appear cheap, not because they need them. David Bach illustrated this wasteful spending propensity very nicely and dubbed it as the "Latte Factor." Let's call it the 'Prodigality Factor,' or to put it in a positive tone, "Frugality Factor." Many folks can save a lot just by taking a public bus instead of a taxi, by reducing their daily snacks and drink purchases, buying less expensive stuff. Do not decide on what to buy when you are at the shopping mall; decide that before you get there, and write the items down, if possible. When making purchases, it is better to think and evaluate your choices before you buy. In Europe, you can save more money by traveling by train than by driving your car most of the time. Remember that "It is not how much you earn, it is how much you spend. How much you earn almost has no bearing on your ability to attain financial freedom."[594] A farmer, when nurturing his crop, pulls out or eliminates every weed in the field? That is what you ought to do with superfluous items you spend money on. What we consider as necessary expenses are often financial weeds. My advice is that you get the financial weeds out. Weed out the tares that are choking and using up nutrients in your investment field. If unchecked, they will always outgrow or be equal to your income, no matter how big it is. That is the law of spending. Increase your Frugality Factor.

The solution is to curtail your prodigality and put on frugality by cutting your expenditures as much as possible. That does not mean living a stingy lifestyle. You can still be generous toward God and people and yet, curtail your unnecessary expenditures. It is amazing to know how wasteful each of us can be.

As a rule, your so-called necessary expenses will normally grow to match up with your income. The more you earn, the more the demand for you to spend. Everything will increase, including those who hide and wait for their own share. That is why Solomon said, *"Whoever loves money never has enough; whoever loves wealth is never satisfied with his income. This, too, is meaningless. As goods increase, so do those who consume them. And what benefit are they to the owner except to feast his eyes on them?"* (Ecclesiastes 5:10-11). You cannot be satisfied because the demand will keep out-running the income.

a) Explore opportunities for discounts and indirect savings. In some countries, you cannot survive the market without sufficient negotiating power. It is part of the business, and you have to learn how to get the best deals—Hunt for discounts in every tangible deal. Most businesses make provision for discounts for customers who pay cash, or buy in large quantities, or pay upfront. You can improve your negotiating power and have more flow to you in indirect savings from your purchases. Paying promptly and avoiding interest or obtaining discounts is a legitimate way of reducing your expenses, as long as the deal is a win-win. Many businesses, such as insurance, medical contracts, automobiles, etc., hire agents to collect their money. Paying directly and by cash is better for them because they will have their money faster and pay fewer service charges to the collection agencies. In that case, they can afford to give discounts.

b) Look for opportunities for reducing expenses on purchases and promotions or credit awards. Some airlines or credit cards accumulate points for free air tickets. Mileage accumulation on air tickets could reduce your overall expenses. If your work involves frequent travel, you could save points for free tickets that could be used for a vacation or personal trip. From 2008-2011, I had redeemed at least *three* free airline tickets, each of which was worth about $900 in value, from my KLM frequent flier mileage accumulation. I had reached over 100,000 miles also on South African Airways a number of times. From the insurance on two cars my family was using in Dallas, I have saved about $600 a year by paying upfront. If you work with certain international organizations that have diplomatic privileges, you can also save on tax and major purchases, such as buying fuel at good discounts. All these save costs and keeps money in your pocket rather than another.

c) You can legally save on your taxes. In some countries, the government reimburses taxes or allows some eligible deductions. Often, I received substantial annual tax payments from income while I was working in Brazil. Many employees lose some of their eligible claims because of their carefree attitude in keeping receipts and documents. In the United States, this is particularly important for ministers. Some expenses are tax-deductible, and some are not. It is important to understand what expenditures qualify for deductions for the purpose of taxation. You could save good money every year by being knowledgeable about the eligible categories. If you work with international organizations or foreign assignments and services, you may also be entitled to tax-free diplomatic privileges.

d) Pay your bills promptly. Many charges are attached by delays in paying bills. This eats into your investment money. By paying your purchases on time from the credit cards, you can avoid the huge interest charges.

e) Flipping unused assets. There are some people who have assets from an inheritance or unused assets. It is possible to have a real estate, e.g., lands, a house, cars, or other assets that could be converted into liquid money for purpose of investment. We need to understand that assets can be converted to a monthly income and that retirement savings are important as a generator of monthly income or spending power.[595] Certain assets can be converted to smart investment that generates passive income. Many of the items we dispose of usually have not spent half of their effective use-life. The truth is that all the disposables you own have no contribution to your wealth. They deplete your wealth as you replace them too frequently.

The decision to sell must be carefully weighed. Some of these assets on their own are important to your future investments. Some wise investors consider what has less value to them but much value to their prospective buyers and sellers. Just selling one asset to buy another one of greater value in terms of return can build wealth gradually. This also requires discipline. There is a tendency to squander plenty of cash that you did not recently work for and think it is free money. You will always find something less worthy to spend it on. Financial discipline is needed. There are many tips available on how to generally cut your expenses and create more wealth:[596] Your options are to buy fairly used goods, rent things you don't need to own, shop garage sales, pay cash, buy the generic brand, prioritize, buy in bulk, pay promptly and shop for value, instead of price alone. However, you must avoid making money your "second religion." Give to God's work, take care of your family needs, and be flexible.

- **Key Actions:** *Save more, spend less, and control your habits*. Your first investment strategy is reducing your expenses: saving more and spending less. Develop skills for frugality instead of extravagance. There are many ways of cutting your spending. Reduce costs on your rent and automobile. Operate on planned and prudent budgets—many people don't plan for most of what they buy. They bought it when they saw it. Emotional purchases are one of the reasons for wasteful expenditures and bad deals. Buy on a cash basis as much as possible, instead of credit cards, "auto-loans," or "cash back" options. Generally, reduce electronic purchases, internet purchases, and using multiple credit cards. Explore ways of legally reducing your payments on taxes and seek discount opportunities. Compare prices before buying.

Scenario 4. Save the surpluses of your income
All the cost-saving scenarios described above are to help you obtain investment money. However, the money you make from this source may

be insufficient to make you rich; it will only improve your situation and allow you some free money for investments. Assuming such money is not available, you will need to save up the start-up investment capital.

Just by reducing your expenses above, you will have started having some surpluses: your newly-discovered hidden wealth. You can even work that out on paper and know that it is extra investment money for you. You need to invest that money first through a savings account. Saving is a form of financial security investment. I encourage you to start with saving at least 10% of your income in a savings account and increase the amount as you go. We have discussed this aspect under the 'Financial Decision Guide.'

During your times of plenty, don't squander. Learn from Joseph's wisdom: save more.

Step 3. Invest your savings and grow it
The purpose for your reducing expenditures and making extra savings is not just for the sake of savings but to provide investment capital for you that could be converted into growth investment. Many investment gurus have noted that "Over time money compounds…over a lot of time money compounds dramatically."[597] You don't need a lot of money to be wealthy or financially independent. You only need consistent savings and investments in profitable systems.

Mere saving is not really an investment; it is just the beginning. Investing involves risk-taking, and the level of risk corresponds to the returns. You need to invest in financial growth and learn to manage risks. In the next chapter, we will discuss investment systems.

The question that comes to mind is what best investment route to take. There is no best answer to it. The best is to evaluate what options you have and decide. The table below gives you an idea of how much wealth could be created by just saving one dollar a day or 30 dollars a month in different investment vehicles at given interest rates:

Table 1 below shows indicative cumulative return on investments of one dollar a day for 66 years, invested in different investment routes and interest rates.[598]

Investment vehicle	% Interest	Potential Returns (Cumulative)[599]
Kept in a safe (or buried)	0	$24,000
Savings account	3	$77,000
Certificate of Deposit (CD)	5	$193,000
Corporate Bonds	8	$1 million
Growth Mutual Funds	10	$2.7 million
Aggressive growth mutual Funds	15	$50 million
Real estate, businesses, stocks	20	$1 billion

Leverage your ability to make wealth

We have discussed the need to cut your expenses and avoid debts, but until you have made deliberate efforts to build your reserves, you are unlikely to be able to have enough capital to invest. It is a conscious and well-planned effort that can take you to where you want to be.

With God's given wisdom, these are all possible. We must see the initial start-up capital as the leverage to our power to make wealth. Archimedes cried, "Give me a lever long enough and a place to stand, and I can move the whole world." If God gives you that lever, in one way or the other, how will you turn your dreams into reality? It is God who provides the lever that we need to create wealth.

Remember that the race is not for the swift, so don't make dishonest money.[600] King Solomon warns that *"Dishonest money dwindles away, but he who gathers money little by little makes it grow"* (Proverbs 13:11).

The Miracle of Compounding Time on Investments

When the Master asked the famous, lazy, and unprofitable servant in Matthew 25 why he had not deposited His money with the *bank* and bring it back with *interest*, He was expecting the power of compounding interest to work for His money, even if the man did not wish to be physically engaged in trading. That is what we have called auto-pilot. The man should have explored autopilot investment opportunities and made more money, even if he could not trade directly. How does this work?

Three things will work for you here when you invest:

i) Your Money;

ii) The Time;

iii) The Investment System.

Compounding interest is known as the eighth wonder of the world. Benjamin Franklin knew this secret when he said, "Money is of a prolific nature. Money can beget money, and its offspring can beget more." His assertion stood the test of time centuries after his death. He bequeathed a sum of $1,000 to Philadelphia and Boston, with the condition that the money should be left intact for at least 200 years. By the time of maturity, a sum of $5 million was paid out to Boston, and $2 million was paid to Philadelphia!

Such dramatic increases in profits can be illustrated in Table 1 below. If you invested $10,000 as a one-time lump sum, over time, how much would that money have compounded and yielded for you?

Table 2. Compounding effects of time on an investment of $10,000 (as a one-off investment)[601]

Rate	5 Yrs.	10 Yrs.	15 Yrs.	20 Yrs.
2%	11,041	12,190	13,459	14,859
4%	12,167	14,802	18,009	21,911
6%	13,382	17,908	23,966	32,071
8%	14,693	21,589	31,722	46,610
10%	16,105	25,397	41,772	67,275
12%	17,623	31,058	54,736	96,463
14%	19,254	37,072	71,379	137,435
16%	21,003	44,114	92,655	194,608
18%	22,878	52,338	119,737	273,930
20%	24,883	61,917	154,070	383,376
25%	30,518	93,132	284,217	867,362
30%	37,129	137,858	511,859	1,900,496

Lessons

- Time is money. The investment grows with time, without the investor doing anything extra.

- The higher the interest rates, the faster money compounds and increases profits more dramatically. Just look at the figures vertically and horizontally; you will realize there is an amazing trigger point at higher rates and longer years; the rates of increase were very dramatic. The longer the years, the greater the multiplying effect of increasing rates of return. It means that if you have identified and invested in a high-yielding investment that is stable and at an increasing rate, leaving it for the long-term is the key to wealth building. That is why properties built 50 years ago are now worth several millions of dollars.

- The two servants who had invested in Matthew 25 might have just put their money in investments that yielded double their money over time, as in Table 1. Money deposited with a 16% return, doubled after five years, or at 8% after ten years. That was what the Master had expected this lazy and unprofitable man to have done.[602]

Beyond A Dollar a Day

You have heard that with a dollar a day, you can become a millionaire in 40 years. Today, you do not need to wait for 40-66 years to become a millionaire. Many have invested a small amount of money and have made millions in less than two years. We are now in an era of exponential growth. Just last year, many became millionaires by investing in some stocks and cryptos, as shown in the simple table below (Table 3). An investment of $10,000 in Ada in early 2020 could have yielded 7000% = 70 times your investment! Assuming you have invested $10,000 in Marathon (MARA)—a penny stock, on 12 April 2020, by 11 February 2021, your investment will have yielded $894,418. Imagine if the investment was $25,000? That is a cool $1.23 million. Even if we want to be conservative, the minimum on the list of the stock and cryptos below could have double or triple your investment in two to three years. For instance, Bitcoin (BTC) was about a dollar in 2011, $10 in 2012, $400 in 2015, $1000 in 2017, $8,000 in 2020, and reached over $60,000 in April to May 2021 before it fell to $29,000 in June 2021, but it has rebounded to $60,000 by October 2021.[603]

Now that is history that may not always repeat itself in the short-term, but you can look for such opportunities in the future. A profit of 20-30% per annum is still a very good investment and can build wealth over time. I bought a meme crypto (Shiba Inu) with small investment in September 2021 at $5.71 when it dropped to its new lowest, by end of October it had reached $86—a gain of 1400% or 15 times my investment. For instance, one of my several small positions was bought at just $50 had yield $750 in less than two months. This is to show that the amount of investment is not as important as the right timing.

Table 3. Return on investment of $10,000 to selected stocks between January 2019 to May 2021.[604]

#	Security	Benchmark		Recent status		Return on Investment	
		Date	Market value	Date	Market value	Return on $10,000 invested	% Gain
1	Apple Inc (APPL)	06.01.19	38.07	11.02.21	135.37	35,558	355.6
2	Abeona Therapeutic Inc	05.11.20	1.03	11.02.21	2.96	28,737	288.3
3	Plug Inc (PLUG)	15.08.19	2.01	17.01.21	66.87	332,686	332.7
4	Marathon Patient Inc (MARA)	12.04.20	0.43	11.02.20	38.46	894,418	8944.1
5	Dell Tech Inc (DELL)	15.03.20	32.49	11.02.21	80.05	24,638	246.4
6	Tesla Inc (TESLA)	26.05.20	32.03	03.01.20	880.02	237,650	2376.5
7	Netflix Inc	15.09.19	270.75	31.01.21	550.79	20,343	203.4
8	Senseonic Holdings Inc	11.10.20	0.37	11.02.20	4.16	112,432	1124.3
9	Face Book	22.03.20	148.1	01.09.21	302.50	20,425	204.2
10	Bitcoin (USD)	27.01.19	3464.01	13.04.21	63,109.71	182,189	1821.9
11	Cardano (Ada)	29.03.20	0.032	15.05.21	2.31	721,875	7218.7
12	Ripple (XRP)	08.03.21	0.154	13.04.21	1.839	119,415	1194.1
13	Doge Coin (DOGE)	10.05.20	0.020	06.05.21	0.685	342,500	3425.0

Today there are many easy brokerage platforms for investing stocks and or cryptos where new investors can start, such as Etoro, Binance, Coinbase, Gate.io, Webull, Fidelity, Charles Schwab, TD Ameritrade, Robinhood, First Trade, etc. Some of these are limited to those who are citizens or reside in the United States, while some are international in scope. Personally, I use Etoro and Binance platforms which are international platforms, and Trouve (Nigeria), and banks for investment. The Etoro platform is very easy to invest and it has a dynamic platform or information exchanges among peer investors and traders. However, I advise the reader to do their own due diligence and research online to make an informed choice on a suitable platform and decisions on what security to invest into, and the right timing. This is a personal financial decision that must not be taken lightly.

How Does This Affect A Borrower?
The compounding effect on the debtor of money borrowed is devastating over a long time. Just imagine someone who took a loan of $10,000 to buy a car fifteen years ago, or borrowed from the bank, or mortgaged a home at an 8% interest rate. The amount accumulated with interest would be $31,722—more than thrice what he had borrowed. It is the reason those who mortgage a home for 30 years will have paid twice or even three times the amount they had borrowed by the time the home is mortgage-free.

How Does This Work for An Investor?
Supposing a young couple, having two children, Joe, and Lucy, have received their pension, life insurance, or Social Security payment, or have acquired money from other income sources and had decided to invest $10,000 each into the future of their children. They have many investment options (real estate, stock with long-term prospects, growth mutual funds, etc.) If they had invested the money into a investment vehicle that had compounded at 16% on average since Joe was seven and Lucy was five-years-old, by the time Lucy would be forty and Joe forty-two, they would have 3.87 million dollars as an inheritance. By that time, the parents would still be in their sixties or seventies. If that money was put in an investment that yielded 20%, each of these folks would have inherited 2.37 million after 30 years. Although this looks unrealistic, it is possible if they invested in good real-estate or good stocks in most countries.

> **Compounding Effect on Landing Real-estate Property**
>
> **Case 1**: In 2001, my cousin bought a landing property in a small city in southern Nigeria (25 standard plots) at US $80 each (calculated at prevailing exchange rates to the US dollars). By 2003, each plot sold at $200, by 2004 it was $400), and by 2006, when I bought three of the plots from him, it sold at $2380 per plot. By 2010, each plot was valued at $5000, and in 2012 it was valued at $5625 each. Imagine if my cousin had kept his holdings till 2012, he would have netted a compounding at more than 40% per annum. His initial investment of $2000 could have yielded $138,625 in just 12 years. Assuming he had bought $10,000 worth of property, his investment would have compounded for him $ 693,125 in 12 years! (As of 2012). In 2021, the same plots worth at $10,000 each. Now the area is a newly developed neighbourhood in a small city and an elite location in Nigeria—a populated nation, meaning that the rate of compounding could be even higher in the near future. This shows how even with small amounts in some countries, the compounding power of real estate can be very rewarding.
>
> **Case 2**: A friend bought a plot of land at Ibadan, Nigeria, in 1994 at $625 equivalent. In 2010 it was worth $10,000. He, too, has multiplied his investment 15 times in 17 years!
>
> You can now understand why my Christian friend I mentioned earlier became very wealthy at a young age due to real estate investment. Real-estate investment in many developing countries does not follow market trends; they generally compound at a higher rate as population increases, demand for accommodation, and income. I noticed a similar trend in many African countries, even in major cities Ghana, Kenya, Tanzania, Zambia, and Mozambique.

Diversify your investment.

Don't put all your eggs into one basket. Without investments, you lose money through inflation. $1 million in 1990 is not worth more than $500,000 in value today, in terms of its actual buying power, whereas the value of $1 million invested since 1990 would be billions today. For instance, according to CNBC calculations, an investment of just $1,000 in Apple stock on 12 December 1980 which was $22 when the company went public or IPO, would be worth around $430,000 as of December 2018.[605] Apple stock has split five times since then. The figure is also staggering if $1 million had been invested in a high-yielding stock such as Microsoft or Dell since 1990, However, it does not mean investing in these stocks today will yield the same result. That is why timing is crucial, but there are always many new opportunities in both stocks and cryptos, but the trend is changing.[606]

I read a fascinating story of diversified investment. A young couple, Ning Wang and his wife, Ting Qian, bought 600 Apple shares (then called Apple Computer Inc.).[607] I have paraphrased it like this:

> Ning and Ting started investment early. First, they bought 100 shares of Apple at $34 per share in 1998. They held on to it despite bust and boom, changes in seasons, recession, and management and refused to sell them. They did not let daily analysis bother them. Thrice, the Apple stock experienced a 2-for-1 split, first in 2000, second in 2005, and thirdly a massive 7-for-1 split in June 2014. It means that their initial 100 shares translate to 2,800 shares today. At $131 per share in 2015, their original $3,412 investment has yielded $363,400 profit—that's 100 times the return on their investment. With additional 500 shares bought in 1999, their investment has yielded over $1 million in profits from Apple stock.

The couple even took two more innovative investment steps: they diversified their investment portfolio by investing in real estate, having purchased and renovated five houses in the Poconos. Four houses were in foreclosure, and one was acquired through a short sale. In addition, they both contributed to their 401(k) and IRA accounts, with a total of $1.5 million (including the Apple stock). Put together, their assets would be several million by the time they retire in the future—they are still in their fifties now and are still working. The point here is: there's no biblical reason why a Christian cannot invest in this way to create finance for family needs and for ministry, except for our own myths.

Salient Points

The *first* way of getting the money needed for investments is to avoid debts; *second* is to spend less and wisely; *third* is to save a proportion of your income and surplus in a reserve account; *fourth* is to invest the money already saved to make more, and *fifth* is to diversify your investment.

Bonus 3 Overview

Auto-Piloting Your Investment

Earning Passive Income, While You Pursue Ministry

Ministry Issue
With little investment capital, how can I multiply my wealth with minimum personal engagement, so I can free up time for ministry or missions?

Ministry Solution
Discover a few auto-piloting routes and invest in them.

BONUS 3

AUTO-PILOTING YOUR INVESTMENT

Earning Passive Income, While You Pursue Ministry
"Money frees you from doing things you dislike. Since I dislike doing nearly everything, money is handy."[608] Groucho Marx

Auto-piloting is a navigational device that automatically keeps ships, airplanes, or spacecraft on a steady course, with little or no assistance from the human pilot. In the early days of aviation, aircraft required the continuous attention of a pilot in order for them to fly safely, just like the driver of a car. But today, a pilot can sleep in the airplane. They have their sleeping bunks, quarters, or compartments, just like the passengers, voyaging across continents on a 10-hour, non-stop journey in the air. Many air passengers can't even imagine that pilots sleep while they are sleeping, too. This practice follows strict rules and predetermined periods, generally less than one hour. The pilot can sleep as "control rest" in the cockpit or "bunk rest" in a seat reserved in the business class for the pilots or in the dedicated pilot bunks on long haul aircraft.

An auto-pilot device is based on a mechanical, electrical, or hydraulic system for keeping ships, boats, or airplanes on course. This is accomplished by attaching a compass to its steering mechanism to guide it.[609] Auto-piloting can also be used to describe any system that can fully navigate or support itself, independent of a human being. This will become more popular in every day as the era of artificial intelligence matures. If your business or money-making system can run without your physical presence, it becomes an autopilot business. This chapter intends to sensitize you to the importance of auto-piloting in full-time, bi-vocational (tentmaking), or workplace ministry, in regard to personal finance.

In a capitalistic economy, people talk of 'making money while you sleep' as an auto-piloting investment route of wealth-creation. Although it is a very attractive maxim, it is also faulty in its logic when it comes to ministry. This is not what this book is about. Our central goal is to use money to create more money, so we can free up the Christian worker's time for the preaching of the Gospel or doing the Great Commission with the money-making system, which would require little or no physical presence. In this case, money becomes your obedient servant rather than a cruel master—we must ride it like an obedient donkey to achieve our God-given dreams.

Many folks have taken the concept of sleeping while money works for them to the extremes in the last decade; they simply put all their money in the investment market and watch it grow during the bull market. Some spend their days idling, vacationing, casinos, clubs, or on other pleasures or sleeping during the day. During the last decade preceding the global financial meltdown, millions resigned from their job and became self-employed, just by living an idle and extravagant lifestyle, and yet, getting good returns from their investment. That worked well during the good years of the bull market.

However, during the years following the global financial meltdown in 2008, the tides changed. Those folks were forced to go back to their jobs or roam the streets in hunger. They lost their life's savings in the financial markets and in real estate. Their properties are worth a third of their purchase prices, and many companies in developing countries became bankrupt without bail-out mechanisms. Listen to a word of wisdom: Money can work for you, but you must not be idle or simply sleep while the money works. Things don't work that way in the Kingdom of God. There's no free lunch. Money can work for you while you work for God, but you still have to be in charge of your investment. Harv Eker, the author of "Secrets of the Millionaire Mind," said, "Rich people understand that "you" have to work hard until your "money" works hard enough to take your place."[610] The more money works for you, the less you will have to work for money. Then you can have both your time and the money, also. The object is not to be idle or have 100% time to yourself but to create enough time for God's work while you earn money in passive streams of financial flows that require less of your physical presence.

You Reap What You Sow
Mark V. Hansen and Roberts G. Allen taught that the ideal money-making system has five characteristics: zero cash, zero risks, zero time, zero management, and zero energy.[611] This is only the ideal situation, as they have put it. But in reality, there is no money-making system that will not require some input from each of these five areas. Even robbing a bank requires some effort and input of planning, cash, risk, time, management, and energy. Getting money as a beggar requires some effort. Winning a lottery also requires the input of each of these, and anxiety can be more than money. I can assert that there is no money-making system that is cost-free or without input.

It is not that I like to be pessimistic, but the truth is that money does not come by any means other than from what is put into it. It works with the principle of sowing and reaping. If you sow sleep, you will reap frustrations and surprises. If you sow to your flesh, you reap corruption. When a farmer plants his crops, he can go home and sleep because God, who brings the rain, supplies the air, and the sunshine will make it grow. It is God who brings the increase.[612] Yet, the farmer is responsible for ensuring that the seed is good, the crop is planted at the right time to get the rain (or irrigate when there is no rain) and the crop is not being choked by weeds and pests. God will not keep the weeds, insects, bacteria, and viruses away from destroying the crop. They are your responsibilities.

The biblical auto-piloting principle is about letting your money leverage your hard work, so you can rest and spend your time on what really matters to you. When you cultivate your field, fertilize your crop, weed your field, and spray your crops, you can go back to sleep. Your harvest will come. The auto-piloting is what happens when you are not there—provided weeds and pests have been eliminated, and nutrients have been supplied. Then God will bring the rain and the dew on your crops.[613] Howard J. Ruff said, "If you tell me your financial troubles, don't expect me to feel sorry for you. You've never lost until you've surrendered...because I know that making money in the investment markets, or a business, or profession, is purely and simply a matter of attitude and hard work."[614]

Auto-piloting is not about spending your days in leisure and living a prodigal lifestyle; it is about organizing your investments in such a way that your money can build a critical threshold of passive income that flows in with minimum physical or mental engagement. It enables you to devote more quality time to your God-ordained *calling*. This is our application of the 'auto-piloting' concept in this book.

According to Napoleon Hill, a capitalistic society was developed through the use of organized capital in order to provide the common benefits available in that society.[615] That implies that there can be no wealth-creation in such a society without *effort* or plowing—in one form of *capital* or the other—including financial, human, social, time, and other forms of capital. I also believe these capital areas must be *tradeable* to generate tangible and intangible wealth.

You actually earn what you are worth: what you put into the system or economy. If all you could put into the market economy is your sweat as an unskilled worker with long hours, you earn the bottom-line, despite having invested more sweat than the CEO, who plows-in his hard-earned years of investment in quality education, decision-making experiences, and organizational skills, integrated knowledge in leadership management. He contributes rare experiences and a considerable amount of social capital. Except for professions such as the sports and entertainment sector, which may appear to violate such economic laws to some extent, your talent—both innate and acquired, experience, skills, education, training, and competence, are compensated by the law of wealth. You earn more wealth in return for your capital input (investments). Even then, the sportsman or artist knows they have to invest thousands of hours in practice for their shows. They have to showcase their skills to their prospective deal makers and viewers. They also have to compete for the prize.

A football player, acrobat, or athlete who needs a few hours of sport at the Olympics must have been preparing for years in advance, with long periods of enduring exercise, practice, and self-discipline. A very good choir at the church on a Sunday service didn't just assemble themselves that morning without having first put in hours of practice together. It is the same with musicians, dancers, symphonists, pianists, and orchestra conductors. This is how money-making is, as well. No billionaire can even boast to only sleep while money makes itself. It can sometimes be easier to lose billions faster than you lose 100 dollars without lifting a finger. So you must stay on top of your investment.

In a capitalistic system, each person in the society has the opportunity to exert his/her influence on the economy, and to capture opportunities, regardless of who they are. Your investment into building skills, knowledge, and experience returns back to you rewards that are in proportion to your input—measured by the products and or services delivered. That is, what you put into the money system.

Nothing Goes for Nothing
The bottom line is that you reap what you sow. You cannot become rich without investing capital into the economy. You cannot sleep and expect money to flow to you steadily unless you have plowed-in sufficient capital into the economy—financial, human, intellectual, time, social and spiritual capital. If it does come while the only thing you do is sleep, the money has a way of flowing back downhill while you are still asleep. The enemy is busy when everyone is *asleep*.[616] It is

after you have plowed in something, that the capitalistic economy aids you in multiplying your investment with little effort. When that law is violated, it automatically corrects itself and metes out punishment to the violator or the society which permitted it to go overboard. That is the reason we talk of the financial meltdown: usually a market reaction to a broken system due to greed.

Most global economy crises can be traced to the 'boom and bubble' in the financial and real-estate capital investment markets around the world. For example, in 2008, real estate properties were overstated, sold, repackaged, and resold many times into obscure financial instruments.[617] Anyone who asked for a loan got it without proper scrutiny, and real-estate gurus *hyped* the opportunities in real-estate investments. Because of the irrational human behavior through unregulated "shadow banking," the instruments ended up in portfolios of most banks and financial firms around the world. Many borrowed several times their worth in cash, and this resulted in huge debts and bankruptcy.[618] In recent years many hedge funds have nearly gone bankrupt because of greed.[619]

Crises developed as money flowed to one sector more than it deserved, and many reaped profits they did not deserve to earn. The result was a global meltdown of the financial sector. The real-estate market collapsed, and the states had to pay the bills because it permitted the situation to occur unchecked. The investors also bore the brunt, while others went away with lottery-type returns. However, as long as they return to business, they will still pay back what they earned in an undeserved way. Real-estate benefactors will end up losing monies in real estate, and if they try to be smart by taking the money to the capital market, the monster of financial loss awaits them through plummeted stock prices, bankruptcy, and inflation. Can they still be sleeping?

In 2008, a Nigerian billionaire listed in Forbes 500 had his businesses and profits at an all-time high. The oil price fell from $146 to $34, hitting him with an over $480 million loss; an additional $258 million was a loss from local currency devaluation, and a further $320 million loss as accrued interest, and a $160 million loss in stock. That is $1.2 billion in debt. That would have been the end of this wealth if he had chosen to simply sleep while money works. According to him, "I had two options, either to commit suicide or to weather the storm. I decided to weather the storm."

The bank wrote off $400 million of his debt. He decided to sell his assets to repay what he owed. His assets included 184 apartments, his shareholding in the banks (he was the largest investor at the time), and he also gave up his shareholding in several other companies. In 2014, his net worth was estimated at $1.8 billion. I have read of a similar feat by a real-estate giant in the United States. Why is it that most billionaires can lose their whole investment and yet rebound in a few years? Success has a pattern that can be learned. If someone can start from zero or even negative and still end in billions, what prevents you from getting enough money you need and rise from where you are to create finance you need to support God's work? There is no excuse.

Earning While You Do Missions
The central message in this chapter is that it is possible to earn money from other legitimate sources to support you while you're doing God's work. With a little investment capital, it is possible to grow your income and multiply your wealth with minimum personal engagement. To do that, you will have to discover a few 'auto-piloting' routes and prayerfully invest in them, with financial principles already described in this book.

As explained earlier, when we talk about money working for you, we do not imply that you fold your arms and do nothing, but that you invest in ventures that will increase and multiply your wealth, using any of instruments that don't require your physical presence. You can simply leverage your income by letting your investment do the hard work for you. You will also be investing your time in selecting the right investments and in managing them. In reality, by investing your money, you have contributed to the system: you have loaned your financial capital or market, and indirectly the company. By managing your investment, you have contributed some intellectual or human capital. By interacting with the company, your bank or the market, even if remotely, you have contributed social capital. With all of these, your full physical capital is unnecessary.

Auto-piloting is a Legitimate Money System for Missions
There are some Christians who have demonized any form of money-making as evil, yet they do not consider that allowing their own money to work for them is even more honorable than suffering in silence or not having the money to do God's work or using unacceptable fundraising methods. Is auto-piloting legitimate?

Let's go back to the words of Jesus. The businessman said to the lazy and unfaithful servant: *"Well then, you should have put my money on deposit with the bankers so that when I returned, I would have received it back with interest"* (Matthew 25:26-27, NIV). A paraphrase of this statement is, "If you know that you are too lazy to work, cannot trust that you have the skills necessary to make a profit, and if you cannot trust that I am a good and merciful master who can forgive your debt, even if you lost your investment money, then you ought to have taken my money to the bank, put it in a low-risk, low return investment, and returned my money back with interest. In that case, you didn't need to be there physically. So what were you doing with your time while you kept my investment money in the hole?"

Your money invested in the bank or stock is contributing, albeit passively, to the running of the company. They use your money to make more money, so you deserve a share. Just as the stockbroker, the CEO, or professionals in the company are working, your money is also working for the same goal of earning more wealth for the company.

Just as the employees in that company or the bank deserve their pay, you also deserve your own share. That is how it works. Because the company is making good money, others are attracted to invest there, so are you, and your money boosts the company's performance. That is why you receive growth in your share and also in your dividends. You have a stake in the company as a stakeholder or shareholder. It is a legitimate earning. If you withdraw your money and everyone else withdraws at the same time, the company is in trouble. That is why every investor matters.

The tenants of a real estate property that you have bought, the employee of your bank or company you have invested stock in and are partnering with you, are creating wealth from your money both for themselves and for you. It is a *win-win* situation, not a *win-lose*. Without the financial capital, no company can operate. Most company owners do not have all the money required to run it efficiently and make more money; even the billionaires do not lay that claim. All of the world-renowned billionaires depend on other people, less rich than they are, even folks with just $1,000 dollars, to co-invest and make their companies work. If they have 10 million investors like that, that is $10 billion! It is more sustainable than when one billionaire puts 10 billion in the company. Why? Because with that, he can use his money to own and control the company, and when he withdraws his money, the company is in trouble. But 10 million people will not take their money at the same time—that will never happen. For instance, in 2020 and 2021, retail investors saved both GameStop Corporation (GME) and AMC Entertainment Holdings Inc. (AMC) from big hedge funds in Wall Street that had bet against those companies in coordinated attempts to force down their prices to levels that could have led to bankruptcy of those companies.

Here you could take your purse (wallet) and your sword and preach the Gospel without having to report to duty on a full-time secular job. For a retiree, if you receive enough regular pension and yet have more than you need from autopiloted investment, you could invest your part of the money and time to do God's work. If you are a salaried minister, you could invest part of the money you received in the ministry in your early years and be weaned from support later, so that such support could be directed to others. For instance, when Rick Warren, Pastor of Saddleback Church in Lake Forest, suddenly became a millionaire from his book, "The Purpose-Driven Life,"[620] he decided to pay back 25 years of salary to his church. Rick Warren says rather than 10 percent, he actually gives more than 90 percent of his income away. That was one way to maintain humility after such success. Some like to call him "Pastopreneur—a kind of avuncular chief executive of evangelism," but the testimonies above show how a Christian leader can make money a slave rather than a cruel master.

According to Pastor Warren, "It scared me.... It's tens of millions of dollars. The money was the easy part. We just gave it away. We said, 'First, we're not going to change our lifestyle one bit.' I still live in the same house I've lived in for 22 years. I still drive the same Ford truck that I've driven for 12 years."[621] That is humility of high order, and it is worth emulation by Christian leaders once God has decided to shine His face upon us.

The "All-By-Itself" Investment Paradigm

Another word we may coin for auto-piloting is "All-By-Itself Investment." It has a sound biblical basis. In addition to Matthew 25 on the parable of the talents, Jesus likened the Kingdom of Heaven to a man who planted and then went home. He puts it this way, *"This is what the Kingdom of God is like. A man scatters seed on the ground. Night and day, whether he sleeps or gets up, the seed sprouts and grows, though he does not know. All by itself, the soil produces grain—first the stalk, then the head, then the full kernel in the head. As soon as the grain is ripe, he puts the sickle to it because the harvest has come"* (Mark 4:26-29).

The scattering of the seed is a term for sowing or investment. The investor also sows in order to reap profits or interests.

Although the Lord was teaching here on the Kingdom, when we, as believers, have sown the Word, God handles the rest. Similarly, when the investor puts his money into a system that works, the market works on the money until it starts to grow and yield profits. Whether the investor sleeps or wakes up does not affect the growth of the investment capital. God's grace can bring the increase on the investment seed, just as He does for our crops.

Your investment money can work all by itself while you do God's work. God can watch over it if your motive is right.

The Law of Sowing and Reaping
You can overcome poverty by faith and action. The Bible gave us a key principle in money-making as sowing and reaping. To reap wealth, you must sow money (investment). The parable of the sower illustrates this. The sower is an investor—he sows to reap. God, Himself is an investor in a sense. He sowed His Son for the world, and He died and multiplied Himself through the Holy Spirit and produced more sons and daughters for God—as the Giver of life. To multiply your income, you need to sow your financial seed, both here on Earth (literal investment) and in Heaven (Kingdom investment). Our God is the provider. He gives seed to the sower, and bread for food, so that we can have an enlarged harvest of righteousness, become rich and generous on every occasion, with thanksgiving.[622]

God provides seed for sowing (investments): the Heavenly seed includes the tithe, offerings, and other giving to God's work, i.e., spiritual seeds. It is an eternal investment that cannot depreciate. Likewise, God's Word has provision for earthly financial investments to grow and multiply your income—financial seeds.

Diversified Income Streams

The most important element is to acquire money legitimately and plan on the appropriate route to invest. It is also crucial to always acknowledge the Source of your wealth (God) by faithfully investing in Heaven.[623] If you become a millionaire today, how much will you give to God's work?

A rich man is not rich because he has a large amount of money in his wallet or in his bank account. It is the gross, net financial income he has accumulated from diverse streams of income that flows continually to his pool of income and keeps flowing and growing.

All financial gurus, experts, and authors agree that there are only three major ways of creating wealth in the world.[624] Most business tycoons and millionaires make their money in these three avenues, which include: Financial Capital investment instruments, Business investment or entrepreneurship and Real estate investment. This first book is to provide insights into possibilities and create intense interest in growing your finances. The next volume will focus on the practical application of these three financial instruments in more detail, and would be less on the scriptural foundation.

Streams of passive and active incomes

These three wealth multiplication principles from above are summarized in an ancient wisdom documented by George S. Clason, that:

"Every gold piece you save is a slave to work for you. Every copper it earns is its child that also can earn for you. If you must become wealthy, what you save must earn for you; and its children must earn, that all may help to give you the abundance you crave."[625]

It follows that every cent earned and invested must reproduce itself to earn and generate a stream of income that flows into the investor's portfolio. The secret is to keep generating both *direct incomes* from your salary or other earnings and also *passive incomes* from your diversified streams of investments, whether it is a full or partial auto-pilot system. If you depend only on your salary or one business, you have limits. A good investor also needs to generate *recurring* income that flows from other sources, regardless of whether she/he is physically present or not.

To earn enough passive income while you are still a salaried employee is important to consider what additional income you may legitimately get on top of your income without violating the policy of your employment contract. In some organizations, the employee is not allowed to be physically engaged in other forms of income other than the job. The investment in financial markets or the real estate route would then be a plausible, if not your best bet. No employer can complain about how you invest your salary or money. Many employers actually encourage their employees to invest. That is how to win in the money game.

You must ask yourself how additional income can legitimately flow to you without your direct or full engagement in the art of making money. You have to figure out how you can spend parts of your spare time, such as weekends or evenings, leave days to make more money? This is the secret. Such an income source is known as passive income. The key to financial freedom is to be able to make passive income that exceeds your active income in the long-term.

To achieve this, you have to think out of the box. You will have to manage your time and prioritize it. It is generally said that 80% of what most people spend their free time on is not important to their goal in life. A successful investor is someone who can manage his own and other people's time to his and their advantage.

Auto-pilot Investment Routes
George S. Clason said, "Wealth is like a tree that grows from a seed. The sooner you plant that seed, the sooner it grows and bears more seeds for you. Nourish and water that tree with consistent savings. It

will bear you the fruit of wealth."⁶²⁶ We have discussed some wealth-creation principles and plans, but they will only work when you work them. Life is a process of discovering and re-discovering, then applying those principles that can work. Making money and investing is an interwoven venture—you can't make money without investing; you can't invest without making money. To do both will fatten your wallet and your financial net worth.

Money can flow to you from any of and is not limited to the following routes:

1. Conventional auto-pilot systems
Conventional auto-pilot systems have been discussed throughout this book. These are the financial capital investments, real-estate investment and businesses. Money can flow from the following:

i) Income from interests, dividends, and appreciation in the liquid capital markets (savings, money markets, bonds, mutual funds, stocks, cryptocurrencies, shareholding, etc.)⁶²⁷

ii) Retirement income and their earnings [e.g., IRA, 401(k), SEP, Keogh]

iii) Insurance vehicles and their earnings (annuities, life insurance, whole life insurance, etc.).

iv) Rent or income from rented, leased, or sold real-estate properties

v) Equity gained on your residential home and real-estate investment properties

vi) Sales and royalties from books, DVDs, CDs, Films, Youtube Videos etc.

vii) Payments from inventions, royalties, patents, franchises, and other intellectual capital.

Wealth can flow to investors through one or more of the conventional routes with less effort, even if she or he has a normal salaried job or work and does ministry as a Christian worker.

2. Non-conventional auto-pilot systems
Some of the non-conventional auto-pilot markets include 'Intellectual capital markets' or the industry which turns ideas into wealth. The knowledge economy is not just about interviewing for or signing contracts to work at high-paying jobs, or collecting consultant fees, or charging hundreds of dollars per hour—those are only the bottom-line opportunities. Moving beyond the bottom-line into creating wealth through ideas is not really a new path, but an ancient one, although it is less traveled by the majority of people in any society. Nonetheless, it is the future of the world economy. Commercializing ideas can exist in different shapes and colors, ranging from designing a 'flying machine' like the Wright Brothers did, and great inventors like Thomas Edison and Alexander Graham Bell, to the Bill Gates of Microsoft, Jeff Bezos' Amazon, Mark Zuckerberg's Facebook breakthrough, Elon Musk's Tesla EV cars and AI, or Anthony Robbins' motivational speaking. These are all idea markets through innovation and technology.

3. Intellectual capital as an auto-pilot system
i) *Commercializing Inventions and patents*
Bill Gates once said, "Intellectual property has the shelf life of a banana."[628] According to Nathan Myhrvold, the former Chief Technology expert for Microsoft, the knowledge revolution that has come from inventions has transformed the United States from an 'agrarian economy into an industrial powerhouse,' comparing the PC-software revolution to the invention industry. "I believe that invention is set to become the next software: a high-value asset that will serve as a foundation for new business models, liquid markets, and investment strategies."[629] His company, Intellectual Ventures, has pioneered and raised more than $5 billion dollars to invest in creating thousands of inventions a year, networking, supporting inventors, and buying and commercializing patents—more than 450 patents were filed in

2009 alone. Several ground-breaking inventions are already emerging from diverse fields of endeavors. This is the future of research-public-private partnerships. The professionals will be better able to operate as entrepreneurs in a sense—making fortunes from their knowledge and ideas.

ii) Franchises from product or ideas
A franchise is part of entrepreneurism or business. What many franchisors sell to the franchisee is not actually tangible products but ideas, models, and knowledge that they have patented in their trade names. For instance, many financial gurus and motivational speakers have not just patented their products to protect them from copyright violators, but they sell 'franchises' to many other motivational speakers, who teach their ideas in seminars in their trade name and at the same level of quality.

iii) Royalty from a high-selling book
The reward for authors who have written books that sell well in the market is their royalties. A royalty is the net profit from the sale of a book after all the costs and applicable deductions by both the publisher and the retailers have been made. Many authors have become millionaires overnight through the sale of books.

iv) Gifts from beneficiaries of your skills
Just as sowing and reaping apply to working and earning, or investing and reaping returns or profits, those who work in the ministry can receive gifts and indirect income, as well. This is supported by the Scriptures.[630] Honorariums are often paid for seminars, training, speeches, and even preaching for many well-sought speakers. However, this should not be demanded or be seen as one's rights—we must see it as a provision from God that we do not deserve. I have been offered this several times, but I have never received it. If I were a full-time minister without another source of income, it would be purely a legitimate income.

I loved the prayer of Dr. Tozer when he said, "And if in Your permissive will, honor should come to me from your church, let me not forget that hour that I am unworthy of the least of Your mercies, and if men knew me as intimately as I knew myself, they would withhold their honors and bestow them on others more worthy to receive them… I am your servant to do Your will, and that will is sweeter to me than position, or riches, or fame, and I choose it above all things in Heaven and Earth. Though I am chosen by You and honored by a high and Heavenly calling, let me never forget that I am a man with all the natural faults and passions that plague the race of men.[631]

v) Awards, prizes, and honors
Marketplace Christians and leaders who have made a stride in their field and are distinguished may receive awards, prizes, and honors that often have monetary values. This is rare but not impossible, and they can help advance the work of the Kingdom.

Other Auto-pilot Markets
vi) Infomercials
Infomercials are a direct-response, television commercial—television advertisements, which generally include a phone number or website.[632] They are also called paid programming or teleshopping (Europe).

vii) Internet marketing and eBooks
Once you have created a winning product, you can build a platform and an online automated business on your products to create passive income, especially when you have a large realm of influence among those who trust in your products. Selling e-books can be best handled in this way. Today, most books are sold digitally as e-books available on Kindle or as audiobook. This will normally have systems for auto-response and be linked to your deposit accounts. There are many professional services with high deliverability and multiple responders. This makes provision for writing automated responses in various steps in sequential order, such that a seamless conversation can be done without physical operation. This is better done with a website, blog, or

Facebook. I must add that e-marketing is the future, and it is already dominating today's business. However, there is an increase in direct selling. Jeff Bezos of Amazon was quoted as having reported that "Over a thousand independent authors surpassed $100,000 in royalties in 2017 through Kindle Direct Publishing."[633] In the account above, traditional publishers are "now missing two-thirds of U.S. consumer e-book purchases and nearly half of all e-book dollars those consumers spend." These e-books are much cheaper and circulate faster. This is good news for independent, new, and less popular authors. The future of e-book publishing increasingly belongs to them. Christian workers can participate in both print and e-publishing industries.

Remember The Grand Cause!
My idea of appreciating 'auto-piloting' as a legitimate means of building wealth is to teach how more money, more opportunities, and more time can be available for preaching the Gospel and mission work. Imagine what God can use you to do if you have all the money you need and have all the time to do it. If money is not an object, imagine what your church can do? Therefore, what we autopilot is part of the critical time and effort that is required for money-making, so we can channel more efforts, time, and investments into doing God's work.

The Lord is looking for men and women of means, who will be so consumed with the business of God that they will be willing to give up their own lives to win souls to Christ, create and desire more time to serve God and His people and to intercede for the lost. He is looking for men and women of means, who will look beyond their own immediate needs—not because they do not need to meet those needs, but they will have enough and plenty more to do God's work and to give for the building of His Kingdom on Earth.[634]

To contact the author, email
armorofgodbooks@gmail.com

INSPIRED TO WRITE A BOOK?
Contact
Maurice Wylie Media
Your Inspirational Christian Publisher

Based in Northern Ireland and distributing around the world.
www.MauriceWylieMedia.com

ENDNOTES

CHAPTER 1
KNOWLEDGE, PROVISION, AND VISION

Getting It Right With Finances

1. Matthew 13:11-12.
2. Proverbs 29:18.
3. John Maxwell, quoted by Perry Noble, "Top Ten Financial Mistakes a Church MakesPart 1."[http://www.churchleaders.com/pastors/pastor-blogs/160324; accessed 24 July 2012].
4. Tim Peters (2012). 10 Reasons Pastors Quit Too Soon. [www.churches.com/mobile/pastors/pastor-articles/161343tim_peters_10_common_reasons…; accessed 28 June 2012]
5. https://www.biblicalleadership.com/blogs/5-reasons-why-pastors-leave-the-ministry/
6. Robert T. Kiyosaki and Sharon L. Lechter (2005). Before Your Quit Your Job. Warner Business Books, New York, p.68.
7. Barna: 1 in 5 Churches Could Close in the Next 18 Months. Jessica Mouser ChurchLeaders.com
8. The author was invited by Dr. Lazarus Chakwera, former President of Assemblies of God in Malawi. He is currently His Excellency, President of the Republic of Malawi. The author went with Revd. Charles Makata, Senior Pastor of the Area 18 Assemblies of God, Lilongwe at the time (under whom he served as a bi-vocational minister for six years.)
9. 1 Kings 3:12-13; 4:29.
10. Perry Noble, "Top Ten Financial Mistakes a Church Makes – Part 1." [http://www.churchleaders.com/pastors/pastor-blogs/160324; accessed 24 July 2012].
11. Perry Noble, "Top Ten Financial Mistakes a Church Makes – Part 1." [http://www.churchleaders.com/pastors/pastor-blogs/160324; accessed 24 July 2012].
12. 1 Corinthians 9:18
13. It is also not unlikely that apostle Paul actually paid rents, but we do not have that information in the Scripture.
14. Matthew 24:14.

CHAPTER 2
FINANCING YOUR VISION

Fine-tune Your Financial Mindset

15. Quoted by Larry Burkert and Ron Blue (2007). Your Money After the BIG-5-0: Wealth for the Second Half of Life. B&H Publishing Group, Nashville, Tennessee, United States, p.27.
16. Gordon Lindsay (1982). God's 20th Century Barnabas, Christ For The Nations, Inc., Dallas, Texas, 1982, p. 235.
17. Kenneth E. Hagin (2000). The Midas Touch: A Balanced Approach to Biblical Prosperity. Rhema Bible Church, p.87.
18. Thomas S. Linscott (1888). The Path to Wealth. B.F. Johnson, Va., 1888, pp.106-110 (cited by Kenneth E. Hagin, 2000, pp.88-91).
19. Ephesians 2:8-9.
20. Ephesians 3:20; 2 Corinthians 9:8
21. Malachi 3:10
22. Acts 4:32-37.
23. Jesse Lyman Hurlburt (1918, last revised 1970). The Story of the Christian Church. Zondervan Publishing House, Grand Rapids, Michigan, United States., pp. 20-21.
24. Bruce L. Shelley (2008). Church History in Plain Language. Thomas Nelson, Dallas, United States, pp.204-209.
25. Ibid
26. 26 Ibid
27. 1 Timothy 6:10
28. James 5:1-6
29. Kennon L. Callahan (1992). Effective Church Finances: Fundraising and Budgeting. Jossey-Bass Publishers, San Francisco, p.3.
30. Proverbs 10: 22; 3 John 2.

CHAPTER 3
JESUS TAUGHT MONEY

Financial Wisdom in The Gospel

31. John Flavel was an English Puritan Presbyterian minister and author
32. Brian Zahnd (2012). Beauty will save the world: Rediscovering the allure of mystery of Christianity. Charisma House, Lake Mary, Florida, 234 pp.
33. An Indonesian friend to the author. Name withheld.
34. Luke 18:22
35. James Richardson is a fictitious name. This character doesn't exist. I have created it for the purpose of teaching.
36. Luke 14:26-27; 18:22.
37. James 5:1-6.
38. A fictitious name, profiled after a true-life situation of medical doctor who is a renowned church planter, astute teacher and evangelist, albeit with some modifications to suit the teaching.
39. 2 Corinthians 8:9.
40. Note this is not the spiritual or theological interpretation of the parable, but are interpreted for the purpose of finances in this book. They should not be seen as being quoted out of context, but a literal application of the parables, not the spiritual sense.
41. Luke 6:38.
42. 2 Corinthians 8:12.
43. Matthew 17:27.
44. The temple tax of two drachma, equivalent of one half of a shekel, which was a levy for every male Israelite 20 years and above. It was atonement money paid to recognize that their life was redeemed by God (Exodus 30:11-16).
45. www.neverthirsty.org/corner/read/r00292.html
46. Matthew 18:23-35
47. Luke 15:8-9.
48. www.truthsaves/articles/value-of-a-shekel.shtml
49. Luke 15:11-32
50. Matthew 13:3-9
51. 2 Peter 1:5-9
52. The focus is not the spiritual or theological interpretation of the parable, but literally applied to finances in this book.
53. Matthew 13:45-47.
54. Psalms 24:1
55. Deuteronomy 8:18

56. John 12:6
57. John 13:29
58. Luke 22:35-36
59. Excerpts from Church, The Power of Words. [https://www.martingilbert.com/blog/give-us-tools-will-finish-job/]
60. Oswald J. Smith (2001). The Challenges of Missions. Edysyl Publications, p.78.

CHAPTER 4
THE KINGDOM INVESTORS MINDSET

Investment Wisdom in Jesus' Parables

61. Doug M. Carter (2007). Raising More Than Money—Redefining Generosity Reflecting God's Heart. Thomas Nelson, United States, p.5. And Ron Blue (2004). Master of Your money. Moody Publishers, Chicago, USA, p.22. [He quoted Pastor John MacArthur, pastor of Grace Community Church, California.]
62. Matthew 25:14-30.
63. Matthew Ashimolowo (2005). Be The Best. Matthyson Media, United Kingdom, p.176.
64. Matthew 25:23.
65. Matthew 25:29.
66. Genesis 49:22-26.
67. Matthew 25:31-35.
68. Robert T. Kiyosaki and Sharon L. Lechter (2005). Before You Quit Your Job. Warner Business Book, p.113-114.
69. Ibid.
70. Ibid.
71. Stephen Spinelli Jr, Robert M. Rosenberg and Sue Birley (2004). Franchising: Pathway to wealth creation. FT Prentice Hall, 234 pp.
72. John E. Girouard (2006). Ten truths of wealth creation. Bethesda, Maryland, 185 pp.
73. Matthew 25:25.
74. Matthew 25:26.
75. Matthew 20:1-15.
76. Ecclesiastes 9:11.
77. Matthew 20:1-16.
78. Galatians 2:11-13.
79. Mark 12:43-44.

CHAPTER 5
TAKE YOUR WALLET WITH YOU

Leveraging Ministry With Your Talents

80. www.historymakers.info/features/missions.html [modified by author]
81. Luke 9:3; 10:4.
82. Matthew 16:18-19.
83. Luke 10:19.
84. Matthew 28:18-20; Revelation 1:8, 18.
85. Mark 16:15-20; Acts 1:8; Matthew 28:18-20.
86. Luke 24:50-52; Acts 1:9-11.
87. Acts 2:41; 4:4; 5:12-16.
88. 2 Peter 1:3-5.
89. Luke 10:17.
90. Luke 9:62.
91. Luke 10:3.
92. Acts 16:14-15.
93. Thomas E. Brewster and Elizabeth S. Brewster (1984). Language Learning is Communication—Is Ministry. Lingua House, Pasadena, CA, USA., p.7.
94. Acts 15:14-16.
95. Acts 16:30-34.
96. 2 Timothy 3:13.
97. Exodus 5:10-12.
98. Genesis 2:15.
99. George S. Clason (1988). The Richest Man in Babylon. A Signet Book, 144 pp.
100. 2 Corinthians 2:14-15.

CHAPTER 6
TAKING YOUR PROVISIONS

Three-Pronged Financial Blueprint By Jesus

101. 101 Ron Sider (unknown source).
102. James 5:1-3; Romans 12:13; 1 Timothy 6:17-19.
103. 1 Chronicles 29:11-12.
104. Genesis 15:14.
105. Exodus 10:24-26; 12:32-36.

106. Elisabeth Bumiller, "The War: A Trillion Can Be Cheap," New York Times Week of Review, July 24, 2010 http://www.nytimes.com/2010/07/25/weekinreview/25bumiller.html; accessed 15 May 2012].
107. Exodus 16:31-35.
108. Genesis 46:26.
109. Exodus 12:37-38, NLT.
110. If each household needed 10 gallons of water per head per day for drinking, cooking and bathing, washing cloths, and water for their livestock, they would require 60 million gallons of water per day, 1800 million gallons per month; and 22 billion gallons per year. That is, 880 billion gallons of water in 40 years.
111. Deuteronomy 2:4-6.
112. An average swimming pool is 20,000 gallons ($100 to fill in Texas, USA).
113. If each person eats 200 kg flour of manna per year, they would consume: 200 kg x 6 million people (1200 million kg or 1.2 million metric tons of flour per year). In forty years, it amounted to 48 million tons of flour!] This is beside the meat they had consumed in forty years!
114. 1 metric ton of wheat flour is $354.48 in 2012 [www.indexmundi.com/commodities/?commodity=wheat].
115. If each household will require at least 50 kg of wood in 3 days, or 150 kg wood per month: 600,000 household x 150 kg x 12 months = 1.08 million tons of wood. In forty years, they would have used 43 million tons of wood!
116. The US Department of Energy Biomass program puts the roadside price of forest biomass and wood waste at $ 20 to 80 per ton.
117. Psalms 105:37.
118. John 6:26-31.
119. Hebrews 4:2-7.
120. "Tent making" generally refers to the dual modalities of working by any Christian worker who receives little or no pay for his or her ministry work and supports him or herself through income earned from a non-ministry related work while simultaneously functioning as a five-fold minister or missionary.
121. Matthew 28:20.
122. For instance, Peter who had been led to convert the household of Cornelius and had boldly defended the need to accept Gentile as brethren (Acts 11:1-18), was later rebuked by Paul for hypocrisy when he tried to dissociate from Gentiles in Antioch because of men (Gal 2:11-21).
123. Luke 10:7.
124. Luke 22:36.
125. Matthew 25:14-30.
126. Matthew 7:7.

127. 1 Corinthians 9:7-9.
128. Acts 18:1-3; 1 Corinthians 9:6, 18.
129. 2 Corinthians 8:1-24.
130. 1 Corinthians 9:4-6; Acts 4:36-37.
131. 1 Corinthians 9:13.
132. Although Barnabas had sold his properties, he still worked for a living while doing ministry, like Paul (Acts 4:36-37; 1 Corinthians 9:6).
133. Luke 10:7; Matthew 10:10; 1 Timothy 5:18.
134. Taking your wallet includes all sources of earning money to do mission, generally termed bi-vocational ministry: Also known as Tent-making, Business as mission, Investments and Auto-piloting of investment.

CHAPTER 7
FAITH FOR FINANCES

Provisions Through Financial Miracles

135. D.R. McConnell (1988). A different Gospel: A historical and biblical analysis of the modern faith movement. Hendrickson Publishers, United States, 195pp.
136. Jesus Last Instruction on Finances and Evangelism must not be confused with the Great Commission, which is the Last Great Command to the Church. In the current context the author is strictly implying the Lord's Last Instruction on Finances. It is also in the context of the previous commands on Finances and Evangelism in Luke 9 and 10.
137. Isaiah 1:19.
138. Matthew 25:14-30.
139. Derek Prince (2006). Blessing or Curse: You Can Choose. Published by Chosen Books, Hampshire Avenue South Bloomington, Minnesota, 318 pp.
140. The name is withheld to protect the pastor's privacy.
141. Ephesians 3:20.
142. 1 Kings 17:1.
143. 1 Kings 17:6.
144. 1 Kings 19:5-8.
145. John 5:5-14, 26.
146. John 6:25-34.
147. John 6:26-33.
148. The story has been paraphrased by the author.

149. Philippians 3:7-8.
150. 2 Corinthians 11:27; Philippians 4:12.
151. 1 Samuel 13:11-12.
152. Collin Whittaker (1997). Reinhard Bonnke—A Passion for the Gospel. Kingsway Publications, Eastbourne, 1997, p. 53-63.
153. 2 Corinthians 9:10-11.
154. 2 Corinthians 9:8-12.
155. Acts 18:1-5; 1 Corinthians 9:6.
156. 1 Corinthians 9:9-12.
157. 1 Corinthians 9:15.
158. Luke 12:29.
159. 1 Timothy 6:10.

CHAPTER 8
FINANCIAL MIRACLES

Amazing Financial Miracles Of All Time

160. Colin Melbourne (2012). Smith Wigglesworth Miracles: Transforming Water into Petrol. Born Again Christian Info. [www.wigglesworth.born-again-christian.info/...].
161. John 6:31-35.
162. The Protestant church of that day generally believed that money and the gospel are antagonistic, and that if you are truly called you have to depend on God for all your finances without asking anyone. Tithes and offering were also shunned, except voluntary offering.
163. A simple purchasing power calculator puts the relative value of $200,000 in 1901 to $5,460,000 United States dollars in 2011. This is obtained by multiplying $200,000 by CPI from 1901 to 2011. That is the real price of that commodity. But the real value is $12.8 million, the labor value using the unskilled wage is $23.7 million, or $33.7 million, if income value is used. [www.measuringworth.com/calculators/uscompare/relativevalue.php].
164. Roberts Liardon (1998). God's General. Evangel Publishers Ltd, Kaduna, Nigeria, pp.175-177.
165. Robert Liardon (1998). God's General. Evangel Publishers Ltd, Kaduna, Nigeria, p.177.
166. Ibid.
167. Ibid.

168. Jeremiah 32:17, 27.
169. Colin Melbourne (2012). Smith Wigglesworth Miracles: Transforming Water into Petrol. Born Again Christian Info. [www.wigglesworth.born-again-christian.info/smithwigglesworth.miracles.1.htm].
170. Colin Whittaker (1997). Reinhard Bonnke—A Passion for the Gospel. Kingsway Publications, Eastbourne, p.61
171. Ibid.
172. Roberts Liardon (1996). God's General—Why They Succeeded and Why Some Failed. Published by permission by Evangel Publishers, Kaduna, Nigeria, p.280.
173. R.W. Schambach (2009). Eye-witnesses to some of the greatest miracles of our times. Destiny Image Publishers, Inc., Shippensburg, PA, United States, pp.19185-197.
174. Joshua 5:12.
175. R.W. Schambach (2009). Eye-witnesses to some of the greatest miracles of our times. Destiny Image Publishers, Inc., Shippensburg, PA, United States, pp.19185-197
176. Philippians 4:19.
177. George Muller, Biography. [http://en.wikipedia.org/wiki George_M%C3%BCller]
178. Ibid
179. Matthew 17:27.
180. Philippians 4:19.

CHAPTER 9
FUNDRAISING FOR MINISTRY

Inviting Partners to Join Hands

181. Milton Friedman, quoted by Doug M. Carter (2007). Raising More than Money. Thomas Nelson, Nashville, United States, p.51.
182. Kennon L. Callahan (1992). Effective Church Finances—Fund-raising and Budgeting for Church Leaders. Jossey-Bass Publishers, San Francisco, United States, p.3.
183. John E. Haggai (1994). Paul Meyer and the Art of Giving. Kobrey press, Atlanta, Georgia. p.66.
184. Reinhard Bonnke (2011). Evangelism by Fire. Charisma House, Florida, United States, p.8.
185. 1 Corinthians 9:7-11.
186. John C. Maxwell (1993). Developing the Leader Within You. Thomas

nelson, Inc., Nashville, Tennessee, United States, p.141.
187. Acts 18:1-4.
188. Acts 19.
189. Gordon Lindsay (cited by Kenneth Hagin, emphasis by authors)
190. Richard Stearns (2009). The Wealthiest Christians in History http://www.charismamag.com/site-archives/572-newsletters/the-buzz/3928-the-wealthiest-christians-in-history. This report indicates 5.2 trillion dollars.
Sandy Gendenhuys (2012). Research and Strategies for Reaching the Unreached. Student Manual, Christ for the Nations Institute, Global Missions Major, p.31. This document reports 10 trillion dollars.
191. Richard Stearns (2009). Ibid.
192. As of 2019, the first is USA, $15.68 trillion, second, Japan, $5.96, third, Germany $3.40 trillion, France, 2.61, fifth, UK, $2.44, sixth, Italy 2.01 and seventh, Canada, $1.82 [https://www.nationmaster.com/country-info/groups/Group-of-7-countries-(G7)].
193. Romans 15:19-20.
194. Acts 9:20.
195. Acts 9:23-30.
196. 2 Timothy 4:13.
197. Titus 3:13.
198. 2 Timothy 4:13.
199. Philippians 4:15-18.
200. 2 Corinthians 11:7-9; 12:14-18.
201. 1 Corinthians 9:6-14.
202. Galatians 1:17-18.
203. Acts 18:1-4; 2 Thessalonians 3:6-8.
204. Titus 3:14.
205. 2 Corinthians 9:1-7.
206. Doug M. Carter (2007). Raising More than Money. Thomas Nelson, Dallas, United States, p.99.
207. 1 Corinthians 6:1-12.
208. 1 Corinthians 16:3-4.
209. 2 Corinthians 12:14-17.

CHAPTER 10
DEVELOPING A FUNDRAISING CAMPAIGN

Five Prerequisites to Developing a Successful Fundraising Campaign

210. Andy Stanley (2004). Field of Gold. Tyndale House, Wheaton, IL, USA, p.122.
211. Doug M. Carter (2007). Raising More Than Money. Thomas Nelson, Inc., Nashville, Tennessee, United States, p.56.
212. Ibid.
213. Kennon L. Kallahan (1991). Effective Church Finances—Fund-raising and Budgeting for Leaders. Jossey-Bass Publishers, San Francisco, United States, p.26.
214. 2 Corinthians 12:14-18.
215. Doug M. Carter (2007). Raising More Than Money. Thomas Nelson, Inc., Nashville, Tennessee, United States, 158 pp.
216. Ibid.
217. 2 Corinthians 9:5-14.
218. John E. Haggai (1994). Paul Meyer and the Art of Giving. Kobrey Press, Atlanta, Georgia, p.102.
219. John E. Haggai (1994). Paul Meyer and the Art of Giving. Kobrey Press, Atlanta, Georgia, p.102-103.
220. Ibid.
221. Ibid.
222. Freda Lindsay (2004). Freda: The Widow Who Took Up The Mantle. Christ For The Nations, Inc., p.8-9.
223. Dr. John R. Mott, Student Mission Power, p.164.
224. Exodus 36:3-5.
225. 1 Chronicles 29:1-9.
226. Nehemiah 7:70-72.
227. Henry Blackaby, Richard Blackaby and Claude King (2007). Experiencing God—Knowing and Doing The Will of God. Lifeway Press, Nashville, Tennessee, p.69.
228. Kennon L. Callahan (1992). Effective Church Finances: Fund-Raising and Budgeting for Church Leaders. Jossey-Bass Publishers, San Francisco, 161 pp.
229. Donald H.F. Gee, cited by Kenneth E. Hagin (2000), The Midas Touch: A Balanced Approach to Biblical Prosperity. Faith Library Publications.; also supported by 2 Peter 2:2-3.

CHAPTER 11
EARNING TO FINANCE MINISTRY

Bi-vocational Model as God's Plan for Missions

230. En.wikipedia.org/wiki/Tentmaking.
231. Ibid.
232. William Ward journal [http://www.wholesomewords.org/missions/bcarey6.html], accessed 11 Nov 2012.
233. William Carey: The Father of Modern Missions. [https://www.wholesomewords.org/missions/bcarey3.html; accessed 18.01.21].
234. Ibid.
235. Bethany Global University [www.BethanyGu.edu]
236. John Wesley (1703-1791). The Use of Money—A Sermon. www.whatsaiththescripture.com/The.Use.of.Money.html
237. Ibid.
238. Ibid.
239. www.durandumc.org/stewardship.htm
240. James Harnish. Simple Rules for Money: Earning, Saving and Giving. Book Reviews on the book, by James Harnish. [www.abc-usa-org/WhoWeAre/Missions/Stewardship/Book/Review/tabid/482/EntryID14/Default.aspx.
241. 1 Thessalonians 2:9; 3:4-13; Acts 20:33-35.
242. Romans 6:3.
243. 2 Timothy 4:11.
244. Colossians 3:14.
245. 2 Timothy 4:10.
246. Acts 4:13.
247. John 12:6; 13:29.
248. Acts 16:13-15
249. 1 Peter 5:12.
250. Titus 3:13.
251. Romans 16:23.
252. Dr. Oswald J. Smith (1959). The Challenge of Missions. The People's Church, Toronto, Ontario, Edysyl Publications, p.55.
253. Ibid.
254. Psalms 110:3.
255. www.weaconnections.com/Back-issues/Business-As-Mission.aspx.

256. Briget Adams (2010). Business as a Mission: Towards a Biblical and Practical Theology of Work and Business. Lusanne Conference, Cape Town, South Africa. And Peter Shaukat (2010). Church, Mission and Business: Roles, Responsibilities, Tension and Synergies.
257. Joao Mordomo (2010). Bossa Nova, The "Beautiful Game" And Business As Mission [www.weaconnections.com/getattachment/58b7e867-adb5-4e58-9…]
258. At the time airplane ticket from Malawi to the United States was probably more than twice what it is today at the time. The author went with his whole family of six at the time. He also knew the author was staying in a very good hotel in Tulsa—a four star close to the venue.
259. Pastor Uzo Obed graciously went to be with the Lord in 2019, and Dr Chy Obed continues the work.
260. Both continued ministry after retirement and focused in international apostolic discipleship ministry.
261. Dag Heward-Mills (1999). Lay People and the Ministry. Parchment House, 171 pp.
262. Dag Heward-Mills (2004). Church Planting. Parchment House, pp.69-94.
263. Dag Heward-Mills (1999). Lay People and Ministry. Parchment House, p.8.
264. Acts 22:3.
265. Acts 13:2-3.
266. Acts 18:3-4.
267. Galatians 2:7-9.

CHAPTER 12
MAKING A DIFFERENCE

Beyond Business As Usual in Bi-vocational Ministry

268. Larry Burkett and Ron Blue (2007). Your Money After the BIG 5-0: Wealth for the Second Half of Life. B&H Publishing Group, Nashville, Tennessee, United States, p.74.
269. www.redcliffe.org/upload/documents/The_Top_Business_As_Mission_Books_25.pdf
270. Bill Peel and Walt Larimore (2010). Workplace Grace—Becoming a Spiritual Influence at Work. Zondervan, Grand Rapids, Michigan, United States.
271. Dr. Tony Merida (Teaching Pastor at the Temple Baptist church, Hatiesburg Mississippi). In Mark L. Russell (2010).
272. The author was at the Assemblies of God church in Zomba for five years and in Lilongwe for about seven years.

273. Festus Akinnifesi. Divine Healing—Biblical Solution to Sound Health (2004), Xulon Press, USA; and ii) Festus Akinnifesi, Spiritual Freedom—Overpowering the afflicter. (2005), Xulon Press, USA.
274. Larry S. Julian (2002). God is My CEO. Adams Media Corporation, Avon, Massachusetts, USA, p.29.
275. Ibid.
276. Ibid.
277. Matthew 6:33.
278. Matthew 6:19.
279. Jeremiah 29:11.
280. 2 Corinthians 9:11.
281. 1 Timothy 6:17-19.
282. 1 Timothy 6:9.
283. Proverbs 10:22.
284. 1 Timothy 6:17.
285. Genesis 42:49.
286. Genesis 42:53-56.
287. Ibid.
288. Acts 20:33-35; 2 Thessalonians 3:6-14.
289. Acts 18:1-5.
290. Dag Heward-Mills (2004). Church Planting. Parchment House, p.69.
291. Acts 20:33; 2 Thessalonians 3:8.
292. Dag Heward-Mills (2004). Church Planting. Parchment House, p.84.
293. Bill Peel and Walt Larimore (2010). Workplace Grace—Becoming a Spiritual Influence at Work. Zondervan, Grand Rapids, Michigan, United States.
294. Roberts Liardon (1998). God's Generals. Published by Evangel Publishers, Kaduna, Nigeria, p.393-394.
295. Patrick Lai (2005). Tentmaking: The Life and Work of Business as Missions. Authentic Media, Colorado Springs, United States, p.4.
296. Ibid.
297. George Macleod, quoted by Patrick Lai. Ibid, p.4.
298. 1 Timothy 6:10b.
299. Lewis Caroll, Alice's Adventures in Wonderland. Superior Publishing House. [In: Todd Ahrend (2010). In This Generation. Dawson Media, p.283].
300. Acts 18:18-19, 26; Romans 16:3; 1 Corinthians 16:19; 2 Timothy 4:19.

CHAPTER 13
MARKETING YOUR SKILLS AND TALENTS

When Your Business is Your Service

301. An unknown source: Quoted by Larry Burkett and Ron Blue (2007). Your Money After the BIG 5-0: Wealth for the Second Half of Life, B&H Publishing Group, Nashville, Tennessee, United States, p.41.
302. Matthew Ashimolowo (2006). Be the Best. Mattyson Media, p.80.
303. Proverbs 13:22.
304. https://www.cnbc.com/2019/11/11/most-expensive-watch-ever-sold-fetches-31-million-at-auction.html.
305. https://www.theverge.com/2020/4/30/21242421/zoom-300-million-users-incorrect-meeting-participants-statement.
306. https://finance.yahoo.com/; https://capital.com/zoom-stock-forecast; https://www.bbc.com/news/business-52884782.
307. https://edition.cnn.com/2020/09/01/tech/zoom-profits/index.html.
308. Anonymous source. Story has been paraphrased by the author.
309. Dr. Faheem Younus (2012). Give Afghanistan Schools Today (or Don't Blame Islam Tomorrow). [www.huffingtonpost.com/faheem-younus/give-afghanistan-schools-today...; 08 Nov 2012].
310. Sandra Wu. (blinkist.com), 22 Dec, 2016.
311. Mike Schultz and John E. Doer (2009). John Wiley & Sons, Inc., p.224.
312. John E. Girouad (2006). The Ten Truths of Wealth Creation. Bethesda, Maryland, United States, 185 pp.
313. Matthew 20:1-8.
314. http://allfacebook.com/zuckerberg-2013-salary-b89538 (14 July accessed 2012).
315. www.forbes.com/real-time-billionaires.
316. En.wikipedia.org/wiki/Mark Zuckerberg.
317. Zechariah 4:6.
318. Matthew 19:24.
319. John C. Maxwell (2001). The 17 Indisputable Laws of Teamwork. Thomas Nelson, Publishers, Nashville, p.1.
320. Ibid.
321. Ibid.
322. Acts 1:8; Luke 22:36.
323. Zacharias T. Fomum (1995). You Have A Talent! Christian Publishing House, Yaounde, Cameroon.
324. Ibid.

CHAPTER 14
REPOSITIONING YOURSELF TO EARN MORE

Reinventing and Rebranding Your Services At The Market Place

325. Statement by Earl Blaik former football coach at the United States Military Academy, quoted by John C. Maxwell (2001), The 17 Laws of Teamwork, Thomas Nelson, Inc, Nashville, Tennessee, p.138.
326. https://en.wikipedia.org/wiki/Pyramid_of_Capitalist_System.
327. En.wikepedia.org/wiki/Nick Vujicic.
328. John Maxwell (1993). Developing the Leader Within You. Thomas Nelson, Nashville, United States, p.viii.
329. Harvard Business Review, September 2010, p.16.
330. John Maxwell (1993). Developing the Leader Within You. Thomas Nelson, Nashville, United States.
331. John Maxwell (2001), The 17 Laws of Teamwork. Thomas Nelson Publishers, Nashville, Tennessee, United States, p.137.
332. Mike Schultz and John E. Doerr (2009). Professional Services Marketing. John Wiley& Sons Inc., p.170.
333. Larry S. Julian (2002). God is My CEO. Adam Media Corporation, Avon, Massachusetts, USA, pp.30-38.
334. Ibid.
335. Napoleon Hill (1926). Think and Grow Rich. Vermilion, London, 302 pp.
336. Jeffrey J. Fox (2000). How to Become CEO—The Rules of Rising to the Top of Any Organization. Vermilion, London, 162pp.

CHAPTER 15
BLOOMING IN A FINANCIAL WILDERNESS

Joseph's Investment Formula

337. Genesis 42:49.
338. Genesis 42:53-56.
339. Genesis 47:20.
340. Genesis 47:13-26.
341. Genesis 47:24-26.
342. Genesis 41:34-35.
343. Genesis 26:12-13.

344. Genesis 41:36.
345. Psalms 1:3.
346. Malachi 3:10; 2 Corinthians 9:8-11.
347. Genesis 41:47-49.
348. Genesis 47:13-26.
349. Genesis 47:20-26.
350. Napoleon Hill (2003). Think and Grow Rich. Vermilion, London,302pp.
351. News.bbc.co.uk/2/hi/Africa/662472.stm.
352. Genesis 30:31-34.
353. Genesis 31:6-9.
354. Genesis 31:43.
355. Genesis 31:10-13.
356. Ecclesiastes 10:10.
357. Mark Victor Hansen and Robert Allen 2002. One Minute Millionaire, Harmony Books New York, p.213.
358. Genesis 26:1-3.
359. Genesis 26:16.
360. https://www.temple.edu/about/history-traditions/acres-diamonds; https://www.temple.edu/about/history-traditions/russell-conwell.
361. Mark V. Hansen and Robert G. Allen (2002). The One Minute Millionaire. Vermillion London, 388 pp.
362. Psalms 25:12-13.

CHAPTER 16
DEVELOPING YOUR FINANCIAL PLAN

Turning Your Dream Into a Reality

363. Dwight D. Eisenhower (1956). Address at Bradley University, Peoria, Illinois, 25 September, 1956 [http://www.eisenhower.archives.gov/all_about_ike/quotes.html]
364. Dr. Jerry L. Williamson (2007). Steps…To The Mission Field. Calvarypress, Jacksonville, p.64.
365. Matthew Ashimolowo, 2005, "Be The Best: 9 Powerful keys to a successful Life," pg.75.
366. Luke 14:28-30.
367. http//overmanwarrior.wordpress,com/2010/10/27/successful-people-that-didn't-go-to-college and 100 Top Entrepreneurs Who Succeeded Without a

College Degree [www.youngentrepreneur.com/blog/100-top-entrepreneur-who-succeed-\ed-without-a-college-degree/]
368. ThinkExist.com.
369. Ron Blue and Jeremy White (2004). Master Your Money. Moody Publishers, Chicago, USA, p p.135.
370. Ibid.
371. Proverbs 16:3, 9; 19:21.
372. Proverbs 21:17.
373. 2 Peter 1:3-4.
374. Luke 4:18-19.
375. Edmund E. Haggai (2006). Lead On—Leadership that endures in a changing world. Kobrey Press, p.
376. Ibid.
377. Anonymous source.
378. Matthew 6:33.
379. Philippians 3:12-14.

CHAPTER 17
BUILDING YOUR FINANCIAL NET WORTH

Charting The Road Map To Financial Freedom

380. Anonymous source.
381. https://fullercenter.org/millardfuller/
382. John Maxwell (2001). The 17 Indisputable Laws of Teamwork. Thomson Nelson Publishers, Nashville, p.25.
383. Life insurance helps protect, care and safeguard for the future. It is also a tax-saving and can be regarded as an investment.
384. Calculated following the financial net-worth method by Blue and White Ron (with modification): Blue and Jeremy White (2004). Master Your Money: A Step-by Step Plan for Gaining and Enjoying Financial Freedom. Moody Publishers, Chicago, p.80-87.
385. Calculated as Total Assets Less Total Liabilities.
386. Liquidity Assets is calculated to include assets that are available for emergencies, bills, major purchases, and investment opportunities. This excludes salaries. It may include cash-value for whole-life insurance, but not for life insurance. Productive assets are those generating or having the potential to generate income.

387. Calculated as all liquid assets less retirement benefits and insurance.
388. Calculated as Total Liabilities divided by Total Assets, times 100.
389. Net-worth divided by years worked (25 years for James, 18 years for Laura and 9 years Julie.
390. Taxes vary depending on country: In the USA, Federal, State tax, and FICA apply. However, one must be aware of tax-deductible items. For instance, your tithe, money paid to church or religious organizations are tax deductible. In many countries, these are not applicable. To legally reduce your tax it is important to understand what applies.
391. Income less expenditure.
392. Proverbs 16:1, 9.
393. Proverbs 3:6-7; 16:3.
394. Proverbs 19:21.
395. Proverbs 15:22.
396. http://thinkexist.com/quotation/if_i_had_eight_hours_to_chop_down_a_tree-i-d/194268.html
397. http://en.wikiquote.org/wiki/Dwight_D._Eisenhower

CHAPTER 18
PATHWAYS TO FINANCIAL FREEDOM

Definite Wealth-Creation Routes

398. John E. Girouard (2006). Ten Ways of Wealth Creation. Bethesda, Maryland, United States, p.xii.
399. Larry S. Julian (2002). God is my CEO: Following God's Principles in a Bottom-line World, Adams Media Corporation Avon, Massachusetts, p.23.
400. Luke 6:38.
401. Dean R. Hoge and Jacqueline E. Wenger (2005). Pastors in transition: Why Clergies Leave Local Church Ministry. Wm Eerdmans Publishing Co., 257pp.
402. 1 Corinthians 9:4-5.
403. 2 Chronicles 29:1-8.
404. Daniel 6:1-7.
405. The Midas Touch: A Balanced Approach to Biblical Prosperity. Faith Library Publications. Rhema Bible Church, United States, 234 pp.
406. 2 Kings 4:1-7.
407. https://www.bbc.co.uk/newsround/25622442 [accessed on 11 September, 2020]
408. T.C.A. Srinivasa-Raghavan (2003). Why America is So Rich. www.rediff.com/money/2003/march/14spec.htm

409. Karl Smith (2010). Why is America so Rich? The Economist, London, 9 November, 2010.
410. Ezekiel 47:8-10.
411. John 6:12-13.
412. John 6:9.
413. Mark V. Hansen and Robert Allen (2002). The One minute Millionaire,Vermilion, London, 388 pp.; David Bach (2006). Start Late, Finish Rich. Broadway Books New York, 348 pp.; George Classon (1926). Richest Man in Babylon. A Signet Book, 144 pp.
414. George Clason (1926). Richest Man in Babylon. A Signet Book, 144 pp.
415. David Bach (2006). Start Late, Finish Rich. Broadway Books, New York, United States, 348 pp.
416. Mark V. Hansen and Robert Allen (2002). The One Minute Millionaire. Vermilion, London, 388 pp.
417. Exchange Traded Fund (ETF) is a type of security that tracks an index, sector, commodity, or other asset, but which can be purchased or sold on a stock exchange the same as a regular stock.
418. George S. Classon (1988). The Richest Man in Babylon. A Signet Book, 144 pp.

CHAPTER 19
FINANCIAL DECISION GUIDE

Three of the Five Investment Allocation Guides for
Achieving Financial Independence

419. The original idea for this table was gratefully inspired by a Student Teaching manual on, "Generational Discipleship" by Pastor Chris Estrada, Christ For The Nations Institute (CFNI), Dallas, TX., United States, p.38-39 [Created along a similar line of thought, but on a different content.]
420. Proverbs 3:9-10; Malachi 3:8-10.
421. Deuteronomy 8:18.
422. Psalms 35:27; 3 John 2.
423. Job 36:11.
424. 3 John 2.
425. Malachi 3:10-11.
426. 2 Corinthians 8:7, 12; 9:6-7.
427. Luke 6:38.
428. 2 Corinthians 9:9.

429. Malachi 2:10.
430. Haggai 1:6.
431. Luke 6:38.
432. Malachi 3:10-11.
433. Philippians 4:17.
434. 2 Corinthians 8:7; 9:6-8.
435. John 1:16-17.
436. 2 Corinthians 9:8-11.
437. The figures in this were column adapted from Mark Hansen and Robert Allen (2002). One minute Millionaire, Vermilion, London, p.4.
438. Charles Swindoll, quoted by Neil T. Anderson Robert Saucy and Dave Park (1998). Higher Ground. Monarch Books, p.65.

CHAPTER 20
THE GRACE OF GIVING

How can we please God with the way we give and spend our money?

439. Deuteronomy 8:18.
440. 2 Corinthians 9:8-11; 1 Timothy 6:17-19.
441. 2 Corinthians 8:2-5.
442. En.wikipedia.org/wiki/John_D._Rockefeller._Jr
443. John E. Haggai (1994). Paul Meyer and The Art of Giving. Kobrey press, Atlanta, Georgia, p.159.
444. Ibid.
445. 1 Corinthians 13:3.
446. Haggai 2:8; Psalms 24:1; Exodus 19:5.
447. Malachi 3:10.
448. Malachi 3:11.
449. 2 Corinthians 9:11, 14.
450. Matthew 6:20.
451. Haggai 2:8.
452. Proverbs 3:9-10.
453. Psalms 4:1; Haggai 2:8.
454. Luke 6:38; Proverbs 3:10; 2 Corinthians 9:6.
455. Luke 6:38.
456. 2 Corinthians 9:6-8; 2 Corinthians 9:6-11.
457. 2 Corinthians 9:6-11.

458. 2 Corinthians 8:3-4.
459. 1 Timothy 3-5.
460. Ron Blue and Jeremy White (2004). Master Your Money. Moody Publishers, Chicago, p.147.
461. Ibid.
462. Malachi 3:11; Ecclesiastes 5:13-15.
463. Proverbs 11:24-25; 13:7.
464. George-Pitt Rivers, The Revolt Against Tithes, The Nineteen Century (1934).
465. Malachi 3:11.
466. Exodus 30:11-16; Matt. 17:27.
467. Ephesians 3:17-19.
468. Ecclesiastes 5:18-19.
469. Ecclesiastes 2:24; 3:13.
470. 2 Corinthians 9:8.
471. 2 Corinthians 9:8-11.
472. 2 Corinthians 8:7.
473. Psalms 1:3; Deuteronomy 28:2-6.
474. Malachi 3:10.
475. 2 Corinthians 8:2-6.
476. Luke 6:38; Malachi 3:10.
477. Luke 16:1-13.
478. Haggai 2:8; Psalms 24:1; 1 Corinthians 4:1-2.
479. Malachi 3:8.
480. 2 Corinthians 9:6-11.
481. Ephesians 3:20.
482. Jeremiah 29:11.
483. 2 Corinthians 9:10.
484. Malachi 3:10.
485. Daniel 7:22.
486. Matthew 13:23.
487. 2 Corinthians 8:1-12; 9:11.
488. Matthew 6:19-20.
489. 2 Corinthians 8:3.
490. Freda Lindsay (1984). Freda: The Woman Who Took Up the Mantle. Christ For The Nations Inc., p.18.
491. 2 Corinthians 8:20.
492. Oral Roberts (1975). A Daily Guide to Miracles—And Successful Living Through Seed-Faith. Pinoak Publications, Tulsa Oklahoma, 366 pp.
493. Acts 4:36-37.

CHAPTER 21
TITHING IN THE MODERN CHURCH

Has Tithing Been Abolished in the Church?

494. Leviticus 27:30-33; Numbers 18:21-25; Deuteronomy 14:22-29.
495. Genesis 14:20-24.
496. Hebrews 7:2.
497. Malachi 3:10.
498. 1 Corinthians 9:13.
499. Acts 1:8; Mark 16:15-19; Matthew 28:18-20.
500. 1 Corinthians 9:9-14; 1 Timothy 5:17-18.
501. Matthew 28:20.
502. Jeremiah 33:17-22.
503. Leviticus 27:30-32; 2 Chronicles 31:5-6; Deuteronomy18:21-26.
504. Ezekiel 43:1-27; 44:15-16; Zechariah 14:16-21.
505. 2 Chronicles 31:4-5; Nehemiah 12:43-44.
506. Genesis 14:19-20; Hebrews 7:1-2.
507. Genesis 28:20-22.
508. 1 Chronicles 29:2-9.
509. 2 Chronicles 34:9.
510. Deuteronomy 16:16.
511. The New Testament Tithe? (Annon.). [http://www.thirdmil.org/answers [accesses 01 Feb., 2021]
512. Russell E. Kelly. The Exhaustive Examination of "Tithes", "Tithes" and "Tithing."
513. 2 Chronicles 23:2-4, 29-32.
514. 1 Samuel 8:10-17.
515. 2 Chronicles 29:2-9.
516. 1 Chronicles 23:25-32; 26:17-28, 30-32.
517. 2 Chronicles 19:8-11.
518. 2 Chronicles 31:3-6.
519. 2 Chronicles 15:18; 16:2.
520. Nehemiah 10:32.
521. 1 Corinthians 3:16.
522. Deuteronomy 12:19, 22, 27.
523. Leviticus 27:30-32; Deuteronomy 18:21-26.
524. Deuteronomy 14:23-27; Amos 4:4-5.
525. Hebrews 7:11-17.

526. Matthew 17:24-27.
527. Acts 21:20-26.
528. Luke 23:2.
529. Matthew 22:15-22.
530. Matthew 23:23.
531. John 20:25.
532. 1 Chronicles 29:11-12.
533. Scott Morton2007. Funding Your Ministry. NavPress, p.242.
534. Ibid.
535. Ibid.
536. https://www.britannica.com/topic/tithe
537. Genesis 28:22-22.
538. 1 Corinthians 16:1-2.
539. Galatians 3:10-14.
540. 2 Corinthians 9:8-11.
541. Philippians 4:1-18.
542. Matthew 23:23; Luke 11:47.
543. Matthew 23:23.
544. Malachi 3:8-9.
545. Galatians 3:13.
546. Genesis 15:1.
547. Malachi 3:10.
548. Luke 6:38; 2 Corinthians 9:8-11.
549. Genesis 14:20.
550. Genesis 28:20-22.
551. Matthew 23:23.
552. Note that if James and other apostles, and Christians expected the Law be obeyed on circumcision it is most likely they would expected or required that people pay their tithes at the temple as well. Those who gave everything they had had fulfilled the requirement of tithing.
553. Hebrews 7:1-7.
554. Matthew 23:23.
555. 1 Chronicles 29:2-5.
556. Pastor David Jeremiah (2012). Always With Thanksgiving: Always Thankful for Prosperity. Turning Point, Nov. 3&4 (email devotional message).
557. 1 Corinthians 9:7.
558. Acts 54:34-37.
559. Genesis 28:20-22.

560. Malachi 3:8-9.
561. Hebrews 8:13.
562. Mark 12:38-44.
563. 1 Timothy 6:18-19; 2 Corinthians 9:7.
564. Luke 18:22-30; 19:15-17.
565. 2 Corinthians 9:11-12.

CHAPTER 22
FINANCIAL REFORMS FOR THE TWENTY-FIRST CENTURY CHURCH

Getting Back On Track With Finances

566. John Maxwell (1993). Developing the Leader Within You. Thomas Nelson, Nashville, United States, p.143.
567. Bruce L. Shelly (2008). Church History in Plain Language. Third Edition, Thomas Nelson Publishers, 532 pp. Jesse L. Hurlburt (1970). The Story of the Christian Church. Zondervan Publishing House, Grand Rapids Michigan, 192 pp.
568. Luke 9, 10 & 22; Matthew 25.
569. Communism is a theory or system of social organization in which all property is owned by the community and each person contributes and receives according to their ability and needs.
570. Acts 5:32-37; 5:1-11.
571. Acts 6:1-4; 11:29; 2 Corinthians 8:12-14.
572. Acts 18:2-4.
573. John C. Maxwell (2001). The 17 Indisputable Laws of Teamwork., p.7
574. Deborah Baum (2011). Estimated costs of post-9/11 wars: 225,000 lives up to $ 4 trillion. [News.brown.edu/press release/2011/06/war costs. Posted 29 June 2011].
575. Wikipedia.org/wiki/Military_budget_of_the_United_States.
576. Christopher Drew (2009). High costs weigh on troop debate for Afghan war. www.nytimes.com/2009/11/15/us/politics/15costs.html?_r=2&hp; published November 14, 2009]
577. Mission Network News, in an article, " Understanding the costs of mission support," posted by Ava Dixon (2015), puts the cost a missionary raise to include salary, health insurance, travel expenses, ministry expenses, cost of education, retirement, and cost of setting up a home overseas.[mnnonline.org; 17 April, 2015, accessed 26 January, 2021]
578. Acts 11:27-30; 2 Corinthians 8:14.

579. Dr. Scott Rae, Dr. Dallas Willard, John Kang, and C. William Pollard. Business is Ministry. Panel discussion excerpt from Leadership Lecture Series. Biblical Wisdom for the Business World. Talbot School of Theology Faculty Retreat, La Quinta, CA, 15-17 September, 2011.
580. William C. Pollard. Business is Ministry. Panel discussion excerpt from Leadership Lecture Series. Biblical Wisdom for the Business World. Talbot School of Theology Faculty Retreat, La Quinta, CA, 15-17 September, 2011.
581. Os Hillman (2012). Equipped for the Workplace. Prime Time With God, TGIF Today God Is First. Vol 1, 12 07 2012.
582. Dr. Wayne Gruden (2011). Theology of Work and Vocation—Biblical Wisdom for the Business and World. Leadership Series, Talbot School of Theology Retreat, La Quinta, California, December 23, 2011. [the author listened to the teaching through Youtube]
583. John C. Maxwell (1993). Developing the Leader Within You. Thomas Nelson, Inc., Nashville, Tennessee, United States, p.144.

BONUS 1
FINANCIAL GROWTH AND OPPORTUNITIES

Last Two of the Five Investment Allocation Guides for Achieving Financial Independence

584. Harvard Business Review, March 2010, p.71.
585. Ibid, February 2009.
586. Harvard Business Review, March 2010, p. 74.
587. This does not imply that real estate is low yielding. For instance, an investment I made in real estate property (a piece of land) a new area with vast development potential at Ibeju Lekki, Lagos, Nigeria in 2017 is worth 350% of the purchase price as of July 2021, and it is still compounding annual interest at a fast rate.

BONUS 2
RECEIVING YOUR INVESTMENT CAPITAL

How to Acquire Your Investment Start-up Money

588. Anonymous source.
589. Ron Blue and Jeremy White (2004). Master Your Money. Moody Publishers, p.63.
590. George S. Clason (1955). The Richest Man in Babylon. A Signet Books, p.110.
591. Ibid.
592. Proverbs 22:1.
593. David Bach (2006). Start Late, Finish Rich. Broadway Books New York, p.29.
594. Robert Powell (2010) Seven Steps to a Sound Retirement. [http://finance.yahoo.com/focus-retirement/article/110951/seven-steps-to-a-sound-retirement?mod=fidelity-buildingwealth] accessed, October 8, 2010.
595. www.mastermoney.org/consolidationarticles/finding money.html
596. David Bach (2007). Start Late, Finish Rich. Broadway Books, New York, United States.
597. Adapted from Mark Victor Hansen & Robert Allen (2002). The One Minute Millionaire. Vermilion, London, U.K., p.6. (with some modifications).
598. Note that this is projected estimates, real life situation will normally be different, and the interest depends on the season.
599. Ecclesiastes 9:11.
600. Estimated using the money chimp online calculator [www.moneychimp.com/firworks/continuous_compounding.htm]. Estimated using the money chimp online calculator [www.moneychimp.com/firworks/continuous_compounding.htm].
601. Matthew 25:27.
602. In March 2010, user on the "SmokeTooMuch" auctioned 10,000 BTC for $50 (cumulatively), but no buyer was found. Likewise, on 22 May 2010, Laszlo Hanyecz bought two pizzas with 10,000 BTC coins in Jacksonville, Florida. In April that amount was worth over $500 million! Analysts are expecting Bitcoin price to reach $100,000 within the next two years, and $250,000 by 2025. Others think it will even reach $1 million per over a long time, but these are projections and speculations based on past performance. Is it too late to invest, I don't think so, but each person needs to do own research and make informed decisions. The right timing is key for stocks and cryptos, as most other investments. Best time to invest is when the market is bearish.

603. Note that all these prices fluctuate, and several have dropped to all-time low in May 2021. These are only indicative of possibilities. Historical performance is not indication of future prices, and the reader must do its own due diligence and acquire proper knowledge or financial advice from experts before investing.
604. Emmie Martin (2018), If you invested $1,000 in Apple at its IPO, here's how much money you'd have now. [https://www.cnbc.com/2018/11/01/how-much-a-1000-dollar-investment-in-apple-at-its-ipo-would-be-worth-now.html; updated, 11 Dec 2018]
605. This is not a recommendation to buy any particular stock, but for purpose of illustration.
606. How we made $1 million on Apple stock, Matt Egan (2015). https://money.cnn.com/2014/09/10/investing/apple-stock-investors-1-million/index.html [posted July 21, 2015, accessed 11, Sept 2020]

BONUS 3
AUTO-PILOTING YOUR INVESTMENT

Earning Passive Income, While You Pursue Ministry

607. Groucho Marx, Quoted by Larry Burkett and Ron Blue (2007). Your Money After the BIG 5-0: Wealth for the Second Half of Life. B&H Publishing Group, Nashville, Tennessee, United States, p.85.
608. en.wikipedia.org/wiki/autopilot.
609. T. Harv Erker (2005). Secrets of the Millionaire Mind: Think Rich to Get Rich. Piatkus Books, London, Britain, p.156.
610. Mark V. Hansen and Roberts G. Allen (2001). The One Minute Millionaire. Vermilion, London, p.268.
611. 1 Corinthians 3:6.
612. Deuteronomy 28:12.
613. Howard J. Ruff (2008). How to Prosper During The Coming Bad Years in the 21st Century. Berley Nooks, New York, 273 pp.
614. Napoleon Hill (2003). Think and grow rich. Vermilion press, London, 302 pp.
615. Matthew 13:25.
616. Chelsea Wald (2008). Crazy money: Humans aren't rational as recent economic crises shows. So why should financier theories assume that they are? Science Vol. 322, pp.1624-1626.
617. Ibid.

618. Some big hedge fund brokers often target flourishing companies such as Tesla, Apple and many others, or companies in financial distress and volatility, by betting big on their stocks, known as shorting—with either a "call option" when they expect the stock price to go up, and a "put option," when they expect the price will go down. Such call or put option gives an investor the right to sell a stock at a specified price. Some literally spend their energy and resources to force the priced down their desired price, including mounting intensive 'smearing campaigns' against that company to bring down the price, so they can profit. This sometimes include misleading analyses and predictions in financial media and social media. Their purpose is to cause panic in the market so inexperienced investors can sell-off their stocks prematurely. Sometimes they go public announcing their intention to cause more fears and further drive the market down. Nonetheless, they too do lose money, and they lose big when investors hold on to their shares against their prediction. Shorting stock itself is not illegal, but it is the manipulation with naked short that is wrong.

619. Over 30 million copies sold, and translated into more than 50 languages world-wide.

620. Mass Appeal, Rob Blackhurst (2011). Financial Times [https://www.ft.com/content/3da2d8d2-c29d-11e0-8cc7-00144feabdc0; posted on 12 August 2011].

621. 2 Corinthians 9:10-11.

622. Proverbs 3:9-10; Deuteronomy 8:17-18.

623. Mark V. Hansen and Robert Allen (2002). The One Minute Millionaire. Vermillion, London, 388 pp.

624. George S. Clason (1955). The Richest Man in Babylon. A signet Book., 144 pp.

625. Ibid.

626. Imagine having invested $1000 in Amazon, Apple or Facebook just ten years ago, that investment will continue to work for you today as those companies grow. Or if you have invested $1000 in Bitcoin when it was $13.9 in mid-2011—two years after it was launched, it would have bought about 72 Bitcoins. Today 72 BTC equals to $3.6 million as of August 2021Today, BTC is worth $50,000, despite having down below its all-time high (ATH) when it touched $65,000 on May 2021. As the price goes up it means you are making money while sleeping because you do not need to do anything more than watch your investment grow! Whether the market rises or falls, those who bought early are not shaken, they remain always afloat while later comers are in red (loss). Blink Charging co. soared to 36 times its value in ten years ago. Tesla's shares were up 22,000% in the past 10 years (220X); Square increased 3000% in the past 5 years (30X)'; Dell went up 200 times its price (200X); Microsoft price was up 154 times! These are hypergrowth portfolios. An investor needs to prepare for the next bull run

in the next years for both cryptos and stocks. The challenge is to look for such opportunities today that will be a BTC, Apple or Amazon, of tomorrow. It is hard to know, and no one can be certain, but with God all things are possible. We must avoid greed in investment, which often lead to losses, and the reader must acquire knowledge before investing.

627. Steven Berman (2011). How To Apply For A Patent. Blog.seattlepi.com/steveberman/2011/07/07/a-bannanas-shelf-life/
628. Harvard Business Review, Mar 2010, p. 42.
629. 1 Corinthians 9:18.
630. Dr. Tozer's Prayer. Haggai Institute, Mid-Pacific Center, Kihei, USA.
631. En.wikipedia.org/wiki/informercial
632. Frank Catalano (2018), Traditional publishers' ebook sales drop as indie authors and Amazon take off. [https://www.geekwire.com/2018/traditional-publishers-ebook-sales-drop-indie-authors-amazon-take-off/; posted May 19, 2018, accessed 16 September 2020].
633. 2 Corinthians 9:8-13.

www.ingramcontent.com/pod-product-compliance
Lightning Source LLC
Chambersburg PA
CBHW071552080526
44588CB00010B/887